Winning Results with
Google AdWords
Second Edition

About the Author

Andrew Goodman is founder and president of Page Zero Media, a Toronto-based search marketing agency offering full-service campaign management for paid search as well as a variety of related online marketing services for growth-oriented clients such as E*TRADE, Canon, Etsy, Business and Legal Reports, Canadian Tire, and Torstar Digital. His blog, Traffick.com, has framed many of the debates in the industry, dating back to 1999. A globally recognized speaker (including an integral role in over 30 Search Engine Strategies conferences dating back to 2002), he has served as Program Chair for Search Engine Strategies Toronto for the past two years. His columns appear regularly in publications such as Search Engine Land, and his sound bites frequently show up in major media, including *The New York Times*, *The Globe and Mail*, *The Washington Post*, *Fortune Small Business*, *Business News Network*, and *Marketing Magazine*. Andrew is also a cofounder of HomeStars, a dot-com startup in the home improvement space. He served as VP, Strategy for HomeStars from 2007 through 2008.

For relaxation, Andrew enjoys inline skating in west end Toronto (sometimes into hostile crowds of picnickers), extreme gardening, watching the Weather Channel, and long walks on Cuban beaches. He shares most of these experiences with his wife, Carolyn Bassett.

About the Technical Editor

Matt Van Wagner is President and founder of Find Me Faster (www.findmefaster.com), a search engine marketing firm based in Nashua, New Hampshire, and product architect for DEKE, an ad simulator and quality control application for the Google AdWords DKI Ad function. Matt is a member of Search Engine Marketing New England (SEMNE) and Search Engine Marketing Professionals Organization (SEMPO), and is a courseware developer for the SEMPO Institute. Matt writes occasionally about the Internet, search engines, and technology for iMedia Connection, *New Hampshire Business Review*, and other publications. He has served as a technical editor for Mona Elesseily's *Yahoo! Search Marketing Handbook*. Matt holds a BS in Economics from St. Lawrence University, Canton, New York, and an MBA from Rivier College, Nashua, New Hampshire.

Winning Results with Google AdWords
Second Edition

Andrew Goodman

New York   Chicago   San Francisco
Lisbon   London   Madrid   Mexico City
Milan   New Delhi   San Juan
Seoul   Singapore   Sydney   Toronto

The McGraw·Hill Companies

Library of Congress Cataloging-in-Publication Data

Goodman, Andrew (Andrew E.)
  Winning results with Google AdWords / Andrew E. Goodman.—2nd ed.
    p. cm.
  Includes index.
  ISBN 978-0-07-149656-8 (alk. paper)
  1. Internet marketing. I. Title.
  HF5415.1265.G656 2009
  659.14'4—dc22

                                                    2008044835

McGraw-Hill books are available at special quantity discounts to use as premiums and sales promotions, or for use in corporate training programs. To contact a special sales representative, please visit the Contact Us page at www.mhprofessional.com.

Winning Results with Google AdWords, Second Edition

1234567890   FGR FGR   0198

ISBN   978-0-07-149656-8
MHID   0-07-149656-4

Sponsoring Editor
  Megg Morin

Editorial Supervisor
  Janet Walden

Project Manager
  Arushi Chawla
  (International Typesetting
  and Composition)

Acquisitions Coordinator
  Carly Stapleton

Technical Editor
  Matt Van Wagner

Copy Editor
  Bill McManus

Proofreader
  Madhu Prasher

Indexer
  Claire Splan

Production Supervisor
  George Anderson

Composition
  International Typesetting
  and Composition

Illustration
  International Typesetting
  and Composition

Art Director, Cover
  Jeff Weeks

For Bill Gates

Contents at a Glance

PART I   **The Paid Search Opportunity**

    1   How Big Is This Market? The Rapid Rise of Paid Search 3

    2   A $21 Billion Afterthought: How Google Entered
         the Advertising Market 33

PART II   **How to Play the AdWords Game**

    3   First Principles for Reaching Customers Through AdWords 71

    4   Setting Up Ad Groups 115

    5   How Google Ranks Ads: Quality-Based Bidding 133

    6   Big-Picture Planning and Making the Case to the Boss 155

PART III   **Intermediate-Level Strategies**

    7   Keyword Selection and Bidding: Tapping into
         Powerful AdWords Features 181

    8   Writing Winning Ads 213

    9   Expanding Your Ad Distribution: Opportunities and Pitfalls 245

PART IV   **Winning the AdWords Game: Advanced Issues**

    10   Measuring Success: A "What's Changed" Report 267

    11   Increasing Online Conversion Rates 283

    12   Online Targeting 1995–2015: Fast Start, Exciting Future 335

        Index 367

Contents

Foreword xvii

Acknowledgments xix

Introduction xxiii

PART I   **The Paid Search Opportunity**

CHAPTER 1   **How Big Is This Market? The Rapid Rise of Paid Search** **3**

Targeted Advertising vs. Surplus Interruption 4

In the Beginning: Advertising on the Internet 7

     Mass Marketing Inertia: Why Do the Old Ways Persist? 8

     Google's Unassuming, Yet Butt-Kicking, Beginnings 9

Search Marketing Facts and Figures 10

     Size of the Advertising Market 10

     Size of the Online Advertising Market 12

The Growth of Search Marketing 16

     Search Engine User Growth 16

     Types of Search Marketing 17

Why Pay for Search Traffic? Isn't It Free? 22

     Screen Real Estate, Location of Listings 22

     Some Ads Are More Relevant 22

     Post-"Florida" Fallout: Algorithmic Changes 22

     Control Over Message, Navigation, Timing, Exposure 25

     Noncommercial Sites and the Organic Results 26

     Organic and Paid Search Strategies: Not Mutually Exclusive . . . 27

CHAPTER 2   **A $21 Billion Afterthought: How Google**

               Entered the Advertising Market **33**

AdWords Gets Its Start 33

     How to "Speak Google"? 34

     Google Responds 35

Predecessors and Competitors 37

     Major Predecessors in Search 37

     Major Predecessors in Paid Search 44

The Growth and Evolution of AdWords   50
    Early Version Challenges   50
    Google as Referee: Complications of Multiple Stakeholders . . .   52
    How Google's DNA Influences the AdWords Game   57

PART II   **How to Play the AdWords Game**

CHAPTER 3   **First Principles for Reaching Customers Through AdWords** **71**
Through the User's Eyes: Profit by Understanding
    Searchers' Love Affair with Google   72
    Do People Really Look at the Ads on Google?   79
    Why Users Love Google   81
    More Thoughts on User Intent   83
Measurable and Nonintrusive: The AdWords Difference   84
    Request Marketing   84
    Google Calls It "ROI Marketing" (Not "Spend and Hope")   85
    Fast Feedback Cycles and Rapid Evolution   86
    Online Advertising Pricing: Why Pay per Click?   87
    Self-Serve, Pay as You Go, and Self-Learning   89
    A Sales-Generation Machine That's Yours to Keep   90
Before You Start: Planning, Third-Party Tools, and a Reminder   92
    Work Backwards: Assess Which Third-Party
        Tools Will Be Needed   92
    Real-Time Auction on Keywords and Phrases   93
Billing   94
Key Metrics and Terminology   94
    Impressions, Clicks, and Clickthrough Rate   94
    Cost per Click, Maximum Bid, Bid Discounter, Total Cost   95
    Ad Position, Bidding Wars, and Reverse Bidding Wars   99
    Limit Vanity Searching Internal to Your Company   100
    Conversion Rates   100
    Return on Investment (ROI)   101
Account Basics   101
    Structure: Accounts, Campaigns, Groups   102
    Entering Basic Account Information   103
    Key Campaign-Level Settings and Possible Opt-Outs   106
CHAPTER 4   **Setting Up Ad Groups** **115**
Why Grouping Keywords Makes So Much Sense   116
    Google's Strange Advice on Ad Group Size   120
    Getting Very Granular with Groups   121
Organize, Organize, Organize   122
    Multiple Persons Managing the Account   122
    Post-Click Tracking   123

Bottom-Line Performance (Ads Match Keywords) 123
Avoiding the Horrors of Overlap 124
Naming Campaigns and Groups 125
You're in Charge: Reevaluate Structure Every Few Quarters . . . 125
Writing Your First Ads 126
Editorial Review 127
Responding to Controversial Editorial Disapprovals 127
Quick Tips 128
Time Lags and Special Rules 129

CHAPTER 5 **How Google Ranks Ads: Quality-Based Bidding** **133**
Encapsulating the Concept of Quality-Based Bidding 135
Quality Scores Are Based on (at Least) Three Broad Types of Data . . . 135
Historical Data 136
Predictive Data 136
Opinion and Arbitrary Determinations 137
Paid Search Ranking Formulas: Past, Present, and Future 137
Paid Search 1.0 138
AdWords 1.0 and 2.0 138
AdWords 2.5 and 2.6 138
AdWords 3.0 139
How Ad Ranking Works: The Letter of the Law, and Beyond 139
The Goal Hasn't Changed 139
Keyword Quality Score for Ad Ranking 140
Keyword Status 142
Landing Page and Website Quality 142
Content Is Separate from Search 143
Case Studies 143
Big Hair and Mistaken Identity: Is Google
Thin-Slicing You into the Doghouse? 144
Case Study 1: Media Company, Slow "Quality
Score Digout" Process 145
Case Study 2: HomeStars, Tighter Targeting
and Speculation on Website Quality Issues 147
Addendum: AdWords 2.7—The Latest Development
in Quality-Based Bidding 150
Fixed Minimum Bids Are Gone, Because Quality
Score Is Now Calculated in Real Time per Query 150
Keywords Are Never, Technically, Inactive 151
"First-Page Bid" Offered as a Data Point 152
Quality Score Detail Intact 152
Glass-Half-Full Reaction: New Opportunities 152
What Hasn't Changed: Strategy 152

CHAPTER 6   **Big-Picture Planning and Making the Case to the Boss** **155**

How Valuable Is Search Engine Marketing to Your Business? 155
    Strategies for Small vs. Large Companies:
       How Different Are They? 157
    What about Affiliate Marketing? 159
B2B, Retail, Independent Professional, or Informational—
    What Is Your Business Model? 160
    Business-to-Business 160
    Business-to-Consumer 161
    Professional Services 161
    Information Publishing 163
Assess Your Sales Process 165
    What's Your Goal: Retail Sales, Leads,
       Registrations, Buzz, Subscriptions? 165
    Cost per Acquisition, Cost per Order:
       Two Brief Case Examples 169
Difficulties in Forecasting 173
    Forecasting Cost per Click and Click Volume 173
    Forecasting Clickthrough Rates and Conversion Rates 175
    An Alternative to Forecasting: A $2,000 "Testing Budget" 175

PART III   **Intermediate-Level Strategies**

CHAPTER 7   **Keyword Selection and Bidding: Tapping into**
       Powerful AdWords Features **181**

How Matching Options Work 181
    Exact, Broad, and Phrase Matching 181
    CPCs on Different Matching Options 185
Keyword Research 185
    The Google AdWords Keyword Tool 185
    Keyword Research Tools and Tips 187
    Keywords You're Already Using 191
    Examples of Unsold Keyword Inventory 191
    Benefits of Being the Only Advertiser on a Phrase 193
Keyword Brainstorming: It's about Them 195
    Solve Your Target Market's Problems 196
    Keyword Variations: Plurals, Verb Forms, and Misspellings 199
    Going Narrow 201
Keyword Progression, Initial Quality Scores, and Troubleshooting 202
    Proceeding with Caution to Avoid Low Initial Scores 202
    Disapproved Keywords 203
Approaches to Bidding and Ad Position 203
    What Do We Know about Ad Position and Visibility? 203
    Do Your Bids Have a Sensible Purpose? 205

Set and Forget? Using Goal-Based Bid Management Tools 205
How to Use Powerposting to Bid at the Keyword Level 207
Making Bulk Changes Quickly with the AdWords Editor 208
Software Saves Time with Keyword-Level Tracking 209
Dayparting 209
Dealing with Foolish (or Rich) Competitors 210

CHAPTER 8   **Writing Winning Ads** **213**
Targeting and Testing: Key Principles of Web Advertising 213
Imagine the "Perfect Ad" 213
Cater to People and Keep Yourself in the Game 214
How Your Ads Look to the User 215
Impact of Media Type and Location 215
Fitting Big Ideas into Small Spaces 216
Adopting the Right Tone 216
Addressing Multiple Priorities 221
Maintaining Accuracy 224
Getting the Most Out of Your AdWords Ads 225
A Technique for Ad Refinement in Stages 225
Getting Help from the Experts 227
Six Rules for Better AdWords Copy 228
Some Ideas for Testing Ads 233
How Split-Testing Works 233
Ideas for What Variables to Test 233
Tracking Results 240
Statistical Significance in Testing 241
Moving from Ad Content to Campaign 242

CHAPTER 9   **Expanding Your Ad Distribution: Opportunities and Pitfalls** **245**
Getting the Most Out of the Keywords You Know 246
Deal with Your Lowest-Quality Keywords 246
Two-Word Broad Matching 248
Expanded Broad Matching: Disable Only if Necessary 248
One-Word Broad Matching + Negative Keywords 249
Advanced Technique: "Go for the Tail" 250
Building on Success: Hypothesize, Extrapolate, and Profit 252
Upping the Bid and Movin' On Up 253
Content-Targeted, or Contextual, Ads: Take a Second Look 254
Ads Appearing near Content 254
Advanced Uses of Content Targeting: Current Affairs 258
Trademarks as Keywords ("Competitor Words") 259
Exporting Your Successful AdWords Campaign 260
Google's Main Competitors 260
Google Ad Planner 261
Offline Marketing 263

PART IV	**Winning the AdWords Game: Advanced Issues**	
CHAPTER 10	**Measuring Success: A "What's Changed" Report**	**267**
	What to Measure, How to Manage: Skinny Summary	268
	How Tracking Works	268
	The World Isn't Perfect, and Neither Is Web Analytics	269
	What You Need to Track: Metrics to Consider	269
	Measuring Success: "What's Changed" Report	270
	Analytics as an "Industry" Has Exploded	270
	Urchin Rules the High Seas	271
	AdWords Conversion Optimizer	274
	Quality-Based Bidding and Instability	276
	Marketers Are Using Analytics to Test Sophisticated Theories	276
	Marketers Understand That "Analytics" (Relevant Statistics) Live Right Inside AdWords	277
	CPCs Have Increased and Competition Has Intensified	278
	What Hasn't Changed (But There Is Always Hope)	279
CHAPTER 11	**Increasing Online Conversion Rates**	**283**
	Conversion Science Isn't a Beauty Contest	285
	What and How to Test Depends on Business Type	286
	The Discovery of Scent: God's Gift to Interface Designers?	287
	Common Errors That Kill Conversions	289
	Error #1: Not Understanding What a Landing Page Is	289
	Error #2: Overloading the Landing Page with Information	290
	Error #3: Assuming That the Best Landing Page Is the Home Page	291
	Error #4: Assuming That the Best Landing Page Is a Bare Contact Form	293
	Error #5: Assuming That the Best Copy Is Brief Copy	294
	Insights Leading to Principles: How Case Study Data Leads Us to Conversion "Schools of Thought"	296
	Case Approaches: Tinkering for Dollars—It Worked!	297
	Are We Plumbers or Persuaders?	297
	Remove Barriers to Conversion (Unclog the Plumbing)	299
	Persuade, Convince, Use Psychology (Persuasion and Storytelling)	300
	Testing Protocols: Best Practice; A/B/C; Multivariate	304
	"Testing" Method #1: Be a Lot Better from the Start	305
	A/B, or A/B/C, Testing	306
	Multivariate Testing	312

What Are Typical Conversion Rates?   320
Retail Landing Page Design: Focus vs. Selection   321
   Category Page vs. Single-Product Page   321
   Ensure Keywords Are on the Landing Page   324
Web Credibility   325
   B. J. Fogg and Stanford Research on Web Credibility   325
   Don't Neglect Site Search   326
Factors Outside Your Control   327
   Seasonality   327
   Hot Sectors   327
360-Degree View: Create a Good Conversion Environment   328
Leveraging Feel and Brand in Small Retail Operations   328
Summing Up   330

CHAPTER 12   **Online Targeting 1995–2015: Fast Start, Exciting Future** **335**
Google AdWords: Emerging Trends   339
Google Projects to Watch   340
   Google Chrome   340
   Google Product Search and Google Checkout   341
   Orkut: The Cool Kids Moved On?   341
   YouTube   342
   Google Labs   343
The Ecosystem: Google's Competitors and Partners   345
   Google vs. Everybody Else   345
   eBay and Amazon   348
   Portal Wars: AOL, Yahoo, MSN, IAC   350
Think Small to Get Big: What Search Marketing
Will Look Like in 2015   352
   The Revolution in Media Buying   353
   A Transparent World   354
   The New Geography   355
Conclusion: What about Peanut Butter?   360

Index **367**

Foreword

In a short time, Google has become one of the most famous companies in the world, with its founders themselves transformed into huge celebrities. Little wonder. Millions of people each day turn to Google for answers to their questions. And Google keeps delivering so well that—yes—"google" is now a verb many people use to say they searched for something. It's an amazing consumer success story.

Google is also famous because those millions of people who google generate billions of dollars in revenue for Google itself. For many searches, Google shows ads. Unlike most advertising, these ads—delivered through the Google AdWords program—don't interrupt what you're currently doing. They don't get in the way of the TV show you're watching, the next song you want to hear on the radio, or the article that you were reading until forced to jump to the back of the magazine, and they don't become the junk mail you toss into the trash.

Google's ads are gifts, solutions, answers to questions that people are expressly looking for. They are the online equivalent of walking into a hardware store and asking for a picture hook that will work on a hollow wall, walking into a dry cleaner to get a stain removed, or walking into a hair salon for that desperately needed cut. No one feels a merchant has "interrupted" them in situations like these. Instead, they likely feel grateful that they got help.

Amazingly, Google offers advertising that helps! Advertising that's wanted. Advertising that can make a consumer think, "Thank you!" Google's ads can be perfectly targeted to an immediate desire that someone is expressing. That's why they convert so well for advertisers; that's why spending on search advertising continues to rise each year. Search is powerful stuff, something no advertiser can afford to ignore.

This leads me to another celebrity: Andrew Goodman, author of this book you're about to read. Andrew is an AdWords celebrity. Indeed, like the star of a hit film, it might make sense for people to refer to him with AdWords as part of his name: Andrew "AdWords" Goodman.

For as long as we've had Google AdWords, we've had Andrew Goodman writing about the system and how it has evolved, giving advice for those wanting more out of it, and nudging Google when it needed to make things better to benefit both advertisers and searchers. Receiving his newsletters is always a delight, despite the fact I need to reserve ample amounts of quiet time to digest the latest amazing insights he dispenses.

Though his work—newsletters, online forum discussions, conference speeches, e-books, and here—the second edition of his "real world" book—Andrew has educated thousands of people. On an ordinary street, he might not seem to have celebrity status. But for those who try to ferret out how the often secretive and complicated Google AdWords system works, Andrew's one of the A-List stars. Indeed, if there were Oscars of the AdWords world, he'd have a lifetime achievement award.

But what's there to explain about AdWords? Write a short ad, pick some words you want it to show up for, decide the maximum amount per click you're willing to pay, and click Submit! Google would have you think that's all there is to it—an almost fire-and-forget process that starts delivering plentiful quality traffic.

Certainly that can happen in some cases. But AdWords has grown and matured over the years, as Google has tried to maximize revenues while simultaneously protecting searchers from seeing irrelevant ads. Quality Score has emerged as a secret weapon that Google employs—in an automated fashion—to stop "bad" ads dead in their tracks. But pity the person with a "good" ad that's accidentally nabbed by the Quality Score arrest squad. Getting out of the "bad quality jail" may be a costly experience.

Quality Score isn't the only trap to avoid. Keyword lists can be too long—or conversely too short! Writing good ad copy when you have a haiku-like maximum of 35 characters per line may sound like a joke. But ad copy does matter, and doing it right pays off. Having the right landing page—what you show to those who click through from an ad—also factors into success. And what is "success"? Have you defined your goals correctly, and are you tracking conversions, when they happen?

That's a lot to digest. For the newcomer, it might even sound frightening. But that's where this book comes in. Andrew has been guiding folks around the AdWords landscape for years. You're in good hands. Read on, and enjoy those winning results you heard about in the book's title!

Danny Sullivan
Editor-in-Chief, Search Engine Land

Acknowledgments

In the three years between editions of this book, changes in the outside world—as drastic as many of them have been—seem to pale in comparison to the rapid changes in our no-longer-little world of search marketing and the business that flows from it. Growth projections for every aspect of the business have been woefully understated, perhaps most of all on the financial side. Google's raw computing power may soon be required to calculate its annual server and food budget. Should the domestic inflation rate pick up, Google's U.S. dollar revenues may soon need to be calculated not merely in gigabucks, but in terabucks or petabucks. (I don't know the difference, and this won't be on the exam.)

Inevitably, then, I have incurred a number of new debts in the past three years, while (I hope) paying a few debts down as well. Those I acknowledge here are mostly those who didn't appear in the first-edition acknowledgments. I'm grateful to all of these friends, partners, mentors, and colleagues, old and new.

I had the privilege of again working with the ever-savvy, ever-patient acquisitions editor Megg Morin. The entire McGraw-Hill crew has been thoroughly professional and I deeply appreciate their talents and support. I have been consistently impressed with technical editor Matt Van Wagner's thorough, probing, invariably helpful technical commentary; nearly as impressed as I was by his pitch-perfect operatic performance lamenting the absence of Dana Todd in the Paid Search 101 seminar at the Search Engine Strategies Toronto conference… complete with red wig.

Page Zero colleague and fellow writer and speaker Mona Elesseily has been remarkable for her consistent drive and appetite for growth, change, and success milestones. In addition, she has regularly provided vital no-kid-gloves copywriting advice for columns and business development pitches, feedback on speeches, advice to smile even when I don't feel like it, and a lead-by-example campaign to adopt the West Coast lifestyle of green tea, sushi, and yoga. What is more remarkable is that I am still walking around in spite of my rampant disregard for nearly all of the above.

It'll be hard to thank the many readers and collaborators who have come into my life as a result of the first edition of *Winning Results*. I've had people tell me the book helped them through decisions to change careers or launch their own agencies; unexpected and flattering. At Fanshawe College, Liz Gray pioneered one of the world's first college-level courses dedicated to search marketing. It's been a pleasure getting to know her, and her students.

Business and personal relationships have also been strengthened by author status that seems to transcend Yet Another Agency Owner status. The growing list on this front is starting to get away from me also, but I'm grateful for the growing bond with old and new friends in the Authors Who Also Run Agencies Club; particularly, Bryan Eisenberg and Fredrick Marckini. Mitch Joel is beginning to write a book, so he counts; more importantly, of late Mitch has been perhaps the leading figure in knitting together disparate groups of digital marketers in corporate Canada.

Along with Mitch and also too numerous to cover completely, other members of the Canadian online marketing scene who have kept the conversation alive include Martin Byrne and Maor Daniel at Yahoo, Eric Morris at Google, Ken Headrick at Microsoft, Sulemaan Ahmed at Apple, Ken Schafer at Tucows, fellow search marketing agency owners Gord Hotchkiss of Enquiro and Jeff Quipp of Search Engine People, and the list goes on at some length.

Moving south of the border, that long list grows even unwieldier. There is only space to briefly thank a short list of those who have continued to knit the industry together in various leadership roles (especially, convening meetings and conferences), who have taken time out to rub elbows as we grab a quick coffee in a fluorescent-lit hallway, or close down another hotel bar or Italian restaurant in places like London, Stockholm, New York, San Francisco, Toronto, and other hotspots: Chris Sherman, Jill Whalen, Kevin Ryan, Jim Sterne, Christine Churchill, Danny Sullivan, Mike Grehan, Ryan Carson, Greg Jarboe, Brett Tabke, Anne Kennedy, Ralph Wilson, Larry Chase, Rand Fishkin, and the "rest of you know who you are" will have to do. Another list, of people passionate about search technology, would begin with people like Chris Tolles of Topix and Rich Skrenta of Blekko, and will have to stop there. I continue to think of Seth Godin as a mentor, and thank him for keynoting Search Engine Strategies Toronto in 2007. Without naming all 50,000 individuals, I'm inspired by anyone and everyone in our industry who has wielded a PowerPoint slide in anger, contributed a pithy blog post, or applauded loudly in the back row of a search conference keynote in recent years.

Without clients, there would be no book, because I wouldn't know anything. I'm thankful to all the Page Zero clients and seminar attendees whose campaigns have helped me and the Page Zero team acquire a business education we wouldn't trade for the world.

And who does the stellar work for the clients? Since I don't work 100 hours a day (only about 25), the fantastic Page Zero team has been a constant source of encouragement, innovation, and support in the day-to-day problem solving that separates book learning from running an actual business.

Over to Google; I've become overwhelmed with the sheer headcount in Mountain View (and their dozens of other facilities around the world). I've had the privilege of interacting with a host of great people. On the AdWords product side, Nick Fox stands out. In addition to patient explanations of the complexities of Quality Score, Nick (like many Googlers) does a personable job of outlining the principles of Google's program to the general public. He, like many Googlers, is often willing to shuck the strict bonds of public relations spin and to give frank answers to advertisers' questions. Also helpful has been Ariel Bardin, who has been involved with, among other things, AdWords keyword tool development, direction of planning and beta-testing new AdWords features, and Google Website Optimizer. Tom Leung is among several others who have provided helpful perspective. Meeting Google salespeople from a variety of global offices, including Germany and Sweden, has been fun and insightful. Diana Adair and several others in corporate communications at Google are consistently patient, professional, and helpful. The same may be said for their counterparts at Microsoft and Yahoo. To pick one at random, I must thank Kristen Wareham of Yahoo.

A key point of contact for larger companies and agencies working with Google is Google customer support. Today, Google employs a "team" approach to assisting large or strategic clients, putting three or more support staff with distinct responsibilities at the disposal of the client. Not only are Google staff helpful in the strictest sense of getting things accomplished, they're highly knowledgeable and have helped me understand many details and nuances of AdWords and marketing in general. I'm grateful for the support of Stefania Pifer and Rachel Greenberg, and their teams.

To find the time to write a book on top of working at least one full-time job, the support and love of family are indispensable. Thanks again, Carolyn, Gary, Jean, George, Norma, and the rest.

Finally, you may find it curious that I've dedicated this book to Microsoft founder Bill Gates. This is meant to be thought-provoking, but not sarcastic. Google stands at the cusp of what is tempting to glibly call "world domination." More specifically, though, the experiences of dominance and monopoly in a key technology field—similar to the path forged by Microsoft—will become increasingly salient to Google's decision-making and identity going forward. With immense power comes an equal dose of responsibility, and a recognition that long-term survival is impossible without a global network of partnerships that creates a healthy business ecosystem, as opposed to a dominant player simply "sucking all the oxygen out of the room." On top of that, it's worth noting that at the end of the day, Bill Gates did not skimp, or pursue what anyone could characterize as a "pet project," when it came to putting his immense wealth to work for philanthropic purposes; much of the emphasis is on eradicating African poverty and disease. Google's founders, for their part, have already shown keen interest in solving universal human problems, such as clean power generation. Should Google grow beyond even Microsoft proportions, the quick-and-dirty moral yardstick "don't be evil" will be nearly impossible to live up to except perhaps in relative terms. As prosaic as it sounds, when the history is written, Google will ultimately be compared with Microsoft. There is always a risk that Google, like Microsoft, will manage to negate a great deal of the good they do, but already balance seems to be entering the equation. Exciting challenges lie ahead for Google, their global partners, and the rest of connected society, who increasingly work and live in Google's shadow.

Introduction

As with the previous edition of *Winning Results*, Chapters 1 and 2 are vital for newcomers and analysts, as they put things into context. If you're an impatient type or already up to speed on the industry, feel free to skip ahead, though you'll be missing some important data. I look at the history of search advertising, and how it fits in with the attention economy as a whole. In addition, I address the current economic proportions of various types of related advertising, along with AdWords. In these chapters you'll get some opinionated characterizations as to what makes many other forms of advertising less effective than AdWords.

Chapter 3 gives you a feel for what a searcher's experience may be like. Here I attempt to address some top-level principles of AdWords marketing as a lead-in to more tactical chapters. I address some myths about searcher behavior, as well. In Chapter 4, I plunge right into the meat of how the Google AdWords interface works and the vital early going of setting up your account with campaigns and groups of keywords. In Chapter 5, I discuss the all-important issue of how Google ranks ads on the page, with a new formula called Quality Score that is a significant departure from their previous AdRank formula. If you don't grasp this chapter, then you won't understand how Google thinks or, for that matter, how customers think, and your volume and campaign economics will suffer. In Chapter 6, for the benefit of folks who have an organization to report to, I address the best ways of making economic projections, planning related initiatives, and getting buy-in at your company.

In Chapter 7, I drill down farther into the world of keyword research strategies and tactics. I also cover another core determinant of success: bidding strategy. In Chapter 8, I provide plenty of ideas for how to write and test ads; both quick tips and examples, and suggested testing methods for those who want to move through intermediate to advanced methodologies. In Chapter 9, I address the "high degree of difficulty" task of taking a profitable campaign and fanning it out to increase total profit.

I discuss analytics, or "measuring success," in Chapter 10. Like Chapter 11, this chapter could have come much earlier in the book, philosophically speaking. I cover what to measure and why, what you can do to pull valuable information easily out of the AdWords interface, and the ins and outs of using core features of Google Analytics, Google's website behavior measurement tool. Chapter 11 could be a book in itself, and again in a philosophical sense you could easily cite it as the most important chapter in the book, as it addresses the issue of converting website visitors into buyers, along with related issues like web credibility, how to test landing pages, and the concept of information scent.

Finally, in Chapter 12, I take another crack at pulling out the old crystal ball to ask what's next, both for you the advertiser and for Google, in an increasingly competitive market for consumer attention and eyeballs. Among topics barely on my radar when I wrote the first edition of this book in 2005 are phenomena like social media and Google's ownership of YouTube.

Part I

The Paid Search Opportunity

Chapter 1

How Big Is This Market? The Rapid Rise of Paid Search

Advertising annoys people. Advertising works. Many in the advertising business have long assumed that both of these statements are true. But the more annoying advertising gets as a whole, the harder it becomes for any particular advertiser to break through the clutter. Tellingly, a grassroots backlash has arisen against the most bothersome ways of interrupting people, to the point where legislation is now being enforced against telemarketing, junk faxing, and email spam.

Ever get the feeling that some big advertisers don't quite get it yet? Recently, I changed home phone providers, now that legislation has paved the way for Rogers (a large Canadian cable company) to offer a local and long distance phone service to compete with the leader, Bell. Evidently incensed at my decision but unable—due to legislation—to phone me to try to win the service back, Bell sent me a nice card in the mail, telling me that they weren't allowed to contact me but assuring me that they'd be calling me when the 90-day legislated cooling-off period ended. Why didn't they just hire kids to throw a rock through my window? I felt stalked.[1] Multiply that instinctive revulsion to heavy-handed marketing messages by millions of consumers, and you get a rapidly shifting pattern of media consumption.

Add to that a new, hyper-pampered mindset. Never before has it been so easy to get precisely what you want. Want the most elusive version of an old live Neil Young recording? An underappreciated new release from Snow Patrol? An inspiring keynote speech from the leader of your trade industry association? Forget the question: if you cared enough, you'd already have it in your MP3 library; maybe it's playing in your ear right now. Want wasabi peanuts or a washing machine part delivered overnight?[2] Click the mouse a few times, and you're done. Writes recovering advertising executive Joseph Jaffe: "The rock group Queen once sang, 'I want it now,' and little did we suspect that Freddie Mercury was prophesying the next wave of consumer empowerment in which they would gain immediate access to information, education, and entertainment on demand on their terms."[3] As rapidly as the consumer and media environments have changed over the past decade, search engine companies have solidified their role as gatekeepers of and facilitators for this robust market activity, for a fairly straightforward reason: if you think you want something, you need to search for it somehow.

In light of the fragmentation of media and the proliferation of products and pastimes, as a marketer, you're dealing with a consumer whose attention has been not only divided, but sliced and diced many times over. Paradoxically, though, once slotted into micro-niches, customers, subscribers, and members of communities are as loyal as ever; perhaps more so. Marketers' abuse of precious attention has led to negative reactions in many ways, but the growing legion of innovative companies that have sprung up to cater to the precise whims of niche markets has achieved unprecedented customer satisfaction on some fronts, leading to demands and expectations that are nearly impossible to fulfill for the mediocre or irrelevant vendor. The death of advertising? Maybe not. But a sea change is well underway.

Web search hasn't just been a passenger in this journey. It's been a major catalyst for changing consumer expectations of media and advertising. Search is a special realm. Because web index search engines arose in a noncommercial phase of the World Wide Web, there is a lingering sense among web users that search is almost like a public utility; an information haven. Internet users have taken to the so-called User Revolution like a diverse population of multicolored, oddly shaped fish, happily swimming in knowledge and community, relatively unimpeded by unwanted commercial messages.[4] Now couple that revolutionary new medium with the opportunity to unobtrusively advertise on the same page as web search results—without annoying searchers. Those little ads are the answer to the $64 billion question: "What if you could come up with a way to advertise that doesn't annoy people and achieves measurable results at the same time—a form of advertising that targets potentially interested customers, yet doesn't bother people needlessly?" This is the underlying premise of Google AdWords and why you should be considering it as part of your ad campaign. (It doesn't generate $64 billion in advertising revenue yet, but it's not far off.)

We know that advertising often interrupts us in the offline world, and, to varying degrees, we accept it. But if you're like me, you've never quite gotten used to being interrupted in "sacred" areas such as your daily work routine on a computer. When I close the door of my office to supposedly get some peace and quiet, I'm still fending off little interruptions such as a pop-up reminder to install security software that I never plan to install. Or if I'm at my parents' house, maybe that pesky animated paper clip is doing the limbo on my screen as I attempt to review a simple Word document. How much is too much?

Targeted Advertising vs. Surplus Interruption

Maybe it's time to propose a distinction between reasonable forms of commercial targeting, on one hand, and intrusive marketing methods that consumers, if given the choice, would actively avoid. No one reasonable would say that all advertising is bad, or even that most of it is bad.[5] But the actions of a company like Google are striking in that they actively take steps to measure negative responses by users to forms of advertising; then they take steps to reduce the frequency of such advertising or eliminate it altogether. In this user-centric role, Google offers us a brilliant example of the distinction between *user targeting* and *surplus interruption*.[6] Surplus interruption, in the user's life, is analogous to pollution in the environment. It might make a profit for some specific actor, but it lowers the quality of life for the citizenry as a whole.

It's significant that I say "user" ("searcher" might be another appropriate word), instead of "consumer." It's presumptuous to define all users of the Internet or web search as "consumers" at any given point in time. Not knowing exact intent, referring to them as "users" reinforces the point that if the user doesn't get the right degree of satisfaction out of the medium or from a given web service, she can switch to another medium, pastime, way of life, or service entirely.[7]

It's worth clarifying further that somewhere in between what I approvingly refer to as *user targeting* and disparagingly refer to as *surplus interruption*, diverse viewpoints abound about what counts as reasonable, as to where you'd draw the line or how you'd define the spectrum. We'd make some lousy assumptions about what people really "want," or what's most healthy for a commercial society, if we had a fixed idea about what's really an "interruption." In an ideal world, wouldn't I see only messages about what I wanted, when I wanted it?

Unfortunately, it doesn't really work that way. I run into commercial messages all the time that do interrupt me to some degree, but which also heighten my enjoyment of the day, or possibly even help me make a buying decision. Recently, I actually picked up the phone for a telemarketer! My Call Display showed that it was Sears Clean Air, and we'd been meaning to get our ducts cleaned for ages. Imagine how shocked the telemarketer was when I said yes to the offer of a free estimate. The secret to that interaction: the targeting wasn't too bad, and some of the reason it wasn't bad was predictable. We live on a street with detached and semidetached homes. We've done business with Sears in the past, though not for duct cleaning. It was spring.

The reversal came, however, when the Sears salesman oversold his company's service when he arrived on-site, at one point raising the specter of us contracting Legionnaires' disease. A few quick searches, including one that turned up an informative page from the Environmental Protection Agency that questioned "sweeping health claims" associated with duct cleaning services, put the salesman's claims on shaky ground. Through word of mouth (family), combined with some online word of mouth (a consumer review site called HomeStars), we wound up choosing another vendor. Happy with that vendor, we considered posting a review online.[8]

That same day, I saw two ads that particularly pleased me. One, a billboard for Milwaukee's Best (inexpensive beer), gave me a chuckle as I drove out of Crosstown Auto (classy carwash). It was a joke at the expense of a Buffalo, NY suburb ("Milwaukee taste at Tonawanda prices") and generally winked at the audience who would get the joke. Many wouldn't, but the alternative— bare bricks—wouldn't have been much better for someone who was, after all, simply exiting a carwash. Good targeting again: more than 80% of the users of Crosstown Auto's carwash would be males of imbibing age, and probably not averse to saving a buck on some beer given the $10 they just paid for the deluxe wash. (Since then, the billboard has been replaced by one touting a video-on-phone partnership between Rogers, a large wireless phone provider, and YouTube, which happens to be owned by Google. Unfortunately, there isn't any good way of measuring the impact of this ad. My gut tells me the ad is wasted on the guys I see coming out of the carwash.)

Another ad seen that same day, a TV spot for Gatorade, was also a delight. Using well-known college football announcer Keith Jackson (doing his best impression of his own distinctly accented voice), it harkens back to the Florida Gators' dehydration in a game long ago. The Gatorade inventor chimes in, in his own stilted voice, stating the baldly obvious and essentially repeating what Jackson said, in a fashion reminiscent of Jason Bateman's superfluous color commentary on "ESPN 8—The Ocho" in the movie *Dodgeball*. For football fans, or merely Keith Jackson fans, the spot works. It also explains (though not in particularly scientific terms) why you might actually need the product. Did the ad interrupt me? Well, I was eating dinner and watching

Seinfeld, and wondering what to write next in this book. In other words, it's hard to say. Did the ad increase Gatorade sales? Or prevent them from losing market share? It's very hard to say.

Some entrepreneurs have proposed unique ways of compensating consumers for interruptions: carrots that go beyond simply offering free content or software. Startups such as Agloco and Attention Trust appear to be revolutionary in this sense, offering people money in exchange for information about themselves and their web surfing habits.[9] On close inspection, these "revolutionary" pay-you-for-your-attention services are often rehashes of the "pay-to-surf" schemes of 1998–2001 that managed to annoy users, bilk advertisers, and disappoint investors all at the same time. In practice, these schemes don't even vaguely approach any kind of advance in the reduction of forms of interruption marketing.

Strict Limits on Advertising? That's for Authoritarian Regimes Only

Depending on who's doing the talking, then, we're often dealing with either (1) a literal interpretation of the concept of reasonable user targeting, or (2) a broad or loose interpretation. Unless we give up on the idea of a society built around choice and pluralism, and decide to follow strict codes of conduct *en masse*, the broad or loose (or liberal) interpretation must be assumed.[10] I could TiVo *Seinfeld*. I could ignore the post-car-wash billboard. But even on the liberal interpretation, there has to be some way for reasonable people to agree on how I can opt out of major irritants so I can be at one with my own thoughts. No one but the most diabolical advertising executive would envision a system that would hijack my car's sound system when I was inside that car wash, unable to escape, pumping a loud commercial message into my ears. Hope I didn't just give someone an evil idea.

Better targeting goes hand in hand with less intrusive marketing, in many cases (but not all). The dividing line between annoying intrusion and reasonable targeting actually isn't a simple one based on the degree of targeting. If that were true, then Bell's wheedling me to come back to their phone service days after switching providers would count as "reasonable," because I am actually very highly targeted to their service—I'm using a direct competitor's exact same service! They know so much about me! (I don't think it is reasonable, perhaps precisely because they know everything about me.) But by and large, the degree of targeting is not only a pretty reliable guide to how socially responsible and nonintrusive your advertising is, but a rock-solid predictor of how much the advertising is worth to you, and its fair market value.

That makes it worth mentioning, as an aside, that all advertisers are looking for bargains. If this book is titled *Winning Results with Google AdWords*, then the way to win by the largest margin is surely to pay less for these forms of new customer acquisition than (1) they're worth to your business; (2) you'd pay in other media; (3) you'll be likely to pay in a couple of years.

So what are all the factors that distinguish reasonable targeting from surplus interruption? It would be difficult to state them all here, because so many reasonable people disagree with what these are. (Walk down a long street and record the percentage of homes that have signs that say "no flyers" or "no solicitors." Would you put up that type of sign? So we have differing levels of dissent against intrusive marketing methods.) In practice, what we've seen is that advertisers will do just about anything they can get away with. At the very least, we can agree that many of these efforts are wasteful, hard to measure, and trigger overtly negative reactions among consumers… er, citizens, homeowners, users… *people*.

And why should you care? Because Google cares. Why does Google care? Keep reading.

In the Beginning: Advertising on the Internet

The idea of the Internet as a marketing medium was so energizing to a growing community of enlightened marketers not just because of its superior targeting and interactive potential, but because of the potential to annoy fewer people. Somewhere along the way (around 1998–2000, when they smelled money), online marketers forgot the promising principles of user targeting and plunged headlong into surplus interruption. Suddenly our favorite websites, search engines, and portals were crammed with intrusive, blinking banner ads. Part of the reason for this is that users hadn't abandoned these sites… yet. And advertisers were paying high rates for this minimal, divided attention, because, by and large, they weren't measuring performance.

Those kinds of ads still "work" in the sense that they get noticed. But research now proves that the most intrusive forms of online advertising might also erode consumer loyalty and do serious damage to the brand image of advertisers and publishers alike.[11]

Until I began my career as an Internet entrepreneur in 1999, I'd never given such issues much thought. Then I discovered a writer who put a new spin on the history of the advertising business: Seth Godin. He changed the world of advertising forever when he wrote *Permission Marketing*. Godin's narrative relegated so-called interruption marketing to the dustbin of history (at least in his enlightened fantasies). Godin's premise was that email marketing would change the way companies developed relationships with prospects by offering a means to contact prospects who had "raised their hands for" (opted into) marketing messages that were "anticipated, personal, and relevant."[12] The skeptical reader might wonder, though, how that permission was going to be gained in the first place. Wouldn't some kind of unsolicited message be needed at some point to initiate the process?

And how do you get off the permission train? Can you really opt out of the relationship, or will the largest database-driven marketers take whatever liberties they can get away with? What if I exited a commercial relationship but still got a "friendly" card in the mail promising to start phoning me again just as soon as legislation allowed. Didn't "no" mean *no*?

I was already beginning to sense the unraveling of the promise of "permission" as I looked with dismay at the clutter building up in my own email inbox.[13] The game of permission marketing seemed to be over before it had truly gained traction, in part due to spam, in part because corporate marketers bent the rules and abused the concept of permission. Everyone wanted in your face, now that your face was stuck in your email box. With no theoretical limit on the number of emails that might pile up, we all wound up receiving too many. People began unsubscribing from opt-in publications, switching email addresses, ignoring and filtering their email. What started out looking like a magic bullet became more like a rapid-fire hailstorm of ammo opening gaping holes in our daily work routines. The recipients of the daily volley of "anticipated" messages ran for cover.

Nonetheless, Godin's theories stuck in my mind because he was evidently working on a broader analysis of the rapidly changing context for marketing and advertising. And he kept publishing these timely ideas. In *Purple Cow,* he explored more deeply how irrelevant big ad campaign methods had become, as they were more suitable for a time (in the 1950s and 1960s) when consumers needed to be trained to adopt leading brands in product categories that had never existed before. Now, with product proliferation, the old "virtuous circle" of the

"TV-industrial complex" (advertise product, take massive profits, and reinvest in yet more advertising) wouldn't work, especially not to introduce new products in old categories.[14]

What does work in this new era? Getting the details exactly right. Understanding your customers' wishes. Word of mouth. Online word of mouth. "Think small," argues Godin. "One vestige of the TV-industrial complex is the need to think mass. . . . No longer. Think of the smallest conceivable market and describe a product that overwhelms it with its remarkability. Go from there."[15] Want an example? How about the PowerBar (now owned by Nestlé), which spread by word of mouth from humble beginnings among a few cycling enthusiasts.[16] Although the energy-bar category eventually became crowded, there was plenty of room for a few more independent growth stories in this same market. The highly successful Clif Bar, the next-generation winner, is worth a mention, as is the more recent LARABAR.[17] But the array of nutrient-packed, low-carb, low-glycemic-index (you get the picture) bars now lined up at the checkout even of ordinary convenience stores just proves the point that product proliferation and rapid iteration work against even relatively fresh brands, even while the power of large distributors to control shelf space lingers. I'm sure someone still eats Wonder Bread, but that's another book.

Mass Marketing Inertia: Why Do the Old Ways Persist?

Food examples serve well as a metaphor for the growing appetite for novelty in the marketplace, and the loyalty that accrues to specialists willing to cater to odd whims. Since the 1980s, American dining tastes have exploded in every direction; along with them, thousands of niche suppliers of unusual vegetables, organic products, and wine and beer (to wash it down with) have sprung up.[18] The online world has simultaneously erupted with a well-organized, searchable outpouring of chatter from foodies and lifestyle junkies at sites like Chowhound.com and Yelp.com. Sometimes you only realize how specific your tastes have become when something is taken away. My local liquor stores appear to no longer stock Anchor Steam, a popular San Francisco–based microbrew. *I'm* steamed.

Another book would also be needed to cover the concept of authenticity. Some mass brands got that way because, like the PowerBar or Under Armour apparel (originally designed to be worn under athletic uniforms such as football pads), they were seen as the cultish province of experts or elites. Under Armour did just as Godin suggests: it went after a seemingly small niche in performance athletic clothing (particularly underwear) and overwhelmed it with its remarkability. The hunger for authenticity as an antidote to bland homogeneity; the need for "my" personalized choice in a world of seemingly endless choice; and a desire for connectedness to stave off an excess of digital anonymity; all of this is hard to exaggerate. In the coming years, these trends will strongly affect marketers' ability to tell their stories and sell their products and services online.

Between you and me—as interested as we may be in AdWords' role in the front row, 50-yard line of online marketing today—it's OK if we accept that larger trends and mass advertising will sometimes continue to drown out our little $30 billion industry. Under Armour is a cool brand; an analysis of why it took off would stretch the abilities of nearly any social scientist, but it would start with young athletes' widespread identification with professional heroes, and mass marketing through major sports leagues and TV. Moisture-wicking undergarments, once the purview of efficient, low-paid, gorp-gobbling Nordic skiers, has reached mass appeal presumably due to the sexier role models who have adopted tougher-looking new brands. The fact that Under Armour celebrated (and maybe perpetuated) their success with a Super Bowl ad in 2008 doesn't make me respect them less. With the advent of "generous" sizing for their various clothing lines, this cult brand now has the potential to literally reach a "mass" market much as Nike and others have done by appealing to semi- and non-athletes. Surely Under Armour is too successful to nitpick. I'm not even running to Google to cook up a scorecard on their use of search advertising. Well, OK, maybe I am. But I'll bury my thoughts in a footnote.[19]

Google's Unassuming, Yet Butt-Kicking, Beginnings

Quietly, and seemingly unrelated to all of this background learning about marketing and advertising, I was writing about emerging search engine technologies. In October 1999, shortly after launching my site Traffick.com (at the time, subtitled "The Guide to Portals"), I reviewed two new entries, Google and Ask Jeeves, that were facing off against powerful incumbents like AltaVista, AllTheWeb, and Inktomi. Google got a positive rating. I concluded the review: "Best of all, the Google site is devoid of advertising. Enjoy it while it lasts."[20]

At that time, the one-year-old startup, led by Stanford computer science doctoral candidates Larry Page and Sergey Brin, had few ideas about how the company would make money. Unlike portal companies such as Yahoo, they didn't scheme about how to "lock users in" or how to "make their site sticky." They didn't spend days in investing seminars spreading hype about how they would "monetize the eyeballs." They basically stuck to improving their web search technology. Based on initially favorable reviews from journalists, researchers, librarians, and enthusiasts like myself (in short, the technorati), word spread rapidly about the quality of search results on Google's site, the lack of clutter on the page, and the speed with which results were served. Google's index passed its challengers in terms of index size at 500 million documents in June 2000 and never looked back.[21]

Many observers assumed Google would make its money by licensing the technology as an enterprise search solution (Google now does this, but earns little from the effort) or by distributing its results through a major portal that required a search index. (Google got its biggest push forward by inking just such a deal with Yahoo, which ended the relationship when Google became a competitive threat.) Today, Google Search is a leading online destination in every country in the world. It may come as a surprise to some readers to learn that 99% of Google's $21-billion-and-growing in annual revenues are currently derived from advertising. Google alone dominates both the online advertising industry and even the advertising industry as a whole in many countries. According to the Internet Advertising Bureau, of a total £2.016 billion spent in the UK on online ads in 2006, Google's share was a whopping 43%.[22] Other recent UK reports show that Google recently moved into second place as the top ad revenue earner overall (online or offline), behind only television station ITV, and ahead of third-place earner Channel 4.[23]

Albeit with a number of modifications, the experience of using Google Search today is not so different from the way it was when there was no advertising. Google wisely realized that their biggest asset was a large population of search engine users, so they released their ad program cautiously, making sure that the ads were in a nonintrusive format. New search services, such as Google News, Google Maps, Google Local, Google Desktop, and Google Earth, and products like Gmail and Google Calendar are released cautiously and without much if any ad clutter.

Thanks in large part to Google's efforts, search engine advertising is now the leading engine of growth in online advertising. Few would argue that, to this point, it's been a genuine success story in marrying the ideal of less-intrusive marketing methods with the ability to build a business by reaching out to interested prospects. In the remainder of this chapter, I'll present additional evidence to prove to you how big a deal search advertising has become. Google is now overwhelmingly the category leader, which means that most online advertisers need to consider Google AdWords as their top priority in any paid search campaign. If you're already aware of these figures, skip ahead to The Growth of Search Marketing.

Search Marketing Facts and Figures

Although my specialty is paid search, and in particular, AdWords, I consider my own consulting shop to be a *search marketing* firm. (Because we offer a variety of services, one day I might make the leap to calling it "online marketing"—but I'm under no illusion that people currently contact us for anything other than our reputation in paid search.) Many of my colleagues are self-described search marketers. Only recently have we been able to gather reliable statistical information about this market. Understanding the size and dimensions of the search advertising market is important because it helps put things in perspective. You don't want to underestimate the power of your search marketing efforts, but you don't want to have unrealistic expectations of the medium, either. It will grow, but for now, it's dwarfed by the advertising industry as a whole.

Size of the Advertising Market

How much do companies spend on advertising in general? As you'll see, this is a huge sector. The spending shift towards the relatively small search marketing arena is well underway, and far from complete. As of this writing, the constantly evolving annual revenue total for Google, nearly all derived from advertising, is projected to be $21 billion for 2008. When this hits $50 billion, no doubt the pace of the shift will begin to slow.

What Large Companies Spend on Ad Campaigns

The size of the advertising market as a whole is enormous, but in the coming decade, much of the fat will be trimmed, and advertisers will look for new ways to spend the remaining funds.

Ad agency veterans view the overall shift broadly in terms of a move from "traditional" media spends to "nontraditional." Overheard in conversation: worried ad agency executives admitting to new media publishers that nontraditional media spends will soon surpass 40% from their current levels. Major conglomerates have recently been devoting fully 20% of their massive ad budgets to nontraditional media exposure; they are also waking up to the fact that their massive media buying power, as leveraged through traditional channels and existing agency relationships, is not leading to expected efficiencies.[24]

Other huge shifts in ad buying behavior are benefiting online media buying models. Today, a growing number of corporate advertisers are spurning "upfront" television ad spend commitments, which means they aim to plan more meticulously, in order to trim fat in their ad budgets and to buy only the media they want, when they want it. They'll also be investigating more performance-based (or at least measurable) advertising strategies.

The TV-industrial complex has some life in it yet, but the days of mass brand campaigns and even mass media are on the wane. Funnily, comparing today's most-watched TV shows with run-of-the-mill episodes of *Carter Country* and *Night Rider*, former Google ad sales strategist Patrick Keane has been among those reminding us that today's top-rated TV shows wouldn't have cracked the top 25 in Nielsen ratings in the 1980s.[25]

This analysis, by the way, can be overdone. Today's top-rated shows, and even middle-tier cable television favorites, still attract audiences in the millions and tens of millions. This must be why Keane recently left Google for CBS: there's life in the old girl yet.

Search isn't the only nontraditional form of advertising that is gaining traction. But it's probably the best-known and most reliable, in the sense that, already, hundreds of thousands of advertisers have search marketing accounts and already track their spending and understand roughly what impact that spend has on business outcomes.

Large companies spend a ton on advertising, generally speaking. In a typical year, the global media buy for just the top four advertisers in the world (of late, that has been General Motors, Procter & Gamble, Unilever, and Johnson & Johnson) reaches as much as $15 billion.[26]

Spending on Classified Advertising and Direct Marketing

Patterns of newspaper ad spending over the past 50 years or so are interesting to examine as part of the whole advertising picture. As a proportion of the entire newspaper ad spend and in absolute terms, classified ads grew rapidly, reaching a peak of $19.6 billion in 2000 before leveling off to their current $14.2 billion of the $42.2 billion total newspaper print ad spend (for 2007). The biggest spenders are in the automotive, real estate, and employment sectors.[27]

No media spending shift has been so abrupt as the shift from offline to online classifieds. The effect on traditional newspapers has been significant, but the dire consequences facing traditional offline publishing models will no doubt be played out over a longer time frame than some doomsayers predict. Many new players in local search and classifieds have sprung up in the past five years, increasingly fueled by venture capital interest. But traditional offline classifieds companies are not necessarily left behind. Many are simply shifting their resources to online properties. An important example is Canada's Trader Corporation, established in 1975. Today, Trader Corporation owns rights to brands like *Auto Trader*, publishing in a variety of offline and online classifieds verticals throughout the world, sometimes in partnership with other shareholders. The company is now a wholly owned subsidiary of Canada's Yellow Pages Group. It's difficult to speculate, but in spending in the neighborhood of $1 billion to acquire Trader Corp., we can assume that Yellow Pages Group saw a classified advertising business that was well positioned to make a smooth transition to an online model.

Depending on whom you talk to, direct-response advertising (of which direct mail is a subset) is another mammoth category. It's also commonly one of the media compared directly with Google AdWords. According to the Direct Marketing Association, total U.S. spending on direct-response advertising was $203 billion in 2003, which represented a 5% increase over the previous year. Total direct marketing–driven sales reached $1.7 trillion in 2003, and this was composed of $904 billion in lead-generation efforts, $635 billion in direct-order sales, and $212 billion in traffic generation.

Since Google AdWords combines elements of a variety of traditional forms of print advertising, it can be useful to stack them up against one another. No matter how you measure it, the size of the online advertising business is no longer considered small. From 2003–2005, online advertising was widely seen as being in recovery mode from a downturn. Today, it's widely acknowledged to be flourishing. By the end of fiscal 2008, Google alone will have generated significantly more annual ad revenue than most observers had predicted for the entire search ads sector just three or four years ago, and more than some had predicted for all of online advertising.

Size of the Online Advertising Market

As the numbers presented in the previous section clearly show, offline advertising still eclipses online advertising by a wide margin. But online advertising is no longer in its infancy. Most of the studies cited in recent years, including those in the first edition of this book, underestimated the growth in online ad spend. The online ads sector came to maturity while prognosticators and media planners were standing around speculating when that would happen. A recent analysis by research firm IDC has global online advertising spending hitting $65.2 billion in 2008; they project $106 billion by 2011.[28] On the face of it, these figures are confusing. Doesn't this mean Google accounts for a whopping one-third of the global advertising spend (on all types of online ads)? In a word, yes. (The accounting may have some complications, as Google reports revenues without subtracting partner referral shares, referred to as "traffic acquisition costs," which makes their revenues from partnerships appear higher than they really are.)

The distinction between online and offline advertising will blur as media converge and as more of the world becomes digital. Microsoft CEO Steve Ballmer stated in a speech in March 2004 that in ten years, all media dollars will wind up online because the separation between televisions, mobile devices, and PCs won't exist.[29]

And what's to say a newspaper company won't offer an automated online auction system to sell part of its advertising inventory? (Or perhaps they'd begin with selling print classifieds through an online interface.) As this begins to happen, advertisers will become more accustomed to online control panels (similar to Google AdWords, perhaps) to manage both online and offline ad campaigns. As early as 2005, one newspaper, *The Boston Globe,* tried a pilot project of this type. A popular half-page ad space that normally sells for $50,000 was auctioned online with a starting bid of $20,000. Stay tuned: we'll be seeing lots more of this. Ad networks and exchanges, some newspaper-owned, are being launched with increasing regularity. Second-tier paid search advertising provider Marchex (the company is something of a holding company with a variety of specialties, including a concentration on domain name inventory) has recently launched Adhere, a "national local advertising network."

Down the road, given the value of the underlying converged online-offline advertising inventory among print publishers and content owners, Google will likely make itself the leading contender to become the platform to run efficient advertising auctions. There is much incentive for other companies—Microsoft, Yahoo, and the content owners themselves—to throw their hats into this ring as well.

The allocation of advertising dollars, at least between offline print ads and online ads of various types, depends in part on how consumers spend their time. We already see marked declines in newspaper readership among young people and marked increases in time spent online. A recent survey of "business decision makers" showed that most spend more than two hours a day online (excluding email), and that a significant reduction in television watching was the main price paid. The Internet is the main medium by which such decision makers access news and information while at work.[30] Media buyers are now rapidly adjusting to these changing sensibilities and information consumption patterns.

Types of Online Ad Formats

Now that advertisers track the return on investment of their online campaigns quite carefully, anecdotal evidence abounds about the effectiveness of various channels and ad formats. For our purposes, we needn't be too comprehensive in the discussion, as we'll be focusing on search, and some other types of ad units also brokered by search companies.

Owners of large content websites are probably the best sources to cite when it comes to trends in user responses to (and going rates for) various graphical online advertising formats.

Academic studies provide fairly conclusive evidence that users don't like intrusive ad formats. That being said, ads pay for a lot of the content available online. So where's the right balance? It's obvious to me that (1) we do need to find that right balance, and (2) there are a lot of publishers and advertisers still trying to stick their heads in the sand when it comes to the viability of intrusive ad formats. Academic usability studies prove negative responses to some kinds of ads, and advertisers can measure poor response, yet do a search for an intrusive format on a blog search engine and you'll find hundreds of recent posts extolling their benefits. But the worst history seems to be behind us in the area of pop-ups and such formats.

Unfortunately, reliable aggregate data about campaign effectiveness in various ad formats can be hard to come by and, in any case, won't help the individual advertiser very much, as results vary widely from case to case. Some mainstream advertisers continue to be content with measures proving *brand lift*—an impact proven to be significant for all forms of online advertising, including search.[31]

Search Ads Don't Win Awards: "Multimedia" Ads Do

In other cases, new "multimedia" formats—almost reminiscent of TV ads—are being touted as the hot new thing. Recently, I was asked to judge a variety of interactive and multimedia ads for the ad:tech awards. Frankly, it felt in most cases like a continuation of TV commercial history. I'm in no position to judge these ads unless I see performance data. I did find that many of them irritated me. Several chose the exact same clichéd themes (insurance, cars, and a shoe care product all with the same basic theme: life is fast!). In a couple of cases, the fact that a multimedia banner ad in the auto industry drove a few thousand clicks and a couple hundred sales leads was touted as a huge win for the ad agency. But at what cost? The media buy alone would have been costly, but then you need to factor in the ad production cost. In reality, many of these campaigns appeared to be huge money-losers for the advertiser. Using paid search with simple text ads, we search marketers would have achieved much higher lead volume at much lower cost. No wonder the ad agencies need to fall back on "brand lift."

In this book, I focus more closely on the directly measurable return on investment that is a hallmark of paid search advertising. (An encouraging sign is the recent establishment of the SES Awards, which judges entries in categories such as "Best Business-to-Business Search Marketing Campaign." The first winners were announced at Search Engine Strategies San Jose in August, 2008.)

Reality Check: Traditional Online Ad Networks No Longer Dominate

The first big wave of Internet advertising focused on banners and email ads. Major portals like Excite, Yahoo, and AOL, and ad-serving middlemen like DoubleClick, earned their keep largely by buying and selling overpriced banners. In the Toronto Google sales office, of the three main people I deal with, two formerly worked in ad sales for DoubleClick, and one was an account manager with Excite. This provides a snapshot of the recent history of the online ad business.

Because the online ad sector focusing on banners and email received considerable funding and enjoyed a financial heyday, assumptions about the relative importance of banner and email ads lingered past their expiry dates. Today, although the exact number is difficult to pinpoint, search advertising revenues are approaching 50% of all online ads. Leading search advertising providers (Google and Yahoo, primarily) have branched out and now serve text ads all over the Web, where blinking banners used to be. They're also fanning out into email ads. In the past two years, Google has begun aggressively experimenting with creating a marketplace for a wide variety of ad formats—not served on Google Search, of course, but in other places, both online and offline. They're even tinkering with radio, print, and TV. In other words, the search advertising providers are essentially the brokers for the second wave of online advertising.

The bottom line? Don't underestimate the importance of search advertising. It's this sector that rescued the online advertising sector as a whole and continues to drive its growth. Whether the Google push into other media will prove successful, or a healthy trend in the fight against surplus interruption, remains to be seen. But there's no question that more efficient media buying marketplaces will provide better deals for advertisers and publishers alike. Some publishers will lose money as overpriced inventory gets discounted.

The fate of first-wave ad network DoubleClick tells the tale of the rise and fall of the traditional online ad business. Once a powerhouse, DoubleClick's June 2005 market valuation of $1.05 billion (in spite of considerable diversification through the acquisition of a variety of smaller, profitable companies) was dwarfed by Google's $78.5 billion valuation. The firm was sold in 2005 to a private equity firm, for about that $1.05 billion valuation. In April 2007, Google's lofty but steady $146 billion valuation (showing a not-entirely frothy trailing price-to-earnings ratio of 47) allowed it to contemplate the acquisition of dying DoubleClick as if it were deciding what to have for lunch (literally). In the end, the pull of consolidation, coupled with Google's growing recognition of their weakness in online display ads and partnerships with "well-lit" online properties attractive to large ad agencies and large advertisers, convinced them to acquire DoubleClick for the gaudy figure of $3.1 billion. The former ad serving powerhouse was able to stick around long enough to be a minor thorn in the new kingpin's side, but it had no hope of victory. Overreacting to the consolidation, an *Information Week* writer argued that Google's deal for DoubleClick could be the end of Yahoo.[32]

Another ad-serving company that experienced both the boom and the bust of the online advertising industry, 24/7 Real Media, was valued at about $500 million shortly before being acquired (in May 2007) by global ad agency WPP for about $650 million; Aquantive, another online ad industry player that combined smaller ad networks and related technology units to form a sizeable force in the sector, was valued at little more than $3 billion shortly before its acquisition by Microsoft for an impressive $6 billion, also in May 2007, a week following the 24/7 acquisition by WPP. Another player in the sector, ValueClick, has seen its value slide from $2.75 billion as of April 2007 to about $1 billion in August 2008. Remaining independent this long, the buyout rumors that gave lift to its valuation have now given way to concerns that a variety of ValueClick's properties are under direct threat from competitors: particularly Google.

Combined, these three traditional online ad brokerages are worth less than $8 billion, compared to the $175 billion combined valuation of their key competitors, Google and Yahoo. What seems to be happening is that Google and Yahoo, along with Microsoft and a couple of other major "portals" (destination sites; those who control traffic flows or own lots of online content), are gaining more and more control over advertising inventory, leaving the other middlemen to mine relatively small and low-margin niches as service providers or operators of specialized advertising and e-commerce platforms. The scale (and scalability) of ad serving works in the winners' favor. The losers fight for scraps, specialize, or exit the space. What's ironic is that the shift was largely financed by the incredible success of search—which started out, in Google's case, with no ads at all. As Google expands its footprint, these small competitors are even more threatened unless they figure out how to operate profitably in Google's shadow. For example, an affiliate marketing exchange operated for years by Performics, a division of DoubleClick, is now offered by Google following the DoubleClick acquisition. This directly threatens companies like Commission Junction, a division of ValueClick.

Despite the threats, brokering a variety of advertising markets can be customized, hands-on work, and Google can't dominate every relationship in every international market. Its competitors will continue to enjoy localized wins and seem currently to be enjoying the fruits of the rising tide that is reviving many hopes in the online ad sector.

Other online ad-serving companies that have at least some search inventory in their portfolios include Ask.com and Miva. Ask.com, widely acknowledged as the fourth-place search engine, is owned by a large holding company, IAC Interactive, and as such, it's difficult to value the company today. IAC's other properties include LendingTree, Ticketmaster, Service Magic, and Match.com. Second-tier paid search provider Miva has struggled to keep pace with the leaders, and has slid precipitously of late to penny-stock status. The company is currently valued at a scant $27 million, even worse than also-ran LookSmart, which has recently rebounded to $51 million.

In light of these trends, to state that Google carries the banner for online advertising today would be an understatement as well as a pun. In recent years, Microsoft and Yahoo have provided able, if not strong, competition. It makes logical sense. Consolidation and scale are driving the online advertising industry. The economics support technologies that combine customization and wide reach so that ad buyers can make efficient buys without running all over the place.

The Growth of Search Marketing

Two things we know for sure are that email is the most popular online activity and that search is second. But how does this translate into time spent viewing advertisers' messages? What levels of ad revenues are being generated by the activity? Let's look at how visits to websites are measured.

Search Engine User Growth

Until relatively recently, an observer would have been hard pressed to get a solid handle on the popularity of various search services. One statistic common to many industry reporting formats has been *reach*. A *web property* (typically a conglomerate or portal that owns many websites and interrelated services) might get credit for reaching a user if that user visits the entire network at least once in a month.

More recently, panel-based web measurement company comScore Networks has been doing more to specifically break out search data, releasing useful reports on monthly "share of searches" and the like. The information is only occasionally made public; most of the detail is buried in custom reports for corporate subscribers. Simply put, *share of searches* is a measure based on how many times a specific user performs any type of search in a month. If hypothetical user Jill used the same search engine to perform 20 different searches in a day, the count would be 20, or if she performed only 1 search on a different day, the count would be 1. Let's say Jill performed 100 searches in a month, where 50 of them were on Google Search, 36 on Yahoo Search, 7 on Ask.com, 5 on Metacrawler.com, and 2 on MSN Search. For Jill, Google's share of searches would be 50% for that month. This is a useful way of measuring the popularity of a search engine, but for some reason, the data haven't always been reported this way in the press.

In January 2007, U.S. searchers performed 3.8 billion searches on Google alone, and 6.9 billion searches in total, according to Nielsen/NetRatings. The average Canadian searches more than the average American in a given month, 40 searches to 35. comScore reports that *search penetration*— the number of Internet users who actually use search engines—is higher in Canada than it is south of the border, at 85%. Amazingly, in their study, only 73% of U.S. Internet users performed any type of search. In the coming years this penetration will no doubt reach close to 100% in most countries.[33] Given the fluid nature of what counts as a "search," and variability among ratings agencies, these numbers should be taken with a grain of salt.

Let's look at some recent numbers. In January 2007, comScore still had "Google Sites" search share as low as 47.5%, with "Yahoo Sites" at 28.1%, "Microsoft Sites" at 10.6%, "Ask Network" sites at 5.2%, and "Time Warner Network" at 5.0%. This confusing bundling of media properties doesn't seem to properly pin down search. Hitwise's numbers seem more realistic. (Hitwise is a major data collection and competitive intelligence research agency that has access to information about the surfing habits of 10 million Internet users in the U.S. alone.) Their U.S. search share numbers for March 2007 put Google at 64.1%, Yahoo at 21.3%, Microsoft at 8.6%, and Ask at 3.5%. These figures seem likely to be accurate within 2–3%, though many individual website owners report even higher shares of search referrals from Google.

In the U.S. market for June 2008, comScore was referring to "core search" market share, giving "Google Sites" 61.5% share, "Yahoo Sites" 20.9%, and "Microsoft Sites" 9.2%. For the same month Hitwise, by contrast, had Google Search at 69.2%, with Yahoo Search at 19.6%, and Microsoft Live Search sharply down from the previous year, at 5.6%. Because the Hitwise numbers focus more literally on pure search on the search engines alone, and because the numbers match more accurately with anecdotal views of the site stats of individual websites I have access to, I, like many of my colleagues, tend to favor the Hitwise numbers specifically with regard to search share.

It's all too easy to take these numbers as gospel. These figures will continue to be a rough guide to user activity, but the definition of a "search" will continue to evolve. In most markets, no matter how you define a "search," Google's share is over 60%. Microsoft is in danger of losing its status as a threat to overtake Yahoo as #2; Yahoo, while it has plenty of turmoil to deal with, remains comfortably situated as a weak second-place contender.

Types of Search Marketing

Marketers have recognized the benefits of search engine visibility for well over a decade. The constantly changing rules of the game of getting seen in or near search results have made it difficult to stay abreast of key trends. Unscrupulous operators continue to take advantage of business owners' naïveté in the field, selling them services they may not need, or scaring them with "ranking reports" that may obscure more than they reveal. As time consuming as it may be, you should try to keep up with the trends. Now that you know that the top three search destinations in the United States (Google, Yahoo, and Microsoft) make up as much as 90% of all search traffic, you're already more informed than many.

Optimizing for "Free" Rankings

So-called search engine optimization (SEO) has been about as widespread and controversial a practice as doping on the Tour de France. The underlying common sense behind optimizing your web presence for search engine visibility hasn't deterred high-profile SEO naysayers from getting in their digs about professional purveyors of outsourced search engine optimization consulting. Jason Calacanis, who sold Weblogs, Inc. to AOL for a reported $25 million, called SEO "bullshit" in a high-profile denunciation of the industry in a Search Engine Strategies conference keynote conversation with Danny Sullivan.[34] Prior to that, fed up with the overblown claims of search engine ranking "scammers," Seth Godin ranted on his blog: "Lucking into (and it is luck) the top slot of a great word on Google is not a business plan. It's superstition. It's blind faith." He went on to praise Google AdWords for being the opposite of luck: "If you can figure out how to BUY (not luck into) keyword searches that bring you X number of visitors, and then you can figure out how to design your site so that Y% of those visits turn into customers, you win. And nobody can stop you from growing all you care to grow."[35]

It goes without saying that strong placements in the regular, or free, search results are important. For some, attempting to achieve them morphs into a full-time job. Unfortunately, the quality of the work performed by many search engine optimization professionals has often left much to be desired. MarketingSherpa, a leading publisher of online marketing information guides, publishes a comprehensive review of search engine marketing firms. Depending on the edition, the Sherpa researchers have attempted to rate the firms' performance and to discuss best practices. The effort has had mixed results.

I myself discovered that it was easy enough to get a high rating (in the first edition of the *SEO Buyer's Guide*) as an SEO practitioner. You can get lucky! One of my clients achieved a very high ranking on a commercially lucrative search phrase, with my help. Of course the client's success story proved temporary, but it was enough to give me a four-star rating as a barely trained one-man search engine optimization "company" in 2001. In general, the causal impact of an SEO consultant's work can be difficult to prove. If you land a Fortune 500 client with a content-poor, poorly designed site, the mere act of bringing the site up to its potential by employing standards-based web design and basic SEO tactics (like clearly written page titles) can make you look like a genius.

Many of the SEO tactics commonly employed by experts are the types of things that might be advisable to do even in the absence of search engines. For example, encouraging partners, suppliers, fans, or journalists to link to your site is something you might want to do anyway, even if Google didn't also reward such activity with the PageRank component of its search ranking algorithm. Self-described "link mensch" Eric Ward has been implementing such *linking campaigns* for a decade now, beginning with a successful campaign in 1994 for a company you might have heard of: Amazon.com.

Many of the survivors in the SEO game—including Ward himself—have set themselves apart from so-called "churn and burn" SEO. Inspired by traditional public relations and marketing disciplines long stressed by industry old-timers like Ward, Sullivan, Mike Grehan, and traditional agencies, new-generation search engine optimization includes detailed public relations strategies such as "blogger relations" (approaching authoritative online sources for relevant coverage), "linkbaiting" (creating clever content that attracts a lot of onlookers), and "optimized news releases." Many later-generation practitioners of nouveau SEO are influenced by today's thought leaders such as Rand Fishkin and Greg Jarboe. Never fear, though, the "churn and burn" contingent is still out in full force, though they often lose their best members to more conservative corporate gigs.

Search marketing and its SEO subset, analogous to the consumer world they attempt to reach, have flowered into a variety of specialties and sub-niches. No one publication or source provides a definitive overview, but many of those who are best known can be found in the ranks of speakers on a multitude of topics at the key conferences in the sector: Search Engine Strategies, Search Marketing Expo, WebmasterWorld Pubcon, ad:tech, and a few others. That being said, many of the basics of SEO do not change rapidly. Shari Thurow, a leading author in the space, has just released a long-awaited second edition of her *Search Engine Visibility*.[36] This material should be supplemented by a variety of online and offline sources, of course.

Paid Inclusion

There are essentially two kinds of paid inclusion today. The first is a fee-based directory listing. The best-known of these is a Yahoo directory listing, which costs $299 per year. The second kind of paid inclusion requires you to pay a fee to have your site included in (but without any guarantee of rankings in or traffic from) a popular search index.

Inktomi (later acquired by Yahoo) was the first major web search index to adopt a paid inclusion model. Webmasters could submit a number of URLs to the index to guarantee inclusion (not ranking). Later, certain benefits of the inclusion programs were trotted out in an attempt to justify them. Webmasters were told that paid-for pages would be "re-spidered" every 48 hours. The Inktomi paid inclusion program was never clearly thought out. Rather, it was something of a panic-button reaction to the growing proliferation of index spam (paid inclusion would help weed out junk pages submitted by marketers hoping to capitalize on the free nature of the index), and an early experiment in how to defray the costs of running a search engine. Inktomi, like many search engine companies, never stumbled on a successful business model.

Others began to experiment with this methodology as well. AltaVista (also later acquired by Yahoo) famously lost credibility when its salesperson offered a marketer higher rankings in exchange for paid submission. AltaVista's public relations department quickly distanced itself from this nod-and-a-wink "rankings for cash" sales tactic, claiming it was an isolated mistake by an individual salesman and that the "trusted feed" payments guaranteed only prompt inclusion in the index.[37]

Today, Yahoo offers the best-known example of paid inclusion, now named Site Match. Like a lot of search monetization schemes, it seems awkward, so I imagine it will be phased out in favor of a flexible new "open formats" scheme Yahoo is now calling SearchMonkey. (SearchMonkey, in my vision, would remain a free upgrade for participating publishers who want to add richness to their search listings. Some larger participants might wind up paying a fee for enhanced-look search results inclusion as high-dollar sponsors.) Costs for Site Match vary; the model is a somewhat confusing hybrid of a flat fee for inclusion and a cost per click once listings are included in the Yahoo Index. (Confused yet?) Larger companies may cut bulk deals and pay only for clicks, depositing a certain amount in advance against a minimum total click charge. Because consumers may be unaware of the nature of these paid inclusion programs and what, exactly, distinguishes "real" search results from the sponsored listings, numerous observers have been critical of paid inclusion programs.[38]

There is no way to guarantee or pay for placement in Google's regular, "organic" index listings. In other words, they remain free. With its newly designed Microsoft Live Search, Microsoft has gone a similar route. As with Yahoo Search, Live Search's search results pages look similar to Google's, with unobtrusive, well-demarcated text ads above and to the right of listings.

Because paid inclusion of a large number of listings can be difficult to manage, third-party software companies and resellers have sprung up to help large companies with so-called feed management. Such facilitators typically also help large retailers get their catalogs included in shopping search engines such as Shopping.com and Shopzilla.

Keyword-Based Advertising, or Sponsored Listings

And then there are pay-per-click ads near search results, the subject of this book. When analysts talk about total expenditures on paid search, they tend to combine all forms of paid search—paid inclusion, pay-per-click listings near search results, and even so-called contextual listings served around the Web by companies like Google and Yahoo. As mentioned earlier, the addition of new ad formats to Google's menu of offerings will make it even more difficult to follow these trends, but for us AdWords junkies, we're still primarily looking at Google's core offering.

What Is an Organic Index Listing?

Over the years, a number of terms have been invented in an attempt to distinguish paid from unpaid search listings. What such terms have in common appears to be a recognition that the average search engine user in the 1990s developed a strong trust for web index search results, believing them to be "scientific" and "unbiased." Industry discussions are peppered with references to "scientific" results, the "real" results, "unpaid search indexes," and so on. There is some debate as to who coined it, but the term that really stuck to distinguish unpaid, algorithmically generated results that appear on sites like Google Search or Ask.com is *organic* listings. No preservatives added. Whatever its origins, the term has been adopted as a favorite by search marketing professionals to distinguish the unpaid results from various forms of sponsored listings that appear near those results.

Safa Rashtchy, formerly an analyst with investment bank Piper Jaffray, is perhaps the best-known Wall Street commentator on the contemporary search business. (Rashtchy recently left Piper.) Before Google's initial public offering (which required the formerly private company to finally disclose its financials in public filings), many analysts had been speculating that Google's 2003 revenues were going to be revealed as coming in around $300 million. When Rashtchy, followed by a few others, began to peg the number at something closer to $800–$900 million, it looked like something big was in the making at Google, and indeed it was. The actual 2003 revenue number blew away even Rashtchy's bold estimate: it was $1.46 billion.

Rashtchy's later projections for the paid search sector as a whole are worth noting. At the October 2004 ad:tech conference in New York, he predicted that total paid search spending will rise to $13.5 billion by 2007 and $23.2 billion by 2010, enjoying rapid growth from its humble beginnings (only $369 million as recently as 2001). He noted that these figures were approximately twice his firm's estimates made only a year earlier. The rapid growth of the sector has caught even the closest observers off guard.

According to estimates by Hoover's (a research company that maintains a database of information on 40,000 public and private companies), Google's revenues as a private company grew from a mere $50 million in 2000 to $125 million in 2002. The real 2002 number was actually a lot better than the outsiders' estimates: according to public filings, it came in at $439 million! As one who had a front-row seat working with excited new advertisers eager to try the new pay-per-click AdWords program after its release in February 2002, I wasn't surprised. Nor was I particularly surprised that 2003 revenues topped $1 billion. Back-of-the-envelope calculations of typical AdWords account sizes multiplied by a reasonable estimate of the number of active Google AdWords accounts gave careful observers good reason to believe that Google's 2003 revenues were in excess of $1 billion, not the $300 million or less that was commonly estimated by the news media.

Two major events caused Google's revenues to explode to their current levels (on pace for about $21 billion for 2008). First, in 2002, Google shifted from an unsuccessful flat-rate "cost-per-thousand-impressions" (CPM-based) ad program to a dynamic pay-per-click auction model. This attracted new interest in Google's ad program, leading to a rapid uptake of the AdWords program and bidding wars for traffic tied to popular keywords.

Second, Google expanded its reach to begin placing text listings near relevant content on partner websites through its AdSense (the name for Google's publisher ad serving system) program in summer 2003. The AdSense program grew at a breakneck pace. Of the $3.14 billion in advertising revenues earned by Google in 2004, just about half of that was generated by ads served on non-Google-owned sites. By 2006, the proportion of revenue generated on Google sites rebounded to 60.35% of the total for the year on significantly higher total revenue ($6.3 billion of $10.6 billion) due to a number of factors, which likely include downward bidding trends on non-Google ad inventory, "smart [lower] pricing" on non-Google ad inventory, rapid growth of revenue from international Google sites, further refinement of the search ads auction, ongoing usability testing on Google sites, and inflation of prices on search ads. In addition to "content" ads, the third-party revenues come from search network partners like Ask.com and custom search offerings for broadband providers like Comcast.

A big part of the Google growth story for 2004 through 2008 has been the many content publishers who began displaying the AdWords ads, making Google a force to be reckoned with as an advertising network, with larger ambitions lurking not far under the surface. Accompanying the explosion of AdSense has been the rise of something of an "AdSense economy." My counterpart on the publisher side, Jennifer Slegg, publishes a popular blog named JenSense, offering tips to webmasters on the best ways to "monetize" website content with publisher partner programs like Google's.[39] With 99% of its revenues generated from advertising, this "search company" could also be referred to as an "ad-serving company."

Yahoo, too, depends heavily on search advertising revenues, though less so than Google. According to public filings, at one time Yahoo's Search Marketing division (which also serves pay-per-click ads, now through a revamped AdWords-like platform code-named Panama) accounted for as much as 40% of Yahoo's advertising revenues. The loss of an advertising partnership with Microsoft (which developed its own paid search system) may now be offset by an improved Yahoo Search offering and the much-improved Panama paid search platform. However, the revenue picture is complex and Yahoo does not currently break out search-related revenues in its financial statements. It's likely that the proportion has stayed at or below 40%. In its most recent annual filing, the company dryly states: "We also recognize revenue from the display of text based links to the websites of our advertisers ('search advertising') which are placed on the Yahoo! Properties and also on the websites of our affiliates who have integrated our search offerings into their websites. We recognize revenue from these arrangements as 'click-throughs' occur. A 'click-through' occurs when a user clicks on an advertiser's listing."

Yahoo is a diversified company, still claiming to be the "world's most-trafficked online destination," that offers a variety of fee-based services (such as paid content, premium email, games, personals, and so on), so it isn't completely dependent on advertisers. If Google is wise, it will begin to diversify its revenue base as well. For the time being, Google has a diversified product offering (Gmail, Calendar, Talk, Docs and Spreadsheets, Google Earth), but it's all used to build Google's general dominance rather than a diversified revenue base.

Why Pay for Search Traffic? Isn't It Free?

If you're actually a visitor from 1997 and have just emerged from your time machine, you might be under the impression that it's enough just to wait around for search engine traffic to reward your business with all the traffic it needs, at no charge. This probably isn't going to happen. Most marketers believe in a healthy mix of paid and unpaid search traffic. Presumably, that's why you've decided to consult this book. There are several reasons why incorporating a paid listings strategy into your online marketing mix is essential.

Screen Real Estate, Location of Listings

At search destinations like Yahoo Search and AOL Search, more and more of the available screen real estate is taken up by paid listings. Although the sponsored listings served by companies like Yahoo and Google are generally marked to separate them from the organic search results, many users click on the most visible listings without pausing to contemplate the distinction between what is and isn't paid for.

Aggregate figures for user clickthrough rates on top-of-page sponsored listings compared with the unpaid search listings just below them are typically not disclosed, but we can assume that the search engines have tested various page configurations with an eye to revenue maximization. The bottom line is that sponsored listings, especially the top two or three, are very prominently displayed and can cut into the amount of traffic received by websites that appear in the first page of regular search results in a given category.

Therefore, the wise course is to pursue a mix of both paid and organic search traffic. In fact, there are some clear advantages to paid search. Advertisers use paid search because they want to, not only because they're "forced" to. Who ever said traffic was supposed to be free?

Some Ads Are More Relevant

If sponsored results were never judged relevant by users, no one would ever click them. The fact is, every so often (at least 15% of the time, Google staff have stated informally, and higher on commercial queries), a user decides that an ad result is more relevant than any of the search results on the page. This is particularly so, of course, for search queries that are commercial in intent. An advertiser who knows just how to present the right ad message to the right user will get noticed (and clicked).

Post-"Florida" Fallout: Algorithmic Changes

To keep ahead of the crowd of *optimizers* and *index spammers*—those who attempt (ethically or unethically, on a wide continuum) to reverse-engineer search engine algorithms so they can flood search results with commercial listings and thus profit from free traffic—Google periodically tweaks its ranking methodology. It changes weightings of various factors that affect how high pages are ranked for a given search query. Sometimes, sites using known optimization or spam techniques are penalized or banned from the index. Historically, sites would be banned for obvious spam techniques like *keyword stuffing* (repeating keywords nonsensically to try to get a higher ranking on a search term).

Google stayed ahead of a lot of early spam techniques because its PageRank methodology was fairly sophisticated. It measured the authority of a site based on how many other authoritative sites pointed to it. PageRank proved vulnerable, however. Some optimizers set up *link farms,* or premeditated interlinking schemes, with the express purpose of increasing free search engine traffic for members. Google periodically banned entire networks of sites participating in link schemes, but the tactics are difficult to stop entirely.

In fall 2003, a most unusual reindexing initiative emanated from the Googleplex, just in time for the holiday season. Suddenly, tens of thousands of commercial websites that had been playing by the rules found their rankings plummeting. Whether it was because it felt like a hurricane, or because the webmasters affected demanded a recount, the reindexing was nicknamed "Florida." Wild theories flew around in an attempt to describe what was going on. Some webmasters talked of a filter that Google was applying on top of its normal algorithm—an additional test that would recognize common patterns of over-optimization. Those who optimize websites for a living can be paranoid, but it turned out their fears were not so far from reality.

What was happening was really just a continuation of an ongoing commitment by Google to what it refers to as "search quality." Peter Norvig, a vice president in charge of search quality, went on record describing some of the tendencies that Google "might" be trying to reward in ranking pages on a given query. Google had decided to emphasize more than ever that the organic search results should be for informational queries, not commercial queries. Even within the commercial, Norvig implied that Google might attempt to make distinctions between what we might call "informational commercial pages," such as company histories, and "solely commercial pages," such as catalog pages. Left unsaid was their nonetheless clear message: commercially oriented pages are most suitable for the AdWords program. Those who want to reach customers should pay for targeted clicks and optimize their paid search campaigns for the best possible results.

Nate Tyler, a member of Google's public relations department, was uncharacteristically candid about the "Florida" fallout, telling me in an interview that site owners need to be aware that "Google Search was never intended as a service whose sole purpose was to generate traffic for commercial sites." He came very close to saying if you don't like it, use the AdWords program. Google was accused of deliberately shaking up their free rankings to send a message to website owners that they needed to buy paid listings from Google. By not vehemently denying those charges, Google seemed to be tacitly admitting that it was not above manipulating its search algorithms in ways that "reminded" webmasters to focus more of their time on paid search campaigns if they wanted their search referrals to continue.

In spite of its push for AdWords participation, there is no direct relationship I'm aware of between buying paid listings and getting better free rankings on Google, though a variety of statistical analyses have demonstrated indirect relationships between buying paid ads and improved search rankings. (This makes sense insofar as any marketing effort should create the types of broader attention that would improve overall search standing; and paid search is a particularly effective type of marketing effort.) In formal terms, the paid ads and the algorithmic search remain unrelated, but as a Google director of ads quality, Nick Fox, put it, "Google's thinking about relevancy and quality in the organic listings and in the paid search rankings are far from siloed."[40] Website owners should participate in the AdWords program because it's a good opportunity for prime exposure on search results pages, not because they assume they'll be getting special consideration for sending Google a "bribe." Guess what: Google doesn't need the money. Their long-term currency, now as always, is editorial integrity.

What Is a Googleplex?

For all of its "virtualness," Google is a company with a strong sense of place. Googleplex is the nickname for Google's headquarters in Mountain View, California, which opened in 1999. Google completed a move to a new, larger facility in early 2004. Along with being a major campus for the world's most-watched technology company, this "plex"—purchased from original owner Silicon Graphics for $320 million—is the home of an annual event called the Google Dance, held in conjunction with the Search Engine Strategies San Jose conference each August.

The name Google is a misspelling of the word *googol* (a word coined by a mathematician in 1938, which means a very large number—1 followed by 100 zeros). *Googolplex,* as it happens, is the name for an even larger number. Visitors to Google's now-legendary headquarters will come across colorful graphical depictions of user search behavior, a fully stocked game room, a large dining area, and other quirks, such as machines that dispense M&Ms. As public scrutiny of the company has increased, puns, practical jokes, and sly references to pornography searches have no doubt been toned down, but Google is unlikely to ever shed its culture as a company that works endlessly and plays together. When I had my first tour of the first-generation Googleplex in August 2002, Sergey Brin's office was pointed out to me. Inside was a large metal waste can containing several hockey sticks whose blades were worn down to a sharp point from Brin's frequent participation in company road hockey games.

As I wrote this paragraph in the first edition in January 2005, most of the company (including the customer service department) was off-site at a ski retreat. In summer 2006 I and a colleague enjoyed lunch with a Google staffer in one of two massive Google cafeterias bursting with themed offerings from a variety of international cuisines. At the Google Dance the same week, I came across an odd sign in the rest room: a cryptic reminder to coders called "Testing on the Toilet." The previous spring I caught a glimpse of the Google New York office, smaller in scale, with a smaller lunch buffet, but with a more than ample supply of delicious eats and an excess of candy dispensers. My host told me that P. Diddy (Sean Combs) had previously owned the floor Google was on. The floor? To me, it seemed like Google was on about six floors of their Manhattan digs, and ever expanding. Today, Google has ever more office space around the world, to say nothing of datacenters. Notably, Google has made significant investments in the local economies of India, Ireland, Michigan, and South Carolina. Glimpses of Google culture are less and less novel for some of us, but the economic impact of the company is hard for anyone to ignore.

Many hard-core optimizers (those who make their entire living from gaming search results, with no provision for paid traffic) want to believe they can still beat Google's algorithm. You'd better be very good at optimizing if you want to act as if you didn't hear what Google was saying in fall 2003, however. Many ordinary business owners, formerly enamored of their SEO consultants' omnipotent powers to generate high rankings in the free index, now realize that Tyler and Norvig meant exactly what they said in the days following the infamous "Florida" update: Google is going to reduce the proportion of commercial websites that rank well in search results. While some lucky ones may continue to do well, it will be a bumpy ride for most anyone who relies solely on unpaid traffic.

Yes, commercially oriented websites will continue to reside in the Google index, and many formerly high-ranking pages have a good shot at continuing to rank reasonably well. But it seems that a great number of informational pages, such as discussion forums, weblogs, university professors' home pages, public radio transcripts, the ubiquitous Wikipedia, consumer review sites like TripAdvisor, magazine articles, and the like, are now dominating top rankings on many search queries. As a result, those who relied on those top rankings for revenue-producing traffic will need to diversify their approach.

Observers may note that on certain types of commercial queries, such as those referring to brand names, the organic results may remain full of commercially oriented websites. However, even here, webmasters sometimes report troubles getting good rankings. At the very least, there seems to be more volatility in rankings than there once was.

It's unwise to become too complacent about the status of organic listings. Even a very popular commercial phrase—**coca-cola**—won't always give Coke unfettered access to consumers' eyeballs. On this query typed into Google Search in 2005, Google actually placed two results from Google News above the first web index listing (which is indeed for the Coca-Cola home page). Today, I'm seeing Coke's site as the first organic listing, but two of my own stored files are listed above that, because Google integrates my own Google Desktop Search results with regular search results. Farther down the search results page, a popular critique site, killercoke.org, is still prominent, and not to Coke's advantage by any stretch. Search engine companies don't think your company has a "right" to any particular visibility profile in their results.

Control Over Message, Navigation, Timing, Exposure

What could be seen as forced diversification into paid search might be the best thing that ever happened to many search marketers, because it compels them to run more disciplined marketing programs. I'm biased, but I do see search as a foundation of any online marketing program. Organic search, however, can be a shaky foundation due to its unpredictability. While more expensive on the surface, paid search offers a more solid foundation in a number of ways.

Organic search has an informational, or content, bias. So, the "informational" pages on your site that are most likely to rank well in the unpaid search results might not be the best types of pages for you from a business standpoint. Search engines can decide on their own how to treat the visible page descriptions the searcher sees, for example. They might choose a snippet of text from the page, as Google often does; choose a selection of text from a major directory such as Dmoz.org; or directly draw on the meta description tag you've placed in the HTML header of your document. In short, the page the engine decides to index might not be a carefully tailored offer page, and the initial messaging (the visible description) might not be favorable to your sales process.

With paid search, you decide on the ad title and ad copy. You tell the system which landing page the user should go to, and install tracking that will confirm for you whether a given paid click resulted in a sale.

You can also control the delivery of a paid search campaign. Different offers and specials can be featured at different times of the year. You can turn campaigns off on weekends if you wish. You can turn off the half of your campaign that performs poorly, while leaving the rest running. Paying for traffic gives you a greater degree of control over your message and the timing of that message.

Furthermore, you can, to a considerable extent, control where your message is displayed. If you want AOL and Ask.com users to see your ad, you can expand your ad delivery to Google AdWords network partners. Or you can just buy exposure on Google only. Now, even more micro-targeting is possible with Google's regional targeting feature that allows you to show your ads only to designated metropolitan areas or geographic areas specified with a latitude-and-longitude tool. You can also specify which countries see your ad. If you're ambitious, you can run ads in different languages.

Noncommercial Sites and the Organic Results

There are some good reasons why certain kinds of informational, content-rich sites do well in search engines and, conversely, why sales-oriented sites don't always do well. Search engines were built to discover topical content—to index text. If your site is not text rich, why try to impress search engines with a lot of content you don't genuinely feel is of interest to your target buyers? By purchasing paid listings, you can quickly skirt the problem of being content poor. Content is king? Maybe. But if you're not in the content business, you needn't buy into this cliché if you have paid search at your disposal to drive targeted visitors to commercially oriented pages.

Another element of many search engine algorithms today, most famously Google's, is analysis of inbound links. Sites with many inbound links from other authoritative sites get better search engine rankings, by and large. But if you're a local paint store, it's not particularly realistic to expect hundreds of other websites to link to you, no matter how great your customer service might be. At one point, as that paint store, you might have stood out from other paint stores by having three or four good-quality inbound links (from external sites pointing to you). Today, everyone does "linking campaigns," so you're seemingly forced to enter into an arms race, where, as that paint store, you're up against another paint store who has gone out and incentivized third parties to the point where that lowly little paint store now has 600 or 1,200 "quality" links pointing to them. To outdo them, you're going to need 1,300 links of equal or better quality. It's reached the point of absurdity. Good public relations makes sense, but you shouldn't have to do it unnaturally, sneaking around and paying folks with high-authority websites to "link" to you, pretending they think your site (that sells paint) is an "awesome resource."

Some categories of business do attract a lot of links by their very nature. Hotels, for example, are often linked from the websites of businesses, trade shows, and associations who may be meeting at the hotel for a conference. Restaurants may garner recommendations from magazines and bloggers who might decide to link to the restaurant's site as a sign of their approval. But some businesses face tough sledding when it comes to getting inbound links beyond the ones that are easy to pay for (such as the Yahoo Directory). Linking campaigns are portrayed as an integral part of a search engine optimization strategy by some service vendors. But these campaigns have become more difficult to conduct, especially for smaller businesses that would have to bother strangers to ask them for a link. When you're selling something and people know you are, a lot of them will be stingy with links, since many website owners now understand that links confer authority. Hence the secondary marketplace where you can plunk down a bunch of cash to have a specialist contrive a way for you to attract thousands of inbound links. In 1999, I thought linking campaigns were cool. Done legitimately, I still do. But the way many of them are conducted today is nothing short of moronic.

The best way to get a lot of authoritative websites to link to your site, of course, is to follow Seth Godin's advice from the *Purple Cow* book: create a remarkable product or service; say something remarkable; do something remarkable; *be* remarkable. Or, you could join a link farm and hope Google doesn't ban your site from the index.

Or, you could integrate a paid search campaign into your strategy. A successful paid search campaign doesn't know if you have 200 pages of quality content on your website and doesn't care if not a single other website links to yours.

Organic and Paid Search Strategies: Not Mutually Exclusive

I often wonder why practitioners of paid and organic search marketing seem compelled to put one another down. Clearly, as a marketing channel, search is good. Without ads, search engine companies would go out of business (as they used to do with regularity in the 1990s). More importantly, paid search has a special discipline all its own. So what is it about veterans in the field of organic search optimization that compels them to treat paid search like an afterthought?

Some of my old friends in the industry are quite "separatist" about it to this day. One well-known expert in writing for search engines—a good friend—was discussing an episode of a client losing rankings in Google Search, and lamenting that instead of sticking it out to attempt to dig their way out of the hole, the client will probably "just hire Mr. Pay-Per-Click here." Another friend, an expert in designing websites for search engine visibility, makes a number of sensible points in her seminars about the need for a long-term view of how to rank well in search engines, rather than hiring hacks to do "cheap tricks" to deceive search engines. So far, so good. Then, she turns to the audience and says, half-jokingly, "or if you're lazy, you can just do paid search—go talk to Andrew." <begin mock indignation> Do you see the bags under these eyes? Do I look lazy to you? </end of mock indignation>

I can't tell you precisely how to allocate your time and resources when it comes to pursuing paid search traffic as opposed to better organic listings. As you embark on your paid search campaign, you'll develop useful new skills and knowledge related to your customer base. More importantly, you'll probably gain customers you never would have seen had you relied solely on unpaid search referrals for generating new business. You'll gain a level of control over your message and the pace of delivery that is simply impossible with unpaid, "stumble-in" search traffic. Paying for clicks is not admitting defeat, as some SEO consultants seem to believe.

Whether the traffic is paid or unpaid, companies of all sizes are beginning to appreciate the unique qualities of search marketing. Google's widely reported business successes have given the whole idea of paid search the credibility it needs to become a real force in the advertising industry as a whole. As this chapter has shown, search advertising is still a small industry when compared to direct marketing and media buying as a whole. But with its superior targeting and noninterruptive format, the planets may well be aligned for continued rapid growth.

Endnotes

1. Apparently, great minds think alike. A couple of weeks after penning this sentence, I ran across a post by Future Now's Holly Buchanan, on her *Marketing to Women Online* blog. In "Do Your Customers Feel Stalked?" Buchanan writes about the unabated tendency of marketers to push consumers into relationships they don't want—in this case, the rabid collection of email addresses, years after many of us got sick of being bombarded by so-called permission-based email communications. Attending a concert, Holly was approached by a liquor sponsor flogging some promotion, asking for email addresses. "You want my real email address?" writes Buchanan. "One I actually check? You have to build a relationship with me first. My email is sacred space. I actively comb it for unwanted messages and report spam diligently. . . . Too many companies take advantage of my permission. They bombard me with emails day after day after day. I feel smothered. I feel taken advantage of. . . . What part of 'no' do you not understand?" She concludes with a question all marketers should ask themselves: "Are you stalking your customers?" Archived at http://marketingtowomenonline.typepad.com/blog/2007/04/do_your_custome.html.

2. Chris Anderson, *The Long Tail: Why the Future of Business Is Selling Less of More* (Hyperion, 2006), is the definitive resource for understanding this phenomenon. What Anderson doesn't do is explain the full history of so-called post-Fordism, as captured by academic observers. These sometimes grandiose scenarios (save yourself time, and go for the Wikipedia version) attempted to explain how capitalism moved onto a new "phase" beginning in the 1970s. Changes in production technologies and, now, communications have evolved with (and in some cases, caused) not only economic shifts, but political, administrative, and cultural changes in all modern societies. Today's capitalism isn't purely defined by mass production of a relatively short list of goods. Rather, producers and consumers (and the social, technological, and political systems that support them) have much enhanced capacity for personalization and specialization. The most obvious example of this economic shift is the rise of a business like Amazon, or the rapid decline of old business models in the recording industry in favor of iTunes and personal media libraries. But the changes to industries are so wide and deep they could fill a few more volumes from authors like Anderson.

3. Joseph Jaffe, *Life After the 30-Second Spot* (John Wiley & Sons, 2005), 38–39.

4. The Piper Jaffray study, Safa Rashtchy, et al., *The User Revolution: The New Advertising Ecosystem and the Rise of a Mass Market* (February, 2007), is so comprehensive I won't be able to resist citing it several times.

5. Although some observers, such as the publishers of *Adbusters* magazine, think of advertising as being so bad that they recommend practices like "culture jamming." The question is: does this mostly constitute a reaction against things some of us don't like, or does it include a coherent model of an alternate lifestyle or form of social organization? The first step

towards advocating a social model, it seems to me, is figuring out the role of people you fundamentally disagree with. If the Adbusters crew have no proposal for how we can all get along, their influence will be unlikely to grow beyond its current cult following.

6. With thanks to Pliny the Elder, or whoever might have inspired me to come up with this concept.

7. In Google's initial public offering (IPO) filing, in the "risks" section, company executives reminded investors that "any user could consign Google to oblivion with little more than a mouse click." (According to David Lagesse, "The World According to Google," *US News & World Report,* May 2, 2004. Craig Silverstein, Google's Director of Technology, emphasized that "the costs of switching search engines are ridiculously low.")

8. Disclaimer: I am a co-founder of HomeStars and remain an adviser. I hold some shares in the company.

9. *The Economist*, "Online Advertising: New Business Models Let Communities of Internet Users Control How Their Personal Information Is Bought and Sold," March 8, 2007.

10. There is little global consensus on many aspects of modernity, including levels of consumption and economic growth, let alone the noise created by the advertising industry. See Benjamin Barber, "Jihad vs. McWorld," *The Atlantic Monthly* 269:3 (March, 1992), 53–65.

11. Jakob Nielsen, "The Most Hated Advertising Techniques," *Alertbox,* December 6, 2004, archived at useit.com. See also Scott McCoy, et al., "The Effects of Online Advertising," *Communications of the ACM,* 50:3 (2007), 84–88. The latter study suggests that intrusiveness of format is disturbing to users, but (referring to display ads near content or on shopping sites, as opposed to ads near search engine results) off-topic or apparently irrelevant offers are not necessarily disliked any more than "on topic" ads, and can be effective.

12. Seth Godin, *Permission Marketing: Turning Strangers into Friends and Friends into Customers* (Simon & Schuster, 1999).

13. In a moment of weakness, a respected business publication allowed me, a small voice in the wilderness, to publish on op-ed piece on the subject of corporate spam: "Corporate America – Stay Out of My Inbox," *The Globe and Mail Report on Business,* September 12, 2000.

14. Godin, *Purple Cow: Transform Your Business By Being Remarkable* (Portfolio, 2003).

15. Godin, "In Praise of the Purple Cow," *Fast Company* 67 (February 2003), 74.

16. Featured as a case study in Emanuel Rosen's *The Anatomy of Buzz: How to Create Word of Mouth Marketing* (Currency, 2000).

17. LARABAR, like many hip brands, annoys me with a plodding flash intro on their website, and virtually unnavigable navigation. It is like pulling teeth to even get from the home page to the company blog, from what appears to be a link. But the bars look yummy.

18. David Kamp, *The United States of Arugula: How We Became a Gourmet Nation* (Broadway, 2006).

19. Now that I've softened you up a bit, OK, I'll admit it. I'm flummoxed by Under Armour's apparent lack of interest in online advertising. Like many large brands, they advertise heavily through traditional channels such as television. (The company's 10-Q SEC filing for the first calendar quarter of 2008 states dryly: "As a percentage of net revenues, marketing costs increased to 17.8% for the three months ended March 31, 2008 from 11.1% for the same period in 2007 primarily due to the film, print and in-store brand marketing campaign driving the introduction of our performance training footwear.") Like many large brands, they are buying AdWords minimally on their main brand keyword terms, such as **Under Armour**, **HeatGear**, and **ColdGear**. But at minimal cost, they could be bidding thousands of additional keywords and creating more incremental customer wins online. A quick audit of the company's online presence does bring to light a key point: strong brands with strong grassroots word-of-mouth and sponsorship strategies will create strong online presences as a matter of course, with relatively little followup and steering. The distinction between online and offline publicity is blurring enough that competence in the offline world coupled with reasonable attention to detail online can be a powerful combination. Powerful, but not quite up to potential, in my opinion. Under Armour's online presence is by no means weak: many athletes, events, and supporters of the company place a logo on their sites, linking to Under Armour's e-commerce site. But given their enormous and difficult-to-measure offline spend, it is still surprising that they are not *maximizing* their online customer acquisition efforts, as surely this incremental growth would lead to both market share and profitability gains at the expense of competitors. (Smaller companies—for whom big brand advertising and big distribution channel expenses are not an option—increasingly turn to the Internet and particularly Google AdWords as a primary channel for reaching new customers.) A job ad I ran across for an e-commerce analyst at Under Armour is one indicator of their comprehensive approach to web marketing, but a read of the ad also shows a typical "short-leash" approach to measuring the return on this relatively small investment—a leash, I gather, is not applied to the rest of the marketing and advertising budget that eats up as much as 18% of company revenues. Among the hundreds of obvious core product terms Under Armour is not showing Google ads for, **football cleats** is one. Football cleats was a highly touted new product line presaging UA's later full-on assault on the footwear market. Luckily for them, in my search they do come up on page one of Google organic (nonpaid) search results for the term **football cleats**, but the page

that ranks well is a generic branded page for www.underarmour.com/click-clack, heavy on Flash animation. The page isn't particularly relevant to football cleats, so it likely won't continue to rank well. (Click-Clack is the theme of TV spots featuring famous athletes and/or look-alikes, "looking the part" in their training.) The Click-Clack landing page, to a web marketer's eyes, looks like an ineffective page that essentially glorifies or justifies the large dollar sums already invested in the TV ads and sponsorships of athletes. The painful irony is that the e-commerce analyst and others on the e-commerce team may be called on the carpet to explain, in this context of a tiny budget being given short shrift by the priorities of Super Bowl advertising and athlete sponsorships, why the "Web doesn't perform." Stock analysts, for their part, cite rising inventory levels and a slowing economy as reasons why Under Armour stock (NYSE: UA) is trading (as of this writing in July 2008) near its 52-week low, valuing the company at $1.2 billion. At as much as 18% of revenues, no one seems to see fit to ask whether as much as half of the marketing budget is pure waste. No one in the financial world asks if a large chunk of profitability could be preserved, and growth rates kept intact, by allocating a tiny fraction of that marketing spend to more effective online customer acquisition (or, for that matter, relatively inexpensive athlete and television sponsorships in global markets). Why? I assume this is because the brand is "successful," this is how Nike does it, and this is the way it has always been done. I predict, though, that Under Armour will soon start to move in the right direction. Their new President, David McCreight, was formerly President of Lands' End, a noted catalog marketer.

20. "Relevant Results: Jeeves vs. Google," Traffick.com, October 18, 1999.

21. Source: SearchEngineWatch.com, "Search Engine Sizes." Google's index has been overtaken in size at times, but generally regains the lead.

22. Mark Sweney, "Google Extends UK Online Ad Lead," *The Guardian,* March 28, 2007.

23. Jonathan Richards and James Doran, "Google Now Challenging ITV to Be UK's Top Advertiser," *TimesOnline,* March 3, 2007.

24. Matthew Creamer, "Johnson & Johnson Seeks Savings with $3 Billion Review," *Advertising Age,* April 1, 2007.

25. MarketingFind.com, "CMA Hits Home Run at Annual Conference," October 21, 2004, archived at www.marketingfind.com/articles/cma_hits_home_run_at_annual_conference .html. I was in attendance so I can roughly vouch for the content of Keane's slides.

26. Sources include Craig R. Endicott, "Top Marketers Spend $74 Billion; Annual Ranking Shows 7.1% Increase with P&G, Unilever Leading the Way," *Advertising Age* 74:45 (November 10, 2003), 26.

27. Source: Newspaper Association of America. These figures are down 16.5% and 9.4% from 2006. Meanwhile, online ad spending on newspaper-owned websites rose 19% to $3.2 billion.

28. Nathania Johnson, "Global Internet Ad Spend to Exceed $106 Billion by 2011," *Search Engine Watch Blog*, June 25, 2008.

29. Stefanie Olsen, "Ballmer: We Fell Down on Search," CNET News.com, March 25, 2004.

30. eMarketer, "The Elephant in the Room: The Online At-Work Audience," February 2003 (PDF), archived at iab.com.

31. Kevin Lee, "Yes, Virginia, There Is SEM Brand Lift," ClickZ.com, Parts I and II, July 16 & 23, 2004.

32. Stephen Wellman, "Google's Deal for DoubleClick Could Be the End of Yahoo," *Information Week* (blog), April 17, 2007, archived at www.informationweek.com/blog/main/archives/2007/04/googles_deal_fo.html.

33. comScore Networks, "Canadians Are More Active Online Searchers Than Their U.S. Counterparts," press release, May 13, 2004, archived at comscore.com.

34. Andrew Goodman, "A Keynote Conversation with Danny Sullivan and Jason Calacanis," *SearchDay,* December 20, 2006, archived at http://searchenginewatch.com/showPage .html?page=3624236.

35. Seth Godin, "The Problem with Search Engine Optimization," *Seth's Blog,* July 1, 2004, archived at sethgodin.typepad.com.

36. Shari Thurow, *Search Engine Visibility, 2nd Edition* (Peachpit Press, 2007).

37. Stefanie Olsen, "Is AltaVista Searching for Top Dollar?" CNET News.com, October 1, 2002, archived at news.com.

38. See for example Danny Sullivan, "Yahoo Reawakens the Paid Inclusion Debate," *SearchDay,* May 18, 2004, archived at searchenginewatch.com.

39. Like myself, Jen is Canadian, hailing from Victoria, BC. Another author on the AdSense phenomenon is Eric Giguere, also Canadian. Completing the Canuck dominance of paid search authorship is my colleague Mona Elesseily, Vancouver-based author of the *Yahoo Search Marketing Handbook*. What can we say?

40. Andrew Goodman, "Holiday Time, Quality Time: Two-and-a-Half Questions About Quality Score Issues for Nick Fox, Google," Traffick.com, Nov. 30, 2006.

Chapter 2

A $21 Billion Afterthought: How Google Entered the Advertising Market

After its incorporation in September 1998, Google's plan was at once humble and ambitious. It included a plan to work on pure search technology—to literally build a better search engine to take on the incumbents in the commercial search engine market—but revenue-generation ideas were vague at best, and it was some time before the company earned significant revenue. Today, its primary revenue stream is clearly advertising. But many casual users, and a considerable number of savvy professionals, are really unaware of the scale of Google's advertising operations. As the company hires ever more employees and rolls out a wide variety of online applications, it seems that they've become a huge, diversified technology company. True enough, but for the time being Google's economic engine is still powered by one thing: ad revenue.

Google did not just appear out of thin air. It was conceived out of the efforts (and stumblings) of a number of precursors, each adding another stepping-stone upon which Google climbed to the top of the heap. As an online advertiser, you will benefit from understanding how and why Google developed and what it took to get where it is. Here I'll also try to add some insight into Google's unique culture, which will not only help you interpret official and unofficial Google policies, but also help you do a better job of dealing with problems and foibles in AdWords as they crop up.

AdWords Gets Its Start

In March 2002, when I first started advising clients on how to use Google's new advertising program, there was much skepticism surrounding this upstart's efforts. It all felt rather unfamiliar: an automated self-serve advertising platform with many restrictive rules and yet rather limited customer support. Complaints were common because few businesspeople had yet come to grips with what type of company Google was. A fair number of Google's first advertisers had learned the ropes on Overture, which structured its program differently. Others were completely new to search advertising. They were Google Search users and were attracted by Google's strong brand. "Hey, we can advertise on Google now! Let's try it!" was the typical thought process. Google invested nearly nothing in marketing the new ad program, focusing most of its energy on technological innovation.

Overture had a serious head start on Google AdWords, but AdWords caught up so quickly it took everyone, including Google, by surprise. Overture's advertiser base had reached 21,000 advertisers by the end of 1999, 37,000 by the end of 2000, and 60,000 by April 2001. By mid-2003, scarcely a year after the pay-per-click version of AdWords was launched, Google's advertiser base had already surpassed Overture's, reaching 100,000 advertisers. Strong global expansion pushed this to 150,000 by September 2003. By the end of 2004, Google boasted over 280,000 advertisers worldwide. Today, Google is reputed to have over a million advertisers, but as this number grows it becomes less meaningful. The important question would be how many advertiser accounts are active at any given time, above, say, $500 in spending per month. The answer is: several hundred thousand, and still growing.

How to "Speak Google"?

In the early days, I found myself acting as something of a translator, explaining to novice advertisers that there were actually key advantages to Google's heavily automated approach and passing along advertiser concerns to staff at Google whenever they would listen. Some of the things that seemed obvious to entrepreneurs muddling along out there in the real world of business evidently didn't occur to Google at all. For example, the tone of many automated editorial disapproval messages struck me as insensitive. Although the messages weren't meant that way, email is a brittle medium at the best of times, and repeated messages of what sounded like disapproval from a company that was supposed to be eager for your advertising business were discouraging to a number of advertisers. It wasn't uncommon at that time for advertisers to give up in frustration with disabled keywords, editorial disapprovals, and the steep learning curve required to achieve a positive return on investment (ROI).

Today, Google is heavily identified with its ad revenue, but what many people don't realize is how cautious the company was in terms of what kind of advertising it would accept in the early going, as well as the format in which it would be displayed. The company's founders and early employees (though not all of its investors) were so convinced of the long-term benefit associated with maintaining search engine user loyalty that they were wary of bending over backwards for advertisers. Sometimes, it was quite the opposite! Sergey Brin's 2003 comments to a *Wired* reporter sum things up fairly well. Asked to imagine what kind of advertising policy an imaginary evil twin to Google might have, Brin responded: "We would be doing things like having advertising that wasn't marked as paid for. Stuff that violates the trust of users. Say someone came looking for breast cancer information and didn't know that some listings were paid for with money from drug companies. We'd be endangering people's health."[1]

The diversified and far-reaching nature of Google's business interests today, however, makes their "strict" editorial policies potentially controversial when it comes to some of the products and services that Google itself offers. For example, Google has been known to ban ads in industries like "streaming television," ostensibly on "legal grounds," that coincidentally seem to overlap with technologies Google itself is developing or has acquired (for example, YouTube).

Many people are also unaware of the extent to which the tone of Google's early advertising policy was set by Page and Brin, the co-founders, or the extent to which complex implementation of the policy was handled by a small number of specialists who happened to work in that division of the company. Outsiders, of course, aren't privy to the detailed debates that carried on inside Google. Was it the case that sometimes, when an advertising exception was referred to a "policy specialist" back in 2003, the case was examined by none other than Sergey Brin or Larry Page? Given the relatively small number of advertisers at the time, and the even smaller number of particularly anomalous cases, it seems likely.

A close inspection of the situation reveals that Google must juggle the demands of many stakeholders and must weigh many variables in deciding how to deal with its advertisers. It's that very lack of overeagerness that has provided such a solid foundation for Google's growth as a favorite destination for search engine users. It has built its brand around balancing the needs of users, advertisers, investors, employees, and other stakeholders.

Google Responds

It's not all just Sergey's opinion, though. Google's collection of user feedback has become increasingly sophisticated with time, but it has always built user feedback mechanisms into the design of both its search and advertising technologies. In an effort to build and maintain its reputation, Google has always consulted its users, advertisers, and a variety of experts in the design of its ad program. Its public relations department regularly facilitates dialogue with those who might be able to provide the types of feedback that will help improve the service. The presence of Google staffers on discussion boards frequented by web geeks has been especially impressive.

Today, there are far more Googlers and far more advertisers than ever before, so Google's challenge is to come up with a more systematic way of incorporating user feedback into the design of the AdWords product—to consult widely in its normal development process while avoiding a "bureaucratic" flavor to the interaction. On this front, Google seems to be holding up very well.

Here's one particularly memorable example of Google's brand of responsiveness. The second-generation (pay-per-click) version of AdWords had begun life in February 2002 with a quirky pricing system. Although the official minimum cost per click was set at 5 cents, many keywords were arbitrarily assigned higher minimum prices. Let's say you had bid 25 cents on a keyword, but its Google-assigned minimum was 55 cents. You'd see that minimum displayed in red, and your ad wouldn't show unless you increased your bid to reach the minimum for that keyword. Talk about frustration.

According to Google, this was based on their study of demand for keywords in its earlier version of the program (also called AdWords). Notwithstanding this supposed market data that implied heavy market demand for the keyword (**derivatives**; likely to be typed by a sophisticated investing audience), there were no advertisers willing to pay Google's enforced minimum of 92 cents. But that didn't mean the keyword had no value. My client, for one, expected to break even if they could bid around 48 cents. So much for market demand! Google's approach to pricing was inefficient to say the least. AdWords, back then, wasn't yet popular enough for Google to force advertisers out of the market-based auction by inventing its own above-market pricing. The program needed more "floor traffic." Just as a house going on the market may sell more if priced lower because more people come to look at it and subsequently engage in a bidding war, I felt that Google would ultimately benefit by lowering its prices on the click auction. By enticing new advertisers to enter the auction at the 5-cent minimum price, Google would ultimately benefit from bidding wars.

At the time, I wrote a couple of complaints about this in my newsletter, and a number of advertisers kept the heat on. Eventually, Google just scrubbed the whole idea of arbitrarily inflated minimums. They had (after spending considerable time pondering) listened to reasoned arguments and to the pleas of their advertisers. Today, the hypothetical minimum bid is now as low as one cent (or other currency, depending on your country), although actual prices have risen significantly overall.

When it comes to third-party feedback about their ad program, is it a question of the squeaky wheel getting the grease? To some extent. But Google listens better to squeaky wheels who make specific, doable suggestions for changes to their program. In many areas, Google takes disparate pieces of user feedback over an extended period and elevates it to the status of principles. For example, Google seems to have an overriding principle to offer AdWords advertisers ways of separately reporting on specific kinds of traffic, and ways of opting out of clicks they don't like on a number of levels. The feature set they've built around filtering and opt-outs seems to surpass many of the early piecemeal complaints by advertisers. In this regard, Google is principle-driven; almost doggedly so. The company's tendency to exceed expectations on feature improvements, going beyond "mere" user feedback, puts enormous pressure on its competitors.

A couple of key points are as clear to me now as they were five years ago. First, a general principle: to understand how to deal with a unique company like Google, you must understand its culture and its power structure. Complex organizations tend to arise under the control of a dominant coalition, and internal power struggles are typically won by that coalition.[2] These patterns will tend to dictate how decisions get made.

Google is rare in that its engineering culture is particularly strong; so much so that even after hiring a large sales force and taking on public investors' cash, the founders still professed a wish (in the prospectus for the initial public offering) to pursue long-term goals rather than chase short-term financial targets. Beyond that, the work habits and characteristics of the people Google hires have lent a certain flavor to day-to-day operations.

Google is stacked with PhDs, and even for the nonengineers who work there, the hiring process is stringent. By all accounts, new hires are judged largely on a combination of raw intellectual talent and the likelihood that they'll fit in with the values and habits of the "well-meaning geeks" who already work there. This isn't particularly remarkable for a technology company, but it certainly contrasts with the sales culture we might expect from a firm that generates nearly all of its revenues from ads.

That said, it's now safe to say that Google's engineering-dominated culture has now eroded in the face of business development and sales initiatives. The size of the advertising division has grown, and the "old way" of acting like search engine purists has fallen by the wayside even though the "old stuff" still generates most of the revenue. Google AdWords customer support reps and product managers are now charged with selling a wider array of advertising products and services. This does lend a different feel to the interaction, even within the AdWords interface. We're now seeing notifications at the account overview level for limited-time-only radio advertising offers, for example.

In any case, the second, more specific principle to keep in mind is that Google's entry into the advertising business was an afterthought to their search engine business. A billboard is a billboard—it serves no other purpose but advertising. The same goes for the Yellow Pages—you don't use it for any other reason except to look for a local business. Google Search, by contrast, is still first and foremost a search engine that is intended to help people find information of various types, especially noncommercial information. No one forces users to visit Google's website. To become preeminent with users, Google's goal has always been primarily to build the world's best search technology. In spite of the fact that 99% of the revenues of this company come from ads, and as difficult as it might be for me and you (as advertisers) to accept this, you can only understand Google if you're willing to see the ads as secondary to Google's primary goal of large-scale user loyalty.

Predecessors and Competitors

Google wasn't the first web search engine, and it wasn't the first pay-per-click listings service. What it has been is the most successful company ever in both of these areas. While this overview is not intended to be a substitute for a full history of search engines and online advertising, it should help put things in context for those unfamiliar with the evolution of the field.

Major Predecessors in Search

The history of web search engines is woefully underpublicized at present, possibly because those involved were (and many still are) too busy building powerful companies to bother chronicling everything they were up to. As such, some of the best resources out there are actually quite limited.[3] Increasingly, web enthusiasts and pioneers are sharing anecdotes in public forums, on blogs, and so on.

Yahoo Directory

Founded in 1994, the Yahoo Directory proposed to simplify the nascent process of finding useful pages that resided on the young World Wide Web. At first, it was little more than a collection of favorite links compiled by two graduate students, Jerry Yang and David Filo. Both were studying electrical engineering and had virtually no training in information retrieval technology. Although it eventually got around to hiring people with some background in subject classification, the company spent years ignoring the importance of developing search technology in-house. (More recently, it has invested heavily in this area.) By calling its staff "ontologists" (a term from library science that implies advanced background in categorization), 1990s-era Yahoo may have appeased a few diehard information scientists, but the reality is, these were mostly entry-level positions. As Yahoo grew in the mid-to-late 1990s, search and information retrieval expertise often took a back seat to business objectives and the imperatives of financial markets.

The company's success in going public as one of the early dot-coms (before they were called dot-coms) gave it the cash and the profile needed to build and acquire additional services, including email and personalized home pages. Yahoo soon became a diversified destination site known as a *portal*. Massive sponsorship revenues enjoyed during the online advertising boom gave the company enough momentum to survive the subsequent advertising crash. Yahoo has become a leading and profitable global Internet brand.

Yahoo (as with competitors such as Excite) did not always realize how important the search experience was to its users. To augment its popular human-edited directory, Yahoo made deals with a number of successive third parties to provide web index search results: Open Text, AltaVista, Inktomi, AltaVista again, and Google. Finally, it decided to get serious about search (and stop helping its competitors). In 2003, Yahoo terminated its partnership with Google Search and acquired Inktomi and Overture (at the time, the latter owned two struggling search engines, FAST and AltaVista, which meant that Yahoo now had access to personnel from three major, but declining, web indexes). Its technology team now bolstered, Yahoo set about releasing its own search index, which has done a decent job of keeping pace with technology trends. Yahoo also has access to insights and technology from a wide range of divisions and properties, such as Flickr photo sharing, shared bookmarking, and much more. Yahoo's continued effort to maintain research-oriented divisions doesn't rival Google's, but has been strong.

The Overture acquisition also brought 100% of the pay-per-click search listing revenues into the Yahoo fold. Overture, a pure "sponsored listings" vendor with no search engine traffic of its own, relied entirely on partnerships to serve its ads and was vulnerable whenever the time came to renegotiate deals with major portal partners. The deal turned out to be beneficial to both companies. Overture would have been at risk of being squeezed, and the deal gave Yahoo ready access to Overture's huge list of advertisers and 100% control over what turned out to be a growing revenue stream.

After some deliberation—and then, renewed investment and commitment—Microsoft launched its own search engine (now awkwardly called Live Search), and its own paid search platform, Microsoft adCenter. There are now three key players in search and paid search, then.

In the meantime, Yahoo Search Marketing (formerly Overture) aggressively expanded its pursuit of advertising partnerships, particularly in its Content Match program. Thus, like Google, Yahoo has quietly become a powerhouse in serving online advertising in various formats on a wide range of partner sites, a business once dominated by traditional online advertising networks. Yahoo spent too long readying its new search marketing platform to replace the aging Overture infrastructure, losing some traction with advertisers and the confidence of Wall Street. However, once released, the new platform (codenamed Panama) was a pleasant surprise,[4] and Yahoo's fortunes seem to have stabilized in the face of Google's powerhouse performance.

From the standpoint of search user market share and search-related revenues, Yahoo is Google's main competitor today. As some of us predicted during the height of dot-com mania in 1999, the portal wars proved very real. Consolidation occurred as users chose the best online services and let the rest die. Competitors like Excite, Lycos, Go2Net, Infoseek, AltaVista, Snap, and many more went out of business or were acquired for a pittance. In the North American market, about five companies—Google, Yahoo, Microsoft, AOL Time Warner, and IAC (owner of Ask.com)—seem worth discussing when it comes to monthly share of searches. The picture is different in other parts of the world, but overall, consolidation has been the name of the game everywhere.

Back When Many Crawlers Roamed the Web...

Search marketing strategies evolved during a time when there existed numerous web indexes, supported by *crawlers,* which would index as many web pages as possible. In the mid-to-late 1990s, as many as eight of these indexes were in play and being actively updated at any given time. The number of web pages available for indexing was relatively small; thus a web crawler project could be supported by limited funds (typically university research projects).

Different indexes had varying degrees of coverage of the Web, and they all ranked sites differently. Because it was often hard to find good information on one search engine, many searchers would try several. This lent the medium a feeling of slight chaos and led marketers to believe that they needed to be "on all the search engines" if they "wanted to be found." Because search usage data was limited, it was tempting to fixate on how high one *ranked* on the various search engines for a given query. The makers of rank-checking tools like Webposition Gold profited handsomely from the presupposition that high rankings were vitally important. Search engine optimization companies convinced clients that they had specialized expertise that would help them rank well on several different engines. Many site owners got so caught up in the rankings game they forgot to build viable businesses.

Arguably, then, the information provided by early search engine optimization experts such as Fredrick Marckini (author of an early book on the subject,[5] and a founder of a leading search engine marketing agency, i-prospect) and Danny Sullivan (founder of SearchEngineWatch.com, Editor-in-Chief, Search Engine Land) was geared towards an audience of webmasters and cutting-edge marketers who needed to know not merely general information about search engines, but specific information about how the different search engines were ranking pages.

Resources put together by research experts like Greg Notess (SearchEngineShowdown.com), Tara Calishain (ResearchBuzz.com), and Chris Sherman (formerly with About.com Guide to Web Search and SearchEngineWatch.com, now Executive Editor, Search Engine Land) also seemed indispensable to anyone trying to understand this cluttered landscape of search tools.

The various search engine comparisons and updates would not have found an audience if not for the apparent importance of a confusing assembly of viable and distinct search engines in the second half of the 1990s. Marckini's first book, for example, received many favorable reviews, but they seem to have dried up around 1999. Coincidentally, shortly after Google's founding in 1998, many of the formerly active search engine indexes stopped being regularly updated, got acquired, changed business models, or simply went out of business. This left a very different (consolidated) landscape: fewer unpaid search indexes, less need to "submit" your site to the various search engines, and fewer optimization techniques to worry about. Techniques like those Marckini had been lauded for explaining were fast becoming obsolete. Even seemingly obvious advice, like marking up the HTML pages on your site with keyword and description *meta tags,* was no longer useful.[6] Marckini's consulting company, like many, began offering an increasing proportion of paid search campaign management to its corporate clients, as was evident in Marckini's shifting focus in columns posted at ClickZ.com.

As the Web grew, and as search technologies became more susceptible to spam, the costs of running a web index had grown significantly. At the same time, venture capital and public investor dollars began to take chances on any company that might become the "next Yahoo." Companies like AltaVista, Lycos, Infoseek, Excite, Snap, Go2Net, and Inktomi had their dreams of dominance fueled by varying levels of investor support. But in spite of their ambitions, they had few good ideas about how to make revenues from running a search engine. Some felt certain that banner ads would be the ticket. Others saw Yahoo become a portal and decided to follow suit, adding many related services to capitalize on their brands.

Excite was a classic example of a me-too portal strategy inspired by Yahoo's marketplace successes. As a user, I found this "#2 portal" exciting indeed, because some of the features it came out with (such as an early intranet platform for the masses called Excite Communities, substantively nearly as useful as today's hot project management apps like Basecamp from 37 Signals) were more full featured than anything Yahoo had on offer.

Building on its early popularity as the well-respected search engine, Architext, Excite kept adding services and advertising over the years, finally merging with cable Internet provider @Home in a promising, but ultimately ill-fated, partnership. A variety of large media companies followed the path of acquiring search engine companies, sometimes to capitalize on inflated stock market valuations. Disney Internet Group acquired Infoseek and launched a portal called Go, in the process building a volunteer-driven directory called Go Guides. NBC Internet went public and snapped up hot Internet companies with names like Snap and Xoom. These efforts turned out to be short-lived. At the height of the boom, Yahoo wannabes like TheGlobe.com went public on scant revenues, making them some of the most overvalued publicly traded companies of all time.

For the most part, the portal model was once again built around banner ads. In most cases, the costs of building these companies exceeded the revenues they brought in. The advertising model failed as banner ad prices plummeted, in large part due to the poor response received from these ads, and in part due to the collapse of a pyramid scheme of sorts—a weakening of demand for the ads from unstable dot-com companies that were going under.

Perhaps the most prominent memory of this wave of search engine technologies is that of their failure to foil relatively simple efforts by porn and gambling sites to reverse-engineer their algorithms and flood the indices with spam. AltaVista, at one time widely considered to be the world's leading search engine, staggered midway through its life when the quality of its results seemed to degenerate badly. Although the technology improved, the public never fully regained its trust in this mid-1990s generation of search technologies. Search engine users would need to hear new ideas if they were to regain their passion for search technology.

The other thing that left the public disillusioned—and again, AltaVista was in the middle of it—was the fact that the search engine companies couldn't seem to focus. People really just wanted to search for information, and yet they were being forced not only to look at intrusive ads, but pages full of clutter and information that they didn't care about. To be sure, the notion of a personalized home page full of news and features like calendars and weather was attractive to many. But few companies other than Yahoo, AOL, and MSN were truly skilled at creating a diversified information service. AltaVista released a decent web-based email product, for example, but couldn't handle the demand on its servers. In the UK, AltaVista claimed to be developing a free, ad-supported dialup Internet Service Provider business, but was later forced to back down from its claim that 100,000 "trial" users were on board. (The real number was zero, and the managing director of AltaVista UK resigned in shame.[7]) AltaVista users, typically a serious bunch, would have been much happier had this company stuck to what it knew best—search.

I emphasize AltaVista's missteps mainly to make it clear how Google has always wanted to be seen by its users: as a great search engine that neither deceives nor annoys the searching public. Remember those two no-no's. Deceive. Annoy. In the World According to Google, you should do neither.

Inktomi, LookSmart: The "Portal Suppliers"

All the while refining their technology, Internet search engines struggled to find the best approach to turning a profit from the exercise. One school of thought had it that pure search technology companies could supply search to large portals who did not want to develop these technologies in-house. Some have called this the "wholesale search market."

Inktomi, founded in 1996 out of a research project by computer science professor Eric Brewer and grad student Paul Gauthier, was widely hailed as an up-and-coming superstar in the field of web search. Initial rave reviews in the press did little to endear Inktomi with end users over the long term. It isn't hard to see why: by acting as the behind-the-scenes engine powering high-profile search brands like Hotbot.com, users were unable to literally "search Inktomi," so they never got behind the company.

Amazingly, an abstract of a speech on the history of Inktomi given by Eric Brewer in June 2004 suggests that "despite having real value, Inktomi was pulled down—not by the 'dot coms,' but by the collapse of the telecom sector...." Were it judged through any normal assessment of revenues and profitability as measured against business risk, Inktomi did not, in fact, have as much real value as its proponents believed. Its briefly profitable period was bestowed upon it by portal partners like Yahoo and MSN, who have proved repeatedly that they are apt to "taketh away" the privilege of supplying them with search results. Inktomi saw its market value plummet and was ultimately acquired by Yahoo in 2003 for relative pocket change ($235 million) because it (like many others) was surpassed by Google as a technology leader and as a favorite search destination by end users. Inktomi had good technology, but it proved conclusively that good technology alone does not make for a viable business.

The problem with the portal supplier strategy, as it turned out, is that by ceding their direct relationship with the public to their big-brand clients, search engines like Inktomi and directories like LookSmart faded from public view and lost leverage in the marketplace, since they no longer had ownership of traffic flows. When portals began to squeeze the suppliers on price (easy to do, since numerous suppliers existed, and licensing the Open Directory was free), these suppliers lost whatever independent brand loyalty they'd developed in their formative stages.

The Open Directory Project (dmoz.org)

Beginning life in 1998 as GnuHoo and then NewHoo, the Open Directory Project (ODP) was conceived as a competitor to the Yahoo Directory. The work was to be done by volunteer editors, and the end product was to be licensed to any portal or site that wanted to take advantage of the information. Doesn't sound like much of a business? Well, it turned out to be a pretty good deal for the founders. The directory's popularity led to its acquisition by Netscape, which was later acquired by AOL.

AOL became the Open Directory's major distributor, but the directory was also licensed (at no charge to the publisher) in many other places around the Web. Google began using ODP data fairly early on, calling it the Google Directory. An innovative feature was Google's use of an "overlay" technique, ranking results in a given ODP category in order based on the site's Google PageRank score. This was illustrated with a green bar (on a scale of 0 to 10, similar to the way the info is displayed by searchers using the Google toolbar). This could have been a very useful feature indeed had there been more consistency to the underlying content in the directory.

Open Directory founder Rich Skrenta and marketing exec Chris Tolles later moved on to a new venture: Topix.net, a sophisticated news search engine that competes directly with Google News. Topix managed to attract majority ownership from a consortium of large media companies relatively early in its growth. Skrenta moved on in June 2007 to found Blekko, one of the few contemporary search startups that is making a serious effort to rival Google. Skrenta and Tolles had used some of their ODP background to build social features into the news site. Topix has thus become part of the emerging and unpredictable category of "citizen journalism," in the same category as startup NowPublic.com.

I was an early critic of ODP for the lack of professional standards in editing and its constant struggles with editorial corruption. The lack of transparency of submission procedures to the public and the huge variations in the degrees of disclosure of editors' biographical information meant, for me, that this so-called open directory was far from it.[8] The construction of a high-quality human-edited directory remains an elusive task, especially as directories like Yahoo have become so commercialized. In the meantime, the world of "rated content" has erupted into a complex playing field, with "news voting" sites like Digg seeming to supersede the singular editorial recommendations of yesteryear.

Fixed "categorizations" of content are now out of vogue as well, with keyword search (sometimes supported by user-based keyword "tagging,"—yes, in a way, the return/revenge of meta keyword tags) serving as a more reliable means for most users to find what they're looking for.

The Google Difference: A Third-Generation Algorithm

If Google hadn't moved to fill the void left by its struggling predecessors, someone else would have. Scientists in various research projects were working on new ideas about how to rank the importance of web pages vis-à-vis a given user query. What Google did was to popularize some of the best emerging ideas about how to design a large-scale search engine at a time when others were losing momentum. Some of these ideas are so central to the task of ranking pages in today's web environment that they were adopted in some form or another by all of Google's main competitors (including Inktomi, AltaVista, and FAST).

The working paper that explains Google's PageRank methodology, "Anatomy of a Large-Scale Hypertextual Web Search Engine," is frequently cited.[9] But the field of information retrieval technology today is rich with ongoing experimentation by hundreds of well-funded scientists, some well known, some not. Google itself has extended the basic idea behind PageRank to dozens of related ideas, many of which can be explored in patent applications.

The idea behind PageRank is brilliant and intuitive. The governing principle revolves around a map of the linking structure of the Web. Pages that have a lot of other important pages pointing to them are deemed important. "PageRank can be thought of as a model of user behavior," wrote

Brin and Page. "We assume there is a 'random surfer' who is given a web page at random and keeps clicking on links, never hitting 'back' but eventually gets bored and starts on another random page. The probability that the random surfer visits a page is its PageRank."

This was a significant advance over previous generations of web search. Although most major engines had experimented with a variety of ranking criteria, many of them had depended heavily on basic keyword matching criteria. Not only did this make good information hard to find because so many pages were locked in a virtual tie for first place, it made it easier for optimizers to feed keyword-dense pages into the search engine in a bid to rank their commercially oriented pages higher. Although this game of keyword optimization is quite effective to this day in ranking pages well on unpopular queries (even on Google Search), it seems to work rather poorly on common queries.

The ascendance of PageRank means that on a Google Search for **auto insurance comparison**, for example, it's likely that a well-known site will rank well here rather than some random site that just happens to contain those keywords.

The calculations involved in determining PageRank are just the beginning when it comes to determining how high a page ranks for a given user's query in the organic search results in Google. Today, Google spokespersons tell us that more than 150 factors go into determining how a page ranks on a given search query. In addition to that, search is now somewhat personalized so that users may see a different rank order of organic search results based on geography; and if they're logged in with a Google Account (which they might have if they're a registered user of anything like Gmail, Google Groups, or any number of dozens of other Google properties), past preferences and habits might be taken into account. Finally, today's sophisticated search technologies—Google calls theirs Universal Search—tries to serve up an appropriate "menu" of information based on what seems like the probable user intent based on a search query. That's why some searches might bring up some Google News results above the regular search results; other queries might result in images being shown at the top of the page; others, maps; still others, an app to check showtimes or flight availability.

The technology alone isn't what vaulted Google to its status of the world's favorite search engine, but it played a big part. In addition to the search results being more pleasingly relevant than what was available elsewhere, many users found the Google Search website to be faster and less cluttered than competitors' sites.

Google Search is far more than PageRank, then. Early innovations included theories about computing power that led to massive increases in processing speed. Vast improvements in crawling technology (how Google's spider, Googlebot, finds pages by following links on the websites it already knows about), combined with a new way for companies to communicate their site structures to Googlebot (Google Webmaster Central), allow Google to continually increase the size of its index. The latter is done through a standardized protocol called Google Sitemaps, which has now been adopted by Microsoft and Yahoo as well (information is available at Sitemaps.org).

The fact that Google did well early on meant that it could tackle many small details with gusto, because it was attracting some of the world's best technical talent. Google kept impressing experts with quiet improvements such as its ability to index various file formats (PDF, ASP, JSP, and so forth). Just when things seemed to be settling into a groove, Google would come out with something new, like Google News, that just seemed to work better and faster than whatever else was out there. Acquisitions such as Blogger (blogging software), Urchin (web analytics service now functioning as Google Analytics and fully compatible with Google AdWords), and YouTube kept the momentum rolling. Many analysts failed to notice that most of these acquisitions and projects sneakily aimed to funnel company efforts and user loyalty back into a single revenue source—ad revenue. Apparent complexity in corporate growth masked an elegant simplicity in the balance sheet.

The second wave of Google innovation was increasingly concerned with complex nonsearch applications such as office software. Taking Microsoft head-on, Google now offers a full-scale calendar as well as spreadsheet, word processing, and slideshow applications in addition to email, all built to function in a fully portable online setting (what Google CEO Eric Schmidt likes to refer to as "cloud computing").

But back to the founding fathers' story for now. The "Anatomy..." paper by Page and Brin shows them to be thoughtful and forward thinking when it comes to the business of search, too. In two short paragraphs ("Appendix A: Advertising and Mixed Motives"), the Google founders provide an insight into search engine bias: "Since it is very difficult even for experts to evaluate search engines," they write, "search engine bias is particularly insidious."

Noting the uproar that ensued when Open Text experimented with a paid placement scheme in 1996, Brin and Page worry that the public may well tolerate less obvious forms of search engine bias. "For example," they knowingly point out, "a search engine could add a small factor to search results from 'friendly' companies, and subtract a factor from results from competitors." Worse still, they argue, poor-quality search results could make advertising listings look better by comparison, providing leading commercial search engines at least a short-term incentive to provide lower-quality results. Over the years, critics have sometimes accused Google of adopting the very tactics the founders criticized in their early paper.

The question of improved disclosure of paid search listings has come up repeatedly in recent years, to the point where the Federal Trade Commission and Ralph Nader have taken an interest in potential harm to consumers caused by poorly labeled paid search results.[10] As Overture's fortunes improved in its early days, for example, it inked deals to display listings on partner sites. Depending on the partner, listings were either poorly labeled or even labeled in such a way to suggest the sponsored listings were particularly important ("featured listings," for example). These ill-advised practices made Google's strict labeling policy stand out even more and no doubt solidified the company's already solid reputation as a straight shooter.

Google's proactive approach to separating search results from sponsored listings is clearly based on their early thinking about the problem of search engine bias. This separation, above all, is the cornerstone of Google's tongue-half-in-cheek credo that "you can make money without being evil." Perhaps unknowingly, the Google founders were heading down a path that had been traveled by media barons of days gone by. No doubt the company will continue to face difficult dilemmas in its attempts to keep "search" separate from the business of search.

Major Predecessors in Paid Search

Google enjoyed something of a late-mover advantage in the field of paid search listings sold on a keyword-triggered basis. Even its own AdWords program floundered in its first 16 months of existence, before being re-released in its current pay-per-click auction format. The idea of paid search was first seriously entertained in 1996, making this a young field indeed. GoTo actually began building a business around it in 1997, but had no customers to speak of until 1998.

Open Text, AltaVista, Metacrawler: Coulda Shoulda Woulda

Open Text, a high-quality search index that came out of research projects at the University of Waterloo (Ontario, Canada) should be lauded for its hard-nosed decision making. It saw before many others did that the search engine market was getting crowded, and that only the innovators would survive. Instead of believing that investor handouts or partnerships with the likes of Yahoo would last forever, Open Text decided to try charging for "preferred" listings on its search engine. It was ahead of its time, unfortunately. The backlash against the move was too strong.[11] Experts and journalists (and to a much lesser extent, members of the Internet-surfing public) wondered about the ethics of promoting search results as "objective" while accepting money from companies willing to pay for prominent placement. Marketing staff at Open Text defended the practice, suggesting that it was largely driven by the steady stream of inquiries as to how a company might appear in the listings, and comparing the service to the Yellow Pages.

Cowed by the controversy, and seeking a stable business model, Open Text subsequently shifted gears, becoming a successful enterprise software company, exiting the crowded web search field as other also-rans lingered too long after the party was over.

AltaVista was the next sacrificial lamb in the process of gauging public reaction to sponsored listings in or near search results. As if it didn't already have enough to worry about, the company floated the idea of selling sponsored listings in April 1999. Like Open Text, AltaVista backed down when the public reaction seemed too severe measured against the effort it might take to build and pioneer the concept in-house.[12] Arguably, AltaVista was more susceptible to user complaints about search engine objectivity because its constituency was made up largely of longtime Internet search enthusiasts who were accustomed to the 'Net being conceived almost as a public utility.

AltaVista might have been better off forging ahead aggressively with a plan to sell sponsored listings on one hand, and a plan to improve its search technology on the other. When it eventually took steps to monetize its traffic through paid inclusion and an Overture partnership, and to court search enthusiasts by launching Raging Search—a "clean interface" search engine site modeled after Google—it was too late. Googlemania—along with the ongoing strength of AOL, Yahoo, and MSN—was cutting severely into AltaVista's share of search engine users.

History buffs may be interested in discovering "the" first attempt to "sell keywords" in an online auction environment. Metacrawler, a popular metasearch engine, did so as early as 1997. I have discovered at least one program (unpatented, sadly for the inventors) that was running as early as 1995. In any case, these proto-GoTo's are strictly for the trivia file.

The bigger picture is that the period 1997–2000 spawned scores of venture-funded schemes that proposed to offer increasingly targeted forms of online advertising. Far too many dollars and column inches in magazines like *Business 2.0* were chasing after the notion of online targeting. Yet the eventual winners in the race to find a targeting model that truly worked—GoTo/Overture and Google—were not fast-talking advertising industry veterans sporting $500 eyeglasses and wielding convoluted flow charts. GoTo was a modest little company building a relatively simplistic experiment. Google barely gave the idea of selling ads a second thought until the money from its experimental ad platform started rolling in.

GoTo.com/Overture: Pioneers of Bid-for-Placement Advertising

If you judged it by its early financials, you would not have expected big things from GoTo.com, which later changed its name to Overture. A venture-backed experiment of Bill Gross's Idealab, GoTo had few users and few advertisers in the early going. While it might have dreamt of licensing its results to a large portal, at first it had hardly any partners, so it had to rely on becoming a user destination in its own right. It achieved only moderate success in that regard, rising to #28 in the Media Metrix rankings of web properties in 1999—an important caveat being that this ranking was probably related to advertisers checking on their listings! In the quarter before its initial public offering (ending March 31, 1999), GoTo.com raked in a trifling $1.4 million in revenues and posted a loss of $7.4 million.[13] Somehow, it managed to complete an initial public offering valuing the company at an imprudent 90 times revenues. The cash from that, and a later follow-on offering, gave GoTo the cushion it needed to aggressively pursue advertisers on one hand and distribution partnerships on the other.

Regardless of the challenges it faced, curious onlookers[14] saw some potential in GoTo.com. Little did we know just how well the company would do in such a short period. By 2003, the smashing financial success of Overture had rescued its founder and investors from some of their other dot-com failures and had made key company executives wealthy.

GoTo.com to Overture: From Small Fry to Legitimate Portal Supplier

In 2000, GoTo began to dig itself out of obscurity—it relied heavily on small webmasters placing a GoTo search box on their sites, which often led to questionable clicks for advertisers—when it inked listings distribution deals with big-name partners such as Earthlink, MSN bCentral, and Netscape.com. The more quality traffic it began to send to its advertisers, the more its reputation would improve, and the more interested advertisers became in the opportunity. As it relied less and less on small-fry sites to distribute its listings, it was actually able to begin cracking down on lower-quality partners, in many cases terminating those partnerships.

The biggest jump in legitimacy came in September 2000, when Overture (it would still be called GoTo.com until September 2001) inked a deal to distribute sponsored listings on AOL Search. The exact financials of the reported "$50 million deal" (the figure is relatively meaningless) were not disclosed, but Overture probably needed to guarantee AOL a minimum cash payment based on a projection of the revenue share from the deal. It appears, nonetheless, that Overture did very well financially from this deal, as bidding wars for listing positions exceeded anyone's expectations. The AOL deal led to rapid company growth for Overture. Other partnerships, including an important one with MSN Search, followed.

Globally speaking, Overture and Google AdWords have played musical partners to an extent, emphasizing the power that traffic owners (portals and large publishers) have always wielded over third-party listings vendors. (This power has diminished as Google itself dwarfs the industry by virtue of its own financial performance and traffic growth, but that doesn't mean it's not still in hot competition with Yahoo and others for publisher partners.) In May 2002, Google formed a partnership with AOL to provide search listings to AOL users and users of other AOL-owned services like Compuserve and Netscape.com. At the same time, AOL also began phasing in

Google AdWords throughout its various properties, replacing Overture as its preferred paid listing partner. But it wouldn't all go Google's way. When Yahoo decided to stop using Google for index results, it also dropped AdWords in favor of Overture.

Simple Click Auction: Paid Search 1.0

For advertisers, GoTo made available a now-familiar bidding process. Advertisers would bid on words or phrases, and user searches would trigger a list of results in the order of how high the advertiser had bid. For quite some time, the price paid by the advertiser was prominently displayed next to a listing. This is no longer done.

Relevance was always part of the mix at GoTo. Editors vetted every submission by hand, looking over each proposed keyword, rejecting or allowing new keywords depending on how relevant they were to material contained on the landing page. This method was uneven to begin with, and is no longer efficient or scalable on its own.

In the early days, editorial practices were particularly uneven. Inexperienced editors sometimes failed to grasp the meanings of industry-specific terms. This supposedly cutting-edge advertising company behaved similarly, in some respects, to the way directories like Yahoo and LookSmart behaved before you could buy your way in. There seemed to be a belief that paying advertisers needed gatekeepers to ensure relevant sponsored listings. Unfortunately, the average editor was often poorly qualified to make relevancy determinations. As we'll see, AdWords offered a major advance on this editorial-centric model.

Inktomi: Paid Inclusion Index

Inktomi, portal supplier extraordinaire, is the search engine most identified with the hotly debated concept of paid inclusion. The idea was that companies could pay to guarantee inclusion in the index, and this would help Inktomi defray the costs of running the engine and help it to weed out search index spammers. Inclusion would not guarantee placement. The ranking algorithm would still aim to present the pages that were most relevant to users in the most prominent positions on the page.

The details of pricing and "feed management" have changed somewhat over the years, but until a major shift occurs in industry norms, not much attention will be paid to this model. Given the persistence of index spam facing Google, we may see a return to forms of validation and authentication of websites to cut down on junk pages in the index. One way that Google could handle this would be by according weight to sites that have Webmaster Central accounts, as the act of signing up with an account potentially conveys at least some of the site owner's history and identity to the search engine.

Modeled on Inktomi's previous efforts, various generations of paid inclusion have been offered by Yahoo up until the present day, under a variety of names. Paid inclusion does seem to benefit large e-commerce sites wanting guaranteed indexing and at least some change of decent rankings on product-related terms. However, this does come at a cost—not only does the website owner pay per page, but the fairness and impartiality of the search algorithm is placed into question in the public's mind, since the distinction between paid and unpaid listings in the organic search results is rarely made clear.

LookSmart, Yahoo: Paid Inclusion in Directory...
(and Then, Pay Some More?)

Yahoo and LookSmart both began life as human-edited directories that employed editors to sort out relevant and useful websites from bad ones. These opinionated categorizations were exciting because they promised to save web searchers time.

Business owners soon recognized the value of these listings. In the meantime, Yahoo and LookSmart, like all Internet companies, were looking for ways to raise revenue. All the relevant dates and policy changes would be cumbersome to pin down, because both Yahoo and LookSmart phased out their free submission options gradually (not unlike Inktomi's early claims that paying for inclusion wasn't "necessary"). In any case, the major changes began happening in 2000.

The evolution of the pricing models was vexing to many listing clients. At first, the submission fees were "one-time-only," and then they went to annual fees. Yahoo's annual fee is now $299 (higher for adult sites), though this figure seems hardly relevant today given the range of other ways you'll pay to be seen on Yahoo, including "category sponsorship" fees that guarantee you a better-looking spot.

Repeatedly, LookSmart and Yahoo appeared to violate unspoken social contracts with existing customers—and likely, the terms of written contracts. LookSmart, for example, wound up paying its advertisers a settlement in response to a class-action suit that charged the company with poor disclosure of impending changes in the terms of its advertiser relationship. Yahoo did not do right by those who had paid for directory inclusion, either. At a certain point, the prominence of the directory listings in Yahoo Search results was sharply reduced to favor the index results and sponsored listings, but of course, no refunds were forthcoming to those who had already paid for their coveted directory spots.

In fall 2003, LookSmart went one better (or worse, in the advertiser's mind) by instituting a pay-per-click inclusion program. Sites would still pay to be included in the directory, but would be unlikely to appear on major partner sites like MSN unless they participated in a pay-per-click auction as well, triggered by relevancy keywords that would potentially help the site rise higher in MSN Search results (which were, at the time, a mix of Inktomi and LookSmart results). Site owners could only look on in bewilderment at a struggling search company laughably asking them to "pay, and then pay some more" into a confusing paid visibility scheme.

Essentially, LookSmart was reinventing itself as a pay-per-click listings middleman to compete directly with Overture and Google AdWords. Financially, this was a sound move, but as so often happens in the business of paid search, it was too late. As advertisers discovered, LookSmart didn't lack for technology, and the bidding platform worked fine. It did, however, make the mistake of designing its program around flat click pricing, and then multilevel flat click pricing. Apparently LookSmart didn't learn from Google's early mistakes with Soviet-style economics.

What LookSmart did lack was quality distribution partnerships, vital to the company's survival because it had long ago given up on the idea of being a destination search site in its own right. LookSmart's one remaining major deal, with MSN, was not renewed in October 2003, so (as had been rumored for some time) it was left only with minor partnerships. To make up the revenue, LookSmart positioned itself as a second-tier pay-per-click listings provider (in other words, it was no longer a directory at all) amenable to partnerships with a variety of small publishers, some aboveboard, others not.

The supremacy of Google AdWords and Overture was cemented by this development, with FindWhat remaining in reasonable shape in third place following its merger with European pay-per-click stalwart Espotting. (In June 2005, the four main divisions of FindWhat—FindWhat.com, Espotting, Comet Systems, and Miva Merchant—were all rebranded under the "Miva" name. The company is now simply called Miva, Inc. and trades under a new ticker symbol, MIVA.) LookSmart dropped off most advertisers' radars, and has gone through a series of caretaker CEOs. Quarterly losses continue. In spite of occasional positive news, the company is on course to run out of cash, and chances, by 2010.

Those Who Own the Traffic Control the Dollars

The fates of paid search also-rans like Inktomi and LookSmart, compared with powerhouses such as Yahoo and Google, illustrate a key principle. Even the former category leader, Overture, saw the handwriting on the wall and allowed itself to be acquired by Yahoo at an opportune time.

The fact is, although the pay-per-click listings services do differ somewhat in their feature sets, probably 80% of an advertiser's decision about which service to use (and how much to use it) comes down to distribution, or reach. A cool online listings bidding platform is worthless if it gives you access to only a handful of potential customers.

The search business is behaving rather like other consolidating industries have in the past. The biggest online destinations (today, these are Google, Yahoo, and Microsoft) can attract users by releasing better search technology. They can also retain them by controlling other aspects of the user experience and by behaving as monopolists do.

As Google has shown, the notion that search isn't "sticky" is a myth; its user base has a serious daily Google habit. Who would you rather be—a godlike economic force who owned all the railroads or asphalt roads at any given point in history, one that was able to pick and choose its preferred vendor of billboard technologies and allowed to charge tolls on usage, or merely one of a number of able vendors of tollbooths or billboards? When you look at it this way, it seems like the future of companies like Google is secure, whereas the chances that a vendor like LookSmart will make a permanent comeback are slim.

Admittedly, Google isn't the only economic powerhouse out there. Its long-term ambitions seem set to clash with those of major players in telecommunications, for example. Thus, Google has developed a growing interest in the concept of "Internet neutrality"—a principle that would prevent telecommunications and network providers from blocking access or discriminating against competitors. In continuing to build its relationships with consumers in the information economy—potentially, as a provider of phone service, for example—Google seeks monopolistic advantages, or at least seeks not to be disadvantaged by unequal rules that favor more entrenched monopolies.

Sudden Reversal of Fortune Unlikely

In light of the consolidation in the search engine business, by 2004 some business owners breathed a sigh of relief, because "pretty much all they had to worry about was Google," even if Google's growing power was a bit scary.

By 2006, though, the consolidation had run its course, and another wave of venture capitalist enthusiasm in "Web 2.0" was gaining steam. Both the leading search engine companies and fast-growing startups were creating new "places to be found." Although no upstart is currently challenging Google as the leading search engine, we're entering a phase where complexity is returning to the picture for any business wishing to conduct a comprehensive public relations and exposure campaign online. New networks, social media, local search options, consumer review sites, and exploding interest in activities like viewing streaming media mean that the relative calm of the period 2002–2005 (from a "getting found online" perspective) may once again return to chaos. Still, business owners take considerable solace in the fact that Google and Yahoo still reap a very high percentage of online advertising dollars.[15]

That some pundits like Robert Scoble recklessly predict the demise of Google Search within four years[16] (at the hands of upstarts like Mahalo and Facebook) doesn't heighten the chaos so much as plant seeds of doubt as to where we may be down the road. Highly touted Google-killers such as Cuil certainly haven't made any inroads in terms of user adoption. The Google brand's strength now wards off competition from even the most perfectly executed startup strategy. But most search startups will fall well short of perfection, as Cuil did. Even if Cuil moved beyond trivial and incremental improvements to search technology to pose a serious threat in terms of superior search relevancy, rapid increases in usage could pose insurmountable performance hurdles. The other barrier to beating Google, then, is that a Google killer would need to invest hundreds of millions of dollars in server hardware. This is why the only companies seen to pose a serious threat are the old familiar biggies like Yahoo, Microsoft, and Amazon, who do have such capacity. And none of them have posed a significant threat of late.

For now, the prudent advertiser will stick to facts: Google's influence and revenues are still growing. While competition is ever-present and the rules of the game can change rapidly, Google has routinely triumphed over or assimilated much stronger competitors than, say, Mahalo. Like the Microsoft Scoble no longer works for, Google's growing status as a monopolist may mean that the biggest threat to its existence comes in the form of government legislation. From a technological or "consumer zeitgeist" standpoint, like Microsoft, perhaps Google's star will someday fade, but that process could take decades.

The Growth and Evolution of AdWords

AdWords is now, and always has been, a work in progress. Let's look at how it grew from a relatively minor experiment to the force it is in today's global advertising business.

Early Version Challenges

The first version of Google AdWords is rarely discussed today. Launched on October 23, 2000, Google AdWords didn't exactly take the world by storm. An opt-in Google Friends newsletter issue on November 22, 2000, covered a number of developments at Google, including the release of a beta toolbar, some magazine awards about the search quality, and instances of Halloween spirit at Google. The mention of the new ad program was included as a brief item. It was almost as if the advertising service was an interesting little hack that would help Google to defray its operating expenses.

Observers still didn't think that Google would earn much more than 25% of its income from ads; it was expected that advertising would be a sideshow to the real business of creating a powerful technology that would somehow be licensed to corporations and power users. Given the time it would take Google AdWords to begin dealing with issues like billing and customer service on an "adult" level, it's safe to say that few in the company knew how much money Google stood to make from its advertisers over the next eight years.

The main trouble with the initial version of AdWords was its pricing model. Overture had enjoyed unexpected success with a pay-per-click auction model that created bidding wars for top listing spots, while allowing small-fry advertisers to stay in the game at a low cost. Google inexplicably decided that it could dictate the terms of its relationship with advertisers by setting traditional fixed prices for ads. A maximum of three ads would be shown on a search results page, priced on a cost-per-thousand-impressions (CPM) basis: $15 CPM for top spot, $12 for second spot, and $10 for third position.

This model didn't take into account the wide variation in advertiser demand for, and the disparities in the potential profitability of, different search words and phrases. Furthermore, if an advertiser really wanted to be visible at the $15 CPM level, there was no way to lock in the position. Ad space would simply be rationed across all advertisers.

So, if a $10–$15 CPM rate was far too expensive for some keywords, Google wouldn't be able to sell that inventory to anyone, leaving too many unmonetized page impressions to earn Google the kind of money they'd need to expand their growing company. Worse (and this happened within a few weeks of Google's launching the program), word would begin to spread that Google's ad program was overpriced and didn't work. By contrast, if that same ad rate was a screaming bargain (priced too low) for some popular commercial keywords, this early version of AdWords left advertisers with no way of competing for maximum exposure. Instead, they'd be apportioned a relatively small number of impressions, being forced to share the slot with others—a recipe for advertiser dissatisfaction.

The worst sin of this fixed-price method, then, was that it left Google no room to raise prices on high-demand keywords. The pricing model Google chose couldn't have been more inefficient. There were clear advantages to Google's "new take" on the online advertising business, however. Google's hacking, experimental, software-driven attitude was reflected in the many small differences between AdWords and Overture in the period 2002–2006.

Although Google's *pricing* method was at first inefficient, the way it chose to operate the program screamed scalability. It was a big plus that advertisers could get up and running in a few minutes by entering a few parameters into the interface. Overture had more human editorial oversight than Google AdWords. Close observers began to suspect that Google was up to something. If it could keep growing and taking in advertiser dollars while keeping a lid on hiring, this increasingly popular search engine could generate fat profit margins indeed. Investors, among others, quietly took notice.

Nonetheless, the program failed to catch fire because advertisers didn't like the pricing model. CPM-based advertising had been badly tarnished in the dot-com collapse, and many advertisers probably had a visceral reaction to the notion of paying $10–$15 CPMs when $1

CPM ad campaigns had failed for them in the past. Overture had done a great job of training advertisers to want *clickthroughs* on paid search listings, not mere eyeballs.

Google's next big move, on February 20, 2002, paid considerable homage to Overture's superior pricing model. After digesting the market feedback on the first version of AdWords for a full 16 months, Google released a new version of the ad program, called AdWords Select, that mirrored Overture's pay-per-click auction in important respects, while diverging from it in others.[17]

The press release announcing the new "Google AdWords Select" program (the name has now been shortened back to Google AdWords) treated this as an incremental change, as "new pricing for [the] popular self-serve advertising program." If you talk to anyone who is keenly interested in search marketing nowadays, though, it's more likely that they consider this as the day that the "real" Google AdWords was born. Advertisers adopted this program quickly, though not without various complaints and more than a little head scratching.

In forthcoming chapters, we'll examine specific examples from the AdWords interface, which has undergone at least a couple of major overhauls since its inception. To keep the momentum going, Google continues to make minor improvements on a regular basis.

Google as Referee: Complications of Multiple Stakeholders

As Brin and Page themselves implied in their early paper, search engines' stock in trade is legitimacy. As a former political scientist, I always grasped this instinctively. Analysts of the 20th-century "welfare state" (the New Deal) often pointed out that a capitalist economy would be most likely to thrive when all participants (including the weaker members) believed that the system was in the best interests of everyone.

Is a search engine really that different? People loved the Internet because of the freedom and power it provided. They loved search engines because they were great ways of acting independently, searching out alternative sources of information, and avoiding biased messages. The objectivity of search engines, much like that of libraries, was something held sacred by many Internet users throughout the 1990s.

We saw what happened when some search engines sold out. Users did anything they could to avoid the clutter and deceit that awaited them on portals like Excite.com and AltaVista.com. The clean, fast, useful Google Search interface came along just at the right time. Google was the Internet's New Deal. Immense user loyalty was the result, and it continues to this day, though not without some reservations.

Advertiser Needs vs. User Needs and the Public Interest

Advertisers, of course, have had their own ideas about what they should be getting for their money. These ideas have often been ignored by search companies at the same time they were busy ignoring users' needs. Wouldn't it be a good idea for a company that derives its revenues from search advertising to pay closer attention to the needs of *both* their tens of millions of users and their hundreds of thousands of advertisers? Don't be so sure. Although Google's massive staff now pays a great deal of attention to advertising sales and support, Google has never "sold out" by relaxing editorial rules. It has continued to test *user* responses to changes in the ad program as the primary yardstick of progress. In the process, it has angered some advertisers.

Individual advertisers, left to their own devices as rational single actors, would always request more prominent exposure for less money. Depending on the prices of the ads, they don't always care that much about relevance. Targeted advertising is nice, but not all advertisers feel it's their job to worry about targeting if they can get their brand out there. Plenty of big-brand advertisers remain dissatisfied with Google as an advertising medium because Google won't sell huge amounts of untargeted inventory to the highest bidder.

That's exactly what Google felt they needed to guard against when they designed the look, feel, and rules of their ad program. From the early days, I was impressed by Sheryl Sandberg's frequent use of phrases like "long-term viability" and "long-term interests of all advertisers" when explaining the emerging AdWords policies. Sandberg served as one of the major early influences on AdWords policy within the company as its Director of Advertising Sales and Services, going on to shine in several roles at Google (including VP, Global Operations) until her departure for Facebook in 2008.

To protect the public, Google knew it needed to clearly label its sponsored listings. It also wanted to make sure that users wouldn't flee Google because the ads were too big or too bold. A muted, understated text-ad design was chosen. Google no doubt benefited from internal discussions as well as external advice from web usability experts such as Jakob Nielsen, who joined the company's technical advisory board shortly after its founding in 1998. In a discussion with Nielsen in 2003 about the AdWords program, I discovered that he remained "unsure" about the program, which to me suggested that he worried even more than Google staffers about the potential for users to become "blind" to the ads.

Moreover, Google decided to build relevance requirements right into the design of the bidding platform, as we'll explore in more depth later. The final step to ensuring that the public was not turned off by what they were seeing was a wide range of strictly enforced editorial policies. Some of these policies were content related, but others related to form. Google prohibited things like repeated exclamation marks or other gimmicks intended to grab the user's attention in ways that might dissuade users from returning to search on Google.

Today's AdWords contains so much automation that the advertiser experience is with a rather slick and smooth environment compared to the alert-laden and appeal-happy environment in days gone by. Google support staff have quietly been transformed into the equivalent of sales reps; their editorial and rule-enforcing role has been quietly diminished. This effectively makes its competitors' editorial processes sometimes come off as harsh by contrast; Microsoft and Yahoo still sometimes behave in ways reminiscent of earlier generations of paid search. Keeping in mind such aspects of the editorial process that Google has gently moved "out of sight" may be helpful as you read on.

Rules against attention-grabbing punctuation and inaccurate claims in ads were developed not only to protect the public, but to protect advertisers from one another. Clearly, Google's "New Deal" for online advertising would have the best chance of succeeding long term if it took a hard line against those who used unscrupulous means of inducing users to pick their ad over another appearing nearby. Then again, the practice of optimizing an ad's text to maximize response rates (as long as such testing is done within the program's terms of service) is vital to a successful campaign.

Addressing User Needs

Presumably, search engine users still expect certain kinds of search queries to be largely unfettered by sponsored links. If no ads at all are relevant to a given query, Google simply shows no ads. Given the past seven years of efforts of advertisers and schemers of various types to find keywords to bid on, at least some ads show for a high proportion of search queries. Recent figures show that Yahoo and Microsoft show ads next to about 75% of all search queries. Google is more cautious in its monetization efforts, at 58%.[18]

If you experiment, you'll find types of keywords that don't tend to show ads. The reason might not be that no advertisers thought of them, but rather that Google's relevancy requirements and user feedback measurements have become ever more refined. Refined or not, if users don't tend to click on ads in some categories of search (say, the names of archaeologists), ads will tend not to show up because Google's system is gently discouraging advertisers from advertising on those terms.

On some commercially oriented queries, clickthrough rates are so high on ads that it's hard to dispute that the ads are more relevant than any other type of result the search engine shows. Indeed, on commercial queries, some sponsored listings are expected by users. Controversies over whether users are "confused" by poorly labeled sponsored listings peaked around 2003, but have dwindled steadily since a scaremongering conference, "Trust or Consequences: How Failure to Disclose Ad Relationships Threatens to Burst the Search Bubble," was held in Berkeley in June, 2005. The confidence and conscientiousness of search engine companies in terms of disclosure, and consumers' consistent high ratings of companies like Google on measures of brand trust and user satisfaction, fly in the face of the claims of public interest groups intended to protect "naïve" consumers.[19]

Whether ads appear on a page or not, Google's users expect the mix of results to be as relevant as possible. Clearly, that balance isn't an easy one to strike. To help users find specific types of information that they might want, but wouldn't be likely to go hunting for unprompted, search engines began experimenting with what Danny Sullivan has referred to as "invisible tabs." A query that might appear to be "newsy" in nature might trigger a couple of Google News results at the top of the page in addition to the regular search results, for example.

With the formal announcement of an approach to search called Google Universal Search, Google has put a name to the experimentation, making it clear that its goal will be to put useful information in front of searchers, and that information today is not necessarily going to be a web page. Various Google information services, such as Google Local, will be featured, but so will objects such as images, audio podcasts, video, and more, as search evolves.[20] Importantly, this will be achieved in an automated, not editorial-centric, fashion, as always. This means that Google aims to offer a helpful mix of "answers" to billions of potential search queries. Presumably those answers will be nearly as useful as hand-built "answer sets" put together by their competitors' (for example, Mahalo, Squidoo) human editorial staff, but available on a much grander scale, and self-learning to customize the response based on the user's preferences and habits.

Working in parallel behind the scenes as a research testbed (perhaps best relegated to that status, as it has such broad ambitions but limited immediate appeal to a definable user base) is a universal discovery service, called Google Base, that would allow submissions of any type of content, information, or object, using categorization schemas decided by those doing the submitting.

In terms of the balance between paid and organic listings, what all of this does is to add complexity to gaining visibility on the so-called organic side, while leaving the status and privileges accorded to the paid AdWords advertiser largely untouched. In a way, then, the paid search program seems like a more certain way than ever to break through the clutter and unpredictability of the search medium, because those sponsored listing positions are deployed consistently.

Taken in this light, it's quite plausible to claim that sponsored links often lead to an *increase* in the perceived relevancy and helpfulness of pages of results. Some queries, after all, truly are commercial in nature.

Google's Profit Motive

Back to the text-based reality of today's Google Search. Google isn't a neutral observer in the pursuit of a better user experience, of course. A very simple formula at least theoretically drives business objectives at a search engine company. Assuming x number of search engine results pages (SERPs) shown on a given day, the goal is to maximize the revenue per page of SERPs. As great as they may be for legitimacy, too many pages devoid of ads are a drain on the search engine company's budget. Pages that contain ads selling for a discount price are also not pulling their weight when compared to pages full of fully priced (or overpriced) ads. And most germane to a pay-per-click ad model: ads that don't get clicks are less valuable to the search engine company.

The pay-per-click auction model, based on advertiser competition for search keywords they want exposure on, is so brilliant because it allows ad pricing to adjust nimbly to the forces of supply and demand. The boom-and-bust cycle of the online banner advertising marketplace happened in part because the pricing and media buying models were so inefficient. One day, everyone was jumping all over overpriced advertising inventory. Seemingly overnight, no one wanted any of it, so prices simply plunged across the board. This won't happen with pay-per-click keyword auctions because the demand for different keywords is so varied, and the bidding platform has so many potential buyers lined up at any given time. Most of all, the majority of today's pay-per-click advertisers are carefully tracking their results, so they won't be making rash all-or-nothing-style media buying decisions.

Keyword Inventory and the Auction Model

What's so interesting about Google's massive "keyword inventory" (the wide variety of search results served on a given day) is that huge parts of this would go unsold if it were priced on a fixed basis. This is certainly what happened with Google's first crack at AdWords. Now, with less-popular inventory available for as little as a penny a click, Google can make at least some money by selling off this vast secondary ad space for low prices. Google's wish to sell off remnant inventory at a discount can be to your advantage as an advertiser. One important task for all advertisers is to seek out the bargain-priced inventory, although this strategy often tends to be out of reach in practice now that competition for keywords has increased. Today, what we're looking for most often is relative bargains and measurable return on investment.

What has made Google and Yahoo so highly profitable, though, has been the serious bidding wars that have erupted on popular keywords. When a dozen or more advertisers are desperate for exposure on a commercially viable keyword, the cost for a click can be driven up quickly in the auction process. The inflated costs of keywords like **mesothelioma** and **personal injury** are often reported in the press. But even in relatively humble fields like enterprise software and specialized professional services like divorce lawyers in prestigious locales, $15 per click is not uncommon for the most commercially valuable phrases. Avoiding the worst effects of such bidding wars is an important goal for you as an advertiser.

Revenue Maximization

Google injected relevancy criteria into its ad program in part to maintain the legitimacy of Google Search and to foster a good user experience. But the prominent role played by clickthrough rates (CTRs) in the ad ranking formula also ensures that advertisers who generate the most revenues for Google are prominently displayed on the page. Those who seek to exploit the system by displaying irrelevant ads may find themselves in less prominent positions on the page, as defined by Google through a quirky measure called Quality Score. (Chapter 5 is devoted to Quality-Based Bidding.)

Another important advance of AdWords when compared with its main competitor, Overture (now Yahoo Search Marketing), was matching options. At the time of AdWords' release, Overture advertisers had difficulty achieving wide keyword coverage, since it treated every phrase as an exact match. AdWords, by contrast, allowed broad matching and phrase matching. This gave advertisers wider coverage with less work and, perhaps just as important, allowed Google to sell more of its keyword inventory without relying on advertisers to dump huge files of keywords into their accounts. Overture later added matching options.

Shareholders, Not Just Founders, Influence Direction

No matter what you read, it seems likely that a sales culture began to grow at Google as it hired more salespeople. It is clear that Google has worked towards goals that involve squeezing more ad dollars out of the daily flow of search traffic, and taking paid search market share away from rival Yahoo. Google's mission statement, "to organize the world's information and make it universally accessible," has led to rapid product development and strategic moves to trump competitors on a variety of fronts—including the biggest competitors, like Microsoft. It seems at times that Google has outgrown even that mission statement as it has grown into a kind of holding pen for the world's top technical talent. It's certainly the case, though, that the engine that drives Google's profitability remains Google AdWords; indeed almost exclusively.

A host of apparently insignificant policies lurk beneath the hood of the AdWords platform, unknown to the average advertiser, or at least confusing and opaque in their impact. Close observers tend to believe that the ad distribution and display policies that are least understood by garden-variety advertisers are in place primarily for reasons of profitability. In many cases I agree with this assessment. For example, Google released a feature called Expanded Broad Matching that is similar to an Overture feature called Match Driver. Ostensibly, this would show your ad on obvious variations of keywords in your account, such as plurals. However, the feature expanded to cover "semantic variations" and did not work very well at first. Google is constantly tuning the workings of Expanded Broad Matching, and at times it appears that broad matches, especially when bid high, lead to erratic performance as ads are displayed unpredictably on "semantically related" search phrases.

Much advertiser dissatisfaction has been directed at the content targeting option in AdWords (called AdSense when viewed from the publisher's perspective—that is, from the perspective of website owners displaying ads paid for by AdWords advertisers). Google was uncharacteristically quick in ramping up this program, likely due to their perceived need to race against competitors like Yahoo and DoubleClick for control over online advertising inventory. In the past couple of years, Google has steadily improved the feature set, transparency, and accountability of this ad program. Most of these changes have come in response to a steady stream of advertiser input, and no small degree of advertiser frustration.

In other instances I tend to disagree with analyses that peg any change to the AdWords platform as "just another Google cash grab." The current Quality-Based Bidding formula is certainly doing no harm to Google's long-term revenue prospects, but the reasons for releasing and refining this formula are complex, and not all tied to pure revenue maximization. The user experience, in my judgment, does remain paramount in the AdWords program. This search engine user satisfaction, in turn, keeps Google in business, and highly profitable.

How Google's DNA Influences the AdWords Game

Let's turn to an overview of idiosyncratic policies and attitudes that will become familiar to you as you play the AdWords game. Many of them stem directly from the values of the founders and their immediate circle. On the whole, though, a certain kind of attitude permeates the company. If I had to boil it down, it might be "never forget the user experience," which in the case of a search engine company means "don't intrude, just help people find what they're looking for." A generalized wisdom also prevails: "don't forget why we're here and AltaVista isn't—don't be dot-com road kill."

Editorial Rules and Banned Items

Google spent a lot of time in the early going debating advertising policies. Today, not only is there less to debate, but the policies themselves may be less transparent than they once were. But you may find yourself running afoul of certain policies. That shouldn't be inherently surprising. Any publisher (online or off) is going to have guidelines for the types of products that they accept advertising for. Google is no different. They must ensure, of course, that ads comply with applicable laws. But they also go beyond the law in areas they worry could become controversial and alienate the general public.

Google has sometimes reminded advertisers that it does not censor search results. Whereas an ad may be banned for something like hard liquor or a certain type of knife that might commonly be used as a weapon, this does not preclude pages about these items from showing up in the regular search results.

If you're curious, https://adwords.google.com/select/contentpolicy.html offers a list of basic content policies. It wasn't published until November 2004. It does not give much detail, and many gray areas are still left up to editorial discretion. In my experience, the list of prohibited industries and ad subjects provided on this page is nonexhaustive. You may run into other problem areas that have yet to officially make it onto the list.

Pop-Ups and Other Poor User Experiences

Pop-up ads, and Google's policy prohibiting sending visitors from your ad to any page containing such ads, is really now just an example of a larger-scale, systematic program Google has implemented to police what it calls "landing page and site quality." In essence, Google once took strong stances against a few things that it believed led to a negative user experience. Now, that iconoclastic approach has been tempered and extended through the collection of years' worth of user feedback. A few of the old policies no doubt remain alongside a richer list of ill-advised practices, such as customer data collection without adequate disclosure of your business credentials.

Since both Yahoo and Google reserve the editorial right to ban any ad just for pointing to a page they deem irrelevant to the ad, it's not surprising that Google has also taken the initiative in banning ads that point to pages that they deem to provide a poor user experience. Want to show your ad on Google? You will pay a premium to point it to a page that serves users an annoying pop-up ad; if your ad shows up at all, that is.

At this point, such specific guidelines shouldn't be taken too literally, in the sense that you can also run afoul of Google's landing page and site quality guidelines by doing other things that smack of deceptive or irrelevant advertising. As mentioned, I'll cover the gamut of ad quality issues in an upcoming chapter.

> **NOTE** *Ironically, this very policy led some entrepreneurs to come up with pop-up-like technologies that were different enough from pop-ups that they passed editorial muster with Google for a time. But "working around" Google's rules is more difficult now because Google looks for a variety of signals of negative user feedback. So much like the Mom who doesn't give her child a pass for saying "Oh, Fudge" (the intent was there!), calling something a pop-in, a pop-around, a pop-a-rooni, or a pop-a-doodle-doo is now unlikely to "fool" a Google policy specialist if it displeases users.*

Privacy Policies

It will be interesting to see just how far Google The Advertising Company is willing to go to collect demographic data on users as competitors attempt to do the same. Google, for now, has relatively strict privacy policies and does not know much about the individual surfer using the Google Search tool, although it does look at the user's geographic location (IP address). Google's history might suggest that it will go slow on offering advertisers advanced demographic targeting, while its competitors forge ahead with more intrusive schemes.

Currently, Google does report limited demographic targeting information to its advertisers, under the auspices of partnerships with (for example) social networking sites such as MySpace. Google does not want to be portrayed as a privacy threat, so its approach is to test the waters gently and to lull competitors into making the first invasive moves (so a competitor, not Google, can take the rap for moving the goalposts).

Because Google The Global Information Powerhouse has now built so many integrated services around its core search offerings, the topic of privacy and Google now seems to exceed the scope of this book! What are we to make of Google Health, a would-be centralized repository for patient medical records? Or Google's steady rollout of a variety of telecommunications services? The apparent mapping and archiving of pretty much everything, as Google's stated corporate mission? When we look at specific policies with regard to searcher privacy, Google looks relatively innocuous. But Google's role in the global information economy could well make it the single greatest potential threat to your privacy. But that's another book.

Are Policies Consistently Enforced?

When it comes to the ongoing quest for top rankings in organic search rankings, many business owners have been torn between so-called "black hat" and "white hat" strategies. A broad consensus has emerged in the industry: you have to be at least "gray hat" to do well. The unwillingness of many businesses to strictly follow Google's webmaster guidelines often comes from observation of competitors bending the rules for years running, apparently benefiting from the deception. "If you can't beat 'em, join 'em" seems to be a constant temptation in the world of search marketing. It takes a strong will to resist temptation. For the record, it's usually best to resist, in my opinion, because that competitor might not be doing as well as you think, and may eventually be subject to catastrophic penalties as Google adjusts their search ranking algorithm or makes manual adjustments to catch certain forms of unreasonable "gaming" of their algorithm.

It was inevitable that a certain degree of this gamesmanship might gravitate towards the paid search program, too. Google combines automated methods with human discretion to weed out and punish advertisers who don't play fair.

The problem with some of Google's policies in the past is that they weren't grounded in any solid principles. Some have been nearly unenforceable; in other cases, Google has chosen not to enforce them—in essence, "looking the other way" on minor violations given the complexity of enforcing the rules to the fullest extent.

One quagmire is the quiet but rarely enforced prohibition on "double serving." If you think about it, an unscrupulous advertiser could open two (or ten) separate AdWords accounts and blanket the page with ads for the same product or service, crowding out competitors. Google prohibits such behavior, but it's not uncommon for exceptions to slip through. There are too many gray areas where it actually makes sense to have two ads showing on the same page from the same company on the same keywords. A large company like IBM might have separate divisions that are both likely to benefit from rather different ads on keywords that sometimes overlap.

More to the point, perhaps, this is yet another policy matter that has now been subsumed under the all-encompassing enforcement mechanism of Quality Score, which is opaque and largely automated. The extent to which human inputs (real policy specialists twiddling the knobs, as it were) affect Quality Scores is not precisely known. Again, I'll be delving deeply into this shortly.

By moving policy enforcement into a "no-tell" zone (into a numerical score that takes myriad factors into account), "bad guys" don't necessarily find out what they've done wrong. Google is under no obligation to tell them, either.

That's led to further uncertainty among conscientious advertisers, wondering if they're being wrongly judged. Where Quality Scores are low, they want to know what factors are causing the low rating. Thus Google is now swinging back towards more transparency. They're studying ways of giving advertisers some clue as to which policies they've violated, or what factors led to their keywords being given low "quality" ratings.

Despite the imperfections that have cropped up along the way, Google is moving in an interesting direction when it comes to policy enforcement. The degree of automation they are attempting to achieve would seem to codify their policies and remove excessive discretion from the hands of editors. The analogy would be with making good laws: judges are needed, but legal interpretations in specific cases should not vary wildly depending on which judge you deal with.

Tight Control of Information Flow

Despite its democratic, fun image, Google is a serious business entity that holds its cards close to the vest. It employs a degree of secrecy that many consider excessive. Some recent political reading that equated undue government secrecy with a deficit in democracy made me sit up and think hard about just what was going on over there at the Googleplex. Google staffers have always told me as much as they possibly can to help me understand AdWords features. But the company's secrecy often precludes them from telling the whole story.

The pressure on Google seems to have abated some now that the nail biting over their IPO is done. (The first trade of Google shares under the ticker symbol GOOG went through at 11:56 A.M. ET, on August 19, 2004, for $100.01, well above the offer price of $85.) In the pre-IPO quiet period, most everyone in the company was terrified of giving away material information or being perceived to promote the stock, since even the suggestion that Google might be a good investment would have violated SEC regulations and led to delays in the IPO. Delayed IPOs, as AltaVista found following 1999, are not good karma for search engine companies.

All Search Engine Companies Are Secretive about Algorithms   Much of the secrecy employed at Google is absolutely necessary. Search engine companies cannot share much about the "secret sauce" of their methodologies on a month-to-month basis, since millions of website owners are jockeying for high rankings in the free results. In this regard, Google is not alone. Its cryptic commentaries about its search engine ranking methodologies are in keeping with the demands of its ongoing battle with index spammers.

Concealing Details of How AdWords Functions, for Competitive Reasons   An unusual quirk of AdWords is that many features are a lot more complicated than similar features offered by competitors. Add to this the engineer-speak combined with public relations spin and you've got some features that are downright befuddling.

Google has opened up their public relations outreach in the past four years, however. Spokespersons such as Nick Fox, a key manager of the "ads quality" team, tirelessly explain new features of the ad ranking formula. Nick has directly answered many of my pointed questions, and has been forthcoming in public conference sessions as well. For example, on the question of whether total advertiser spend or length of account history (in terms of time) affect account-wide Quality Scores and performance, Nick was clear in stating that Google "does not believe in perverse incentives, so it doesn't include time or spend in the Quality Score."[21] I believe him.

Google also has more products in the marketplace today than they did two or three years ago. This has evidently led to a more systematic outlook on how to communicate with the public. Google Analytics (a website analytics service) and Google Website Optimizer (a landing page testing tool) are key examples of products used by paid search marketers. The outreach effort has evolved towards a mature dialogue with affected businesses and interested commentators and journalists, with heads of the product development teams making their insights widely available. Google's recent move towards *glasnost* has been refreshing. It appears that they have counseled their key public faces to give direct, clear answers to questions about how products work, while maintaining confidentiality only where absolutely necessary.

In fact, it's the substance of their complex, automated systems that leads to most of the apparent obfuscation. No amount of spokesperson explication or number of oversimplified PowerPoint presentations can make up for the fact that the AdWords program has always been complex, and has shifted from generation to generation quite rapidly, with nearly no external actor being competent enough to distinguish between a small feature change or a major new release.

For example, in the early days of AdWords, Google invented a sliding scale to measure the exact minimum threshold of clickthrough rate (a relevancy requirement) that advertisers were required to meet to keep keywords enabled. Officially, the cutoff was 0.5%. But Google emphasized that this was actually "0.5% normalized for ad position." This means that the relevancy policy, as measured by clicks on your ads, is relaxed as your ad moves down the page to a less visible position. (The 0.5% is no longer part of the formula, but the threshold for what counts as a "good" CTR is still normalized for ad position.) Many advertisers wanted to know exact numbers for CTR cutoffs in different ad positions, but Google never disclosed this. In part, this was because this CTR cutoff would vary by keyword (industry norms). Therefore, disclosing all the figures would have disclosed proprietary search behavior information. Google is unlikely to disclose this level of detail on such matters, at least for the time being. While literal-minded advertisers often found this coyness frustrating, pretty much everyone's gotten used to it by now.

In fall 2003, Google claimed to be raising that cutoff to 1.0% on some keywords in some situations, but the explanation for that was so confusing that virtually no one understood it. The 1.0% cutoff formula, whatever it was, was quietly dropped.

Google policy gets a lot more complicated than that. Many features have not been amenable to straightforward description because they're based on proprietary algorithms and predictive formulas. Pricing on content targeting, for example, is subject to a so-called Smart Pricing formula, where Google's software determines the cost of a click (subject to your stated maximum bid) based on a predictive or actuarial formula that looks at which kinds of pages online are more likely to return a higher conversion rate to sales.

Three motivations have underpinned these elaborate feature designs. First, the brilliant Google engineering team always wants to take a stab at solving a problem through software. Second, Google wanted to design AdWords as an elaborate, proprietary system to muddy the waters in its drawn-out patent dispute with Overture. Finally, the more difficult Google made AdWords to copy, the less likely competitors would be to ape it. Certainly, Overture and FindWhat moved quickly to duplicate some of the most compelling features of AdWords—particularly matching options. But it takes considerable experimentation and development time to copy the more arcane features. Is *feature* even the right word for a formula based on complex interrelationships among a host of variables? Google AdWords is not only multifeatured, it's multiformulaed.

Not Disclosing Details of AdSense Program   Content targeting has been an ongoing source of concern for advertisers. Like Overture, Google is content to boast of major publishers and certain "poster child" publishers who have participated in its AdSense program. But there is poor disclosure of not only the full list of participating publishers, but many other details of the AdSense program, such as how pricing is determined, what the revenue share is, and more. Advertisers see click costs, and publishers see basic reports and receive checks in the mail, but a lot of detail is missing.

Failure to Break Down Reporting of Ad Spend by Country of Origin   One thing I always found curious was that Google will let you choose which countries you show your ads in, but the reporting interface doesn't break down your click costs by country. I'm sure that's one feature Google has on its to-do list, but it does stand out as an example of an area of nondisclosure that was left to linger too long. There have been numerous others.

Google's Service Revolution, or "First We Take Chelsea"

Relative to the program's popularity, AdWords was administered by a skeleton staff of customer support and editorial staff in the period 2002–2004. Since that time, Google's headcount has exploded. The new staff complement runs the gamut from engineering talent, to advertising sales execs, to customer support reps. Their Manhattan office space in the trendy Chelsea area, still a novelty to many longtime observers of the Mountain View, CA–based juggernaut, seemed to me considerably more labyrinthine and bewildering in March 2007 when I visited it than it had been only a year previously.[22] As always, the food is tasty (organic or vegan if you want), and a fun-looking selection of confections and beverages is always on hand. Mountain View meets Manhattan, in style. Google appears to believe that if you've made it into the *Village Voice*, you've really made it.

Google added nearly 7,000 employees in the period between May 2007 and the same time in 2008, when quarterly financial reports are published for Q1. This brought the company's total headcount to over 19,000. Prior to that, headcount grew at least 80% in each of the previous four years. That's a breakneck pace. While there may be some slowing of that pace due to the consolidation of acquired DoubleClick employees, as Google expands into completely new fields, its ravenous appetite for talent may well continue unabated for some time. It's likely that this trend will eventually put a damper on profits, in spite of the notes of caution formally offered by company management. It's also worth noting that much of this growth is international.

At the end of 2002, the year AdWords' pay-per-click version was launched, the company had only 682 employees. None were stationed in a chic Manhattan neighborhood.

As a result of the buildup, advertisers have noticed significantly increased service resources. Many of us who run agencies with multiple clients have permanent "agency reps" who assist in expediting troubleshooting and answering difficult questions. Sometimes, however, this has spilled over into meddlesome behavior. Accustomed to "self-serve," some advertisers find Google's growing customer service staff "salesy" just by virtue of their very presence. Achieving a consistency of tone and behavior across the board becomes a challenge with such rapid growth.

In light of all this, the company's early technical orientation—automate where you can—is actually a strength, buffering advertisers from the most pesky effects of salespeople with too much time on their hands. At the root level of AdWords is a "product" that works consistently (if in complex fashion). Fundamental decisions about the advertising auction are driven by product managers incorporating feedback from advertisers and users, with only minimal input from this "growing headcount."

Google Underestimated Need for Customer Service   At first, by using software to facilitate editorial review, Google assumed that it was onto something big: a business model that could reap revenues even greater than Overture's, while spending far less on human support. As the program grew, it became difficult to ignore the huge gulf in service. Google became aware that advertisers need a lot of hand-holding, and the pace of hiring accelerated. Today's attitude towards service appears to be nearly a 180-degree reversal from the early "don't call us, we'll call you" approach. Because Google can attract good people and is so stringent in its hiring process, their new commitment to service could make it tough on the competition. That being said, new concerns are now being raised about Google's overhiring cutting into profitability.

What about Rewards for Good Customers?   There doesn't seem to be a conclusive policy on how to provide dedicated support for agencies and advertisers who spend more. The overall level of service and attention is now so high that pinpointing exactly what criteria are used becomes less important, but for some literal-minded folk, the process may be murkier than they'd like. It's important to recognize, in any case, that few advertisers spending any decent amount are denied time and support, because Google has such vast resources. So make use of it, no matter how big or small you are.

Certainly the "sales potential" of an agency or large advertiser (how much can Google expect them to spend in the future) appears to be a large part of their internal criteria for how much extra dedicated support to provide.

Uncertain Relationships with Advertising and Marketing Agencies   Third parties often advise clients on how to use AdWords, or directly manage complex campaigns. (That's what my firm does, for example.) Observing Google's progress in dealing with the environment of marketing and advertising agencies, they have never fully given up on the idea that advertisers really should be coming directly to them for advice. However, this situation appears to be improving.

A Google Advertising Professionals (GAP) program, launched in November 2004, was an interesting initiative that was supposed to sort out qualified from unqualified individual AdWords campaign management practitioners. A company wide (agency) version of this is also available. This is more of a training and indoctrination program than anything else, however. The reward to the qualified professionals and agencies is minimal at best, though ostensibly it helps advertisers avoid working with "hacks."

Agencies certainly get much less out of Google in terms of financial rewards (such as a commission) than they have in any relationship in the history of advertising. On a variety of fronts, including the Google-agency relationship, observers have asked the question: is Google sucking the proverbial oxygen out of the room? While consultative relationships have improved and become more formalized—a key improvement, to be sure—many of the leading AdWords consultants and evangelists must make their living from service fees alone, putting them too close to break-even for comfort, while Google's extreme profit margins continue to fuel the company's growth. There are practical hurdles to be addressed before such traditional advertising industry practices can be adopted, particularly in the "geek culture" which has served Google so well. However, the goodwill and indeed survival of the search marketing agency community, in particular, may hinge on a recalibration of their financial relationship with Google.

In its formative years, having the right (geeky, iconoclastic, world-beating) attitude at the right time was a big part of what made Google into a global powerhouse. Some critics predict that this same attitude could be its undoing. Experts believe that the degree of Google's cooperation with the developer community (and I would add, the marketing ecosystem) will determine whether the company has the staying power of a Microsoft.[23]

Coexisting with "Resellers" and the Ecosystem in General

Through the back door, Google may be studying ways of responding to the above analysis. Beyond AdWords, the company has new, highly technical products, like Google Analytics and Google Website Optimizer. It has initiated partner and reseller programs for these products. By instituting criteria for membership, working closely with that community on product development, and figuring out ways of steering valuable consulting business to such resellers and partners, Google can study the ins and outs of forming such productive relationships. Such relationships seem to be founded on classic models common in the software industry, especially in high-ticket enterprise software. What makes this unorthodox (as usual) is that Google's products are often free, and many of the customers for them are small to midsized businesses. What will it mean for my consulting firm to "resell" Google's free product to a small customer, I wonder? Like many others, including Google themselves, I can't wait to unravel that puzzle.

Google's survival may well require it to balance its secretiveness (against increasingly feisty competitors like eBay and Microsoft) with a new openness in its dealings with certain partners. And as it enters adulthood, it might need to shed its laid-back attitude and become more strategic in forcing users and advertisers (and welcoming reseller partners and application developers) into proprietary, but widely shared, information technology architectures. These architectures may allow new uses of Google's products, but when the goals of third-party applications conflict with Google's, Google can always block access or raise prices on certain types of usage. An example might be the recent acquisition of aQuantive by Microsoft, making it the owner of Atlas, a popular third-party bid management tool. Microsoft owning a tool that can gather a huge amount of search behavior and economic data about how real businesses are faring on the AdWords platform may have caused some initial alarm at Google, but it doesn't seem to have helped Microsoft gain market share. Regardless, through their ownership of Google Analytics and now DoubleClick, Google has trumped competitors in the race for dominion over business data pertaining to advertising performance across wide swaths of the online world, regardless of whether that advertising is going through Google AdWords.

Another model Google could pursue to ingratiate itself to the developer and business ecosystem is to release more thoroughly open-source products, as it has recently done with its new browser, Google Chrome. Such initiatives can be advantageous to the community and even competitors, while solidifying loyalty to Google as a source of innovation.

With specific regard to paid search, the introduction of the AdWords Application Program Interface (API), is promising insofar as it signals a heightened commitment to cooperate with third-party developers and agencies. But it's clear that Google does not view all third parties as cooperative with its own goals and its customers'/users' needs. When it comes to third-party "layers" such as bid management technologies, Google can price API tokens (the price for any automated access of the AdWords interface) and set the API terms of service in such a way that it is costly to build certain kinds of software overlays. Such overlays may be seen as superfluous annoyances, given that Google is also developing new features to help advertisers directly within the AdWords platform.

Google will likely need to create more formal partnerships in the future, and invite more developers and agency types into ongoing dialogues about features and business relationships. They have already begun to formalize this process, putting together new "blue-ribbon" panel groups to assist in ongoing feedback about their products (including the AdWords interface) that will coexist with older means of gathering feedback from forums, users, and webmasters chosen for limited beta tests.

In the past, the dialogue with the "affected community" often appeared to be limited to select groups of beta testers and informal chatter mediated by the likes of anonymous Google employees posting on forums, such as GoogleGuy. These means of communication did little to forge long-term adult relationships with Google's agency advocates, resellers, and technology partners. Google has now begun to reach out to these latter players, which augurs well for Google's long-term survival because it is more aligned with the lion's share of online advertising dollars. Geek-speak will never be out of vogue in this medium, but it will now be tempered by business focus.

Google's unique culture was shaped first and foremost by its founders, moderated by technology veteran CEO Eric Schmidt. The company's ability to focus depends heavily on the ongoing involvement of top management in steering what has become an increasingly diversified enterprise. To paraphrase the "risk factors" sections of the company's SEC filings: If Google should lose the services of Larry, Sergey, or Eric, it could be in big trouble. Time will tell, but there is no reason to believe that Google's top people have anything in mind other than overseeing its continued breakneck pace of growth and change. By building a sound and consistent means of interacting with partners, Google will also build allies for the long term, allies who bring more resources and perspective to the table than the first wave of geeky foot soldiers who helped Google cross the chasm to global search supremacy in the first place.

Endnotes

1. Josh McHugh, "Google vs. Evil," *Wired* (January 2003), archived at www.wired.com/wired/archive/11.01/google_pr.html.

2. A useful primer on such matters, covering the whole range of contemporary administrative theories, is Charles Perrow, *Complex Organizations: A Critical Essay, 3rd ed.* (McGraw-Hill, 1986). Chronicles of dot-com startup desperation, greed, and excess such as

Po Bronson's, *The Nudist on the Late Shift: And Other True Tales of Silicon Valley* (Broadway, 2000), don't seem appropriate to grokking the Google work culture, which has always seemed relatively settled and self-confident as opposed to chaotic. As nerdy and unconcerned as Google employees may appear to be about the traditional goals and structures of large corporations, keen observers (see David Vise, "Following a Rich Tradition: Under the Avant-Garde Veneer, an Old-Guard Startup Strategy," *Washington Post,* June 24, 2004, E01) have argued that this powerhouse is very much a traditional Silicon Valley "insider" company. Key early investors and advisers—including Jeff Bezos, John Doerr, and Michael Moritz—were all seasoned members of the Silicon Valley elite, and the hiring of Eric Schmidt as CEO introduced a degree of settledness to a group that was already arguably mature beyond its years. Of course, some sensationalistic press reports have suggested otherwise.

3. For example, Danny Sullivan, "Where Are They Now? Search Engines We've Known & Loved," *Search Engine Report,* March 4, 2003, archived at searchenginewatch.com.

4. For the whole story and a detailed how-to guide to the new Yahoo Search Marketing platform, see Mona Elesseily, *Mastering Panama* (Page Zero Media, 2007).

5. *Search Engine Positioning* (Webware Publishing, 2001). An earlier iteration, *Achieving Top 10 Rankings in Search Engines: Insider Trade Secrets from Positioning Pros*, a spiral-bound self-published effort, was released in 1999. Marckini has explained to me that a book distribution partnership with rank-checking software provider WebPosition Gold fueled rapid growth in his business.

6. See Danny Sullivan, "Death of a Meta Tag," *Search Engine Report,* October 1, 2002. This is not to say that metadata are unimportant, just that webmasters were still worrying too much about keyword tags in particular, when Google likely ignores them. Description meta tags are still visible in many search results and are therefore worth using. A proper discussion about the future of metadata would fill a book.

7. Claire Woffenden, "AltaVista MD Resigns Over Unmetered Fiasco," vnunet.com, August 30, 2000. The credibility of AltaVista's claims had been challenged by a technology "critique" site, *The Register*. See Kelly Black, "AltaVista's Unmetered Access Hoax," InternetNews.com, August 22, 2000.

8. "Why the Open Directory Isn't Open," Traffick.com, March 30, 2000.

9. Sergey Brin and Lawrence Page, "Anatomy of a Large-Scale Hypertextual Web Search Engine," Stanford University Department of Computer Science, 2000. Jon Kleinberg, widely considered to be the leading contributor to this generation of search technology,

has published many important papers on search, including "Authoritative Sources in a Hyperlinked Environment," 1998.

10. For those interested in such issues, Danny Sullivan, "The Bumpy Road to Maximum Monetization," *Search Engine Report,* May 6, 2002, archived at searchenginewatch.com, is a must-read.

11. Nick Wingfield, "Engine Sells Results, Draws Fire," CNET News, June 21, 1996, archived at news.com.

12. Jim Hu, "AltaVista to Auction Premier Ad Placement," CNET News, April 15, 1999.

13. Steve Harmon, "GoTo.com IPO Set to Go This Week," InternetNews.com, June 16, 1999.

14. "Paid Search Is Here to Stay," Traffick.com, March 27, 2000.

15. eMarketer offers a convincing summary of relevant online ad market share stats that serves to re-emphasize points made in the first two chapters here. See eMarketer, "Portals Dominate Online Ad Take," April 24, 2007, archived at www.emarketer.com/ Article.aspx?id=1004838. Stats include Google and Yahoo now accounting for 91.9% of U.S. paid search spending and the same two companies accounting for over half of all online ad spending.

16. Robert Scoble, "Why Mahalo, TechMeme, and Facebook Are Going to Kick Google's Butt in Four Years," *Scobleizer*, Aug. 26, 2007. Rejoinders include Dave Winer, "Google and Search," Scripting.com, Aug. 27, 2007; Rand Fishkin, "I Used to Respect Robert Scoble's Opinion," SEOmoz, Aug. 26, 2007. Archive locations: http://scobleizer. com/2007/08/26/why-mahalo-techmeme-and-facebook-are-going-to-kick-googles-butt-in-four-years/; www.scripting.com/stories/2007/08/27/googleAndSearch.html; and www.seomoz.org/blog/i-used-to-respect-robert-scobles-opinion, respectively.

17. Indeed, the formats were similar enough that Overture contended that Google violated key Overture patents. Following Yahoo's acquisition of Overture, the two companies settled the ongoing dispute out of court. In August 2004, on the eve of its IPO, Google awarded Yahoo 2.7 million shares of Class A Google stock as a lifetime license payment covering any relevant patents for the pay-per-click auction model.

18. Figures from comScore qSearch, as told by James Lamberti in a presentation at SES San Jose in the panel on "The Search Landscape," Aug. 20, 2007.

19. See Kevin Ryan, "SearchTHIS! Paid Listings Under Fire," *iMedia Connection*, June 7, 2005.

20. Mike Grehan, "Optimizing for Google Universal," *ClickZ*, July 9, 2007.

21. Andrew Goodman, "Holiday Time, Quality Time: Two-and-a-Half Questions About Quality Score for Nick Fox, Google," *Traffick*, November 30, 2006, archived at www.traffick.com/2006/11/holiday-time-quality-time-two-and-half.asp.

22. *Gothamist*, "Google Eats Up More Office Space," September 1, 2007, archived at http://gothamist.com/2007/09/01/google_eats_up.php.

23. Charles H. Ferguson, "What's Next for Google," *MIT Technology Review,* January 2005.

Part II

How to Play the AdWords Game

Chapter 3

First Principles for Reaching Customers Through AdWords

This chapter is intended to illustrate how small, unobtrusive AdWords ads fit into the typical user's journey in a given online search session. (Actually, the first thing to realize is that there is no "typical user," *per se*. Luckily, advanced forms of segmentation that might have cost oodles of cash in the old days are relatively easy to approximate at little cost in time and money through AdWords.)

Even if you're well versed in online advertising, this chapter is worth reviewing. In the effort to master the finer points, it's easy to lose sight of the basics of how and why people are using Google Search, and what you can realistically expect them to do when they come across your ad. It's all too easy to make stereotypical assumptions that there is one way of searching the Web, or one typical model for making sales to online audiences. The examples I'm about to give are intended to convey a sense of the diversity of this medium. There are many different ways to succeed, and also many ways to fail.

In addition, I'll briefly review recent developments and happenstances that have conspired to put Google and its AdWords program in the leadership position they enjoy today. Google's visionary path towards search market dominance has created special opportunities for advertisers, but the medium also poses some difficult challenges.

The following two chapters are also fundamental, as they pick right up on the basics provided here. If you happen to be super-impatient, skip ahead to Chapter 4 for my philosophy on "setting up ad groups," but recognize that you may be missing important background by skipping ahead.

Chapter 5, on how your ad will rank on the page in competition with other advertisers for various keywords, is far from basic. Because Google now ranks ads with a complicated formula, I had to devote an entirely separate chapter to it. I'm afraid you can't really get away with skipping that one!

Through the User's Eyes: Profit by Understanding Searchers' Love Affair with Google

For millions of Internet users, search is an habitual activity, performed daily. According to recent figures from comScore Networks, the average U.S. user performs 35 searches per month. The average Canadian user is a bit more active, at 40 searches per month. Keep in mind that these are averages; many users search much more frequently than that.

The detailed data about user behavior gathered by panel-based web measurement companies like comScore are not actually all that easy to come by. comScore has a proprietary dataset it calls qSearch. To get access to all of the information about the complex daily patterns of search behavior, you would either have to subscribe to comScore's premium info service or have direct access to the same search data that some employees of companies like Google and Microsoft do. Various web metrics vendors like Hitwise offer increasingly accurate, detailed information. Again, though, for Hitwise's best stuff, you'll pay a fee.

We don't always know what is running through a user's mind when he or she undertakes a web search, so stereotyping or prejudging is unwise. But we do know that the purchase process is largely about navigation and usability. Web usability experts write articles, convene at corporate seminars, and do in-depth studies to assist companies in their efforts to make it easier to navigate through the website to the point of purchase. But what we as search marketers need to do is to extend the thinking about the user experience back one step, to the very first stage of finding your site listed in a search engine. Users can't use what they can't find, obviously. And how they encounter your listing makes all the difference in initiating a positive contact with them.

To provide a feeling for the process, I'll offer a couple of straightforward examples of a typical search-to-purchase scenario.

The prospect of sitting in the same place long enough to write a book brought back painful memories of graduate school, eyestrain, and lumbar pain. A new monitor took care of the eyestrain. But oh, my aching back! I decided I'd put off my purchase of an Aeron chair long enough, but I also wondered if there were any alternatives to Herman Miller's pricey design. Surely I could get a chair of the same quality for less with just a few minutes of research and a little shopping around.

What to do? As I and millions of others do every day to solve such problems, I went to Google.com and performed a keyword search. The first query I tried—**aeron-like**—could have been too clever for its own good, but it turned up a fair amount of useful material.

I suppose one of the wondrous things about searching the Web for information using a tool like Google is that nearly anyone can do it without a lot of specialized instruction. Google has advanced features, but no one is forced to use them. Arguably that's a big reason why search has spread so quickly throughout the population. It's easy. With a few keywords and a couple of clicks of a mouse, ordinary users find even the most unusual information quickly, a scenario that would have been unthinkable a few years ago.

As you can see in Figure 3-1, a number of relevant results appear. The left-hand side of the page contains what are commonly known as *search results*. I often call these *web index results* because they're pages drawn from an enormous database of pages created when Google's spider,

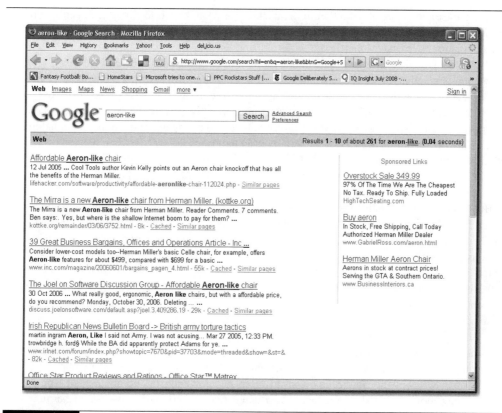

FIGURE 3-1 Typing **aeron-like** into Google Search yields a list of useful and interesting results.

Googlebot, crawls the entire Web. These are the pages that Google's technology deems the most relevant to my query. (Web index results means the same thing as "natural search results" or "organic results." Some simply call them the "free results.")

> **NOTE** *Google's search technology uses an algorithm that uses several weighting factors. Early versions of this algorithm may have drawn on PageRank—a complex analysis of which important pages on the Web link to other pages, about which topics. (But some speculate that Google no longer uses PageRank per se.)*

None of the web index results are paid for by advertisers. There is no way to pay your way to the top of the regular search results, or even to guarantee that your website is included in them. Google currently maintains an index of over 15 billion web pages, and on any given keyword query, Google will determine how many pages match. On popular keyword queries like **new york hotel**, there are thousands of matches. In fact, on **new york hotel** (without quotes), there are about 22.9 million matches. On **"new york hotel"** (typed with quotes by a web searcher to denote a phrase), there are about 3.6 million matches, for what it's worth. Good luck getting your website onto the first page of results there! Anyway, since my query, **aeron-like**, was so quirky, it turns out that only 261 pages matched.

Over time, Google seems to be pursuing a number of interrelated strategies regarding information demand and user expectations. Google is at once trying to respond crisply to what users expect to see on the page, while playing an active role in shifting those expectations over time. One interesting thing that Google has been doing recently, some believe, is ensuring that a higher proportion of the search results are informational, educational, or governmental in nature. Google may be treating obviously commercially oriented pages differently when it comes to its ranking algorithm. A major reindex in fall 2003, now dubbed "Florida," elicited howls of protest from webmasters on discussion forums and was covered in the technology press such as CNET as well as in the mainstream press.

But this is an oversimplification of what is really going on. As Google made more explicit when it formally announced its approach called Universal Search, the key today is to attempt to show search results that respond well to the user's intent on any given search query. As search technology experts have half-joked for years, the perfect search engine would guess what you wanted even before you typed in any keywords.

With Universal Search, web page results from Google's index of the Web will remain in the forefront. But, depending on the query, Google may serve up other types of "objects" or modules on the page to show information it thinks you might want: movie showtimes; weather forecasts; local listings with maps; news results; your own desktop contents if you have Google Desktop Search installed; photos; videos; and much more.

Meanwhile, on queries with strong commercial intent, there is a high probability that AdWords ads will show up, and as time goes by, users develop expectations about what types of things they should see in the designated advertising area, as well. As I'll discuss further in Chapter 5 (on how Google ranks—and sometimes rejects—ads), if it doesn't fit the mould of a retailer, technology service provider, or some other typical and expected type of business, users tend to squawk to Google that they are getting annoyed. Google takes this to heart, and has developed a system to disincentivize certain kinds of unconventional business models from advertising at all. The more ads Google rejects, it seems, the more money they make. Google today continues to work this paradox as much as they ever did. If anything, they've become more self-aware of the sources of their success.

Many queries are not commercial in intent. Others are highly so. Google doesn't really want shopping sites to appear high up in the index search results if a query is obviously informational. Where the query is commercial, Google would hope to fill a little more screen real estate with advertising. They conduct subtle experiments all the time, figuring out how to show more ads where appropriate, and less where inappropriate. Want to get a sense of whether search engines guess that a query is commercial? Try Microsoft adLab. For background research purposes, they offer a tool (Detecting Online Commercial Intention is its current name) that will tell you what the Microsoft Live Search engine thinks of a given query. On the term "Cleveland irons" (a golf club), for example, Live Search (via adLab) believes this query has a 92.6% chance of being at least somewhat commercial in nature. The first time I tried this a couple of years ago, that figure was 96%. As more data comes in for a whole range of search queries, these predictions are likely to become more accurate. Among other things, they can help search engines determine how many ads it's appropriate to show on the page for different kinds of queries, as part of their long-term planning processes.

Some time ago, Google's director of search quality, Peter Norvig, confirmed that for the purposes of organic rankings, Google might attempt to assess not only the degree of commerciality of sites, but different types of commercial intent (a catalog page versus an "About Us" page) and rank pages accordingly. It might even, Norvig told me, look for data such as how long a company has been in business, or how long a website has been operational, for cues to the quality or reputability of a given page. Practically speaking, this may be putting more pressure on commercial sites to use the pay-per-click AdWords program if they want to generate targeted traffic. But, AdWords is not a get-out-of-jail-free card for businesses wanting to promote themselves without being scrutinized by some kind of algorithm. Nowadays, Google applies to the paid listings some of the same criteria of quality, credibility, and relevancy that they apply to the organic search results. Users demand quality control no matter which side of the page a listing shows up on.

There has been endless speculation about which factors are most important in Google's algorithm. That Google uses some form of link analysis seems unquestionable, but like most leading search engines today, Google's means of ranking websites goes beyond published formulas. Search engine ranking methodologies are a moving target—deliberately so, as marketers try to exploit knowledge of algorithms to achieve the best possible "free" rankings. To put together a strategy for improved organic traffic, today's marketers are best served by dividing up ranking factors into "action buckets" such as good content, external reputation, site architecture, user experience, basic labeling, and the like, and pursuing the improvements that seem most likely to please not only search engines, but customers or readers.

In any case, this book is *not* about getting your website well ranked on that elusive left-hand side of the Google Search page. It's about paying to place your advertisements in the right-hand side of the page (and sometimes, at the very top of the page in the highlighted premium sponsor area) *near* those search results so that you might grab the attention of customers typing in relevant keywords.

On my query, **aeron-like**, you can see (Figure 3-1) unobtrusive-looking text listings in the right-hand margin. These are clearly marked as "Sponsored Links." The ad from BusinessInteriors. ca caught my attention, as did an ad from Backs, Etc., which has a strong local reputation and a convenient showroom on Eglinton Avenue in Toronto. (Due to search personalization and ever-evolving search algorithms, the current screen shots may not sync up entirely with your experience, or mine prior to or subsequent to writing these paragraphs. Backs, Etc. is just an example of a company that did catch my eye in real life.)

I didn't click on any ads at first, though. I read a couple of the articles I noticed in the regular search results. I also noticed that the very top link in the search results was to a page describing a new, less expensive, stylish Aeron-like chair from Herman Miller called the Mirra. That's about as close to the definition of **aeron-like** as I could come. Is Google clairvoyant? Anyway, more research was still needed. I had three choices: spend all day reading articles about Aerons, zip directly to an online store and order one right away, or something in between. I chose the middle path: do just enough research to decide which chair was more or less right for me from the standpoints of form, function, price, reliability of retailer, and convenience of purchase. Once I got those issues settled, I fully intended to make my purchase in a physical store because I feel more comfortable making some purchases in person.

I point all of this out to show how easily a businessperson and an advertiser can fall into the trap of making assumptions about how people search and shop.

Above all, you can get lulled into believing that everyone is naturally going to do what you want them to do: buy your stuff online at the price you're asking, seconds after seeing your offer.

This might be nice, but it doesn't always happen. You can't control how people behave, and often, unless you're a large company with plenty of reliable data on hand, you can't even guess very well about what motivates them to act on your offer. Don't get too narrow in your thinking; just realize that your target audience—as my Aeron-like chair example shows—may behave in a reasonably orderly but ultimately untidy, unpredictable fashion. In particular, it's safe to say that many purchase decisions take time. Consider that a sales cycle—be this a week or a year—is a normal part of doing business online, and that repetition and consistency, along with targeting, are the bedrock of any online advertising investment. If you're looking for some confirmation of this latter point, consult Jay Conrad Levinson's *Guerrilla Marketing*. It's the bible for the fundamental principle of repetition in advertising. To succeed with online advertising you must, at a minimum, *be bullish about advertising* and understand why you advertise.

Although you can't totally control or predict your target customer's behavior, you *can* control many aspects of your AdWords campaign, which is what makes an AdWords campaign so different from traditional advertising. Here, you can analyze your data with reasonable degrees of precision, but then again, the data can't tell you everything. I never traffic in stereotypes like "no one shops at night," "they're not buying because the ad copy isn't exciting enough," or "everyone is looking for the lowest price." Relax. Backs, Etc. got my (offline, walk-in) business, even though I probably never explained to them that some of my searches were done at night; even though the ad copy didn't make me come to any sudden revelations other than that they were in business and eager for mine; even though Backs, Etc. is not a discounter but rather a trusted local fixture that focuses on good service.

Back to the Google Search results screen. In addition to the text listings in the right-hand margin, advertisements appear in one other place on Google Search. Depending on the query, how much you bid, and other factors (Google doesn't completely disclose these, nor many other, details of their formulas), Google AdWords may also appear at the top of the page in bold text on a colored background, as you can see with the **"new york hotel"** example query in Figure 3-2. These ads are not treated any differently from the ads on the right-hand side. Your ad might show up in these spots in the normal course of your AdWords campaign. This position is all part of the same keyword auction.

When I originally searched for **aeron-like**, some of the ads that appeared on my screen applied to Canada only, as shown in this illustration.

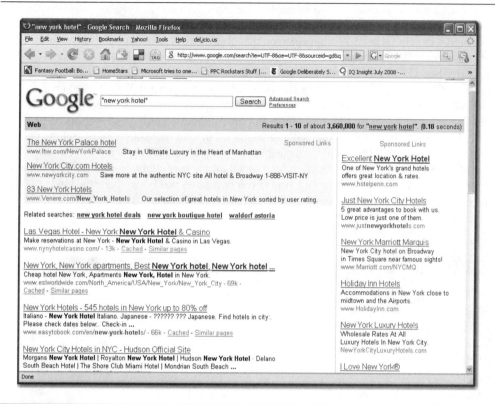

FIGURE 3-2   The phrase **"new york hotel"** attracts many advertisers. Google displays ads at the top of the page, above search results, as well as in the right-hand margin.

A different set of ads, however, would have appeared for my **aeron-like** query to a user in the United States (as shown here).

Different sets of ads are shown to users in different countries because advertisers have control over which countries their ads show up in. (A Google AdWords feature called geotargeting also allows advertisers to limit their ad display by geography on a variety of dimensions, including state or province, metropolitan area, or even a specific radius or shape on the map.)

After my **aeron-like** search, I followed up on one of the articles I'd run across, a product review on Wired.com for an Aeron-like chair, the Ypsilon. As directed by the article, I went to the vitra.com website to find out more about the Ypsilon, but found it difficult to navigate, and returned to Google to search under the phrase **ypsilon chair**. The first thing I learned, after poring over a few regular search results, is

Sponsored Links

Aeron Chairs - $849
Fed-Ex Delivery - Quick Shipping
Financing Available On All Aerons!
www.healthyback.com

Aeron Chairs- On Sale Now
All 2004 & Classic Colors Are In
Stock. Free Shipping Via FedEx
www.OfficeDesigns.com

Aeron Chair Sale
You Deserve It - Floor Model Sale
12 Year Herman Miller Warranty
UltimateBackStore.com

Aeron
Herman Miller Classics. Over 12,000
items online. Free Shipping
www.unicahome.com

Aeron
Compare Prices at 40,000 Stores.
Find Spring Deals at BizRate.com!
BizRate.com

that the "real" Ypsilon chair is an avant-garde wooden chair designed in 1950 by Hans Wegner. A reviewer declared it to be without "faults or mendacious pretences."

The high-tech 2008 type of Ypsilon chair, on the other hand, is widely available and, at a retail price of $900 all the way up to $3,000, must generate fat margins for the designer and retailer alike. But when I typed **ypsilon chair** (Figure 3-3), only two or three advertisers typically showed up for the U.S. market. At later points in search history, no advertisers showed up at all. This will vary over time, especially depending on how many advertisers can keep their ads enabled on the broad match for the word **chair**. In Canada, there are still no advertisers on this term. No doubt this search results page will eventually fill in with more advertisers. But the point is, when potential ad spaces go unfilled on such a high-margin product, especially when you consider that advertisers don't pay for the advertising until the user clicks on their ad, you can bet someone is missing out on an opportunity. And if you're reading this book, that's the kind of void you'll be looking to fill. There are many such opportunities on Google AdWords if you know where to look.

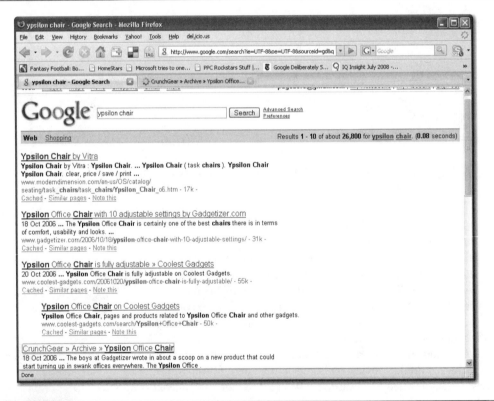

FIGURE 3-3   Few advertisers take the trouble to show up on the query **ypsilon chair**— an opportunity missed, since such an ad would likely attract a high-income customer.

Do People Really Look at the Ads on Google?

In conversation I frequently hear observations like, "I never look at the ads when I do a Google search." The observer will then typically generalize his own experience to conclude that search engine advertising is a waste of time and money. Of course, proving that people not only look at the ads, but also click on them, and then move from click to purchase, is not difficult. These days, this stereotype doesn't carry much weight in an era when Google's stock price has vaulted over $700. Its megabillions of annual revenues coming from ads tend to be a fairly good answer to this silly type of comment, especially given that the majority of advertisers do track whether the money they spend on AdWords converts directly into sales.

The reality is, your eye often avoids the ads when you're researching something noncommercial. But a higher percentage of people typing **Dallas tax attorney** would likely be looking to form a business relationship, and would be more open to the sponsored results (possibly even seeking them).

The incontrovertible proof of people not only looking at, but also clicking on, ads is found in data from any given Google AdWords campaign. I've had the opportunity to access data from more than 300 client campaigns and to peek at briefly at least as many again. I can tell you that users are clicking on these ads, usually at a consistent rate somewhere between 1 and 10%. That is, for every 100 times a client's ad appears next to the search results for a given phrase, it will typically be clicked between one and ten times. That's not bad considering that users usually see between 10 and 20 search results on their screen, and as many as ten text ads. For them to click on something that is clearly marked as a sponsored link even once out of a hundred times is something of a small miracle.

Google once claimed that its ads are clicked on 10 to 20 times more often than the typical online ad banner, even though such banners are becoming increasingly large and obtrusive. The disparity between search ads and banners might be even greater than that. Recent figures from DoubleClick put average clickthrough rates (CTRs) on banner ads at under 0.5%, whereas at least one of the ten Google ads that appears on a page of search engine results pages (SERPs) might be clicked on something like 15% of the time. That's 30 times more often than banners.

Eye-tracking Studies: What Can They Tell Us?

Even the question of where people's eyes are looking when they're scanning a page of results can be answered with some degree of certainty. Some major search engines and portals, including Google, maintain usability labs that can graphically display where users' eyes go on a screen and how long they maintain their gaze at any given place (see Figure 3-4 for an example). What users are typically trying to do is to find whatever most closely matches what they're looking for.

Different eye-tracking studies may show different results, and these are nowhere near as important as the actual clicks on your ads, along with data that tell you whether there is a return on investment on those clicks, at reasonably high volumes. I don't need to make abstract predictions about whether a fifth- or sixth-position ad on a popular term will be seen or clicked, or whether this translates into a respectable return on investment. I see account data and financial data for clients that clearly show even the fifth or ninth ad position is big business and generates many leads at an identifiable cost per lead every day.

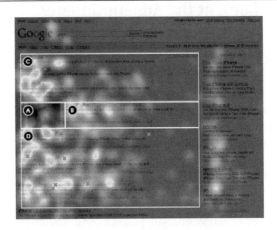

FIGURE 3-4 A heat map from an eye-tracking lab study by Enquiro Research. This shows where users' eyes go on a page of search results.

The question of whether users pay attention to the ads is no trivial matter and is so important to Google that they've paid attention to it with a fervor sometimes approaching paranoia. The history of online advertising seems to follow a pattern: first, there is a high degree of user interest and attention to advertising presented in new formats; then, a phenomenon of unconscious ignoring (sometimes called "banner blindness") takes hold, and clickthrough rates (the number of times a user decides to click on an ad divided by the number of times an ad is shown) begin to plummet to levels approaching zero. As this happens, advertisers eventually move to devalue the advertising. As demand dries up, ad rates plummet, and publishers—especially large publishers like AOL, Yahoo, and Google who depend heavily on advertising income—find themselves in trouble. This happened following 1999 as the dot-com honeymoon ended. As ad revenues plunged and hopes of growth for online media companies were dashed, stock values plummeted.

Google depends heavily on the advertising program, and they are watching closely for signs that users are becoming "blind" to these ads. So far, this hasn't happened, but it explains why Google puts so much emphasis on relevancy and the user experience.

In his Alertbox column ("Will Plain-Text Ads Continue to Rule?" April 21, 2003), Web usability expert Jakob Nielsen wonders if banner blindness will give way to text box blindness. He argues that the low-tech text ads are currently enjoying the same novelty effect that previous advertising formats did, but that they "are not guaranteed a bright future outside of their native search engine habitat." But Nielsen does admit that the low-tech format that requires advertisers to be highly relevant *might* be able to hold user interest for the long term.

Thus far we are not seeing any major drop-off in clickthrough rates on search ads. In part, this is because of the uniqueness of the search medium—the fact that the ads are often exactly what the user is actually searching for. Probably more importantly, Google's ad system is ruthless about relevancy; this isn't left to chance.

Why Users Love Google

In Chapters 1 and 2, I demonstrated how dominant Google has become in the marketplace. Take a second to reflect, though: amidst all the competition from companies like Yahoo, Microsoft, AOL, Ask, yellow pages companies, and feisty startups that seem to come along every month, *why* do so many users display such loyalty to Google? Arguably, it's what Google Search *isn't* that has attracted so many users to it. The clean design and singular focus is what people want. Google has done a remarkable job of appearing clean and simple even as it has added a host of new services. The home page today looks remarkably similar to older versions.

In the portal era, emboldened by inflated stock market valuations, every search company wanted to become the next Yahoo, which had grown from a small directory service to a large media company with many offerings. Unfortunately, also-ran portals were not compelling to users. They were simply ad-cluttered, unfocused messes. Taking advantage of the Wayback Machine at archive.org, you can look at old screen shots of Excite.com (see Figure 3-5) and AltaVista.com (see Figure 3-6) and understand why these companies didn't win the search wars. (These screens actually fail to do justice to how banner-cluttered many pages on these networks became, and they predate by a couple of years the desperate shift by online ad agencies and publishers to oversized, page-dominating banners.)

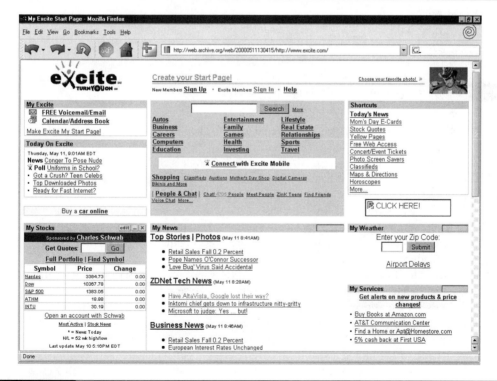

FIGURE 3-5   Excite's home page got too exciting for its own good.

FIGURE 3-6   Portal clutter got the better of search specialist AltaVista.

As other search sites admonished beleaguered users to shop until they dropped, Google quietly entered the fray in 1998 and gained momentum in 1999–2000 with a simple search box and new-generation search technology. AltaVista, one of Google's chief rivals at the time, lost market share quickly. Evidently, it had changed courses too many times. What a terrible time to give up on search! Google filled the void and soon took over as not only the leading search engine, but one of the world's best-loved brands.

In May 2000, AltaVista tried to copy Google's simple layout with a new, standalone site for "search enthusiasts" called, of all things, Raging Search (see Figure 3-7), but it was too late. Google had already won too much mindshare.

Users flocked to Google's oasis of simplicity and relevance for good reason: they wanted to search, not be shouted at. If an advertiser shows up near the search results and delivers something that's at least as relevant, users seem to see that as a fair compromise. But Google has never taken this for granted. The founders of the AdWords program had the vision to forge that compromise from scratch, taking Google from a company with virtually zero revenue to one raking in close to $21 billion a year from advertising without alienating that notoriously fickle user base. Unbelievably, as recently as 2005, media analysts (including Forrester Research

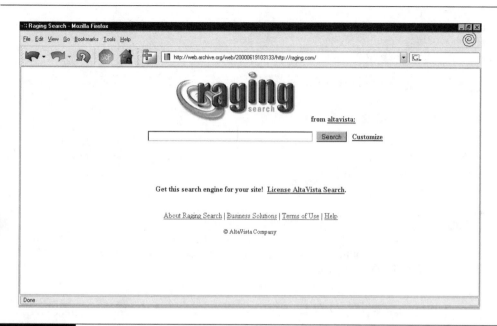

FIGURE 3-7   AltaVista copied Google's look and feel with Raging Search, but no one
noticed; they were too busy getting acquainted with Google Search, the new
whiz kid on the block.

analyst Charlene Li) peddled the faddish view that the "big portal companies" like Yahoo would
eat Google's lunch sometime soon as Google failed to grow beyond its "one-trick pony" status.
Obviously, this prediction was wildly off base.

More Thoughts on User Intent

Even a search that's informational in nature can ultimately result in a commercial transaction.
A computer user hears through the grapevine that Windows XP has a security vulnerability
whereby any user with an old Windows 2000 CD can circumvent the admin-password-protection
on Windows XP. Is it true? She searches on a specific query such as **windows password
vulnerability** or a broad term such as **windows 00** to find out. In the midst of her research, an
interesting, free "Windows tips" newsletter, Brian's Buzz by Brian Livingston, is advertised (see
Figure 3-8). She clicks on the ad and signs up for the newsletter. As it happens, Livingston's
subscribers are typically so delighted with the free information that a predictable percentage of
them turn into paying subscribers. Advertising near search queries that are largely informational
in nature nonetheless produced a measurable return on investment for BriansBuzz.com.

Given Google's experience of winning with clean, uncluttered search, more search engines
are erring on the side of conservatism when it comes to how much advertising they show. This
can pose a challenge to many advertisers who won't be getting the volume they'd like to see.

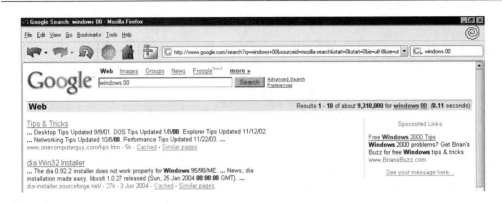

FIGURE 3-8   Official Microsoft bulletins appear prominently in the main search results for Windows-related queries, but some searchers are eager to receive a third-party viewpoint, so they click on the nearby ad for Brian's Buzz, a biweekly newsletter about Microsoft Windows.

Recent figures presented by James Lamberti of comScore (at the SES San Jose conference in August 2007) indicate that Yahoo and Microsoft "monetize" (show ads next to) in excess of 75% of queries on their search engines. Google monetizes less than 60%, meaning more white space in the ad area. That likely increases aggregate user satisfaction. But it's not just about white space. By ensuring that the ads are more relevant than they once were, all three leading search engines have taken major strides towards increasing user satisfaction.

Measurable and Nonintrusive: The AdWords Difference

AdWords is such a different environment from what advertisers have traditionally encountered that many have had trouble adjusting their strategy to suit this new medium. Here I'll outline what makes it so different and groundbreaking.

Request Marketing

The idea of customers finding you after searching for something related to your offering turns traditional media and advertising metaphors on their heads. Seth Godin's 1999 classic *Permission Marketing* alerted marketers to the difficulty and rising cost of reaching consumers amidst the cluttered landscape dominated by old forms of "interruption" marketing. However, his proposed solution to the clutter problem, developing relationships with customers through opt-in email marketing, still rests on the assumption that a company will broadcast messages to large numbers of people. Such marketing is getting much tougher to do effectively now that the inbox has become another site for clutter. And the problem remains: how do you get users to opt-in in the first place? Godin envisioned contests and incentives run by companies with fairly large marketing budgets, or perhaps he simply assumed that a lot of free search traffic would generate visitors to sign-up pages, and people would be eager to sign up. Those assumptions are no longer valid ones. Only nine years later, consumers are worn out from being permission-marketed to death. The theory of permission clearly had a few holes in it and was too easy to abuse, as Godin now acknowledges.

Godin's book, *Free Prize Inside!: The Next Big Marketing Idea* (Portfolio, 2004), takes the argument against interrupting people to a new extreme. He lauds companies like Amazon.com who have eliminated their television advertising budgets in order to spend the money on product improvements or features that would generate excited word of mouth among consumers. (In Amazon's case, they used the money to offer free shipping.) Marketers are trying to find a happy medium between not spreading the word about their company at all, and wasting money annoying people who are not interested. That's what makes search marketing such a good compromise: you're advertising, but you're doing so in a way that seems relevant to the recipient. And the minute it stops showing a *measurable* return on investment, you can choose to shut it off. More to the point, you can keep it showing to the prospects who are likely to be interested, while showing nothing at all to those who aren't. Not only will that help keep you in business, but superior relevancy means people will keep coming back to Google and paying attention to the results they find there.

Jakob Nielsen, in an October 2000 article called "Request Marketing," made a seemingly radical statement:

> The Web and permission marketing work in opposite directions. Whereas permission marketing is business to user, the nature of the Web is from the user to the Website. It is the ultimate customer-driven medium: He or she who clicks the mouse controls everything. It is time we recognize this fact and embed it in Internet marketing strategy.

> Request marketing basically means that customers ask the company for what they want. You can't get more targeted than that. You can't generate hotter leads. And, from a usability perspective, request marketing entails a design that works with the Web's fundamental principles, not against them.

What foresight! This is the kind of thinking that governs today's most successful search marketers. Users have choices. To fight this reality is not an option if you want to succeed in search marketing.

Google Calls It "ROI Marketing" (Not "Spend and Hope")

With pay-per-click advertising, almost everything is measurable. Advertisers don't have to be content with a lot of traffic that might or might not be good for their business. Advertisers don't have to console themselves with "exposure." (That's spending money, not making money.) Mark Stevens, in *Your Marketing Sucks* (Crown Business, 2003), offers a powerful argument against the typical company's approach to marketing: earmark *x* amount, and then "spend" it. The opposite of spending money is actually making a positive return from your investment, thus paying for the marketing costs in a short time period after they're incurred. Make no mistake: this is revolutionary. Ad agencies and television networks have a lot at stake when it comes to defending the presence of million-dollar Super Bowl ads that may or may not pay for themselves. Big ad agencies pushed Google to develop a premium program so that agencies could swoop in with expensive media buys for their large clients. After all, the larger the buy, the larger the agency commission.

In summer 2003 when Google made the decision to put an end to the premium sponsorship program, their spokespersons told me that they felt that the advertising community had not been quite ready for pay per click at first, so the CPM-based (cost per thousand page views, or impressions) model had been used as training wheels for ad agencies and large interactive agencies (to placate them so they'd spend their clients' dollars with Google). But, they continued, now that large and small advertisers alike see the benefits of "ROI advertising," the premium sponsorship program is no longer needed.

Fast Feedback Cycles and Rapid Evolution

Google AdWords provides you with a powerful tool to reap competitive advantages from rapid feedback cycles. Advertisers who religiously implement a dozen or so of the most important checklist items for optimizing their accounts, and do so repeatedly, can find themselves zooming ahead of their slower-reacting competitors.

It's not really all that difficult a concept to grasp. Think about golf clubs. Over the past 20 years, the average driving distance in pro golf has increased by 40 yards, making mincemeat of formerly formidable golf courses. Even the average player is hitting the ball farther today with the help of better clubs and balls. Because distance is generally seen as a good thing by buyers of golf clubs, manufacturers have bent over backwards to add yet more of it each year within the limits of golf's rules. So they've tested hundreds of small influences of materials and construction on the ball's flight, making changes to their technology every year to squeeze out that extra bit of performance. Companies that chose not to do this would have been selling measurably inferior equipment. It's pretty hard to argue with a tape measure.

In addition, advanced players now take on more of the responsibility for the process of equipment refinement. They actually match their equipment to suit their own unique swing patterns and ball flight, as measured with increasingly sophisticated instruments. Senior tour players employ personal trainers and undergo deep stretching exercises to maintain their edge. Better use of available research has also exploded old myths about the types of club lofts and shaft flexes that are likely to maximize performance for the average player. In a world of rapid improvement, those who stand still find themselves falling behind.

Playing the AdWords game involves a similar process of refinement with the aid of a rich set of data that is available to you nearly instantly. There are probably a dozen different key *aspects* of a campaign in play at any given time. Depending on how you play, you can address a lot of data in a short time (potentially being aware of a universe of millions of data points, but acting on only a tiny percentage of them requiring your judgment and input). You'll have to assess and then reassess your bidding strategy, keyword selection, ad wording, and other major determinants of campaign performance. If you do so on a reasonable schedule, you'll evolve into a superior being that survives as slower-learning competitors perish.

Companies that take care to consider these elements not only at the outset, but iteratively (again and again) as part of a process of ongoing adjustment, may beat the competition not just in narrow AdWords terms, but in the marketplace. Seth Godin, in a management theory book called *Survival Is Not Enough: Zooming, Evolution, and the Future of Your Company* (Free Press, 2002), teaches larger companies how to manage change by learning to "zoom." A summary of the ideas is contained in the April 2002 edition of *Optimize* in an article entitled "Chief Change Officers." In essence, Godin argues that too many companies generate mountains of data, but don't give the chief information officer the authority to act on it quickly enough. So, the competitor with a reactive culture—the one that zooms—starts to open a performance gap over the slow-moving company, until it's impossible for the slow mover to catch them. In Godin's words:

> Generational length is a powerful thing. If Project X resets every six months and Project Y resets every two years, X will produce eight generations of feedback in the time it takes Y to yield two. It's up to you to figure out how to dramatically increase the pace of change within your organization by making every generation of information of shorter duration than the last.

Google AdWords offers you powerful feedback as long as you're willing to use it to its fullest by creating a smart campaign, testing its performance with a decent monthly ad spend, and then reading and reacting. Your competitors are testing and improving their campaigns. So must you.

Let's turn to a deeper exploration of pay-per-click advertising. Advertising methods and pricing models for advertising have always been in flux. If you at least understand what you're paying for and how the online advertising industry got to this point, you may be better prepared for not only the current generation of paid search, but whatever comes along next year.

Online Advertising Pricing: Why Pay per Click?

No pricing model for online advertising is totally satisfactory to all parties in the transaction. This young industry has been through various fads, and I like to think it's learned something. The dominant model for online advertising pricing—both in email newsletters and banner campaigns—was, until recently, CPM, or cost per thousand impressions. This presupposes a certain value in "eyeballs." This model was touted in mostly self-serving fashion by portals like Yahoo and AOL that wanted to portray themselves as networks, as big media companies that can help advertisers broadcast their messages to a mass audience. They're still clinging to this image, but have also experimented with a wider variety of revenue models.

The problem with CPM is that it doesn't guarantee any type of performance. If an ad is shown, the advertiser is charged for it even if hardly anyone ever clicks on it to find out more. To put it mildly, many advertisers concluded that this type of pricing was a rip-off. But it hasn't vanished entirely, so it must be performing for someone. CPM has its place. It's also important to note that you can check out the CPM equivalent in your AdWords campaign. Since there are "impressions" involved, users seeing a page of search results and clicking *x%* of the time, you can calculate a CPM rate on your campaign, even though you pay per click. In fact, this is now published in the Account Snapshot view of your campaign. This will help you compare apples to apples in your overall marketing plan. Often, search is much more expensive on a CPM basis because it is so targeted. The cost and, ultimately, the targeting are probably good reasons why paid search was somewhat slow to gain acceptance, but then underwent rapid adoption as the secret of extreme targeting got out.

At the opposite end of the spectrum from CPM is cost per acquisition or cost per action (CPA). This is the purely performance-driven model: a commission is paid on a sale or lead that can be traced back to the user's visit to the publisher's site. What is the problem here? What self-respecting publisher wants to be reduced to a commissioned salesperson or affiliate for their so-called advertisers? This might be fine as incremental income here and there, but large publishers have principles to uphold, so they can't afford to give advertisers too much of an upper hand by agreeing to too many CPA deals. Neither side should be allowed to offload all of the risk onto the other party. Presumably, quality content (and pages of search results) is in short supply, so publishers should be able to set some of the terms of the advertising transaction. Enter cost per click: advertisers pay whenever a user sees the ad *and* clicks through to the advertiser's website.

How, in the past, did search engines envision charging advertisers? They've tried a number of ideas, but the fact is, paid search hasn't been around very long, and no one, until recently, had any idea that it would even work at all. Search companies have experimented with paid inclusion as well as targeted ads near search results. (As discussed in earlier chapters, Inktomi, AltaVista, LookSmart, and the new Yahoo Search have charged websites anywhere from $10 to $299 per URL to be listed or included in search indexes or directories. Today, Yahoo Search offers paid inclusion that charges a flat fee *plus* a per-click charge, and that does not even guarantee your website will be ranked well in the search results.) Metacrawler, a metasearch engine, was selling advertising on a CPM basis near certain keyword search results as early as 1998.

Paid search itself had no precedent, and until just a few years ago, few publishers even believed in the model, let alone espoused a particular pricing system as the best. When Yahoo moved from free inclusion in its directory through various phases of paid inclusion ($149 one time, $299 per year), the message was something along the lines of "pay up or else." Little rationale was given other than the need to pay editors for their time. Those who had paid for inclusion weren't too thrilled, either, when Yahoo moved to downgrade the prominence of directory listings in their overall search mix. This directory inclusion model, then, is an example of an imperfect model that didn't seem to work well for the advertiser, yet didn't allow Yahoo to maximize its revenue from its advertisers without completely alienating many of them.

What really got search and portal companies interested in charging advertisers on a per-click basis seems to have been the wild success Overture had with the model, especially as bid prices rose on popular keywords. Even here, it took several years for the industry as a whole to catch on, as discussed in Chapter 2.

The reason pay per click caught on is likely that it presents a sensible compromise between purely performance-based ad models (these would make the publisher simply an agent of the advertiser, a degree of risk to which many publishers wouldn't stoop) and CPM-based models that place too little performance onus on publishers.

Google itself piloted the first, CPM-based version of AdWords beginning as far back as October 23, 2000, following the launch of a premium sponsorship program in August of the same year. That so little was written about the program in the ensuing 16 months, and the fact that advertiser uptake was so slow, says a lot about how ineffective the CPM-based AdWords program was for the advertiser.

Self-Serve, Pay as You Go, and Self-Learning

The whole notion that an online ad program could be self-serve, and allow advertisers to choose their own pricing, campaign duration, and a host of other campaign elements while sitting in their pajamas at 2:00 A.M., seemed to pique the interest of the early adopters. Some of these were true Internet pioneers, like Bob Ramstad, who has operated Condom.com (also known as Condom Country) since 1996, making him one of the world's pioneering online retailers. When I first corresponded with Bob in summer 2003, he had already developed an extensive keyword list for his Google AdWords campaign and had generated plenty of data about the return on that particular marketing investment.

Thousands of forward-thinking entrepreneurs like Bob were all over pay-per-click advertising from its earliest days. People like Ray Allen, a former advertising executive who founded a wildflower seed company called AmericanMeadows.com, Jimmy Hilburger of Switchhits.com (he sells switch plates), and Stephanie Leader of Leaderpromos.com (corporate promotional products), have been able to grow their businesses with pay-per-click ads by tapping into a degree of flexibility and cost-effectiveness that usually isn't available to the small to midsized business. Many others are now catching on, which reinforces the need to develop a sound strategy to deal with an increasingly competitive keyword auction.

No haggling with the ad department over prices; no scheduling the campaign according to availability. Instead, we get to play with a cool little ad-serving machine built by Silicon Valley engineers. Google AdWords' designers created a little universe for the entrepreneur to play in. "Knock yourselves out," they seemed to be saying. The true entrepreneurs among us loved the idea that you could change your ad copy on the fly, if it wasn't performing well or if you simply didn't like it. Don't want to run your campaign on Saturday? You can pause it. Want to change all your bids, or pause or delete just some of your keywords? You can do so instantly. How about ensuring that your ad is only shown in certain countries and not others? That's part of the campaign setup process. No problem. While AdWords can be complicated, and actually now does come with a larger human editorial and service staff complement than Google once envisioned, it can be very simple to operate. Paradoxically, there can be as much complexity to the process as you like, too, since the interface offers an incredible level of control. It's that control we find addictive, since without it, we don't make as much money.

One important aspect of this control is the money part. Advertisers enter their credit card information but are only billed after they've incurred a certain dollar value worth of clicks. Since reporting is real time (with typically only an hour or so delay in detailed statistical reports), you can usually step in and take action quickly if things aren't going well. With a tiny outlay of cash (under $50), then, advertisers can get started with their AdWords experiment. Larger companies can apply for credit terms and invoicing if they wish.

Increasingly, services like AdWords want to make their systems easier to use for advertisers who don't want to fiddle around too much. As we'll see later, AdWords has a number of rules, and the determination of ad placement is based on a dynamic auction process that takes into account several relevancy factors, not just how much you bid. That's not as frightening as it sounds. You can rarely "break" AdWords, and in many ways, the rotten parts of campaigns take care of themselves—they simply wind up being shut off. There are a number of training-wheel-style features in AdWords. Advanced advertisers will want to disable some of them, as we'll discuss later.

A Sales-Generation Machine That's Yours to Keep

Seth Godin (in *The Big Red Fez: How to Make Any Web Site Better,* Free Press, 2002) has likened a website to a Japanese game called Pachinko—a game that involves dropping a disk at the top of a game board full of pegs. The disk bounces around and, if you're lucky, lands in one of the scoring areas. If you consider that disk as your prospective customer, Godin argues, you want your website to get the customer from the top of the game to the scoring area with a minimum of bouncing around, to increase the odds that he or she will actually take action while on your site as opposed to leaving. The good thing is, of course, that you don't have to let some random arrangement of pegs dictate whether you score or not. Here, we can rely on some known issues about website navigation, some of which Godin outlines in his book.

Better, though, is the fact that the game—both your and your prospect's participation in it—does not begin when your user arrives at the website. It begins when the user first types a query into Google and sees the first page of search results. For you, it begins in your construction of an orderly, compelling AdWords campaign: keyword selection, campaign organization, bidding strategy, advertising copy, tracking URLs, the selection of appropriate landing pages, and more.

This is very different from the typical ad campaign because you have so much control over the minute adjustments needed to get the "machine" well oiled. Imagine running a local television campaign and calling up the TV station in mid-campaign to ask whether they'd be willing to run a split-test to determine whether you sell more product when the pitchman wears a red sweater as opposed to a yellow one. Good luck!

With AdWords, and better yet, in combination with a website improvement tool called Google Website Optimizer, you can for all intents and purposes test the impact of that proverbial red sweater.

Such testing became the norm in avant-garde direct sales companies such as QVC, the home shopping channel. Jim Novo, formerly a vice president with the Home Shopping Network, now runs an online measurement firm called drillingdown.com. "If our data showed that people were more likely to buy microwave ovens between 3:30 and 4:00, then we'd sell microwave ovens between 3:30 and 4:00," Novo remarks dryly. But such testing capabilities have rarely been available to the small to medium-sized enterprise. For big clients, many ad agencies actively discourage such quantitative methods, instead touting softer "branding" benefits.

Some think of direct marketing methods such as direct mail as most analogous to Google AdWords, because considerable testing can be done to measure the effectiveness of different elements of the direct mail offer, right down to the envelope color. Successful direct marketers no doubt feel that their carefully honed, carefully timed mailings constitute a "system" or even a "sales-generation machine." But consider this: Google AdWords allows you to do the same kind of testing, but on a much more rapid cycle. Direct mail campaign feedback can take weeks or months and will cost several thousand dollars with each mailing. With AdWords, you have useful response data typically within 24–72 hours, and can make many small improvements at low cost.

The best thing about it is that once this machine is built, it's yours to keep. Yes, it will require maintenance, bid adjustments, competitive intelligence, and further testing, but your past refinements carry over fairly well. The initial effort of building it is well worth it. The fact that you are building not just a one-off "campaign" but a sophisticated lead-generation or sales-generation machine that weeds out the worst prospects and sends you the best ones at the lowest possible cost should justify your time investment in Google AdWords. The knowledge gained here can carry over to future campaigns in other media, as well. Because your prospects are coming to you based on a search for certain keywords, it's a great way to learn what's going on inside the minds of your customers.

Collective Action Problems in (Non-Search) Online Advertising

With the growth of search marketing, you don't hear people expounding on the virtues of intrusive pop-up ads and gimmicks nearly as much as you once did. Or do you? Theories about invasive forms of advertising haven't died. Many are alive and well at conferences like the popular ad:tech. Targeting is a primary focus of much of the programming at ad:tech, but if you wander into the exhibit hall, be prepared for a shock. I suppose advertisers who sell solutions that help you knock customers over the head and drag them off screaming are not going to be shy about approaching you in the same way. My advice: if you attend this conference, run at top speed through the exhibit hall, wearing full pads.

I believe there's a community responsibility to err on the side of nonintrusiveness in advertising, due to the classic Tragedy of the Commons problem. This is the old economic argument based on a common pasture with a few sheep grazing in it. There is individual incentive to add more sheep and reap higher profits, since additional usage of the pasture costs nothing. But, if everyone did this, the pasture would be grazed out and all the farmers would lose. Costly sheep would starve, or would at least need to subsist on feed that had to be purchased. In this scenario, a sense of collective responsibility, if upheld, is rational even on an individual level (unless you know where to find more free pastures). It's the same for the Newfoundland cod fishery. Individual trawlers have no disincentive to vacuuming up fish as quickly as technology allows. However, depletion of fish stocks leaves no fish for anyone.

User attention is like the fish stocks or the pasture. The example of email shows just how averse the user can become to being contacted in certain online formats. Individual corporate marketers may protest that their correspondence is legitimate, but too many have gone just over the line and communicated with customers too often, or on terms that were broader than those the customer agreed to. The result: people overcompensated. They started ignoring and filtering their email. Email marketing performance—measured in terms of open rates—declined as a result.

The same has happened with pop-ups and other intrusions. Today's Internet user doesn't particularly care that some marketers find them measurably effective, or that some are less intrusive than others. What they know is that they "hate pop-ups." So while a few pop-ups continue to be served, many others are blocked by technology asked for by consumers. And companies that continue to profit from them—both publishers and advertisers—run the risk of alienating people and destroying brand equity built up over decades.

(*continued*)

Bad actors in this ecosystem violate user expectations and conventions. We need to ask ourselves: did the user request or expect this form of interaction? If advertising is part of the user experience, is it in a format that they might reasonably consent to? By visiting a website, you are not giving the site owner tacit permission to employ intrusive or unexpected navigation conventions on you. (That's why even a musical theme playing on your website is considered tacky. What if the user's baby is sleeping, or what if they're at work, on the phone with head office?) Recently, I saw an animated Honda car ad jump out of a page at me as I attempted to mouse over a photo of something completely unrelated (a campus scene), connected with educational content. I couldn't believe it! Don't the publishers know that if they push it too far, they'll have no website audience to sell ads against?

Ad serving companies sometimes resort to the defense that intrusive formats are "relevant" to what the user wants. That argument doesn't wash, because relevance doesn't confer *carte blanche* to break all manner of social conventions. A shiny new Honda is highly relevant to me, but I don't want to be run over with one. (If it helps to drive the point home for you, feel free to think of racier examples.)

Before You Start: Planning, Third-Party Tools, and a Reminder

Dynamics will differ depending on how many stakeholders are involved in managing an account. Whether a succession of marketing managers over a couple of years, just the boss and one staff member, or a third-party paid search management firm or agency, in many cases there will be multiple people working on an account and trying to pull data from it. Therefore, it makes sense before starting that you step back briefly and resolve to make sure the campaign is tidy and orderly. Don't overplan, but don't just wade in and make a mess, either.

Work Backwards: Assess Which Third-Party Tools Will Be Needed

You may have already heard sales pitches for bid management tools and other types of software you might need in order to do a good job at this task. Step back briefly before plunging in (and review the material on third-party tools in Chapter 6). If the tools themselves create more work than they save, they may be a bad idea. AdWords is meant to be self-serve. Many of the bid management features and campaign reporting options built into AdWords give you everything you need. Google offers a tool to track sales conversions after the click. Google Analytics, an increasingly sophisticated and user-friendly web analytics product (developed from the core of Urchin, which Google acquired in 2005), works very well when integrated with your AdWords campaign. Privacy is one key reason to consider third-party tools over Google's. Do you want Google to have your sales conversion data?

In the early going you will probably need to know this much: many systems that will help you track sales back to their exact source will require you to tag your ads—specifically, the "destination URLs" that tell AdWords to which page on your site to take users after they click—with special tracking codes. You can also do this at a precise level, tracking sales by exact keyword or phrase. Whether or not you have to tag ads, you'll generally need to install JavaScript code on some or all of your pages for conversion tracking to work.

At the very least, make sure you do *not* build a large campaign with thousands of phrases and dozens of ads with the wrong tracking codes; do *not* build a large campaign with tracking codes designed to suit the needs of an inferior tracking tool that you'll need to change later. It can take a full day or two of work to reformat everything with correct tracking URLs should you set this up incorrectly from the start.

So yes, you are probably going to need to decide which post-click conversion tracking software is best for you before you begin. (A discussion of services to help track ROI and campaign performance is in Chapter 10.) If you already have something installed, or your IT department tells you they already have back-end systems that "work fine" and "track everything," don't let that dissuade you from doing more due diligence to ensure that what you do have can actually give you the data you need in a format you can use.

Another common type of third-party tool you may need is *keyword research software.* It's less crucial to decide on this right away, but I want to emphasize this much: vendors of software have everything to gain from overselling the role such software may play in the success of your campaign. Keyword research is important, but don't let a software vendor confuse you into believing that it's the only determinant of success. The methods I'll teach in this book typically outdo one-sided software-driven efforts that rely on brute-force lists of thousands of phrases. Also, be aware that Google's own keyword suggestion tool is free, and it has improved by leaps and bounds. Moreover, the data that are used to signal real user search frequencies are, well, real; third-party tools cannot duplicate the accuracy of Google's search keyword database. Take advantage of this in the setup phase.

Real-Time Auction on Keywords and Phrases

As discussed earlier, a traditional media buy might involve constructing a few campaign elements, negotiating a price, and then broadcasting a campaign, which will hopefully achieve desired results. In this model, advertisers don't have much control, but they may have a stronger sense of how much they're paying, for what type of exposure.

AdWords is different. Prices fluctuate constantly depending on the presence of other buyers. Much of your strategy—and your good and bad results—will revolve around the fact that this is an auction-based environment. You're not just bidding for exposure across the board, though. Each keyword or phrase is treated separately, and the positioning of your ads on the page is determined in part by the amount you bid. Fluctuating prices create budgetary uncertainties, but the benefit is, the pricing model is more efficient and creates economies for the advertising community as a whole.

At the most obvious level, then, you'll soon become aware of the high prices on certain keywords and phrases. To achieve prominent placement (ad position 2 or 3, let's say) on

new york hotel, for example, you'll need to bid as high as $5 per click on Google AdWords. In a business with thin margins, that's a steep cost to pay for a click unless a high percentage of those clicks convert to sales.

Let's move on to the nitty-gritty of paying Google; key terminology; how accounts are structured; and what you need to know to lay out your core objectives and get moving.

Billing

Google's billing method is to bill you only after you generate a set dollar amount of clicks. This billing increment might escalate from $50 to a recurring charge of $500 or more depending on your spending pattern. Customers can be billed in a wide variety of currencies, but you can't change the currency you're billed in after you establish an account. If you decide to change currencies, you'll have to start a new account in the currency of your choice. Therefore, set up your billing preferences with care. Depending on the size of your account and your account history, you may be able to apply for credit terms. Currently $10,000 per month over at least three months is the standard for allowing credit, although Google's finance department may relax that standard at its discretion. Since policies change from time to time, you should check the Google FAQs for the most current information.

Make sure you keep your billing information up-to-date to avoid problems. For example, if your credit card is declined, your AdWords account will be suspended after a brief grace period. Google will send an email to the primary contact, but you will still lose a certain amount of exposure until you can remedy the situation. A great fail-safe in this regard is the secondary or backup credit card Google allows you to enter when you're working in the Billing Preferences area under My Account. Take advantage of this. If your first card fails for some reason, your backup card gets billed, thus preventing interruptions in traffic.

Key Metrics and Terminology

Since your success will be measured based on key metrics generated in the course of the AdWords campaign, I'll review some of the Google terminology along with how certain statistics are calculated. You'll notice that some of these stats are best interpreted in terms of averages or aggregate totals. For example, your ad's position on the page might fluctuate during the day depending on what your competitors do, whether you've changed your bids, how relevant your ad is, and so on. So at the end of the day you'll be able to look at the stats for that day and see your *average* ad position—something like 2.4 or 5.1. Recall that this is not a typical media buy, but rather a dynamic environment, so the stats can look a little unusual to the new user, but most get up to speed quickly.

Impressions, Clicks, and Clickthrough Rate

If you're advertising on popular keywords, you should notice early on that your campaign generates a high number of impressions each day, possibly in the hundred thousands or more. Don't get too excited by those numbers. Remember, the number of people who see your ad is not what counts, but how many are motivated to take action when they see it. The majority of people who see your ad are probably not your customers and probably never will be. In some ways it's a brutal numbers game, but fortunately, it can be a consistent numbers game that yields an unusually devoted customer base when all is said and done. An *impression* is counted whenever your ad is shown, regardless of whether a search or a content page serves it up to a user. Although you aren't billed for impressions, they are part of the calculation of clickthrough rate (CTR). When a user clicks on your ad and comes to your site, that's a *click.* You will pay no more for that click than your maximum bid on that ad group or on that specific keyword.

As you saw in the example earlier, your clickthrough rate is determined by a simple formula:

CTR = clicks/impressions

Therefore, if your ad receives 8 clicks after 100 impressions, your clickthrough rate is 8% (8/100).

Note that some statistics programs may interpret the measurement of a click differently. Whereas the company charging you for the click (for example, Google) might feel they've earned the right to charge the advertiser as soon as the user has seen the landing page beginning to load, your stats program might not count it unless the whole page loads. If a user leaves very quickly, then, that user might not be counted at your end. It's not uncommon to see discrepancies of 5% to 10% in the number of clicks counted by Google and those counted by your analytics package. And different analytics services will show discrepancies among themselves, as well. Also, Google doesn't charge you for every click, and clicks that aren't charged may not be counted in the AdWords stats. Their antifraud technology looks for duplicates and other anomalous click patterns in an attempt to charge you only for bona fide clicks. Your web analytics package, on the other hand, will count most of these as clicks.

Cost per Click, Maximum Bid, Bid Discounter, Total Cost

As you've no doubt already figured out, each time someone clicks your ad, you pay. Your *cost per click (CPC)* is calculated on individual clicks in real time, and when those costs are added up, that's the total amount you'll pay Google.

As you interpret your data, you'll typically be looking at *average* CPC in relation to various parameters: the average CPC on a particular phrase, the average CPC for a particular ad group or ad within that ad group, the average CPC on a campaign, and so on. There is a slim hope that you might pay the absolute *minimum* CPC of .01 on any given click, or you could pay several dollars. This depends totally on your bidding strategy and the market competition for any given word or phrase.

Don't ask what a normal CPC is, because there is no such thing. In spite of SEC disclosure requirements, disclosure of average CPC by Google and Yahoo is spotty.

Fathom Online, a pay-per-click consulting firm, publishes a keyword price index that looks at the average price for a click in a variety of hot sectors. The methodology used to produce this study isn't entirely clear. The survey evidently focuses on brand-name clients often bidding on expensive keywords. In any case, the average CPC in this survey in 2007 hovered around $1.50. Your mileage will vary significantly.

The best explanation of variations in click pricing is that since this is a competitive auction, some keywords are more valuable in the marketplace than others. Clearly, **colocation hosting** and **insurance broker**, for example, are commercial words that are subject to hot competition. Less commercially relevant keywords like **arboretum** don't seem to have as much commercial value, although certainly a local museum or public facility such as an arboretum could do worse than to advertise on this term if they're looking for local paying visitors, tourists, or even donors. For now, few advertisers show up on words like **arboretum**.

Some words, like **cure**, are difficult to generate enough user interest on because they're too ambiguous, even though they might have huge commercial potential; so the ad space next to searches involving those words lies dormant, or as some in the online advertising industry would say, "unmonetized." When I typed in **cure**, I saw an ad for the nonprofit Christopher and Dana Reeves Foundation (looking for ways to help those with spinal cord paralysis), but it was the only one. By contrast with **cure**, a similar phrase, **the cure**, sometimes attracts the odd advertiser because it's the name of a popular 1990s band, and **cure for cancer** attracts several advertisers.

Often, specific phrases cost more than general ones because advertisers have decided (sometimes using their sales data) that the person typing **colocation hosting seattle** is usually a better customer than the person simply typing **hosting seattle** or **colocation hosting**, so they bid more on the more specific term. More obviously, **buy lobster online** or **lobster delivery** will attract a higher bid than simply **lobster** or **lobster recipes**. Phrases with which the user is signaling an intention to make a purchase are frequently referred to as *buy-words*. Buy-words might be worth five to ten times as much as a generic word unadorned with clear commercial intent.

Like keyword searches themselves, click pricing is very *granular,* a term which is often used by search marketers to convey a sense of getting into the nitty-gritty. Search engine users can be considered granular because they sometimes type very specific queries. When LookSmart was a new, educationally oriented directory with many subcategories, they boasted of the granularity of the information they provided. See Figure 3-9 for a depiction of that old LookSmart directory, drilled down to display several subcategories. You'll do better if you understand what it means to "get granular" with your AdWords account.

You needn't be discouraged even if you're in an industry where clicks appear to be expensive, because prices vary a lot even within your own list of keywords, and you can always discover cheaper ones. If you plan to do a lot of keyword research in the hopes of uncovering words that other advertisers have missed, you'll discover a rewarding fact of life: the less-traveled keyword inventory is often less expensive. By broadening your portfolio of keywords, you'll hopefully mix some bargain 5-, 10-, and 25-cent clicks into the average. By doing this, in no time an average CPC of $3.00 can be whittled down to, say, $1.80, even assuming that you're shooting for a comparable degree of targeting on the whole. Less expensive traffic isn't better in and of itself, of course; the goal is to find less expensive keywords that provide a solid return on that investment.

Be aware that Google, like several of its competitors, uses a *bid discounter,* so you never pay more than you have to for a click. Let's say you're in ad position 2 with a bid of 0.95 and the advertiser in position 3 is bidding 0.90. If a user clicks on your ad, you only pay 0.91, one penny more than the next advertiser's *maximum bid.* Here's the best part, though. What if that third-position advertiser decides to shut down the account and the fourth-position advertiser only bids 0.15? Without the discounter, you'd have to monitor your account constantly or use third-party software to "close the gap" so you didn't pay the 95 cents of your bid. With AdWords, you will simply pay 0.16. That's why your average *actual* CPC will typically be significantly lower than

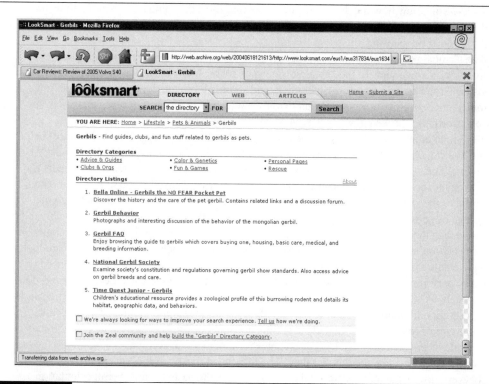

FIGURE 3-9   LookSmart was a granular directory. That's the nature of search: it gets very specific.

the amount of your maximum bid. That's also why the steady, persistent advertiser may pay less than expected to stay listed all the time.

It's worth noting that for people who don't like the concept of a "maximum bid," Google has added an option called "preferred bid." That's not worth the time to go into. Suffice to say, there are a wealth of choices in the interface for advanced advertisers. Some features, though, seem to have been created to head off the complaints of some particular cranky subset of deep-pocketed advertisers. The functionality adds little, but fortunately is buried quietly in the interface so the rest of us don't have to fuss with it.

When all of your click charges are added up at the end of a given day, week, or month, that's your *total cost*. Total cost figures taken in conjunction with your sales data (or other post-click data) will be used in measuring return on investment and other metrics such as cost per action, cost per lead, cost per order, and so on. Using your total cost in conjunction with the number of impressions of your ad served over a given time period, you could even measure your CPM to compare how your AdWords campaign is priced in the "old math" (how banners were typically priced in the past).

Unless you know how much money you're making from the campaign, there really is no good way of determining what counts as a high or low CPM or CPC. It's those CPA and ROI numbers you'll be focusing on.

The Campaign Summary view, shown in Figure 3-10, will quickly become familiar to you. It provides a bird's-eye view of the key aggregate stats for an AdWords account, including average ad position, total cost, average costs per click, and so on, all broken down by campaign. You can get much more specific information than that, by navigating to different screens that show ad group performance broken down by keyword, by ad, and so forth.

Be sure to adjust the date range of the stats to display the information that will be most helpful to you. You can choose the exact dates or terms such as Today, Yesterday, Past 7 Days, Last Week (Mon–Fri), This Month, Last Month, or All Time in the drop-down box. Often, the numbers for a single day (especially Today, because stats reporting may be delayed by up to two hours) aren't as helpful as the stats for Yesterday or Past 7 Days. Also, don't let your All Time stats be your sole gauge of performance. What your account has done in the past week or month probably tells you more than the all-time performance, particularly in cases where the first couple of months of experimentation were costly. One of the most common mistakes new advertisers make is to look at just one date range (particularly, the All Time stats). When I'm trying to come up to speed on an account's performance, I might look at the Past 7 Days statistics to see what the account has done for me lately as compared with the same week in a prior month. Or I might compare entire single months six months apart, or look at trends month to month for several months in a row. This would be an informal means of quickly assessing account performance. I'd rather assess trends that include recent data than just look at averages for the life of an account.

For many advertisers, the number they'll be looking at most closely every week, and some, nearly every day, is the number for total cost, as it forms the basis for the overall calculation

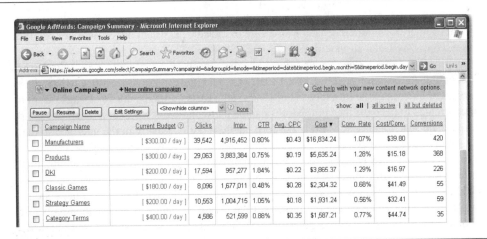

FIGURE 3-10 Aggregate account data—most advertisers will be paying close attention to total cost.

of ROI. Other numbers, like average ad position and even average costs per click, may be relatively trivial in comparison to total cost. By now it should go without saying that you'll also be heavily focused on CTR, but you will usually need to drill down further to look at breakdowns of CTR by keyword to see how the account is truly performing.

Ad Position, Bidding Wars, and Reverse Bidding Wars

On Google Search pages there are approximately 10 to 12 ad positions—they experiment regularly, so this changes. Recently, I saw 11 positions—three premium spots at the top of the page, and eight ads in the right-hand margin—for the phrase **seattle flights**, which is fairly indicative of a hot query in a fast-moving, commercial sector. If more than 10 to 12 advertisers are bidding on a particular keyword or phrase, advertisers further down the list (in terms of Quality Score, discussed in Chapter 5) will be shown on subsequent pages of search results. You can be pretty sure you're not making it onto the first page if, when you check your stats, you see your average ad position reported as a number higher than 12. On my screen, fully nine of the ads for Seattle flights were visible "above the fold," so don't assume that ad positions 7–9 or so make you "invisible." But experience tells us that most users don't get beyond the first page of search results. Therefore, you're not going to get many clicks if your ad falls into a position beyond 12.

While ad position is clearly important, it is not the only factor you need to consider. One of the misconceptions many new advertisers fall prey to is the need to be #1. While it is considered by many to be the optimum position, it is by no means a guarantee of success, especially considering the financial extremes to which many advertisers go to ensure that their ad appears in the top spot.

One of the least productive exercises an advertiser can engage in is a bidding war for that #1 position. A typical scenario might include a group of advertisers content with modest bids on a given phrase. A new advertiser enters the fray and is determined to be #1. Unfortunately, the advertiser in the top spot decides to hold on to its advantage. What invariably happens is that the two bid one another up to an outrageously high bid, 10 or even 20 times the modest high bid of the remaining bidders. Because Google's ranking formula is somewhat opaque, fortunately bidding wars like this don't play out in an accelerated fashion, as they once did on Overture, where every advertiser could check everyone else's bids throughout the day. Resisting this "openness" and sticking to their more subtle auction format is one of the best decisions Google ever made.

The result of a silly bid war is that the two competitors spend an unnecessarily inflated amount for the advantage of appearing in the top slot. Since many advertisers claim to get better results with lower ad positions, this is at best a crapshoot. Eventually one of the high bidders will relent and settle for second place, which costs only a fraction of the price that the top slot commands due to the bidding war.

When cooler heads prevail and both top competitors begin to realize the cost savings of settling for second place, a new bidding war may take place, only this time for second place. The reverse bidding war continues until the top bids approach the former modest bid range; however, they generally remain somewhat higher than they were before the original bidding war started.

Usually, Google is the real winner in bidding wars. So, my advice is to stay out of them and let the others battle it out while you keep your eye on the primary issue—making money! When I set up accounts for advertisers, I shoot for a slot somewhere between ad positions 2 and 9, with 2–5 being more typical. Bidding strategy is an important topic that I'll address in more detail later in the book.

Limit Vanity Searching Internal to Your Company

Anyone who has managed campaigns for any length of time is aware of "restless CEO syndrome." For CEOs as well as some regular people, if it isn't tangible, it isn't real. Hence the common tendency to just "double check" if the ads really are showing, by constantly typing in your own target search words.

This is a bad idea for a number of reasons. Generally speaking, using personalization technology, Google will tend to avoid showing ads to users who don't click on them, unless that advertiser bids very high. While your ad might already be in a high position for many users, the vanity-searching CEO goes and instructs the campaign manager to bid ever higher, so *he* can see the ad. Bad idea. The only known cure is to change the ad copy for these terms to read: "Take it easy, boss. Yes, our ads are showing!" But seriously: real and accurate insight into campaign performance is to be found inside AdWords reporting and financial reporting, not on the search results page.

Conversion Rates

Conversion rates, which can be measured in a number of different ways, are a pivotal measure of a campaign's success. Let's start with a basic definition and the typical method of measuring conversion rates. The *conversion rate* is the percentage of clicks that result in either a sale or some other direct action that the ad has been created to induce. If your ad is selling a product, your conversion rate formula is as follows:

Conversion rate = number of sales/total clicks

Therefore, if you make three sales on 200 paid clicks one day, your conversion rate on those clicks is 1.5%. To ensure that your conversion rates are accurate, you need to be able to verify that those sales resulted from your AdWords ad rather than a customer who just happened to stumble onto your site. You can use Google Conversion Tracker, Google Analytics tweaked to set up custom "goals," or tracking URLs and third-party tracking software to identify those sales generated by your Google ad.

Of course, sales aren't the only type of action that represent a meaningful conversion. Some advertisers measure application forms, new subscribers to a free newsletter, and so on.

As with other metrics, there are no hard-and-fast benchmark conversion rates for a given industry. In reality, conversion rates are often quite low. I see 2% or less more often than I see 10% or more. The best advice I can give you is to keep your conversion rate goals subservient to your long-range goals. Don't set a conversion rate target and follow it blindly.

You want your own conversion rates to improve, to be sure, and you certainly won't make money if nothing's converting. However, aggregate conversion percentages can be misleading if they don't take into account the cost of the traffic.

Return on Investment (ROI)

ROI, while simple to calculate—total revenues divided by total cost—is not a short-term measurement. By that I mean you can't calculate it on a daily basis and worry (or celebrate) based on the numbers. Give your ad(s) a chance to perform before you start to panic. Smart marketers know that you need to spend on marketing up front to see benefits down the road. They also know that repeat business is important and that acquiring a new customer is worth a certain amount, no matter how little that customer spends at first. This is especially true if early adopters are likely to spread word of mouth.

As for the formula, total cost is the total cost of your AdWords campaign over any given time period. Total revenues is the total dollar amount of the sales that can be attributed directly to your AdWords campaign during the same period or some reasonable period of time after the initial click. As you may have deduced, this isn't an exact science.

For example, if you spend $300 over three weeks on AdWords to attract new subscribers to an information service, and by week three, you've converted two of the free-trial subscribers to paying status for total revenue of $150, your ROI thus far would be 50%. That technically means you're losing money, but as I mentioned, you might be on the right track if you're patient. Some of the free-trial customers generated in the initial three weeks might convert to paying subscribers next month, bringing the total revenues attributable to that first $300 worth of clicks to $375. Thus the ROI for the initial period would have reached 125%—in other words, a positive ROI. Your campaign would already be in the black. And that wouldn't even be factoring in the lifetime value of each customer—the possibility of advertising revenues, consulting income, sales of related products to the subscriber base, or next year's subscription.

This is the way in which smart businesses make the most of the clicks they're paying for. Those who rely heavily on initial sales to turn a profit, and who have a poor capacity for repeat sales, will find it more difficult to afford AdWords as the average cost per click rises.

Some campaigns really do pay for themselves as they go—revenues always exceed click costs on any given day. Some have referred to this as a "self-funding campaign." A positive ROI from the get-go means you're "playing with the house's money" and may give you incentive to aggressively search for ways to widen the distribution of your ads.

Let's get into the account interface and start getting set up properly.

Account Basics

The first thing you need to understand is how your account is set up and the various components that go into it. Today, Google offers interactive tutorials on this stuff to new advertisers, so this is just my condensed take on it.

Structure: Accounts, Campaigns, Groups

Your AdWords account consists of two key organizational components—campaigns and ad groups. As you can see in Figure 3-11, the account appears at the top of the flow chart, with at least one campaign underneath that, and then one or more ad groups in each campaign. (Technically, there is one level above that. Some large companies and agencies like mine have multiple accounts that they're managing, so they sign up for a multiple-account management console that Google offers, called My Client Center. Do *not* set up multiple accounts unless you have an extremely good reason for doing so. When my colleagues and I have taken over an account that was actually broken up into multiple accounts, we saw that the client had muddled up accounts with campaigns, creating such a mess that we had to re-create the account from scratch.)

The ad groups, which are the basic building blocks of your campaigns, consist of one or more ads, a maximum bid, and a list of keywords or phrases. When you're comfortable with bidding, you can go ahead and enter specific bids for particular keywords, but the convenience of setting a single bid for all keywords in a group is tempting, at least at first. For more on this structure, see the AdWords FAQs on Google's website, which include the table illustrated in Figure 3-11.

If you're wondering why you would want to use multiple campaigns, there are several good reasons. The first is simply organization. Having all your ad groups under a single campaign can

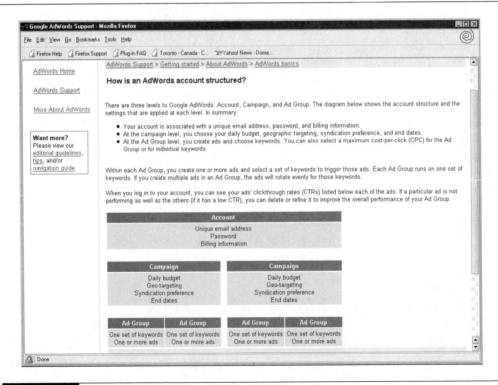

FIGURE 3-11   Google provides an overview of the account structure.

get chaotic and confusing, especially as the number of ad groups increases. For simple accounts, two or three campaigns is often sufficient, because the AdWords interface is now designed well enough to allow data to be accessed quickly no matter how many groups of keywords are listed under a single campaign. Having more campaigns becomes essential as your product list increases or if you want to keep a clear separation between certain themes, geographical target markets, content-targeted ads, or the work of different account managers.

The second reason you may want to break things into several campaigns is for better control over budgeting. You can have a "go-slow" campaign with a daily budget of $15 and an "already working, full speed ahead" campaign with a daily budget of $800, if you like.

Third, having separate campaigns also allows you to set different country parameters, regional targeting parameters, and language parameters for different parts of your business without having to set up a separate AdWords account with a separate login. A national real estate company may offer packages in 30 cities, for example. It'll probably want campaigns for all 30 cities; in fact, it will have to have separate campaigns if it wants to geo-target each campaign to a particular metro area. (I realize in real estate, people might be relocating; let's not get too caught up in the particular example.)

Google places an official upper limit on the number of campaigns allowed. This varies, but a recent check shows 100 ad groups by 25 campaigns as limits. Regardless, unless your spend is high or you qualify through special permission, Google will also warn you as you approach an upper limit on keywords. This is typically 50,000. (It's important to realize that for certain special requests, Google will make exceptions. They won't let some untried affiliate marketer jack up their number of campaigns into the stratosphere, but I certainly hope they'd consider allowing more than 25 campaigns for a legitimate company that doesn't want to hassle with multiple accounts. If there are different websites and very distinct business objectives involved, by all means open multiple accounts, and work with your Google reps to place them under a common My Client Center interface.)

Advertisers who advertise in multiple countries will find that this can save them money. In less competitive markets (from the standpoint of advertisers' bids), such as Canada and Sweden, for example, some keywords are much cheaper than they are in the United States. Instead of showing a single campaign to both countries, having a separate Canada-only or Sweden-only campaign might allow you to bid very low on some fairly popular keywords.

You can also name campaigns. By and large, the best approach is to label them as informatively as possible; for example, "Arkansas Real Estate."

Ad groups, the basic elements of an AdWords campaign, are the key to sound organization and strong performance. They're covered in depth in Chapter 4. Why do I love ad groups? Maybe that's just the kind of brain I was born with. Some scientists like atoms, others like subatomic particles, still others get off on molecules, and yet others study the properties of matter. I like ad groups.

Entering Basic Account Information

At the account level, you'll set the key parameters of who you or your company are, credit card information, billing preferences, and so forth. Of course, the first thing you have to do is access the AdWords site.

To get there follow these steps:

1. Open your web browser and access the Google website. (For U.S. users, this is www.google.com.)

2. Click the Advertising Programs link to open the Google Advertising Programs page. Information about Google AdWords appears on the left side of the page.

3. Click on Start Now.

4. You'll notice that Google now gives you a choice between something called the Starter Edition and the Standard Edition. By removing functionality and coddling you, Google seems to believe they can reduce the anxiety levels of small or timid advertisers. The problem is, you lose control over key features. I have no real comments on the Starter Edition. In business, people who use training wheels aren't going to be winning any Tours de France. In fact, they're probably going to get run over. Go with the Standard Edition is what I'm telling you. If you want to play with Starter Edition, hand over your copy of this book to someone who can really use it!

Whoops. Forgot one thing you should probably consider before you get going on all of the above. You'll be asked to associate your AdWords campaign with a Google Account. Google Accounts may include a variety of Google services you use (much as Yahoo accounts worked as Yahoo grew from search engine to portal), such as Gmail, Google Talk (instant messenger), and so forth. Personally, I find it inconvenient to overlap my business dealings (AdWords) with private information (chat accounts, email, and the like). So at this stage I would recommend that you start an entirely new, "clean" Google Account and associate this with your AdWords account when you set that up.

The basic account setup is supposed to be self-explanatory and straightforward, but it's actually not as simple as it looks, because a lot of variables are hitting you in the face at once. Yes, you should be able to get through the basic parameters and activation steps OK, but even here, you can sort of get off on the wrong foot. I doubt you want to waste too much time doing this, but if you like, you can play with Google's interactive tutorials prior to getting started. If you have specific problems in midstream, support is always available at 1-866-2GOOGLE.

In the midst of setting up your first campaign and ad group, it's already possible to get off on the wrong foot because Google now assesses your website (using automated and human means) as well as your keywords and ads just as soon as you get started! So let's say you point to a malfunctioning destination page, throw in a bunch of irrelevant keywords in your very first ad group, or write a gibberish ad as a "placeholder." Unfortunately, everything you do—especially with new accounts that have no data with which to give Google's algorithms confidence of your status as a high-quality, relevant advertiser—can affect something called your Quality Score (QS). I devote all of Chapter 5 to this topic.

At a minimum, then, you should heed the suggestion to "work backwards," in at least a couple of senses. You want to make sure you know to which landing pages you're going to be sending traffic from different ad groups, and you want to make sure those pages are high quality (and importantly, not doing anything to block Google's AdsBot from assessing those pages, such as a robots exclusion file that excludes all spiders, something that isn't out of the realm of possibility) and relevant, with at least some relevant text or offer on them.

Earlier in AdWords history, I used to throw up a default "dummy" campaign very quickly, paying no particular attention to its content, and then pause it pending further client instructions (or payment). You shouldn't really do this anymore.

One important thing to keep in mind is that you'll need a username and password to access your account. If multiple people will be accessing the account, you'll need to provide them with your login information as soon as you set it up. But a few words on that.

Sharing Access

You don't have to give out your Google Account login information in order to share AdWords campaign access. There is a better way to share access (see Figure 3-12). Under My Account | Access (tabs at the top of the page), you have the option of inviting other users. They can have Administrative, Standard, or Reports access. That basically means they can have the same functionality as you (including the ability to invite and uninvite others); they can fully manage the account in all facets; or they only get to run reports and look at data, but not manage the account.

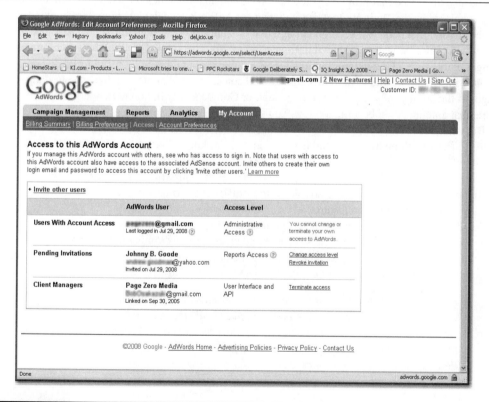

FIGURE 3-12   Setting account access levels.

Unless you specify otherwise, your username is tied to a single email address as the primary contact. This is the only person who gets "alerts," typically.

Key Campaign-Level Settings and Possible Opt-Outs

Many important settings are determined at the campaign level. You'll find yourself frequently returning to the Edit Campaign Settings screen (see Figure 3-13) to check on things like daily budget, ad distribution, and more. This will be a staple of your account. Review your options carefully as you get started. Initially, you may want to accept the default settings Google offers, to simplify your setup. As you gain experience, however, you'll probably want to take more control of your campaign. Therefore, I'll discuss some of the more important options in detail.

Daily Budget Setting

Understanding how unusual the daily budgeting feature is will help you to use it properly. Because it doesn't necessarily work in a way that's intuitive, you can easily misuse it and end up wasting both money and time.

In addition to enabling you to enter a specific dollar amount in the Daily Budget option, Google also has a tool that provides you with a recommendation. Click the View Recommended Budget link below the Daily Budget box and wait for AdWords to calculate your "recommended" budget. If you already have it set high enough that Google considers your amount to be "maxed out," it will return the message shown in Figure 3-13, "Your budget is OK. We don't recommend changes at this time." Google might also suggest a dollar amount that will ensure full delivery of your campaign. Pay attention to this amount and consider simply entering that as your daily budget. If the number of phrases in your account, or Google's distribution network, grows in the future, that amount could become too low. You should recheck this setting periodically.

But what does "daily budget" actually mean, how does it work, and how should you proceed? The first thing to understand is that Google is looking at the keywords and bids you have in your account, along with settings like country and distribution preferences. Using these parameters, it estimates how much you'll need to budget to ensure full delivery of your ads. By "full delivery," I mean that your ads show up virtually every time a user types a query that matches the keywords in your account.

Anything less than full delivery means your ad is being shown only sporadically. If your budget is set anywhere below Google's recommended amount, AdWords might respond by beginning to turn off your ads sporadically during the day in order to keep you within the budget; you might even find them turned off completely late in the day.

NOTE   *If AdWords fails to keep you inside your daily budget limit, you may or may not be entitled to a refund. Officially, Google promises only that you will receive a refund on click charges if you spend more than your daily budget multiplied by 30 over an entire month's period. However, if you feel that a particular daily spike was too far over your daily limit, you might convince them to offer a refund anyway.*

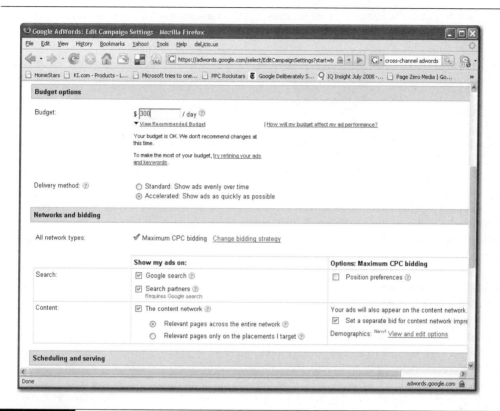

FIGURE 3-13   The Edit Campaign Settings screen is your ad campaign headquarters.

When you're just getting started, it isn't such a bad idea to set a conservative daily budget. This will limit how quickly you spend money while you get up to speed on how well your account is performing. But you don't want to spend too slowly, or you won't collect the data you need in order to improve your account based on market feedback. And there is a whole list of reasons why the low daily budget is a poor strategy.

Allowing your ads to be apportioned by setting a low daily budget takes control out of your hands and may help your competitors save money. One of the biggest mistakes novice AdWords advertisers make is bidding too high on a hastily constructed set of keywords and then, in a panic, drastically reducing the daily budget to compensate. The problem with this strategy is that it doesn't improve performance—it just keeps your ads from showing as often. You're not saving money on a per-click basis with this strategy, and your ROI does not improve. You're simply doing less of what you came here to do: advertise.

In the case of a money-losing account, all a low daily budget does for you is to help you lose money slowly, which means you waste not only money, but time. Running your account as if it were a "slow leak" helps you put off making important decisions, and that can cost you. To create value with AdWords, you'll want to implement a range of sound targeting techniques and bidding strategies. Instead of using the daily budget to fix a problem account, I recommend turning down your bids, tracking your conversions, and optimizing your ad copy. There are many ways to change the economics of your account. Learn how to use the power of the tools available to you.

While it's true that Google's recommended amounts can be quite scary looking, more often than not the final tally is substantially less. That's because of the wide range of variables involved in predicting daily amounts. Remember, you're paying for something you can't control: thousands of users typing in queries that match your keywords and then deciding to click on your ad. Your competitors are bidding against you, and they might be changing their bids. User behavior fluctuates day to day and seasonally.

As a result, it's not uncommon for you to actually wind up spending less than 50% of the "recommended" budget. So when Google tells you to set the budget at $500, you'll be spending a lot less in most cases. It's really more of a worst-case number that ensures your ad delivery will be turned on "max" regardless of what users and competitors do. Now, having said that, there is always the possibility that the worst-case scenario will turn out to be the one that you encounter. Therefore, you must monitor your campaigns and make necessary adjustments before you run up a large bill that you're not anticipating.

In conjunction with the daily budget setting, Google confuses you with another option: you get to choose between "standard" and "accelerated" ad delivery. First, know this: if your daily budget is set high enough to accommodate all relevant user searches in that day, "standard" and "accelerated" delivery work exactly the same, according to my Google contacts. For low budgets, standard delivery will spread your ad delivery out temporally so that you're as likely to receive an ad impression late in the day as you would be early in the day (you just won't show up as often as you would if you had your budget sufficiently high to show your ad to all relevant searches). For low budgets, accelerated delivery will show your ad more consistently in the early part of the day, and therefore exhaust the daily budget sooner. At that point, ad serving would be slowed drastically or stopped. Don't be confused by the names "standard" and "accelerated"— again, they don't apply at all when you have your budget set to the appropriately abundant level.

Ad Rotation Optimizer: Ad Scheduling and Serving

Also adjustable at the campaign level is a tool that Google uses to automatically show the ads that are your best performers. We'll get to ad rotation and testing later in the book, but for now, you should be wary of using this feature. Since Google allows you to show multiple ads "in rotation" in relation to a given ad group, this tool automatically shows the ads that generate the higher CTRs. In some ways this helps you, especially if you don't plan to manage the account actively. But for those advertisers who actually want to run extended tests of their ads to look not only at CTR data but sales conversion data, this "optimizer" can take control out of your hands, making it difficult to run an informative experiment. You'll find this feature on the Edit Campaign Settings page. It's the Optimize: Show Better-Performing Ads More Often option, under Ad Serving in the Scheduling and Serving section of the Edit Campaign Settings page.

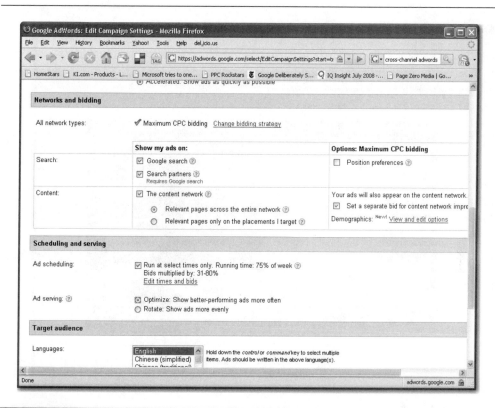

FIGURE 3-14   Consider the Rotate option. Google makes Optimize the default.

If you plan to test ad copy over extended periods, you'll want to leave this option unchecked. As shown in Figure 3-14, the default is set to Optimize, so you need to change it to Rotate.

There are also some more advanced bidding strategies and options that I'll cover later in the book.

Search Network

Search network partners include Ask.com, Infospace (Metacrawler and Dogpile), and AOL Search. But be aware that additional partners that you don't consider to be "search" (but Google believes are "navigational in nature") may be part of the search network. An important example is parked domains. Let's say you go to Guacamole.com (see Figure 3-15) and it's owned by a "domain bank," a company that simply places ad links on the domain names it owns, in case anyone happens to type these in or stumble on them somehow. At Guacamole.com, there is a list of rather pointless links to categories. Click again (say, on the "hotel reservations" category), and you get a list of hotel-related advertising links. Click once more, and you might wind up on, say, the Expedia or Orbitz site. Do these major travel companies know they paid (say) 55 cents—to be split between the Guacamole.com publisher and Google, Yahoo, or some other provider of

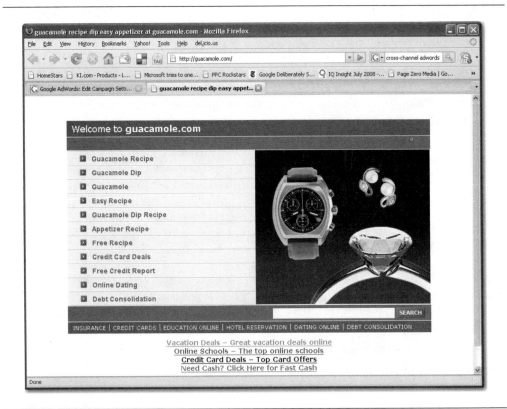

FIGURE 3-15   Guacamole.com

ad links—for this particular type of click? Some advertisers don't much care, as long as the overall ROI works out for them. Others wish there were more transparency about the search network, and the ability to opt out of parked domains.

As is typical with Google, after years of us advertisers complaining about this, they have been responsive. You do now have more opt-out control when it comes to a variety of content types, and significant visibility into the performance and extent of those types of clicks.

Advertisers usually find search network traffic to be beneficial, since it does mostly come from brand-name web properties with wide distribution. Therefore, even though it's optional, I recommend you keep this box checked.

Content Network

Content targeting, on the other hand, is another matter entirely. Revenue from "non-Google properties," most of which comes from the content network, has essentially doubled the size and scope of Google's search engine advertising operations. This has at different periods of time accounted for over 50% of Google's revenues. In fiscal 2006, it accounted for just under 40%.

Google no doubt has high hopes to grow this back to 50% or more, as the definition of "content" expands into a variety of media that might be amenable to booking placements through an auction platform like AdWords.

This program places your AdWords ads on pages of publishers' websites, ranging from large publishers like CNET, the New York Times, and About.com to smaller content sites published by small independent publishers of high-quality content—and yes, even on blogs and junky MySpace pages. Due to the improving quality of the content network, and its continued growth, it offers an opportunity for advertisers in terms of both quality exposure and additional reach. Many advertisers put considerable effort into researching and building their accounts, and into ongoing bidding strategy and analysis of results, so the added reach is always a good way to make that effort worthwhile. You should be aware, however, that content targeting is quite different from search-based advertising. It should be treated more like banner advertising, even though the ad displays are triggered by the keywords in advertisers' Google AdWords accounts.

Speaking of banners, the choices available in the content program are increasingly impressive (if bewildering). The content-targeting program started with plain text ads, but now allows a variety of sizes and shapes of banners, animated banners, video pre-roll advertising, and more.

You may hear the term AdSense used interchangeably with "content targeting" (or a term that others have used, "contextual advertising"). AdSense is the name of the interface that publishers use to place the Google AdWords ads on their sites to receive revenues from Google (ultimately from you, the advertiser) when users click the ads. Figures 3-16 and 3-17 provide examples of the different ad formats used on content sites.

Pricing for content targeting is based on proprietary semantic matching technology developed in-house at Google that actually determines which ads to show on the fly as a page loads. The key criteria are how closely the meaning of the content on a page matches the keywords you're bidding on in any given ad group in your AdWords account. We can also presume that your reach is heavily influenced by your maximum bid. Bid high enough on content, and your ad will show up on far more pages—although relevance will suffer.

CTRs for content targeting are typically much lower than they are on search ads; however, these CTRs are *not* factored into the CTR that determines your ad rank score for the purposes of ranking you on the page. Don't worry too much about these low CTRs regardless of how bad it makes your stats look.

In spite of the lack of negative consequences attached to these low content-targeting CTRs, some advertisers will see cause for worry when they attempt to interpret their stats for periods when content targeting is turned on. In statistical summaries for given ads, periods of content-targeting usage will frequently drag down the aggregate CTR number. Thus the strong performance of an account may not be immediately evident without scrutinizing the data more closely. Also, turning content targeting on and off can make comparing the CTR performance of ads difficult. Newer ads that were showing during periods of heavy content-targeting use are difficult to compare head-to-head over, say, a month-long period, when pitted against ads that were showing with content targeting switched off (or simply left on for a shorter duration). Until Google improves this reporting, you can be easily misled about ad performance unless the ads you're comparing have been running with the same settings applied to all. Keep this in mind when testing ads.

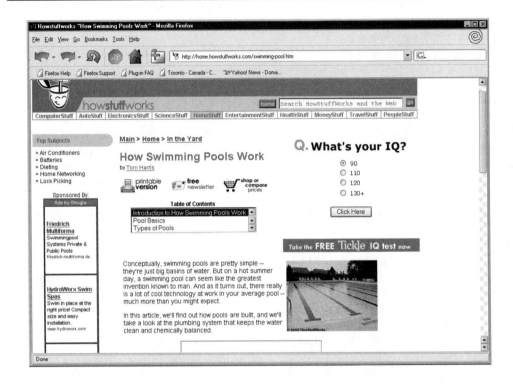

FIGURE 3-16   A typical AdSense publisher, HowStuffWorks.com, displaying text-based ads in the left margin. These ads are served by Google AdWords.

Don't mistakenly stop an ad that may be doing well but appears to be a slow performer due to content targeting.

Ads near content perform differently than search ads, because user behavior and expectations are usually different when they're casually reading articles rather than actively searching. Thus the economic worth of content ads to advertisers may be lower than what we see from ads placed near Google Search results. Since the inception of content targeting, Google has maintained that conversion rates on content ads are comparable to those on search ads, even if CTRs may be lower, so the value should be about the same.

In April 2004 Google introduced something called "enhanced smart pricing" for content targeting. Many advertisers had asked if they could bid separately on the content-targeted ads or even create separate ad copy for content targeting. Although this smart pricing stopped short of those demands, it used a formula to adjust click prices based on their expected value to advertisers. This expected value is based on information Google may have about the probabilities that certain types of pages (say, a page containing reviews of digital cameras, as opposed to a feature-length

FIGURE 3-17   Google AdWords ads for golf-related products show up in a text box in the
middle of this article on the About.com Guide to Golf.

article about the history of photography) have of converting to a sale for the advertiser. Google says
it uses "all possible pieces of information" to determine the expected value.

Following this advance, Google later did release something called *content bidding*. This
is absolutely vital. In the Edit Campaign Settings interface (Figure 3-14), if you don't disable
content targeting entirely, you'll at least want to enable content bidding, by clicking the check
box to "Set a Separate Bid for Content Network Impressions." You then have the choice of
adding separate content bids to your account's ad groups now or later. Content bidding only
takes place at the ad group level. An example would be a keyword group full of terms like "forex
trading." These are valuable terms when found through a Google Search, so assume I bid $3.00
on most of them individually, and leave a default bid on of $2.00 for the ad group for any other
keywords I don't bid on specifically. I know that my ad does perform somewhat decently in
the content-targeting program, but the ROI is sharply lower. I don't want to give up the sales
volume; I just want to bid 70 cents on content clicks, to even out the outcomes. So I do, using
content bidding.

Content targeting is a different animal from search targeting. If you're unsure, opt out of it for the time being by leaving the Content Network option unchecked at the campaign level. As you become more experienced, you may decide to try experimenting with it, since it can significantly expand the reach of your existing campaign. The power of large networks like Google's is that they are certainly far easier to enable and test than is possible under the traditional media-buying methods of negotiating ad buys with individual websites or traditional ad brokers.

Google actually now has multiple "flavors" of content targeting. Two options are most prominent in the interface: keyword-based *content targeting* (what I often call classic content targeting, because it was a key product innovation at Google) and a newer program, site-based *placement targeting* (formerly called site targeting). Placement targeting is really a separate program in itself. To keep us moving here, I'll discuss placement targeting and other Google network initiatives in more depth in Chapter 9.

Country and Language

Many of you will be focusing most of your efforts on the original and largest AdWords market, the United States, in English exclusively. Unfortunately, running campaigns to attract viewers who are using Google set to display other languages is not an automated process. For each language, you would have to run a separate campaign, choose different keywords, and write the separate ads.

By and large, you'll find that displaying ads to all countries is a money-losing proposition. Your mileage may vary, but not all English-speaking markets are equally responsive from an economic standpoint. More importantly, of course, your company might only ship its products or perform its services in the United States, or the United States and Canada. Unless you're prepared to do business in other countries and you know your product is marketable in them, you might want to take a cautious approach and go with the United States only, or United States plus Canada. For those who want to branch out a bit further, a typical approach seems to be to add the UK (one of the largest AdWords markets), and perhaps Australia and New Zealand, to the mix.

For business-to-business and professionals as well as midsized to large companies (especially those with a strong international base), it may make sense to run ads in English in a variety of target countries in the hopes of influencing decision makers in those markets. As a general rule, though, such efforts can be a waste of money, and my instinct (honed by client anecdotes from the past) is to be cautious.

Chapter 4

Setting Up Ad Groups

From what I've observed, at least half of all new AdWords advertisers make the same set of predictable tactical mistakes. To help you avoid these, let me review some of the most common errors.

There seem to be a few common patterns here. Most revolve around a couple of tendencies: first, the desire to create an enormous list of keywords at the beginning rather than a smaller "beginner set" of keywords that fit logically into groups; and second, an interrelated belief that with the right amount of effort in the planning (prelaunch) phase, the campaign can explode out of the starting gate, generating huge numbers of customers right away. Small problem with the "explode out of the gate" mentality: Google has more than 500,000 advertisers. Lots of them already exploded out of the starting gate, and you'll be competing with them. You'll need to ease into this process at first and then build on your early discoveries. This process rewards smart "guerrilla" advertisers who can learn from feedback, not just those with a bigger marketing bazooka.

There are some historical reasons why many paid search advertisers seem bent on doing things in a certain way (the way that I consider to be "wrong" for AdWords). Advertisers who had experience with Overture became accustomed to the idea of large numbers of keywords. One reason for this was that Overture didn't offer broad matching options in the past; so unless your keyword or phrase matched the user's query exactly, you didn't show up.

There is nothing strictly *wrong* with using every possible word combination of hundreds of words, culminating in a file of five thousand or more keywords. But the reason for doing it was initially because you couldn't capture enough search volume without wild card–type matching options. Those who overdo it on the keyword generation front today are banking heavily on the value of infrequently searched keywords, sometimes to the exclusion of balanced priorities, campaign organization, and thoroughness with more important keywords.

Keyword research tools come in various shapes and sizes. There are some "gray market" aids that will even help you determine what competitors are bidding on. To come up with *extra* keywords to *add* to a well-functioning account, to test their effectiveness, is a great idea. But don't dump them all in at once.

Another historical reason for large keyword files was that Overture's early interface was a first-generation utility with limitations in the usability department. The cumbersome process of dumping large files of keywords into the account without any really convenient or intuitive way of then managing or editing them seemed worthwhile to early Overture advertisers, who felt like they were getting in on the ground floor of something exciting. It certainly delighted the makers of third-party account management software. I never much cared for it. When Google AdWords came along, it gave advertisers better tools for keeping everything straight—most of all, an intuitive way of grouping keywords. In any case, the result of all that history is that an orthodoxy sprang up whereby marketers felt they could impress one another by sending each other gigantic Excel files of keywords.

Let's take some time to explore *ad groups,* then, which I consider to be the core of Google AdWords.

Why Grouping Keywords Makes So Much Sense

When my colleagues and I use software to track what users are doing after they click through to a client's website, we don't overanalyze the performance of individual keywords, especially those that generate low volumes of searches. Because the infrequently searched words can't give you statistically significant feedback on their own, we often prefer to track no finer than the "ad group and specific ads within those groups" level, because, if the groups are designed logically, tracking the results by group actually provides highly actionable and meaningful data. Sometimes we track everything right down to the return on investment on individual keywords and phrases, but this is not always necessary or even beneficial.

Keeping the data well organized seems to oversimplify things, but you have to "apparently oversimplify" AdWords accounts, because your ability to correctly influence events is actually tied to a lot more complexity than you are likely to be able to handle. Machines can do some of it, but you need to free up as much of your time as possible for "softer" analytical work that explores the full range of potential responses to the data you're seeing.

Think about the analogy of an American football playbook with 500 or 1,000 plays in it, grouped according to different types and situations. The quarterback and the coaching staff need to master and memorize these plays so that they can deploy them correctly at the right times. These plays are difficult to digest even for many quarterbacks—hence the tiny crib notes you see written on many quarterbacks' wrist guards. With the play clock ticking, it wouldn't help that quarterback at all to receive a giant Excel file of new plays, or an even larger file of past and probable outcomes for 10,000 other plays. Not only must coach and quarterback choose among a relatively small universe of courses of action in calling the next play, but once the quarterback steps up to the line of scrimmage, he must have the ability to call an "audible" (a new play based on the defensive formation he sees). The number of possible audibles is typically tiny—there might only be two or three alternative plays to choose from. I don't think the analogy is so far-fetched. To reduce confusion, reduce the number of potential decisions you need to make. Then make those decisions with full consideration and as often as you can feasibly make them to improve your performance.

Granted, AdWords isn't a football and you don't have to physically throw it while avoiding human tacklers, so as you get more advanced, you'll want to explore ways of automating decisions where this makes sense. For now, thinking about doing it all manually will help you understand the underlying principles.

Ad groups give us that manageability we're looking for. I tend to believe that each *group* of keywords expresses an idea of something a user is searching for. That might be a big idea or a very narrowly conceived idea. The idea could require only one keyphrase to express (let's say the exact match for **goat cheese**), or it could require 250 phrases covering a long list of low-volume but highly targeted industry jargon words. So, when someone asks me how many keywords is a lot, I usually avoid that question because I believe campaigns need to be thought of in terms of ad groups. I sometimes think in terms of this analogy: putting just a few of the most obvious keywords in a few groups is OK at first, because you'll find the process of expanding to more words within those groups quite natural. They'll almost multiply like bacteria (icky, but that's kind of how it works). Actually, you'll be using your own brain and keyword suggestion tools, but the basic idea is that ad groups often start off small and grow larger over time.

This can be an intuitive process, because you'll also give names to those groups within your account; so, you'll be able to glance at them quickly and say something like, "I see the 'Last Minute Travel' group is generating a higher than usual number of clicks today," or, "The 'San Jose Sharks apparel' group is generating a low CTR lately; better figure out why." For my money, that's better than poring over huge files of keyword-specific data, because the intuitiveness of groups with sensible names allows you to read and react steadily to changing conditions. If you structure your data analysis task so that it's more daunting than that, you might find yourself putting it off for weeks and months, and that'll cost you.

Think of this as a kind of sorting or filing. The database-driven nature of the AdWords application is actually not too far different from the idea of a directory, with multiple levels in a logical progression.

As librarians and search technology experts sometimes say, categorized directories (think of Yahoo or the Open Directory, or anything with categories and subcategories) possess an *ontology*. In other words, a professional categorization team needs to create a tree that breaks the world down into different levels of meaning. Your account won't be that comprehensive, but I hope the analogy helps you to understand that your job in creating a little "meaning tree" for your account will help you to do a better job of sorting out search users who see your ad after they've expressed meanings of their own by typing a query into Google Search. This structure will also make the campaign easier to make sense of down the road.

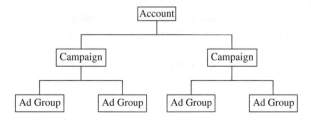

Ad groups express a thing (the "soup bowl group," for example) or an idea ("agricultural pesticides litigation" and 40 other ways to say that). Your advertising copy (or multiple ads) are *tied to* the keywords in that group. Different groups, different ads. Sure, you could use the same ad all the time, but it's best to write different ones, as I'll show later. Basically, whatever ad (or ads) you enter for, say, Ad Group #3 (or the "Tile Flooring Group") will show up whenever a user's query matches one of the phrases in that group, assuming your campaign is active. That ad won't show up for your other ad groups unless you specifically create the same ad in those groups, as well. The AdWords interface allows you to control exactly which searchers are seeing which ads.

Once you've got a few phrases that all express something related to an idea or thing, you're on your way with your first ad group. It should be easy to set up several groups in no time as long as you aren't fussing with huge keyword lists. You can edit everything later as much as you like.

Not only will you write separate ads tailored for each group, you'll notice that you'll be bidding separately on each group. All the words and phrases in an ad group are tied to a global maximum bid. That makes it convenient to change the bid for the whole group, although there is also an optional feature called *powerposting* that allows you to set individual bids on keywords or phrases (more about that in Chapter 6).

This advice, then, ties into advice given later in the book about how to write winning ad copy. There should be less mystique about how to write successful ads once you understand that your ads' performance will improve almost automatically by dint of the fact that you've written a variety of tailored ads that closely match or reflect the ideas or exact phrases in each ad group. The question won't be only "which ad works the best" across the board, but also, in many cases, "which ads work the best *with which groups of keywords.*"

You'll want multiple ad groups for two key reasons, then. First, ad groups offer the convenience of tying your maximum bid (the highest you're willing to pay for a click) to all the keyphrases in a group, to save you the trouble of bidding individually on every keyword. Most of us use a mix of keyword-specific bidding and groupwide bidding. Figures 4-1 and 4-2 show two key views inside the Google AdWords interface: the summary view within a campaign showing a list of ad groups, and a fairly typical example of an ad group.

The ad group shown in Figure 4-2 has a maximum bid of 80 cents that applies to all the phrases in that group, and as you can see, the 2 phrases in the group resemble one another. (Of course, 2 is an unusually small number of phrases to put in a group. It could just as easily be 5, 20, or 50, but this suffices for illustration purposes.) A single ad applies to this group of phrases, although this advertiser had previously tested multiple ads with this group to see which one performed the best. He has also made his ad timely, telling readers that the site contains specific information about planting tips for the month of June (not a common month in which to plant), which likely conveys freshness and expertise. This may be part of the explanation for the robust 10% clickthrough rate on this ad.

In this reporting summary, various performance data, including CTR, are broken down by keyphrase. Note that this advertiser is using the classic approach to bidding, using the global bid for the group so that all of these keywords have the same maximum bid. Many advertisers now make finer adjustments, adding specific bids to keywords within groups, which is often necessary to adjust bids to market demand. Still, there is a certain tidiness to the classic way of doing it.

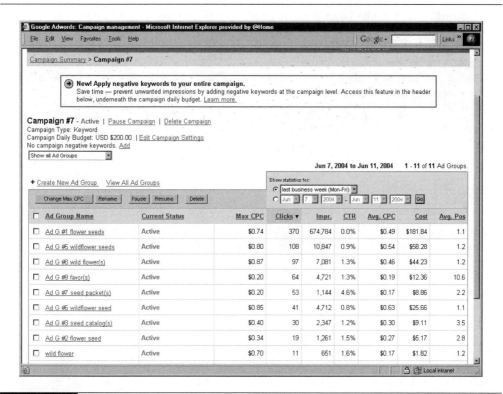

FIGURE 4-1   A list of various ad groups within this advertiser's "Campaign #7"

A second, and not unimportant, reason that organizing around ad groups is helpful is to ensure that each group of keyphrases linked to any given idea is linked to an ad (or multiple ads) that closely targets users searching for whatever that idea or thing might be. The closeness of the match to users' interests, and those users' feelings of being catered to (basically, extreme relevancy in search), seems to improve campaign performance. If Google is giving us the ability to micro-target users with an offer that might really appeal to them based on what they're typing into the search engine, should we run a generic campaign that acts more like the traditional run-of-site banner ads? No! Groups remind you to target your ads more tightly to the user's query.

As I'll explain in more detail in Chapter 8, within an ad group you can run multiple ads at the same time. (Some call this split-testing or A/B testing.) So even within a tightly focused area, you can still experiment with different ways of catching searchers' attention to find out what works best, and the independent impact of variations in ad title and ad copy will be measured accurately.

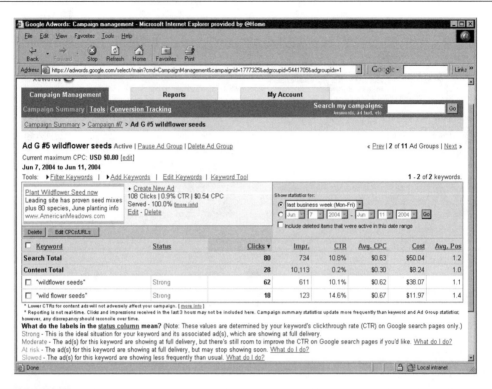

FIGURE 4-2   A summary of AdWords campaign data for a week in the life of "Ad Group #5 Wildflower Seeds"

Google's Strange Advice on Ad Group Size

Oddly, Google staff do (verbally) tend to give you strong advice to limit the number of keywords per ad group. Why? The unspoken reason is that very low-volume keywords muck up the system and give Google data overload they can do without, given that it costs you nothing to add 100,000 of them to your account. Google won't make much more revenue out of all that keyword inventory, as long as their various matching options are causing ads to show up on a lot of queries at good average CPCs as advertisers bid things up. So Google, from a purely selfish standpoint, isn't going to applaud huge keyword lists.

The overt reason, according to comments made by various Googlers, is that the same keywords are being interpreted by the content targeting algorithm that attempts to match the overall semantic meaning of your ad group with the overall meaning of text on a web page. More than 10–15 keywords starts to dilute the effectiveness of that matching, supposedly. That leads me to wonder whether the tail isn't wagging the dog. Should our ad group sizes be dependent on the foibles of a content program that came out after the search ads program, layered on top of that program in an idiosyncratic way by Google product managers? So on this front, you probably should march to the beat of your own drummer, and figure out other ways of maximizing your content performance, such as setting up separate campaigns or using placement targeting (discussed in Chapter 9). Ad group sizes shouldn't be unwieldy, but limiting a group to 10–15 words is unrealistic in many cases.

While there is ultimately no single rule of thumb for how many keywords in a group is unwieldy, you will soon get a feel for this from your actual campaign data. Certainly, over 100 keywords is probably too high. If the bottom 75% of your keywords combined doesn't get a single click in a month, that might be a sign you are overdoing it! But that is not the only way to have too many keywords in a group: the other way is to have too many keywords with different meanings, with different user intents, jumbled together. Again, then, rather than merely counting, just do what makes sense from the perspective of users seeing relevant ads, and from the perspective of ease of reporting and interpretation long term. In some cases it might make sense to place only one or two keywords in an ad group, if these are particularly high volume. This might sharpen your focus in reporting on, and testing ads for, your main drivers.

Getting Very Granular with Groups

How fine-grained you want to make your group structure is up to you. A large retailer with 20 ad groups in a textiles-related campaign might do better if they subdivide those into 80 more-specific groups.

When called upon to improve my clients' campaign performance, one tactic I'll try is to take a medium-grained ad group and break it into more fine-grained groups. Let's say, for example, that the various words for *fabric* have all been dumped into one group. There are six main ways (let's say) to express the concept of fabric. For some reason, people typing in those different terms might respond differently to different offers. Working with different ads for each, and tracking their performance separately, might lead to better performance. It's not as if the advertiser was lazy before—given their various other products, having a "fabric" group was reasonable. Just not 100% optimal.

Let's say you can use six different keywords that mean something more or less the same as *fabric,* and you want to build commerce-friendly phrases around each (*cloth, pattern, material,* and so on). Make sure you use six different ad groups, each one revolving around a different way of saying *fabric,* and then build related phrases onto each. It also helps if your ad title contains that keyword. Your clickthrough rates are usually higher if there is an exact match between a word in your title and the phrase the user has typed in; even very close synonyms don't seem to do as well.

You'll probably want to write ad titles that are different for each group, for example:

Fabric for Less
Wholesale Cloth
Looking for Patterns?
Buy Unusual Material

Using a single ad title for all of the diverse keywords in the campaign usually lowers performance (CTR), and this can cost you money. The same goes for the written copy that goes with the title. It should be tailored as much as possible to the keywords in a logically sensible ad group.

Advanced Tip: Couldn't You "Set" the Level of Granularity Somehow?

Wouldn't it be cool if some kind of tool were available to help break down big campaigns with big ad groups into finer-grained ones? Obviously, the tool wouldn't be able to rewrite all your ads, and it might get things a bit wrong, but it would be cool. My hunch is that Google support staff already have beta versions of such tools available now to help them advise advertisers on account improvements. In the future, such a feature might even find its way into the AdWords interface.

Depending on your objectives, each of these ads might actually take the user to a different part of your website, or a different *landing page* (the target URL for the ad). When deciding on the target URL to enter with each ad, consider the user experience. Is the searcher's experience going to be intuitive and seamless? Does the "buy unusual material" ad take her to an appropriate page on your site, or just the home page? If you want, you can even test both to see which performs better. As a rule of thumb, this process is always about improving your targeting. Secondarily, it's a matter of usability and sensible navigation. Think carefully about targeting at each step of the process. Sales conversion rates generally go up when users get the exact information they were looking for right away rather than having to hunt for it.

Currently on Google.com, on advertising as well as regular search results, the search engine user's search words are being highlighted in bold, so this may also lead to higher CTRs (bold text is eye-grabbing) if you focus on making sure your ad titles and copy contain relevant keyphrases.

Organize, Organize, Organize

A fastidiously organized account leads to faster AdWords success and prevents headaches later. Let's review four reasons for being careful about how you organize your campaigns, groups, keywords, and ads. The kind of organization I'm referring to here is basically what we discussed in the previous section: the idea of carefully piecing together a meaning tree within your account, with sensible labels on everything. Pretend you're the corporate librarian and assume that your job is to set things up so that the average person could understand where to find everything.

Multiple Persons Managing the Account

At the beginning, it might be just you managing the account, but that's rarely the case over the long haul. In many companies, a succession of people will be involved at one point or another. Even if it's just you, you'll find that things go much more easily if you organize carefully in the beginning. The "later-on you" might have real trouble figuring out where the "old you" put various keywords, or why certain bidding strategies were employed. Haste makes waste.

Post-Click Tracking

Depending on your goals, you will usually track user behavior after they click on your ads. Most typically, you'll want to trace a specific type of conversion event (did they convert to a paying customer, a lead, or a newsletter subscriber?) back to the assessment of how well different ad groups and ads performed. Analytics can be a breeze when you've set up ad groups based on a logical structure of meaning, whether it be product line or different variations of similar words. By contrast, data can seem meaningless and random if you've built the account hastily, piling disparate phrases into various ad groups rather than organizing them thematically. If you set things up carefully, strong performance in a particular ad group is easy to interpret, and you can build on that knowledge.

Set up tracking URLs (destination URLs with custom tracking codes) to represent each ad group, or preferably every ad and ad group. (Again, tracking URLs aren't really required if you use certain tracking solutions, especially Google Conversion Tracker.) I recommend figuring this out right at the beginning, because the setup of tracking URLs is busywork that can eat up the better part of a day for larger accounts. You don't want to have to do it twice. If you do nothing about tracking at the beginning, with a logical campaign structure, you can, at least, come back later confident that it will be easy to add different tracking URLs to represent each different ad in all of your groups.

Tracking URLs are not hard to enter and don't require any complex math or programming skills, just a numbering system (often one you invent yourself) that will help you keep score later. We'll come back to this.

Bottom-Line Performance (Ads Match Keywords)

All the major search engine advertising representatives will tell you this: CTRs go up when your ad title matches exactly with the keywords typed in by the user. For the time being, there is no disputing this, although I think it's a little too pat. If that were the only secret to good copywriting, everyone would do it, and everyone would have the same ad titles on any given search query. Zzzzz. Taking the general principle to heart is the important thing. The better you organize your ad groups and the keywords in them, the easier it is for you to write a variety of different ads to achieve granularity. In other words, by writing differently worded and differently titled ads for each group, you'll wind up with ad copy that is closer in meaning to the keywords you're targeting. This almost invariably creates a higher CTR across your campaign. There's a very good reason to shoot for a higher CTR: it's the predominant factor in the Quality Score algorithm that rewards advertisers with higher rank on the page for ads that are more relevant to users. In some cases, ads may not be shown at all if your Quality Score multiplied by your bid fails to reach what Google terms a "bid requirement." I'll cover this fully in Chapter 5.

By doing everything right from the standpoint of organization and granularity, your campaign will become easier to run and make you more money. This frees up your time to work on other things while your competitors are killing themselves managing their pay-per-click accounts. They might also be goaded into bidding too high, then wind up shutting down their accounts in a panic, because they don't understand one of the big secrets behind your high ad positions: proper campaign structure.

Avoiding the Horrors of Overlap

I'm often asked if you can put the same keywords and phrases into different ad groups or even different campaigns. The answer is yes, but the result isn't exactly as you might expect. If you sell eight different products that are all relevant to the same keywords, guess what, you can't have eight of your ads (or even two of them) showing up on the same page of search results. Google calls this *double serving,* and it's against the AdWords terms of service. As you can imagine, many advertisers would take advantage of this to crowd out competitors with multiple ads, and this goes against what the user is expecting to see in that space—a choice of different vendors. So, in the case of overlap (the same keywords in different ad groups or different campaigns), the AdWords system will choose to show a single ad from your account corresponding to only one of those keywords. How is that choice made? As with many such questions, Google is evasive on the point, preferring to emphasize the relevancy aspect over any messy talk about simply choosing the one where you've bid the highest. Strictly speaking, the ad chosen is the one from the group where that keyword has the highest Quality Score.

So why do I speak of "horror"? After all, nothing breaks if you overlap. Your ad is shown. No problem. Usually it isn't a problem. If you happen to get forgetful and create some limited overlap, nothing terrible will happen.

But with significant overlap across different groups and campaigns, an account becomes virtually impossible to comprehend and manage, especially when multiple stakeholders come on the scene. You (or others) will find it difficult to interpret tracking data, to know which ads are going to show up, and to get a handle on how much you are paying for the keywords. If you're caught in an account that already looks like this, pause some campaigns and groups until you've built a cleaner campaign.

The Tale of the Impatient Client

Overlap in the early going can be particularly troublesome, because highly targeted ad groups compete with clumsily built, more general ad groups. In Google's new Quality Score regime (again, see Chapter 5), new accounts may be held to rather harsh scrutiny, so getting high CTRs out of the gate is a must.

My team built a very focused, granular campaign for a B2B client. These campaigns are typically low volume with very high CPCs. They have a number of other unique qualities.

Impatient with the volume, the client built their own general ad groups around our more specific ones, not bothering to check out where keywords were being duplicated. They enabled those, and promptly began contributing bad Quality Score karma to the account. With the very low CTRs that are inevitable when marketing to a niche audience using very general keywords, they made it harder for the account as a whole to generate the positive user feedback signals Google is looking for.

Don't "go scattergun" first, and refine later. In the new era of AdWords, especially for tricky accounts, go narrow first, and build out once your Quality Scores are proven to be OK.

Magic Candles: Accounts That Need Repeated Deletions

A typical example of what can happen with rampant overlap is the advertiser who decides she's paying too much for some of her keywords and wants to lower the bids on them by up to 60%. Her trusty AdWords consultant goes in and lowers those bids significantly, hoping the total daily spend will be slashed from, say, $800 to $400. It seems OK for a few hours, so the consultant takes off for the long weekend and the client thanks him for his help. Lo and behold, like those gag birthday candles that never blow out, the same keywords "pop up" in another campaign and start working to display ads for approximately the same cost as before. The following week, it's discovered that some higher-volume keywords are hiding in no fewer than six campaigns, and they must be ferreted out and deleted. Yikes!

The same thing can happen even when *similar* keywords are in different ad groups or campaigns, if they are using broad matching. If you shut off **college loans** because it isn't converting well, but leave **school loans** on somewhere else, **school loans** may "pop up" unexpectedly—unexpectedly because previously it had been dormant due to **college loans** siphoning off most of the impressions. This is a bit complicated; I discuss Google's "expanded broad matching" in Chapter 9. The only easy takeaway from this description of the magic candles syndrome is that one round of bid adjustment is never the last word on your account performance. Your campaigns will need regular monitoring regardless, but require particularly close monitoring after you make a round of bid changes whose intended effect is to lower bids, or after you pause or delete certain keywords entirely with the expectation that this will improve campaign economics.

Various bad things happen with too much overlap. Avoid it, and build a clean campaign in which the vast majority of your ad groups have a clear purpose, with keyword lists that do not also appear in other ad groups. You should also consider focusing on Google's *phrase matching* option as opposed to *broad matching*. See Chapter 9 for more.

Naming Campaigns and Groups

Just a friendly reminder: giving memorable labels to campaigns and groups is part of the process of staying organized. To go back and name or rename an ad group if you forgot to do it at the beginning, you'll drill down to the campaign level of your AdWords account to see the list of existing groups and click the check boxes next to the groups you'd like to rename. Then, from the gray buttons at the top of that list (Change Max CPC, Rename, Pause, Resume, Delete), click the Rename button.

To rename a campaign, go into Edit Campaign Settings and edit the first field, labeled "1. Basic Information—Campaign Name."

Your naming system should be one that will jog your memory later. It might be based on different product lines, different words (*fabric, material, cloth*), or even different AdWords strategies. I sometimes name groups "experimental," or even more specifically, such as "low cost experiments," "developer jargon," "competitor meta tags," "unconvincing AdWords keyword tool suggestions," after any number of nefarious strategies I might use to generate and test innovative keywords. The naming should dovetail with the structure as a whole—it should remind you to group similar keywords together, whatever *similar* means for you.

You're in Charge: Reevaluate Structure Every Few Quarters

As you add keywords to groups over time, you might find your groups becoming too cluttered once more. Some phrases might merit being "hived off" and put in groups of their own. At that point, you may want to consider starting new groups revolving around such phrases, especially if you've discovered new ones that generate high volumes of clicks—new concepts or terms that might be worth building on in their own right.

Writing Your First Ads

The first advertisements you write might not prove to be your best, but you do have to get them written to get things rolling. The AdWords interface will ask you to enter at least one ad right at the start. Later on, when setting up new ad groups, you'll simply drill down to the ad group level of the AdWords interface and click on Create New Ad.

As the interface will show, you have a very small space to work with: 25 characters for the headline, and 35 characters for each of two lines for the two-line description. The display URL (the web address that users will actually see below your ad) can only be 35 characters. However, the landing URL gives you plenty of leeway. It can be up to 1,024 characters. Some advertisers have very long tracking codes or complicated URLs for their catalog pages, so this helps.

A few tips on format first. For the *display URL* you'll typically just put in your home page URL. The user may be taken (by the landing URL) to a specific page on your website, but the URL displayed in your ad needs to be uncomplicated and, hopefully, should look trustworthy; for example, www.legumes.com. Sometimes I experiment with capital letters where appropriate in two-word URLs; for example, pagezero.com versus PageZero.com. I haven't seen any conclusive difference in user response. Google won't allow you to misuse capitals. You can't alternate caps manically just to grab attention (www.GiLoOLy.BiZ), for example. Not that you'd want to make a spectacle of yourself in this way, but you'd be amazed at what some folks dream up.

Choose the landing URL with care. You need to ensure that every ad you write uses a landing URL that gets two key things right: first, it must send users to the corresponding page on your site (this is preferably a targeted page that gets users to the information they need without an extra click); second, it must contain the correct tracking code based on whatever tracking nomenclature you've decided to use. If forced to do this, I use a unique tracking code for each ad. We'll return to this, but an example of a landing URL would be something like this:

http://www.legumes.com/lentils.asp?source=gaw&kw=23b

Always Be Testing

Advanced Tip: Don't prejudge the impact of any element in an ad. What do the consumer response numbers say? The display URL is actually an element to test, if you have high click volumes and the guts to try new things. Some advertisers have the flexibility to try different domains. Others use descriptive keywords in a subdirectory name, such as www .mysite.com/pencils, and Google doesn't seem to mind if your real URL doesn't look exactly like that. Another tip you may have completely overlooked is that if you're running out of characters for the display URL, you can leave off the "www."!

Nowadays, though, I rarely use this hand-crafted approach. I'd either use Google's tracking or use a tracking tool that automates the process of inserting the correct codes into destination URLs using the AdWords API (Application Programming Interface).

As for the ad itself: now the challenge begins. You have to squeeze your message into a small space. Some call it a haiku. But it's really no different from traditional classified ads, except that here, you have the ability to test response in real time. Once you've entered that first ad, a maximum bid, and a couple of keywords just to get the account set up and running with your first ad group, you're on your way—well, almost. Google has some fairly extensive editorial policies to contend with.

Editorial Review

No one has ever sent me a Google organization chart, but I've been fortunate enough to talk individually with dozens of Google staffers and executives at various levels of the organization and thus believe I have a decent feel for the company's workings. Certainly, as with any industry, there is competition for good people. Google is one of the most prestigious companies in the technology world, and many good people want to work for the company. This works to Google's advantage. Competitors such as Yahoo also have sufficient experience and prestige to attract top-quality staff.

I point this out because customer service plays an increasingly important role at Google. That said, in the past three years, it looks like their jobs have been subject to significant standardization and automation. Automated editorial "warnings" stop you from breaking the rules even before you enter mistakes. And written and verbal "decisions" are rare. Today, everything is moving in the direction of opacity, even though human oversight is as important as ever.

In the increasingly rare event of editorial disapproval alerts (best visible at the Account Snapshot level), you have the choice to either correct the problem or contact your Google rep to ask for clarification. Often, staff will show you the courtesy of requesting a review by a policy specialist, but there are no guarantees. Most, but not all, of the rules are fairly clear.

Responding to Controversial Editorial Disapprovals

Sometimes, you can be the victim of a misunderstanding or localized bias of some kind, resulting in an unfair editorial disapproval. To head off potentially condescending responses from editorial staff who may not fully appreciate your depth of knowledge about your own business and the advertising business in general, try making an initial email contact to identify yourself fully, possibly with a brief bio explaining your background. Politely explaining small distinctions about your industry or your campaign that staff may have overlooked may be required, too. With so many advertisers to deal with, staff might simply assume that your case isn't worth looking at too carefully, since many editorial disapprovals are fairly routine. You might have to remind them of your brilliance and convince them to squint harder at your correspondence. Unfortunately, this is a fact of life in dealing with customer service people who may be accustomed to receiving a large volume of inquiries.

The online medium can lead to brittle communications, and there is no more uncomfortable feeling than receiving several warning emails that your advertisement has been "disapproved." I think that's probably why Google has chosen to sharply reduce the number of such messages in recent years, by offering automated warnings that happen as you enter the ad, and also by burying more of their biases and policies within the Quality Score algorithm. It's just plain harder to quibble with an algorithm.

Many of us have a deep psychological aversion to disapproval. If you work for a larger company, you'll probably be stunned that someone would nitpick you, given your big ad budget. But consistent policies are obviously better for everyone concerned, even though they might be applied or interpreted too rigidly in some cases. So the best advice is to treat a disapproval as a minor setback, and either adjust your ads to make them conform to the rules, or politely appeal.

Why were so many minor editorial rules enacted in the first place? The history is interesting. According to Sheryl Sandberg, an early director of the Google AdWords Select program, Google was from the beginning trying to set an industry standard for advertisers. Pressure to do this increased as Google entered negotiations to form a syndication partnership with AOL, a partnership that they won away from their rival, Overture. A standards-based approach was not implemented simply to appease AOL or imaginary consumers, though. It was also intended to protect advertisers from one another. (The concept is one of a level playing field for all participants.) If an advertiser breaks one of the editorial rules, it may be creating an artificially high CTR at the expense of one of its competitors. Google wants to reserve the right to disapprove ads for that reason as well as for reasons of quality control and consumer protection.

Quick Tips

The full list of editorial policies is at http://adwords.google.com/support/bin/static.py?page=guidelines.cs&topic=9271&subtopic=9277.

Probably the most important idea is mentioned near the top of the guidelines list: "As a basic rule, use clear, descriptive, and specific ad content that highlights the differentiating characteristics of your product/service." Proper targeting generally makes gimmicks unnecessary.

Google does a good job of describing its own rules, so I won't duplicate everything they say; just a few words about them. Quite a few of the guidelines are basic matters of form—almost like the style guides reporters must follow when writing a news story. No repeated or unnecessary punctuation; don't use all capital letters for anything except an acronym; spell words correctly.

Some punctuation styles that were verboten in the early days are actually now recommended by Google! (How easily we forget how disdainful we used to be about things that actually work.) One example is the practice of capitalizing the first letter of every word in body copy. It used to be banned. Now, it actually appears as a favored example on Google's editorial guidelines page. This is likely because it increases CTRs slightly in many cases, upping Google's revenues (without bothering users unduly). It might not work for you. My colleagues and I tend to think this looks unprofessional, but if you insist, we'll test it.

Some guidelines are designed to prevent you from making misleading claims. Some forms of "come-on" might be disallowed—especially if they're clearly inaccurate. Phony low prices designed to induce clicks might be a waste of your money, so Google might actually be doing you a favor by asking you to reword your ad.

Google has a set of policies aimed at making life tough for affiliate advertisers. At one time, they were actually forced to identify themselves in ad copy with the designation "aff." From there, things have gotten a lot quieter, but mainly because Google has launched a deliberately quiet campaign to reduce the numbers of affiliates who advertise.

> **NOTE** *An affiliate is someone who sends referral traffic to, say, a parent company like eBay, receiving a commission if that traffic results in a purchase. They might publish recommendations with their affiliate links (including a code, so they get credit for a sale) in an email newsletter or a website or blog. Or, they might spend money on AdWords clicks, hoping to pocket the difference between the cost of the paid search clicks and the commissions they make from sales.*

As a result of too many affiliates crowding the page of sponsored listings on some queries, Google enacted a rule that limits the number of advertisers appearing for a given display URL to one (so there won't be four ads for eBay.com on the same page, for example). But that's really just the beginning. Manual intervention and automated means of assigning low Quality Scores to affiliate sites are all part of the process, too.

Over the past three years, I think it's safe to say that Google's evolving policies have been, in large part, designed with an eye to making it harder for affiliates to advertise. If there is the slightest "seedy-looking" thing about certain offers, or if there are too many ads from (let's say) eBay on a page, consumers tend to react negatively. Examples of Google's human evaluation methods circulate around the Internet from time to time. These methods—applied, I presume, to both paid and organic search results, and websites vying for rankings on either side—have shown that Google coaches its human "landing page raters" to grade affiliates harshly unless they offer something unique. (For example, human raters might be offered descriptions of "what a 'thin' affiliate site" is.) Examples of sites and pages that typical human raters don't like are fed into the AdWords Quality Score algorithm to train the system to recognize signals of "seediness."

Anyway, on the editorial front, if you feel you've been the victim of a gray area ruling that goes against you, by all means reply to Google's support emails with a polite request for more information, clarification, and possibly an appeal of the ad disapproval.

> **NOTE** *Depending on your geographic location, your reply will be to AdWords-support@google .com, or if in the UK, AdWords-uk@google.com. Or just reply directly to the editorial messages you receive by email.*

My final word on this subject: don't spend your life swimming against the current or tilting at windmills. Make your views known, to be sure; then, get back to work!

Time Lags and Special Rules

Some foibles in Google's editorial process are never explained in any documentation. There are certain background considerations that need to be kept in mind. In particular, you may find yourself tripped up by delays in getting ads running for new accounts, or new ads within an existing account, or even in unpausing an account that has been dormant for some time.

Google vs. Search Network Partners

Editorial approval delays are sometimes attributed to differential editorial standards at network partners such as AOL. You tend to hear stories circulating around about how "instant" ad activation is on Google.com, and that it takes a bit more time to show up on partner sites, but the routine isn't really disclosed as far as I know. You should become concerned if your ad isn't approved and generating impressions on your keywords within 24 hours; 48 hours in busy times, allowing for weekends.

Automated vs. Human Review; Ramp-Up Timelines

Many people assumed (based on how AdWords was marketed in the early days) that ads get "up and running right away." Indeed, many advertisers found it exhilarating that they could see their ads running nearly immediately and that editorial review mainly consisted of automated tests to see if ads broke any rules, followed by a *post facto* checkup by a live editor as Google's software deemed necessary.

Not so fast, though. While the process has often worked basically like this, Google has now deviated significantly from it, especially on popular keywords with many established advertisers. Although ads may be given a few token impressions and clicks (for what reason I do not know—to confuse advertisers further or to throw Google's competitors off?), it's been confirmed in support calls that new ads can sometimes sit in an editorial queue for up to a week. The most glaring example of this will be over the Christmas holiday period. After December 10 or so, don't count on getting any new ads approved in anything less than ten days. Plan ahead to avoid disappointment.

Over the years, I've also come to suspect that (for reasons I can't explain) new accounts and new keywords undergo a "ramp-up" process (even taking into account delays in syndication through network partners or content targeting). They're served only partially at first, gradually increasing in volume, until one day, a week or several weeks later, they finally reach full delivery. Again, no one at Google will confirm this, but plotting the number of daily ad impressions over a period of three to four weeks for any new campaign or ad group containing new keywords would offer some proof of this. The exact pattern just changes from year to year. Now, new accounts and new parts of accounts are subject to an opaque "buildup" phase wherein they are evaluated on all kinds of variables (primarily CTR) in order to establish Quality Scores for keywords. It's not clear whether that evaluation phase also limits delivery until there is some certainty level about the readings.

As if it weren't difficult enough to project your monthly spend prior to launch, you may have difficulty getting any kind of consistent feel for how much you're spending until everything has been running steadily for a few weeks.

Established accounts tend to have fewer hiccups and "phase-in" issues, but if you're doing anything involving "turn on a dime" seasonality, I'd budget for a week or more of slow initial delivery.

No Double Serving

As mentioned earlier, Google won't allow you to use multiple AdWords accounts to run several ads on the page at the same time on the same keyphrase. Admittedly, this can be a gray area. A large diversified company won't be able to prevent its various divisions from bidding on the same keywords, and if the lines of business are distinct enough, Google likely has no problem with it. However, case studies I've seen from companies like IBM have shown that it can be bad economics to bid against other divisions of your own company!

Even in smaller companies, there can be allowable forms of double serving. For example, a division might target consumers exclusively with one site, and a separate division might be using the same keywords to send traffic to their B2B site. If you're trusting, you'll turn to your Google rep and ask for clarification as to whether this might be allowed. If you're a shoot-first, ask-questions-later type, you'll just do it, avoiding messy questions, and hope that Google doesn't discover or have a problem with the double serving. Rest assured, though, that in 99% of cases, Google knows what you're up to.

The principle here is simple: allowing companies to blanket the page with their ads by creating multiple AdWords accounts would be an abuse of the system, unfair to other advertisers, and a bad deal for users, who expect to see some choice in listings. The terms of Google's arrangement with advertisers do not, of course, include the right to buy up all of the screen real estate devoted to advertising. Evidently, Google prefers the competitive auction process because it provides users with more choice and drives up Google's revenues. Hey, they're the publisher and it's their website, so that's their right.

Chapter 5

How Google Ranks Ads:
Quality-Based Bidding

As I showed in early chapters, the manner in which search engines display query results is becoming increasingly complex. Google's ranking algorithms for the organic web index are constantly evolving. In addition, Google now organizes a lot of different types of information: news, video, local and map results, weather, Google Groups discussions, and much more. To display an appropriate mix of information, Google (like other search engines) attempts to discern user intent through a mix of personalization and guessing at what a query's intent means in part by going on past data. So if you were to type a common news-related query, Google might show news results above the web index results. For some local vendor queries, Google might show six or more local listings, pushing everything else further down the page (see Figure 5-1)!

Google calls this blended approach to showing search results Universal Search. It has changed marketers' assumptions about what they can expect to accomplish by optimizing websites solely for the web index results. Fortunately for your focus in the paid search realm, the screen real estate taken up by paid search ads hasn't changed a whole lot. Paid search ads are relatively easy to trigger in the familiar slots in the areas above and to the right of the organic search results.

Phew, so all that increasing complexity in the search world won't affect our paid campaigns, then? Sorry, but the clever engineers at Google have ratcheted up the complexity of their keyword advertising system, too. There is now a whole formula that affects both *how high your ad ranks* on the page in relation to other advertisers, which affects the visibility of your ad and therefore your click volume, and *keyword Quality Score for the purposes of meeting a newly designed Bid Requirement*, which can make your ad ineligible to show up at the time of the query. I explain all the generations of ranking formulas, leading up to the present one (released late August 2008), in the current chapter.

This formula used to be relatively simple in the period 2002–2005. Even so, it required several pages of explanation in the first edition of this book. The concept of multiplying your bid by your clickthrough rate (CTR) to arrive at your "AdRank" was not intuitive to many advertisers.

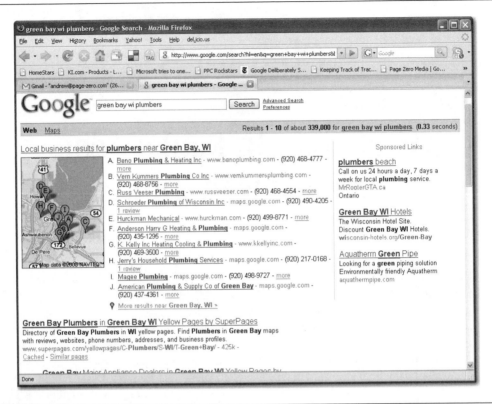

FIGURE 5-1   Google guesses at user intent, displaying a large number of Google Local
listings for the search query "green bay wi plumbers."

Eventually, folks got used to it. In August 2005, a newly announced formula led us down the
path towards an increasingly complex and opaque bidding regime. CTR was replaced by Quality
Score (QS), and the method of calculating QS has been changing steadily. It's not entirely unlike
the mysterious and changeable proprietary algorithms Google uses to rank other types of search
results, most notably the unpaid listings in the web index.

In this chapter I will delve deep into the concepts of Quality-Based Bidding (QBB),[1]
covering the current principles that drive the system; the historical evolution from then until
now; and the basic ranking factors that affect your ad rank. To illustrate the practical side of
succeeding in this environment, I'll also offer case studies.

If you get lost, well, I'm a big fan of Occam's razor. So keep in mind that two key principles
behind the auction—relevancy or tight targeting, and catching bad guys—can help you simplify
all the detail. The other thing to remember when you get lost is that there is considerable

continuity in the system's operation from 2002 to this day. *CTR is still a core driver*. If you don't get clicked, it'll be hard to make your keyword stick.

A quick heads-up: what counts as a good CTR is relative, not absolute. A good CTR in ad position 2 is not the same as what constitutes a good CTR in ad position 11. Typical CTRs vary by industry and by keyword, too. In Google-speak, they "normalize" CTR based on such factors as ad position, so don't get caught up in thinking that you have to be in a very high ad position solely for the CTR benefit. Google's formula attempts to compare apples with apples.

Encapsulating the Concept of Quality-Based Bidding

Much of the advertising world is based on loose targeting. Put another way, it's mass or broadcast advertising, dreamt up by old-school advertising moguls from the days of the TV-industrial complex. These were the sorts of chaps who, if asked off the record, might tell you that they love the smell of napalm in the morning. Metaphorically speaking, of course.

If you watch TV daily, not a day will go by that you won't say to yourself: "Why are they showing this to me?" You might be offended by a given ad because it's talking about some embarrassing ailment you don't have. You might even get a bit angry at such loose ad targeting! It's the napalm of the airwaves.

This is the opposite of what Google wants the search experience to be like. So they've built some serious disincentives into their auction to discourage loose targeting and to encourage tight targeting.

To put it in a single sentence, Google's ad system is a complex auction that takes into account your bid amount (on any given keyword) along with a variety of other (mostly relevancy-related) factors, which, put together, is called your *Quality Score*. Quality Scores are assigned *by keyword*, but ads, landing pages, and account history may affect Quality Scores. So when we speak about Quality Scores, assume that we are talking about an individual keyword or phrase, but don't assume that the keyword's performance alone is what influences that keyword's quality. (OK, so I admit, that was more than one sentence, but you could have stopped reading after the first sentence.)

Under this system, the lowest possible minimum bid is actually lower than it has been in the past; it's one cent ($.01) or the equivalent very low amount in your currency unit. That's mostly window dressing, however. You'll likely have to bid considerably higher to reach a desirable ad position.

Quality Scores Are Based on (at Least) Three Broad Types of Data

Googlers often stress that this process is nearly 100% automated. Decisions on where to rank ads, and whether keywords are active at all, are complex and data-driven. Here are some guidelines to the broad types of data Google looks at when it comes to keyword performance.

Historical Data

Accounts with a lot of past history have generally come through the new era unscathed, especially if they have a history of strong CTRs and other indicators of relevancy. Historical data on a keyword—and on the entire account—make it relatively easy for AdWords to assign a "true" Quality Score to any given keyword. The more known information Google has about keyword and account performance, the more accurate the Quality Score is likely to be.

Predictive Data

Setting up a new account poses much different challenges than managing an account with a strong history. Google has no data for your keywords. Technically, they don't know how relevant your campaign is to users because you haven't run it yet. But don't think that'll stop them from trying! They'll use past search data and data from other advertisers' campaigns to assign initial Quality Scores to your keywords. This is significantly more precise (and in many cases, less generous) than the old version of AdWords, which assigned new keywords a default CTR based on industry averages. Whereas in the old days your initial ad positions were often skewed a bit to the generous side, in many areas Google's system now takes a "show me" approach to your account. Google now has more than enough advertisers (and in case you hadn't heard, enough money to keep the lights on), so your account is going to have to prove its mettle a bit at first. That's probably going to require you to bid a bit higher than you'd like in the early going.

Google began experimenting with a "suspicious outlook" on new accounts at least a year prior to the switchover to full-on Quality-Based Bidding. In part because a minority of advertisers—in particular, affiliate advertisers bidding low amounts on a large number of irrelevant keywords—were wont to flood the system with junky campaigns that would show bothersome ads to users during the data evaluation period, Google took steps to make sure these ads rarely made it live in the first place. For new keywords in new accounts, Google—with the help of AdsBot, which scans your landing page and website for content—now uses a host of means to check out the predicted relevancy of your keywords, ads, and web pages.

On the keyword front, Google uses (among other things) historical data from past advertisers' campaigns to try to guess at whether the keywords you're choosing have any commercial viability. They also look at how well your keywords, ads, and landing pages relate to one another. Gone are the days where you can try to show your ad on keywords about the daily lottery if you're trying to sell home equity loans. Sure (as the UK-based advertiser who tried that told a panel at SES London a couple of years ago), there is some logic to this—someone's worried about money, so they buy lottery tickets, so they might be interested in a loan. Apparently, though, on certain queries, people really just want what they said they wanted—in this case, lottery results. This advertiser would have found he garnered low CTRs on his terms if he advertised against lottery results keywords. Using predictive data, Google disincentivized this advertiser from even finding out. Google had so much data on poor CTRs for similar irrelevant ads showing up against lottery results keywords that it imposed a Quality Score hurdle on any advertiser who wanted to experiment with such loose targeting.

You're certainly free to buy "loosely relevant ads" around the Web—if you do display advertising and want to negotiate ad buys with publishers and networks that are eager for your dollar without regard to how closely your offer is related to their content. Not so on Google Search proper, though. Google currently works on the premise that users are unequivocally looking for ad listings that are relevant to their queries, and Google has found that off-topic "diversionary" ads make some search engine users irate. So Google won't risk killing the golden goose, which, as I've already established, is searcher loyalty.

Opinion and Arbitrary Determinations

Editorial rules and human assessments of keywords, ads, and websites were always a big part of the paid search auction. For whatever reason, Google has taken steps to reduce the level of human enforcement of rules. By "human enforcement," what I really mean is that Google has reduced the frequency of direct staff interaction with advertisers when it comes to infractions; and Google has reduced the number of "on-off" and "yes-no" policy determinations. Both trends have resulted in more decisions being moved into the opaque world of Quality Score, allowing Google to set a sliding scale of incentives that raises prices on advertisers to varying degrees as opposed to triggering a confrontation.

For example, whereas in the past certain types of keywords might have been banned either across the board or selectively in response to complaints, now Google simply discourages advertisers from advertising on those same words, by making high Quality Scores relatively hard to attain on them.

Another example: in the past, Google editorial staff (as always, aided by automation) might have looked for a short list of user experience violations on an advertiser's website. Pop-ups and a few other things were discouraged. Now, a wide range of such experiences might be included in the increasingly complex formula for determining landing page quality. Google still uses a combination of automated and editorial means to catch "no-no's." But because the new system is so slick and opaque, advertisers today sometimes think everything is automated. Not entirely so. Sometimes editorial decisions are made outright about a given company, its products, landing pages, or messages. These can be human-driven decisions. Getting anyone to admit this, or to explain exactly what the problem is, can be like pulling teeth. To be sure, major problems are rare. But they happen.

Paid Search Ranking Formulas: Past, Present, and Future

The key to understanding the basic workings of paid search ranking formulas today, in my view, lies in recognizing the continuity of today's model—to be precise, what I refer to as "AdWords 2.7" below—with the previous approach used by Google from 2002–2005 (what I'll call AdWords 2.0). Here are some brief reminders of what past models looked like leading up to the current one.

Paid Search 1.0

At its peak, Overture maintained partnerships with AOL Search, Microsoft, and several other prominent search engines. Today, they're wholly owned by Yahoo (and called Yahoo Search Marketing). They were ousted from the AOL partnership by Google in 2002. At the time of this writing, Yahoo has rebuffed a buyout offer from Microsoft, who subsequently took that offer off the table.

Under Overture's system, highest ad placement went to the highest bidder, and in the early days, bids were published right on the page. Today, that model is a thing of the past.

What has remained intact is the "pay only for a click" model. Although Google and others are now experimenting with a variety of pricing models in their ad platforms, on the paid search side, pay-per-click remains dominant.

The Overture model was keyword- or keyphrase-centric. Advertisers would associate a separate bid and an associated ad with every single keyword in the account, even if they had 10,000 keywords. This and other quirks spawned the rise of third-party bid management software.

AdWords 1.0 and 2.0

In 2001, Google had quietly rolled out a relatively unsuccessful experiment in monetizing Google Search results pages. Called AdWords (I'll call it AdWords 1.0), it was initially based on fixed CPM (cost per thousand impressions) rates, and only three ad slots were available on a page. The pricing wasn't favorable and advertisers didn't take to it.

A year later, Google rolled out a more sophisticated offering. In some ways, it mimicked Overture's auction (Google later paid Yahoo a hefty settlement for patent infringement). It was pay-per-click, and bids were one facet of how visibility on the page was determined. But this version—initially called AdWords Select, then back to AdWords again, so I'll call it AdWords 2.0—incorporated relevancy in the formula for determining placement on the page. The higher your clickthrough rate on a given keyword, the better as far as ad positioning went.

Google also introduced some new ways of interacting with the system. As we've seen, instead of one keyword, one bid, one ad, you had "ad groups"—multiple keywords in a group associated with a single ad and bid. You could also specify individual keyword bids. A level above the ad group was the campaign level, which offered a number of settings such as daily budgets, language, country or region, and more. The platform was far more flexible and intuitive than Overture's, so Yahoo was continually playing catch-up by patching features on top of an old, clunky interface.

AdWords 2.5 and 2.6

In 2005, Google introduced a new wrinkle: a so-called Quality-Based Bidding initiative (I'll call this AdWords 2.5), adding other relevancy factors to the mix, including keyword relevancy. Later, landing page quality (AdWords 2.6) was incorporated into the formula for determining keyword status and ad rank.

In late 2006, Yahoo finally completed development of the replacement for its outdated Overture platform, code-naming it Panama.

In many ways, Panama closed the gap in terms of functionality differences between Yahoo's and Google's paid search programs. Although there are still significant differences between the two, the differences aren't as great as they once were. Yahoo, like Google, now ranks ads using what it calls a Quality Index. To date, landing pages aren't always factored into the formula, but it's likely that they increasingly will be. The Googlification of Panama was nearly complete by March 2008, when Yahoo introduced "reserve bid prices" similar to Google's minimum bids.

AdWords 2.7 was added by surprise fairly close to press time, so see below for the Addendum section of this chapter, where I provide an updated take on the latest formula.

AdWords 3.0

While the numbering systems describing phases in the program may be arbitrary (I don't know if Google has used their own names for releases), it is the case that AdWords is working on a future upgrade to the system, and it's also the case that some Googlers have informally called this future update "AdWords 3.0." Although some elements of this system have crept into full view—a proto-version of the Account Snapshot; a new hierarchy of ad types that allows a more global classification system that can take account of various kinds of offline ad programs; and more—a great many other features are being tested and debated. Google solicits some stakeholder and user feedback on features through a newly formed AdWords Beta council. AdWords 3.0 is just a nickname for a future interface upgrade. It is unlikely that any major ranking formula changes are being saved for any given period of time. Changes to the Quality Score formula will be ongoing and shouldn't necessarily be associated with any given version or era in interface design.

How Ad Ranking Works: The Letter of the Law, and Beyond

The current ad ranking system has a number of complexities to it that are fully covered in Google's easily accessible help and FAQ files online. The following is intended to summarize and put that information into context.

The Goal Hasn't Changed

The goal, as it has been since AdWords was born, is to get your ads into the most favorable possible positions on the page (which leads to higher click volume) for the lowest possible cost per click.

We are finding that the same "winning results" generally come through practices honed to take proper advantage of AdWords 2.0—with a few wrinkles. You need to be more cautious with account buildout; more cautious of website and business issues; and more willing to accept tight targeting orthodoxy over more experimental, loose targeting. Ultimately, in many accounts, some of your testing efforts will come at a cost: that's the "experimentation tax," if you will, that is now transferred directly to Google's bottom line in the form of increased profits.

At the end of the day, building a relevant campaign helps save you money.

But to be clear, on the "ad ranking formula," a fairly straightforward shift has taken place: clickthrough rate (CTR) has been replaced by the more multifaceted Quality Score (QS), which does include CTR. In fact, on mature accounts, Google has said that CTR is still the "predominant" factor in QS. Or they might have said "*a* predominant factor," which, like many Googlisms, is hard to pin down. (Speaking of Googlisms, if you're wondering how frequently Google updates the Quality Scores on your keywords, under AdWords 2.6, a Googler once said that Quality Score calculations were made in "relatively real time." Today, these calculations are all done per query, fully in real time—an impressive feat of computing power.)

First, let's look at the ranking methodology with some examples. That involves your bid being multiplied by your QS to determine AdRank. After that, we'll look at the Quality Score (yes, a second one) that determines keyword status—that is, your minimum bid that determines whether your keyword is active.

Keyword Quality Score for Ad Ranking

A recent version of Google's FAQs stated: "Quality Score for **ad position** is determined by a keyword's clickthrough rate (CTR) on Google, the relevance of the keyword and ad to the search term, your account's historical performance, and other relevance factors."

CTR

Densely written indeed, but the point is made. Google confirms that CTR is a key component of QS, and that historical data are used when they become available. "Other relevance factors" is a catch-all term to cover anything that falls outside of the official definition. This could include, for example, a whole class of keywords, such as trademarked terms or celebrity names, being deliberately given worse QS than other kinds of keywords. The connection of the keyword and ad is brought up, and is part of the concept of tight targeting.

You'll also notice the pithy phrase "on Google." That means data from search partner sites is not taken into account. In other words, a low CTR on Google Search is bad; a low CTR on a partner site, such as a cobranded Verizon search result, won't hurt you.

To illustrate the fate of advertisers with high and low QS, the following examples might help. The cost savings associated with high QS, all else being equal, can be substantial. Note that these examples are fairly closely adapted from the previous edition of this book, which referred to CTR instead of QS.

Where will your ad show up on a given search query? AdWords works on an auction system to determine how high on the page your ad will be shown, but it's not a "pure" auction. Google combines your bid on a given keyword with the current QS associated with that keyword, to come up with your AdRank.

Ad position on a given keyword or phrase = [your QS on that keyword or phrase] × [bid]

In other words, your ad position is determined by your score relative to other advertisers based on a calculation of your QS and your bid. To be precise, Google no longer refers to any notion of "multiplying" the QS by your bid—preferring to use the word "and" in their descriptions of the formula. "And" could mean "multiplied by," but it leaves them more definitional wiggle room, as usual.

Let's take an example. Let's say your company is called Bunky's Bikes, and your ad is showing up near search results whenever users type **bicycle tires**. Your maximum bid is $1.08.

Your CTR on that phrase is 2.0%. There are some other elements going into that keyword's Quality Score, but because we don't know what those elements are and because I have never been shown what a typical Quality Score number might really look like in absolute numerical terms, let's just say that Bunky's has a QS of 2.0. For our purposes, this gives your ad an "AdRank" score of 1.08×2.0, or 2.16. Now let's say one of your competitors, Mike's Bikes, is bidding considerably higher than you, at $1.53, but only has a CTR of 1.4% (and thus, for this example, a QS of 1.4). Not bad, but still, their ad rank is only about 2.14, slightly less than yours. It's very close, but in terms of positioning on the page, your ad would rank slightly higher than Mike's in this particular case.

Now let's say a third advertiser, Dread's Treads, is vying for placement on this same phrase. Dread's comes in with a maximum bid of only 48 cents, but their ad is so effective, users click on it 4.7% of the time (we'll say their QS is 4.7). This advertiser outranks you both, with an AdRank score of 2.26, which puts Dread's above both yours and Mike's ads.

Finally, let's consider the efforts of a fourth, novice advertiser in this space, Spunky Spokes. First of all, Spunky's doesn't sell retail bicycle tires at all. They are a spoke wholesaler that only sells to other manufacturers. This advertiser also unthinkingly sets their maximum bid at $8.00, which is probably irresponsibly high. Spunky proceeds to write an ineffective ad that only gets clicked on 0.3% of the time. In spite of the much higher bid, Spunky would come in with an AdRank score of only 2.4. That's not the final score, though, because Spunky's "loose targeting" and poor relevance, according to Google's system predictions, invokes a downgrade of the QS in this case to only 2.15. This puts Spunky in third place, below you and Dread's, but still high enough to be ahead of the fourth-place contender, Mike's. To achieve that position, they had to bid $8, whereas you only bid $1.08. Table 5-1 summarizes the company standings. (I've added some also-rans, Spike's and HandleBarz, for added realism.)

Your Account's Historical Performance

Google's documentation notes that "your account's historical performance" is used in QS. This is not the same as individual keyword performance. In addition to the performance of an individual keyword, an entire account can establish a good or bad history across the board. Consider this another layer of the formula that comes to affect initial Quality Scores across the account. In short, a strong account history can help "green light" newly added keywords so that they begin

Advertiser	Max Bid	QS	Ad Rank Score	Downgraded for Poor Relevance?	Rank on Page
Dread's	0.48	4.7	2.26	No	1
Bunky's	1.08	2.0	2.16	No	2
Spunky	4.30	0.3	2.15	Yes	3
Mike's	1.53	1.4	2.14	No	4
Spike's	0.74	0.5	0.28	Yes	5
HandleBarz	0.20	1.4	0.15	Yes	6

TABLE 5-1   Rankings Based on the Google Formula

life with a high QS—a nice bonus to have. As the new keywords develop their own history, their own performance will factor more heavily into the determination of QS.

Note that historical performance doesn't include money spent or the age of the account. Google has stated that those would create "perverse incentives" and thus has not included these as factors.

Keyword Status

As I'll explain in the final section of this chapter, "Addendum: AdWords 2.7—The Latest Development in Quality-Based Bidding," Google has quite recently eliminated the notion of "minimum bids" applied to keywords. Formerly, under what I am calling AdWords 2.5 and 2.6, any keyword could be rendered "inactive for search" if your bid was lower than the required minimum. This minimum bid was calculated based on Quality Score (but confusingly, a separate Quality Score from the one used to determine rank). Now, the Quality Score affects ad rank, period, and does not generate any minimum bids.

What this means is that there is technically no such thing as an inactive keyword in your account. All keywords are theoretically eligible to have ads shown against them. There are several other nuances to this update that I will cover in the final section of this chapter.

Landing Page and Website Quality

Expanding from modest editorial initiatives that banned things like pop-ups, Google has taken an aggressive stance towards so-called landing page and website quality. Indicators of a poor user experience on your site will lead to a poor landing page Quality Score. Again, look to Google's official documentation for the full list of guidelines.[2] I'll highlight the keys here. For positive advice on landing pages and website design generally, see Chapter 11.

Annoying User Experiences

Annoying user experiences include things like pop-up ads and other intrusive elements. They also include frequent site outages, and, recently announced, slow page load times that can result from anything from a technical malfunction to an elaborate multimedia Flash-animated welcome. These things will result in lower Quality Scores.

Poor Relevance

Whether it's done to be deliberately misleading or through negligence, pages that are completely irrelevant to the ad shown are, not unexpectedly, likely to result in lower Quality Scores.

Deceptive Business Practices; Lack of Disclosure

"Data collection" is a category of business model that Google takes very seriously. Most major online businesses are in the business of collecting consumer information; Google certainly is. But you must uphold high disclosure standards and privacy policies in any situation where you're asking for users' private information. Google spokespersons like to give the example of the "come-on" ads that promise a free iPod that only comes after disclosing reams of personal data, inviting five friends, and entering a draw. Such offers are intrusive, deceptive, and annoying. And they rub off on Google. Google doesn't want to show ads like this.

Similarly, to a lesser extent, "email squeeze pages" that promote some sort of digital offer without fully disclosing the use of your private information, or the quality of the offer, are on the outs.

For those selling digital information, Google provides specific guidelines, such as a recommendation to offer a sample issue for free, so buyers understand the type of information they're getting.

Google is certainly wading deep into judgmental territory here, in spite of their sometime claim that the system is "all automated" based on "what users want." Perhaps users do react in certain ways to certain user experiences online, but there are whiffs of affect and caprice in the guidelines that refer to business models that typically run afoul of the Quality Score algorithm, including "get rich quick schemes," "travel aggregators," and "comparison shopping sites."[3] Types of sites that are *unequivocally* banned are: (certain types of) data collection sites, malware sites, and "arbitrage sites that are designed for the sole purpose of showing ads." Given that Google adds qualifications to nearly every definition, the "banning" isn't nearly as unequivocal as it seems. I'll explore this more in the case studies.

Content Is Separate from Search

Quality Score tallies are maintained separately for the content network. That means poor quality on content won't hurt your search campaigns. If you see low CTRs on your content clicks, do not worry too much. This also means that it might make some sense to run separate campaigns for content, in spite of the convenience of content bidding in today's system that partially mitigates the need for separate campaigns. Different ads, different bidding strategies, and even different landing pages might perform differently on content than they do on search.

Case Studies

I could probably regale you with hundreds of case studies of long-running accounts that have carried on pretty much as normal under AdWords 2.5, 2.6, and soon, 2.7. They had established CTR histories, no major website problems, and no major relevancy problems. Such case studies can't help new advertisers and exceptional advertisers work through the rough patches, though.

So the first case study below will walk you through the minefield of trying to manage a challenging campaign in a "gray area" business model that Google is holding up to greater scrutiny than normal.

The second case study will look (quite optimistically) at approaches and tactics we used to achieve high initial Quality Scores, some cases in new campaigns set up within accounts that had lain dormant for some time due to low Quality Scores or company reorganizations.

Getting in tune with the rhythm of how you can successfully go from having initially poor Quality Scores to OK and Great Quality Scores may be instructive. How some hard cases look in real life doesn't often resemble what life looks like in official Google documentation.

Big Hair and Mistaken Identity: Is Google Thin-Slicing You into the Doghouse?

First, at a high level, let's explore the experience faced by a sizeable minority of unlucky advertisers in a realm of "heightened security" intended to catch "bad guys."

The high-level issue we are dealing with in the case of many advertising campaigns is that you might have a sensitive business model that is vulnerable to Google's Quality Score policy whims. On one extreme, there are so-called "pure click arbitrage" sites that are sending AdWords clicks to pages of limited value whose sole purpose is to list more advertising links. Google dislikes the arbitrage model because users don't like the extra clicking. So they've actively tried to slap "poor landing page quality" scores on such sites. Did I just say slap? Yes, some in the affiliate marketing community call this the Google Slap. That's a tad melodramatic, even for me.

Somewhere in the middle, you have what I call high-class arbitrage. The reality is, many businesses make money from the difference between the costs of advertising on one medium and ad revenues that they make from the resulting visitors. Ever heard a local radio ad for a local publication that sells advertising? Well, that's ad arbitrage, isn't it? We're advertising to you, the potential business owner, with a pitch to advertise in our publication. The radio station takes the ad, because they're not fussy about the business model, as long as the advertiser pays. Many online media sites are buying other online media. Just because this sounds somewhat circular in the abstract doesn't mean it's necessarily wrong. We live in an attention economy, and media companies are often buyers of ad inventory from other media companies.

To the other extreme, you have content-rich, popular sites that may already do well in organic listings, and that Google would be pleased to allow full rein in the paid search program as well. The only reason this might not be called "arbitrage" is that the content-rich site chooses to monetize less with advertising. Or it's just such a lovable, content-rich, branded site that we and Google are less likely to question their motives for putting up an AdWords ad.

The situation is far from black and white. And many cases, like it or not, fall into that muddy middle ground.

The problem is, Google is using a combination of human assessments and algorithmic checks to screen for the most undesirable types of pages in their overall world view. The assessments can vary, but given the strength of the mandate from higher-ups at Google to weed out the "bad guys," it seems quite possible that low-level quality raters and higher-level editorial staff might get overzealous in their assessments of a given site, to the point of tunnel-vision prejudice when those biases are baked into an algorithm. Hey, snap-judgment stereotyping happens to the police—is Google immune?

In *Blink: The Power of Thinking Without Thinking*, Malcolm Gladwell provides a graphic case study of an innocent man gunned down by New York police, largely based on assumptions coupled with rapid "thin-slicing" observation as opposed to deeper observation.[4] Gladwell fans also know that he provides further background of a personal nature on his blog. Gladwell, a light-skinned African-American, describes his experience with police prejudice based on his physical appearance: it began happening after he grew out his hair. As he strode along 14th Street in Manhattan, police mistook him for a rapist who was in fact "much taller, and much heavier, and about fifteen years younger," continuing the interrogation for twenty minutes.[5]

Snap judgments based on limited data are common. Using heuristic formulas to cut diagnosis times in life-or-death medical scenarios, for example, has been shown to save lives. Even without prearranged formulas, experienced human brains seem to have a tendency to make snap decisions based on limited cues. Gladwell calls this process "thin-slicing."

In police work, the debate may rage on about the need for thin-slicing in certain situations, because police are often put in life-and-death decision-making situations chasing suspects in the dark. In broad daylight on a crowded street, the case is much weaker. And in non-life-threatening cases where we're deciding whether a web page is "evil," surely we owe it to business owners to ensure that the punishment for "looking like the bad guys," if any is warranted at all, fits the crime. On the whole, *Blink* is about encouraging decision-makers to distinguish their good rapid cognition (it exists) from bad rapid cognition. Now that Google has so much to say about ad quality and website quality, it has created a similar challenge for itself.

There are plenty of potentially perverse effects of botching the thin-slicing process. For example, what if the majority of new AdWords accounts are started up by amateurs or large-scale system abusers? If Google is looking at past user response data largely based on the fumbling efforts of marketers who don't yet understand how to generate quality user experiences, they might be inclined to disrespect savvier marketers' efforts, pulling them aside and interrogating them for something as trivial as the proverbial Gladwellian big hair.

Case Study 1: Media Company, Slow "Quality Score Digout" Process

To protect client anonymity, I'll refer in a "composite sketch" to a couple of companies we worked for who wound up with similar trajectories in their Quality Score patterns. Both were media companies attempting to drive traffic to local search or news content sites. So, for example, they might have information on local night spots, and wanted to drive traffic to their local entertainment listings and reviews section. In other cases they might simply have classified listings and a few reviews, for a business category like accounting. To alert users to the quality of their listings, they might still buy accounting-related words in AdWords.

For the sake of this case study, let's assume the media company buying AdWords lies somewhere in between a "pure click arbitrage" model and a "beloved content site" model. In other words, they would probably qualify as "high-class arbitrage." As such, either Google's algorithms or human raters, or both, may lean towards a suspicious take on the quality of the landing page. This leads to low initial Quality Scores.

Phase 1: Very Poor Quality Scores

In this phase, we found that many keywords were in Poor Quality Score territory. Only a few keywords were working well. We continued building out the account.

Phase 2: Following Google Advice

I assumed that Google (again, either algorithmically or in human terms) had something against the site because the site was showing a fair number of ads and didn't yet have much content. Without knowing the company's intentions to build more content and user interaction, Google's assessment might stay poor. I conveyed the full story to a Google rep, explaining that the company had a number of plans to build rich local content. To some extent, this was sticking my neck out for the client, because what if they never followed through on that claim? Had I attempted to make this case for a company like TrueLocal, for example (one of the most notorious "evils" in Google's anti-arbitrage sweep), I would have been seen walking around with a Pinocchio nose for years to come.

Our Google rep stayed pretty close to boilerplate "increase your relevancy" advice. For example, I was told to take some of the specific ad groups and make them even more granular. To improve on an ad group about Greek restaurants (selecting this group was perhaps an in-joke, as the Googler's family happens to own a Greek restaurant), I was instructed to add keywords about souvlaki or subtypes of Greek food. Clearly, this is ridiculous. No one needs to build a campaign that granularly. But to their credit, Google's frontline reps don't fully know how to manipulate that Quality Score algorithm much better than you or I do—all they can do is cautiously give stock advice.

Another thing they, or higher-ups, can do, though, is to manually tweak site and landing page Quality Scores. You are never told that this is happening.

In this case, I instructed my client to show as much goodwill as possible, and to improve the user experience of their site by removing some of the ad units and working to improve page load times. I believe this had the dual effect of showing Google's algorithms that the user experience was improving on this site, and showing both the algorithm and human raters that this site was not just all about the worst type of click arbitrage.

I made a few of Google's recommended changes—adding new ad experiments, more granular phrases, and so on. But I'm not at all convinced that in this case my changes had any major independent impact.

What happened, I believe, is that someone at Google reviewed the account and made enough of an adjustment to the landing page Quality Scores that we would have the opportunity to get more of our ads live, so we could begin seeing some results.

Within three or four days, Quality Scores improved; many were still poor, but the account was moving in the right direction. A week after that, they moved again. Here, I believe some combination of initially positive CTR and user behavior data (which would have been impossible to collect had someone at Google not manually tweaked the QS enough for us to at least show our ads some of the time), and some Invisible Hand pulling some Quality Score levers at Google's end, allowed this account to crawl out of the Very Poor Quality black hole.

Phase 3: Data + Adjustments + Manual Help = Great Quality?

Still, our average CPC remained high for another 3–4 weeks. But as the account's momentum built, as we tested and adjusted our campaigns, and as positive CTR and user behavior data were gathered, account-wide and campaign-specific data were positive enough that another significant move happened to the Quality Scores on this account. Eventually, we tended towards "Great"

Quality Scores on the majority of keywords in the account, allowing us to bid low enough to get the average CPC below 30 cents, in decent ad positions.

This pattern isn't the only one you'll see, but it's one we've seen repeated on these types of accounts. Along with lobbying and best practices, time must elapse to allow Google's algorithms to give you credit for building a strong account history.

We've seen enough of this pattern to realize that we can risk only so much of our political capital as an agency in going to bat for a client who lies in that murky middle ground of high-class arbitrage. What if we tell one story about a client's intentions, and it turns out to be untrue? So I'm not inclined to just pass along a new client's version of events to Google—I'm also going to do my own investigating, unfortunately, much the way legal counsel interrogates his client before defending him. We'll support those who have strong brands and those who are telling the truth, but we have to be extra cautious about being "used" by bad guys who just want us to talk Google into taking them seriously.

To an unknown extent, the judgment of website and landing page quality is driven by mysterious human assessments (assisted by automation). As marketers, we'd rather be focusing on doing a better job of writing copy, targeting customers, and improving the user experience on websites, than dancing around, trading euphemisms with Google account reps. But if the shoe fits.

The next mini-case-study is intended to make the case for meticulous account setup, and to show that paying attention to relevancy and campaign organization details in the setup phase does, indeed, matter to initial Quality Scores.

Case Study 2: HomeStars, Tighter Targeting and Speculation on Website Quality Issues

Keep in mind the informational value of the fact that you can see your keyword quality status instantly upon setting up ad groups (all you have to do is Customize Columns when viewing under the Keywords tab at the ad group level). Chalk another one up for the paid search laboratory. When the scores come back "Great," especially for an unusual, newer, nonretail type site, I figure there must be something positive to learn.

This case study is about HomeStars.com, a website that features consumer reviews of home improvement companies. (Disclosure: I began as an advisor to the company and remain a shareholder.)

I finally got budget clearance to resume building AdWords traffic for HomeStars. Because I own a piece of the company, I have some incentive to get in there and build it myself. I've seen so many initially Poor Quality Scores for a variety of accounts in the past few months, I decided to be as careful as possible and execute the type of advice I so blithely give to others but all too rarely have the chance to execute for myself.

Step one was to have a superior landing page strategy. The HomeStars site lends itself to very targeted pages in a coherent information architecture. There is meaty content on these pages and they are well labeled. The key would be to send visitors to highly granular landing pages only. For example, an ad for "Boston Architects" for searchers looking for **Boston Architects** would send users to a page containing actual consumer reviews of Boston architects—a fixed category on the site with a fixed, keyword-rich URL.

Step two was to hand-build the ads, including granular topical keywords in title and body copy, as well as some geo-specific cues that matched up with the custom metropolitan-area geotargeting I'd set up with the campaign.

Step three was key: start with highly targeted, commercially relevant keywords. If there's one thing I know, it's that setting up really broad words, or tossing in all the keywords suggested by a keyword tool, is a great way to develop low quality in a hurry, even if you don't get slapped with it at first. Why not tighten down and just try to cherry-pick visitors who are going to be the most targeted ones for these landing pages? Among other things, this would raise conversion rates to desired actions and annoy fewer people. What's interesting here is that these are the visitors who might click and use your site in such a way as to build up strong Quality Scores for you over time; but somehow Google is getting better at predicting just this even when there is no data. In this case, I might have used a very short list of keywords like **architects** or **architectural firms**. I might have bid on **boston architects** as well, though it wouldn't have been strictly necessary, as I was targeting the Boston area with this campaign.

These may seem like obvious points. Putting account history aside (this one was so-so from past efforts), why did I see "Great" for so many keywords and for a brand-new campaign, when so many similar campaigns start out in the high end of OK, trending towards Poor? There must be a few things about the website that AdsBot likes.

AdsBot?

As you set up ad groups, a jaunty set of multicolored balls dances across your screen as you're informed, "We want to be sure your website is functional when a user clicks your ad. We're also making sure your ad text complies with our Editorial Guidelines. This can take several seconds. You'll be taken to the next page when we're done."

Making sure the site is up? Checking the ad text for violations? Twelve seconds?

What else is AdsBot doing, do you suppose? In terms of landing page and website quality guidelines, the bot could be doing anything from checking to see if there are specific signals of evil on the landing page, to checking for evidence of broader evil being done by your company or website(s). AdsBot doesn't say. Like Googlebot, the organic search spider, AdsBot reserves the right to return to your site frequently.

One thing AdsBot now assesses, according to Google's documentation, is landing page load times. Slow-loading pages or pages with various redirects and intrusive advertising formats provide a poor user experience, so Google is now considering this in landing page QS.

In this example, Google gave my keywords mostly Great initial quality assessments. Here are a few theories as to why. Google may have data about the website as a whole that indicates real user satisfaction, or some kind of vibrant community. That could include things like bounce rates or time spent on the site. HomeStars has strong stats, particularly in terms of the average number of pages viewed per user.

AdsBot, or Google in general, might also find the semantic meaning of our Boston Architects landing page understandable in the context of a good site architecture: more than just body copy, the site drills down nicely to the landing page in question, with good quality headings, title tags, well-formed keyword-rich URLs, and breadcrumb navigation.[6] In other words: common sense dictates that taking a reasonable approach to creating your site layout and landing pages is all you have to do; some attention to logical hierarchies and keyword-based labeling cues is definitely worth it from a user experience and conversion rate standpoint regardless of the search ranking algorithm *du jour*. I go into user experience issues in more depth in Chapter 11.

No red flags were found to derail this happy picture AdsBot initially saw. For example, there aren't tons of text link ads on the site, so the goal isn't pure arbitrage. We haven't registered a bunch of domains, hoping to map out some kind of ill-conceived "cookie-cutter campaign" strategy, and our company information is verifiable in our domain record. We aren't part of any kind of "link farm." (That's just the initial "cut" at quality. The data that builds up from there, such as low CTR, or editorial interventions, could sink your Quality Score like a stone.)

Five Key Takeaways

There are at least five takeaways from this case study.

First, landing page and website quality are increasingly important.

Second, related to the first point, there is increasing evidence that Google engineers think about similar relevance issues in paid search as they do on the organic side. One example in this case study was the strong effort we put into information architecture (which included keyword-rich page titles, headings, and well-formed URLs) for the HomeStars site. This effort seems partly responsible for the high initial QS.

Third, the principles of tight targeting and granular campaign organization are borne out by this success story.

Fourth, the little extras in terms of segmentation and granularity—in this case, targeting particular local areas with campaigns that mention the city in the ad copy and on the landing page—seem to be advantageous.

Finally, all of the above points to the value of a cautious, two-stage account buildout process. Building loosely at first and then tightening up later is bound to give you poor account history that will reflect on your whole effort going forward. A strong, tightly relevant campaign will, by contrast, give you the firm foundation that will allow you to gradually search for ways to expand your ad distribution without incurring a whole lot of extra cost.

Unfortunately, as more and more complexity is added all the time (as you'll see from the next section, the eleventh-hour "Addendum"), I feel less confident in boldly offering a universal strategy. Now more than ever, every account is different. Google's concern with tight targeting and CTR just won't leave us alone, it seems, so I worry that the final phase of broadening an account's reach risks creating a "backslide" effect, removing the positive benefit of a strong established account-wide quality. If we are to take Google at their word, accounts that attempt to boost total profit by expanding into broader keyword areas and tangentially targeted keywords will potentially pay a premium across the entire account, not just on the broad areas. In light of this, it's disingenuous for Google to claim they are not raising prices by constantly coming up with new ways to penalize loose targeting. By forcing narrower targeting on us, Google appears to be limiting our remaining options for volume expansion; certainly, an obvious avenue must include increasing bids. That said, I'll try to explore the non-bid-related expansion options in Chapter 9.

Then again, given the opacity of the latest version of the AdWords Quality Score system, it is potentially the case that established accounts that attempt to "get broader" will not find poor quality evaluations bleeding unduly into the robustly performing parts of the account. This would be the ideal scenario: a system that determined Quality Scores and auction placement in real time, with precise reference to recent performance, and the specifics of the exact query and ad in question, without weighting unrelated account-wide performance too heavily. That way, parts of an account that are built meticulously can coincide with more experimental parts of an account, so that efforts to test, experiment, and expand do not trash the Quality Scores of the established parts.

It's my hope that the new version of Quality Score does attempt to reach this ideal, but it's not entirely clear at this stage. I describe this latest version in the following, final section.

Addendum: AdWords 2.7—The Latest Development in Quality-Based Bidding

In late August 2008, Google announced more sweeping changes to the Quality Score system. The addition of landing page and site quality to the mix had been enough to prompt a new informal "version number" in my count—2.6. I'll call the latest formula, which eliminates fixed minimum bids in favor of a new way of calculating and reporting on Quality Score, AdWords 2.7. It's a significant change, but perhaps not a fundamental one. Some of it is cosmetic, and some of it actually improves transparency. But because of the added power of the dynamic, real-time calculations, most lay observers are saying it feels like the system is even more opaque now, because it is so hard to describe in a few words.[7]

By my reckoning, there are four main elements of this new approach:

- ▪ Fixed minimum bids are gone
- ▪ Keywords are never, technically, inactive
- ▪ "First-page bid" is offered as a data point
- ▪ Quality Score detail remains intact

I'll discuss each of these elements in turn next, and then give you my thoughts about the overall effect of this new approach.

Fixed Minimum Bids Are Gone, Because Quality Score Is Now Calculated in Real Time per Query

The nub of the change—and probably its main motivating factor—is to make Quality Score calculations more precise. When you think about it, a broad-matched keyword can accumulate a global Quality Score based on all the past data relating to it, but should that same fixed evaluation apply to your ad's placement on a variety of different search queries that might trigger your ad, in a variety of geographic locales, in different situations? Not necessarily. For example, if you run the broad match for the keyword **medical jobs**, but your ad and landing page are mostly for part-time medical jobs, some specific queries triggered by that broad match (say, an expanded broad match that shows your ad against the query **casual hospital work**) might warrant a particularly high "real time" Quality Score for your keyword. And other queries would be less closely related to your offer or ad, and Google would be warranted in assigning a lower score and showing your ad farther down the page.

It's difficult to speculate whether there were many serious problems with inaccurate Quality Scores in specific instances in the past, or whether this is just Google pursuing a level of precision that would elude most comparable companies.

In any case, once again, Quality Scores are now calculated in real time per query, so Google has had to eliminate any notion of a static, global minimum bid applying to the keyword.

This potentially creates a cascade of issues and strategic implications. First, it puts additional, nearly chaotic, pressure on vendors of third-party bid management solutions. It will require increasingly sophisticated paid search bid management software to bid accurately in each real-time auction, aiming at the maximum efficiency these vendors purport to achieve in exchange for a significant management fee. Few will be up to it. Solutions of middling sophistication may be hardest hit, because they will not be able to invest the resources to adapt to Google's subtle formula, yet their fee cuts significantly into the advertiser's profit margins and makes it less cost-effective to hire qualified human analysts. In the meantime, the strategic benefit of using a less-invasive, alert-based approach to bid management that makes less-frequent bid changes and gives the human analyst more control remains intact as ever under the new system. Seasoned human analysts will also do fine under the new system. Google, in a sense, is taking some of those bidding decisions out of your hands—and out of the hands of third-party systems not privy to the opaque real-time Quality Score calculations. You'll need to know a general level that is appropriate to your keyword, but your ad positions could be even more volatile than before from query to query. A bid management tool wouldn't know whether to bump that bid up, down, or tie itself in a knot and take a leap off a cliff at Big Sur. Like a human analyst, it might know enough to bid generally in the right area, keeping the campaign more or less on track to a target cost per action.

As a corollary to this first change (as I'll explain in the next section), keywords can never be marked inactive for search.

Keywords Are Never, Technically, Inactive

Since no fixed minimum bid level is reported for keywords now, even keywords with low Quality Scores won't be marked inactive for search. You might conclude from this that Google is content to give your keyword very low ad positions if your keyword is very low quality—thus giving you a fighting chance to at least get some traffic. To some extent, yes, but it's also the case that Google retains a "bid requirement" that will be in force in real-time calculations. Come in below the bid requirement, and you don't show up—in any ad position. In other words, you can be inactive for search instantly at the time of the query—just not across the board for that keyword. In some penal systems, the parole board maintains a "faint hope clause," allowing any criminal, no matter how heinous, to apply (and be rejected for) parole. For very low-quality keywords, this system is a little like that. In part, it probably means that Google now has enough computing capacity to once again allow certain rogue advertisers to clog the system with inane experiments. Rather than definitively deactivating them, Google lets them hang around and be inactive for nearly every actual query. For the hair-raising explanation, check out "Is there a bid requirement to enter the ad auction?" in the AdWords Help Center.

"First-Page Bid" Offered as a Data Point

This one is actually less significant than it seems. The information supplied by the minimum bids—especially the very low ones like 2 cents, 5 cents, etc.—was pretty minimal. If most advertisers were over the threshold, that piece of data told you generally that your quality was high, but gave you no inkling of what bid amount would be required to get on the first page of search results, typically. So, Google now provides first page bid information. It is only an estimate but may be helpful for advertisers wishing to gauge the real impact of the combination of their own Quality Scores and the competitiveness and bid levels in the auction.

Quality Score Detail Intact

The notations of Poor, OK, and Great will not only be kept, but Google will provide additional information in the form of a scale of 1 to 10. You'll need to customize columns or run reports, as outlined in the AdWords Help Center, to look at this information. As I've discussed, Quality Score for the keyword in a particular context is calculated at the time of the query. So the reported scores are aggregates.

Glass-Half-Full Reaction: New Opportunities

Although the new system undoubtedly poses unforeseen challenges, it's possible that old blind alleys may be illuminated once more. Google has indicated in the past that certain classes of keywords were considered less relevant, and would likely clock in with poor Quality Scores, especially in new accounts. Such keywords included trademark and brand terms, famous people's names, and unusual or emergent keywords that Google has little data on. It's quite possible that you may now show up on such keywords situationally, given the new real-time calculations that replace the old "fixed minimum bid" regime. In addition, and perhaps even more significantly, you won't be knocked out of the auction entirely if you have a low-CTR broad match (especially one-word broad match) such as **jobs** in your account. Instead of being forced into inactive for search status by a high minimum bid (of, say, $5.00), you might show up from time to time, where you're deemed relevant. This might also take the pressure off you to create long lists of negative keywords, but this is pure speculation at this point.

What Hasn't Changed: Strategy

You can breathe a huge sigh of relief that, at least, the strategic lessons outlined in the earlier section "Five Key Takeaways" have not changed. Although often shaken by Google's experimentation and secrecy, for us as marketers with bottom-line concerns, the foundations of our understanding of targeting and testing for success have not crumbled. But there are storm clouds and distant thunderclaps on the horizon: a background rumbling noise that Google feels that it would be better than you at managing your campaign. Increasingly, in help files and elsewhere, Google recommends that you "work on improving your Quality Score through account optimization." Account optimization means any number of things: it might mean a few guidelines in a help file; it might mean taking principles and applying them on your own initiative, with your own testing protocols;

or it could come to mean a kind of orthodox hand-holding provided in rote fashion by a Googler who has been trained to believe he knows what's best for you. Let's hope it isn't the latter.

I firmly believe that it is our job—your job, as a company owner or professional, or my job, as a professional in an agency that represents the best interests of clients—to take needed steps to optimize an account. The Quality Score formula itself sends subtle messages that we are not up to that task; its complexity and opacity all but ensure that only a minority of us will be able to get the most out of the system. Clearly, there is a significant role for Google's expertise in helping guide advertiser strategy and in helping befuddled advertisers overcome roadblocks. But how much is too much? Now, more than ever, you need a strong in-house professional or third-party agency to take a firm hold of your account, and to work diplomatically but firmly with Google. Weak account management may lead to a sort of humiliating exercise in going cap in hand to Google, practically begging them to meddle in your advertising and business strategy. Even the strongest and best of us sometimes find ourselves overly dependent on Google for explanations for peaks and valleys in performance and volume. Good luck—and hire well.

Endnotes

1. This chapter contains considerable technical advice and technical detail. Some, to be sure, is conjecture, but quite a bit of it is based on hard-won consensus among search marketers trading information and campaign data. In particular, I'd like to thank Nick Fox, Google's Director of Product Development for Ads Quality. Nick has been accessible for many briefings and follow-up interviews and has publicly responded to many detailed advertiser questions at search marketing industry conferences. Not least, Nick made himself available for 11th-hour detailed Q&A about the AdWords 2.7 changes, on August 26, 2008. Other Google spokespersons such as Frederick Vallaeys have also provided useful insight. I've followed Quality-Based Bidding closely since inception. Any mistakes of analysis remain mine.

2. Google AdWords Help Center, Landing Page and Site Quality Guidelines, https://adwords.google.com/support/bin/answer.py?answer=46675&hl=en.

3. On the official AdWords blog, Google provides insight into business models that have often run afoul of the Quality Score algorithm. See "Websites that May Merit a Low Landing Page Quality Score," *Inside AdWords*, September 18, 2007, archived at http://adwords.blogspot.com/2007/09/websites-that-may-merit-low-landing.html. For my discussion, see "AdWords Quality Score: Can Your Business Model Be Banned?" *Search Engine Land*, September 25, 2007, archived at http://searchengineland.com/070925-140955.php.

4. Malcolm Gladwell, *Blink: The Power of Thinking Without Thinking* (Little, Brown and Company, 2005).

5. See www.gladwell.com/blink/.

6. Breadcrumb navigation is a visual layout format that helps users recognize where they are in a site hierarchy. A designer will use text cues to point to category levels. An example of breadcrumb navigation would look like this: Home > Cities > Cleveland, OH > Architects. This subtly informs users they could navigate up to the general Cleveland page to discover other categories for the city, and that they are currently "three levels in" from the home page in the (arbitrary) logical category hierarchy of the website.

7. See Trevor Claiborne, "Quality Score Improvements," Inside AdWords blog, August 23, 2008. Archived at http://adwords.blogspot.com/2008/08/quality-score-improvements. html. See also the detailed Frequently Asked Questions file referenced in that post, for a sense of just how much detail Google has felt it necessary to share to explain this change.

Chapter 6

Big-Picture Planning and Making the Case to the Boss

Before you launch your online marketing campaign, you'll need to make a number of strategic decisions. In earlier chapters I covered the pragmatic aspects of launching a campaign, since that's what most marketers are most interested in. However, if your job is as much political as it is operational, or if you're an executive trying to weigh the AdWords initiative among competing priorities, you'll want to pay particular attention to this chapter.

How Valuable Is Search Engine Marketing to Your Business?

First, you'll want to satisfy yourself that search engine marketing (SEM) in general, of which Google AdWords advertising is a subset, is a smart investment of your marketing dollars. I've attempted to set the stage for such decision making in Chapters 1 and 2. You might also find useful supporting materials at the website of an industry group called SEMPO (Search Engine Marketing Professional Organization)—www.sempo.org.

Studies by the Interactive Advertising Bureau (IAB) point to the effectiveness of search engine marketing. For example, an IAB-commissioned study performed by Nielsen/NetRatings in 2004 showed strong brand recall for companies who attained listings at or near the top of a search results page.[1] An IAB-commissioned study performed in 2006 by comScore Networks showed strong performance for local search listings and online classifieds for blue-chip advertisers like CareerBuilder, Ford, and others. Ford Rental Car realized a 7.8 ROI (measured as the ratio of generated revenue to advertising expense) on local search ads, with about 40% of those conversions taking place offline and 60% taking place online.[2]

Recently, Yahoo released a study about the role of Internet research in consumers' "road to purchase"—this is often nicknamed the "Long and Winding Road Study."[3] No one customer profile makes sense, but several typical scenarios have strong empirical support. In particular, Yahoo believes that sustained exposure in search results, both paid and unpaid, builds brand equity and recall.

Thinking through apparent counter-examples in my own buying habits, ironically, ultimately strengthens my conviction that gaining mindshare through search presence is an underrated activity. As a business-to-business buyer of computer equipment (obviously, an extremely popular monthly activity for many business owners), I rely on a small number of vendors with whom I've developed a trusting relationship. One of these is Tiger Direct (in Canada, TigerDirect.ca). When they don't have an item in stock (it happens), there are a couple of others I use as backups. In the case of Tiger Direct, I might easily conclude that since I have so much loyalty to them, and directly navigate to their site of my own accord or based on reminders from their weekly special emails, search plays no role in my decision-making. But the real answer is quite the opposite! In the longer period of time that it took my vendor preference to congeal, a continual presence in search listings was part of what influenced me to give Tiger Direct a try. And because I developed that long-term business relationship with them, the lifetime value of running those search ads is probably a lot higher than even the most optimistic forecasts would project, if an analyst were forecasting too conservatively based only on measurable direct-marketing results.

Even if you stick to measurable direct marketing results, top management should have plenty of reasons today to test AdWords. Check out what Seth Godin, author of *Free Prize Inside!: The Next Big Marketing Idea* (Portfolio, 2004),[4] had to say back on July 1, 2004 on his blog. He noted that the South Beach Diet spends "more than $1 million per year on online promotion (keywords, etc.)." Godin calls this "marketing that pays for itself... no magic, no superstition. Just planning and measurement and hard work." (That was part of Godin's critique of unscrupulous search engine optimization firms who want you to believe that success is easy if you can only luck into a #1 search ranking on Google.[5] Don't let it be about luck.)

In July 2004, MarketingSherpa wrote a case study of Edmunds.com, the automotive information site. After having some success with optimizing the site for free referral traffic, but reaching the limits of that strategy, Edmunds now spends nearly $500,000 per month on keyword advertising with Google and Yahoo Search Marketing, employing full-time in-house staff to manage the campaigns. This initiative made a multimillion-dollar impact on Edmunds' business, providing the catalyst for recent rapid growth.

Once you're satisfied that SEM is right for you, and Google is your preferred venue, the next step is to determine what percentage of your search engine marketing budget should be dedicated to AdWords. Obviously, this proportion may vary depending on the opportunities you can discover in other forms of paid search, such as Yahoo Search Marketing, Microsoft adCenter, Ask.com, Business.com, and Miva. Because opportunities for keyword-based advertising are often fairly scarce, I've found that allocating 70% or more of your search marketing budget to AdWords is quite realistic. Google maintains over 65% search market share in many markets, remember, and their ad program is the most developed. Many advertisers devote upwards of 80% of their paid search budget to AdWords.

Strange as it sounds, you may find it difficult to spend heavily on AdWords in the early going. Unlike the expensive TV and print ads that many advertisers are accustomed to buying, large chunks of AdWords exposure can't be bought in advance for a predetermined price. Those large media buys are the reason many larger companies have bloated advertising budgets. They know advertising works, and they know that it's more likely to work (at least from a top-line, market-share-maintaining perspective) if they throw more money at the problem. Putting together a media buy in such scenarios (either by outsourcing the job to an agency or negotiating a few large buys themselves) does a terrific job of "spending the budget."

This entrenched mindset is so strong in the agency world that Google has had to develop a feature in AdWords called Budget Optimizer. At the risk of putting words in Google's mouth, my take on this feature is that if you have a high monthly budget, this tool will do things like raise bids, seek out more content-targeting inventory, and broaden your broad matches, to "help" you spend more on less-targeted ads. Here's an excerpt from a recent version of Google's help from the AdWords Help Center, on the Budget Optimizer feature. After explaining roughly what the tool does, Google warns: "Please note that we don't recommend the Budget Optimizer for advertisers focused on measuring conversions or values of ad clicks." Yikes!

The big media buy is a no-surprises method that may keep everyone in a company happy because there are few internal planning questions left unanswered, except for the most important one, of course: "How can we measure and improve on the profitability of our ad campaigns?"

The rest of this chapter will serve as a reminder that the planning process for a Google AdWords campaign is different from what many companies are accustomed to. But the risk of missing your "targets" is worth taking because the *material* risk is so minimal, and the potential upside is attractive: you may discover a new, high-ROI channel.

Many companies today need little convincing to embark on the uncertain path of experimenting with AdWords. The fact that their competitors are already highly visible in that space is enough to spur them to action. If anything, I'm finding that marketing managers who are asked to consider an AdWords campaign may handcuff themselves unnecessarily because they overestimate the career risk of dramatically "underspending" the budget at first. No, the process won't be predictable, and at first you may not be able to give your boss those simple answers she might seem to want. But consider that many companies today are more entrepreneurial than ever before, and senior management might actually reward those who take chances, make mistakes, and champion unorthodox paths to growth.

Strategies for Small vs. Large Companies: How Different Are They?

There needn't be a radical difference in the way an AdWords campaign is developed just because a business is particularly small or particularly large. Campaigns tend to run on a basic premise that calls for gaining one customer at a time, one search at a time. Campaigns will vary quite a bit in terms of breadth and ad spend, but I see more similarities than differences in the general approaches taken.

Large companies will want to consider budgeting for more sophisticated web analytics software, consulting help from an outside agency, additional staff time or full-time hires, bid management software where appropriate, and of course, more money for clicks.

Furthermore, additional time can be spent on usability testing, site development, ad testing, landing page tests, and so on. But the remarkable thing is that companies of all shapes and sizes are doing all of these things in much the same way, albeit at different budget levels.

Given that a typical AdWords sales process takes the user from a brief text listing to a tailored landing page (reminiscent of the ultrasimplistic "Pachinko machine" described by Seth Godin,[6] which imagines the Web as the ultimate, super-simplified direct marketing channel), there is no reason why a smaller company can't make a big impact with limited dollars. Indeed, one reason that larger companies sometimes agonize so long over the decision to move forward with a pay-per-click campaign is that it can be so inexpensive and accessible as to seem insignificant. Surely there must be more to it than this! It's simple in some ways, but deceptively complex in its number of moving parts. But nope, there isn't "more to it" in the sense of a need for massive overheads and massive amounts of wasted spend that you need to justify after the fact with vague "lift" metrics.

One thing large companies will need to do is sort out who is responsible for what. Multiple stakeholders and long meetings are the norm in large companies, but this should be avoided wherever possible. Turnaround time is paramount. Somebody must be given the flexibility and authority to test and tweak as steadily as possible. This perhaps explains why more large companies are willing to pay substantial salaries to senior search marketing experts to manage affairs in-house rather than hiring junior trainees whose decisions must be second-guessed. Failing that, outsourcing the job to an integrated, multitalented marketing agency that can implement and understand various elements of the campaign strategy (business analysis, copywriting, keyword discovery, tracking, landing page design, and so on) will help to avoid slowdowns that inevitably crop up in situations where responsibility for project results is made too diffuse. You're not going to hand over your whole company to a third party, of course, but giving that third party more discretion and more freedom to achieve results is one way of signaling that the AdWords campaign is a high priority. Increasing the budget is another way.

Large companies with centralized IT systems or laborious processes of gaining approval for the release of website stats will also need to consider streamlining their procedures. In some cases, it's easier to set up a separate website for the AdWords campaign to allow direct supervision of the project by those who understand the need for quick response and hands-on control of landing page copy, tracking codes, and so forth. One of my clients, an international bank that offers an international debit card, runs the AdWords campaign through a separate site called TheirCompanyDemo.com (fictitious name, obviously). This makes it easier to deal with shifting priorities in marketing the product without undue involvement from globally dispersed managers. At the same time, the CEO can remain quite hands-on in his oversight of the campaign results as implemented by the marketing managers and the outside agency.

Another difference with large companies is that they can afford to "lose money" (or at least to bid so high as to seem to be losing money) on a campaign. By locking down exposure in a key channel, you can keep competitors out of that channel. Bidding high enough to be #1 or #2 on the page for popular search queries might be a high priority for a large company, whereas it could be suicide for a small company. Expedia isn't just selling "flights to Jamaica," they're also selling "not the competition." When McDonald's puts a franchise in a key location next to the service station on the turnpike, they're not only selling burgers, they're making sure the other guys aren't selling them. And Expedia is (or should be) taking up valuable screen real estate that it can afford to buy, and that keeps them in the forefront of the consumer's mind. Pursuing the Expedia example of a query for **cheap Jamaica flights**, actually, I see several smaller competitors outbidding Expedia. That could mean that specialists in cheap Caribbean vacations are actually able to justify bidding higher because of their specialized focus. Alternatively, though, it could signal a complacency on Expedia's part; underbidding relative to the hidden value that might lie in pushing upstarts down the page. Or it might mean the smaller companies are engaged in kamikaze bidding in an attempt to gain a toehold in a lucrative space, and will soon fall out of sight.

If your company is particularly small, in spite of the increasing cost of keywords, AdWords is going to be a relatively comfortable environment for you because you can pause it anytime you don't like the way it's performing. You can monitor results on a daily or even hourly basis, if you want. I offer a couple of key pieces of advice to small companies. First, understand your limitations. You won't have the resources to hire staff to monitor and adjust everything constantly. And while you might already be in the habit of saying, "I'll do it myself," you won't be able to keep up that pace forever. So if you plan to do it yourself, be kind to yourself, and plan to do less. A simpler approach to campaign management and tracking is better than a convoluted one. Simpler does not just mean abdicating the role of campaign manager to some automated software.

To those special small business owners who really do have the energy and curiosity to spend hours every week poring over every detail of their campaign, I advise them to use those admirable energy levels to better advantage by not allowing themselves to become full-time AdWords junkies. Eventually, you'll burn out. Even if you don't, a fanatical obsession with squeezing every last ounce of productivity out of your campaign could be a symptom that you have more important work to do in other, more fundamental areas. It could mean you're in a dying industry, or need to change your overall marketing strategy. In terms of the amount of time you budget to spend working with AdWords for your small business, then, be realistic from the start. Work on your business, for heaven's sake, not just your AdWords campaign. If you want to play, crack out a nice game of online chess or fire up some tunes and Return to Castle Wolfenstein on your computer. Really, AdWords can be fun, but it isn't a game! Don't use AdWords obsession as an excuse not to visit your mother or water your plants. End of lecture.

What about Affiliate Marketing?

At the small end of the small-business spectrum is the aspiring affiliate marketer. This is someone who joins a parent company's affiliate program, receives custom linking codes that are used to credit them with sales, and then goes out and finds customers for the parent company. I've no doubt that for a clever minority, the math can work—attract targeted clicks by placing AdWords ads and hope enough of them convert to a sale to make you a profit. Just don't ask me for tips. If I could tell you how to turn a passive profit in your home in your spare time, then why wouldn't I set up all those affiliate codes and keywords myself, shut down my computer, and take a nap?[7]

Certainly, if you already have a following on your website or newsletter, affiliate sales can be a nice bit of residual income. Think about how many folks attach affiliate codes when they recommend a book that's available for sale on Amazon.com, for example, as part of the Amazon Associates Program. I happen to love various software programs and online services, such as Basecamp from 37signals, and if I love them enough, I'll recommend them and take a little percentage of the action by joining their affiliate program (too bad I can't stick that code in this sentence). Why not? I'm not down on affiliate income in general, but I don't think much of the idea of individuals with limited business experience trying to turn an easy profit by playing affiliate roulette with no website at all by buying AdWords clicks and sending them directly to the parent company's site. Some such "marketers" have complained to me that my writings aren't "advanced" enough for them—they're looking for the latest get-rich-quick mumbo-jumbo, I guess. This confirms for me that many "top dogs" in the multilevel marketing area want you to believe that black is white and up is down.

B2B, Retail, Independent Professional, or Informational—What Is Your Business Model?

Campaigns are often run very differently depending on whether they're niche-focused business-to-business (B2B) or retail-focused business-to-consumer (B2C). A third category is the independent professional firm, which may fall on either side of the B2B/B2C divide, but which most often conducts its campaign and customer acquisition effort as if it were B2B. A fourth category is information publishing. There are many business models and they all have their quirks. The following discussion is an overview of a few things to watch for.

Business-to-Business

Business-to-business campaigns are some of the most profitable types of Google AdWords campaigns. The targeting is so tight, you won't often waste a lot of clicks. A key hurdle, both real and psychological, is the limited feedback you receive as compared with a B2C campaign. With "lumpy" sales patterns often based on high-ticket, long-sales-cycle purchases, testing periods take longer and more-arbitrary decisions need to be made. You'll simply have less data to go on.

In planning such a campaign, be bullish about potential profitability but take heed that an apparent challenge—if you correctly micro-target your keyword list instead of reaching too broadly into generic search queries by the masses—will be to spend enough. If you're just targeting a few purchasing managers and C-level execs, you have to wait for them to type relevant terms into a search engine, and that may take months or years. You might generate very few clicks, but the value of those clicks could be high.

Don't be alarmed, then, when you see costs per click in the stratosphere for niche terms in your industry, especially not if a successful lead could be worth half a million dollars to your company! Costs per click of $5, $10, and $20 are not uncommon in some areas. You can lower the average by experimenting with the techniques offered in this book, of course.

A very effective model for a B2B campaign is often to request that interested parties fill out a contact form in exchange for receiving a valuable white paper or some other professional incentive. This is a lead-generation model and will help you operate the campaign based on a cost-per-lead metric.[8]

Business-to-Consumer

Online retail seems to occupy the most real estate when it comes to pay per click. Campaigns can vary from a single product (acne medication), to a product line (contact lenses), to a diversified storefront from a major retailer carrying 10,000 or 1,000,000 items. As the scale grows, my earlier advice about meticulous campaign organization becomes all the more important.

In forecasting, begin with a test of one product or category before expanding the campaign, to get a feel for cost and performance.

Online retailers face special challenges. Margins are often slim and competition fierce. As a result, careful bid management, possibly even dayparting, is a must. Meticulous attention to tracking URLs and landing pages is time consuming. Depending on the size of the campaign, you will need to write dozens, hundreds, or even thousands of different ads. To manage this task properly, large-scale retailers need to look carefully at available software and services to make the task more manageable, and some will need to hire full-time staff or a third party to handle it.

One thing worth mentioning about conventional retail models as they intersect with Google's priorities is: Google loves you. No, I don't mean you personally. But the very literal and unambiguous facts of your business model are helping you sync well with Google's objectives—a searcher types in **bag of hockey pucks**, and you sell hockey pucks. No one's being deceived, no one is confused. The ad is relevant and gets lots of clicks, and those users are satisfied with what they find on the site. As a result, conventional retail campaigns tend to garner high Quality Scores across the board. In the above example, when I try the query **bag of hockey pucks**, actually, some of the ads are for retailers selling hockey bags. Not perfect, as is so often the case when matching options are being used. But hockey pucks sometimes go in hockey bags, don't they?

Compared with B2B and localized professional services, you're probably spending quite a bit, too, and are quite serious about your business (not playing games with Google's system as some affiliates do, for example). For that reason, Google likes you just fine. Expect solid account support and don't hesitate to ask for help from Google reps if something seems off with your Quality Scores, or if there is any other hiccup in performance. You're Google's bread and butter, and they know it.

Professional Services

Individual doctors, insurance brokers, accountants, realtors, lawyers, electricians, and the like, often have trouble with online marketing. The problem lies partly with economics and partly in these types of professionals being poorly suited to make decisions about outsourcing things like web design and marketing. It's one thing to hire a receptionist or purchase supplies—professions have long histories in this area. It's quite another to delve into new media, user interfaces, and response rates. Many professions were also historically banned from advertising, or simply didn't consider it "ethical," but that's a long story. In other cases, say regulated professions or home improvement contractors in hot markets, service providers have grown accustomed to working with a full slate of customers—in "backlog" mode—with limited marketing effort. When competition heats up, that type of assumption must give way to an active online lead-generation effort. Sending out calendars isn't going to cut it.

When you're uncomfortable with hiring help in an emerging area, it's easy to make a mistake. One variant of this mistake is placing too much trust and allocating too much budget towards a web design firm that can only get you part of the way towards your goals. Some interactive services firms are sectorally focused—they build, for example, medically oriented websites. Beware of "cookie-cutter" web development processes that treat a whole bunch of clients in your sector "equally" and don't figure to help you battle your way to the top of the heap.

Another variant of the "uncomfortable with finding web marketing talent" syndrome is for the professional (the doctor, the electrician) to try to do too much themselves. Without hiring a trusted web-savvy associate (even if that's just a consultant), copy doesn't get written, decisions don't get made, and projects get stalled. Of course, the answer is not to just farm out this all-important building block of your business to a receptionist or technician in your professional services company. They may be junior colleagues with available time, but often they have zero expertise other than their own hunches and what their cousin told them at a wedding last month. You get what you pay for.

Small-scale professional offices will find it difficult to afford online marketing, but that's partly because they'll often waste too much on unprofitable activities before finally getting it right. A prosperous real estate broker, dental office, or plastic surgeon, on the other hand, can even afford to make a mistake or two, as they're multimillion-dollar operations. Most companies of this size should be investing seriously in online marketing. It becomes cost-effective with persistence, though it's unfamiliar territory at first.

Think Locally if You're Local

A huge hurdle here is the sheer number of "me-too" practitioners. In a mobile society, patients aren't even restricted geographically when it comes to things like plastic surgery or experimental noninvasive cancer treatments. The cost of a flight is built into the overall (expensive, but worth it) cost of the services. But the dentist or ophthalmologist who doesn't offer much differentiation from a hundred other practitioners in a given city may be best off with a simplified web strategy, including working with Google Local Business Center listings and the like. Detailed local search marketing strategies are somewhat beyond the scope of this book, but it's worth pointing out that some local listings, through integration with services like Google Maps, can actually be free. Other variants will cost you on a per-click basis because they're integrated with a standard Google AdWords campaign.

Local review sites, such as Yelp, CitySearch, OurFaves (focusing on bars, restaurants, salons, bookshops, and other trendy "local hotspots"), and HomeStars (focusing on home improvement contractors) are often good places for professional services providers to build an online reputation. Encouraging customers to write reviews in these places is one way to tilt the balance of opinion in your favor. You can also buy "enhanced" listings on the review sites. Typically, these don't buy you a better image directly, but allow you to gain additional visibility and to provide more information. Some companies might even find these enhanced listings nearly as useful as having a standalone website.

Sometimes, when people lack savvy in a specialized area like web marketing, they make the mistake of overspending as opposed to underspending. Savvy online marketers understand that they need to avoid overpaying on any given component of a web project so that they can budget for everything that is needed. "Getting the Web," then, doesn't mean paying an exorbitant amount for a one-off site design, but rather, understanding the nature of the sales process. A simple yet effective site can be designed (without sacrificing an arm and a leg in sunk costs) to capture leads. That way, sufficient funds can be kept in reserve for the marketing effort, which might include testing multiple landing pages, ads, and so on, as well as monitoring ROI in detail.

The minority of professionals who "get the Web" can clean up. To do so, they must recognize that online marketing is an ongoing process, not a single event. It is not a matter of "how much" is spent, but "how" your budget is spent. If you get it right, there is enormous opportunity to succeed online in a professional niche.

Information Publishing

Selling subscriptions or e-books, or driving traffic to an informative website that sells advertising in its own right, are natural online businesses, since, after all, "search" is inherently informational in nature.

Hundreds of interesting examples of how information changes hands for a fee come to mind. For example, when I was looking for models of self-publishing how-to information, I was stunned to see how much money even a modest self-publishing company like Self-Counsel Press was able to make. The founder, Diana Douglas, started selling divorce how-to kits in the 1970s, and her company took off from there. When I spoke to Ms. Douglas about the evolution of her business, she stressed that nearly all of Self-Counsel's revenues continue to come from print, not online, information sales. This is due in part to distribution agreements with the bookstores that carry Self-Counsel's titles. Although Self-Counsel doesn't currently disclose its annual revenues, and the founder is quite modest about the accomplishment, they deserve credit for growing from a single handbook title into a publishing business with hundreds of titles that has remained a going concern for 30 years.

While Self-Counsel didn't reap its success online, the model is the same. Online publishers, indeed, may have more flexibility. Whether or not she'll admit to being a great success, the growth of Diana Douglas's Self-Counsel Press was an inspiration to me when I decided to distribute niche information online. The voracious readers in niche information markets, coupled with low overhead costs, make it an attractive risk for an online venture.

MarketingSherpa (which recently merged with another online publisher called MarketingExperiments.com) has built a business around selling specialized information that includes marketing reports, buyer's guides, email marketing data, and more. On a grander scale, media giants like Bloomberg and Thomson are all about packaging and selling information. Thomson has divested itself of some high-profile mass-media assets, focusing on acquisitions of niche information providers you've never heard of in fields like medicine and accounting. Thomson is worth billions. For one example of a powerhouse B2B information publishing division of Thomson, visit TechStreet.com, which sells things like technical specifications and drawings. "Rules for Construction of Nuclear Power Plant Components" will run you $3,940.

One of my clients, a business journal published by a major university, focuses on selling subscriptions. But an interesting additional revenue stream is one-off articles from their content library. They use Google AdWords in a limited way to promote both subscriptions and article sales. A side benefit is keeping the brand name out in the forefront. Selling a $5 article for $6 worth of clicks, in the right circumstances, is an inexpensive way to spread a trusted name in business research, not even counting potential repeat business for articles.

You're limited only by your imagination when it comes to putting together an information product, particularly in consumer areas where much disparate information is available that has not yet been aggregated into a coherent package. Not only those who have proprietary information and big budgets can succeed, but so can those like Diana Douglas, who put together her first product, the do-it-yourself divorce kit, on the strength of personal experiences and research. The positives of information publishing as an online business model include low overhead, the ability to find highly specific keywords for low cost, ease of delivery of the product (digital), and plenty of examples online of companies that have created compelling landing pages for selling an information product.

To do more background research on what has come to be called the content business, check out Anne Holland's ContentBiz.com and subscribe to the newsletter. The leading guru in the economics of online content in its broadest sense, however, is likely Rafat Ali, publisher of paidContent.org. It should go without saying that if you are in the "content business" (are an online publisher of any sort) and have the money, you can also try buying AdWords ads to draw attention to your

Keyword Arbitrage: Scam or Rational Business Strategy?

A current practice among online publishers that have high advertising rates is to buy inexpensive keywords to drive more traffic to their sites. This is frequently due to the fact that their advertisers are willing to pay for more impressions than the publication can currently generate from name recognition, bookmarks, and free search referrals. One name-brand business magazine contacted me to discuss the tactic in connection with a growth plan for their website division. Some take a dim view of this "keyword arbitrage" and feel that only scammers are involved in buying ads low online and selling them high. Not necessarily. It's a perfectly rational strategy for a major business publication to remind people of their expertise in an area in order to build a long-term subscriber base, and failing that, to generate 20 cents in advertising revenues out of a 10-cent keyword buy. The fact that they can do it with 5- and 10-cent AdWords clicks is downright clever. If you're going to break even on a marketing initiative, I can't think of a better way to do so than to generate more mindshare for your magazine. Longer term, that's going to do better than break even. When keywords were as cheap as a penny on Overture's predecessor, GoTo, I sometimes used to buy them up for popular keyword searches like **Yahoo** just to drive traffic to my site so people would read my articles. Talk about vanity! Talk about a money-losing proposition! But I think that showed foresight, and it paid off in the long run. A practice that seemed crazy back then would be adopted by just about any writer or blogger today, because you can pay a heck of a lot more than a few pennies to introduce new readers to your unique content these days.

ad-supported online content. Large media companies, in particular, are beginning to do this. Get the feeling that this might be a controversial practice, because Google is also a large media company directly competing with some of those large media companies wishing to find cheap ad space on Google? That's the feeling I get.

Because driving "paid traffic to ad-supported content" is a respectable cousin to the less-respected "thin content" strategy of click arbitrageurs (recall the discussion of *click arbitrage* in Chapter 5), it is a trickier area because of the arbitrariness of Google's approach to quality-based bidding.

Information sales in general have been tougher to achieve through AdWords lately because of the risk of falling into "false positive" territory, whereby a legitimate offer is being painted with the same broad brush as business models that Google now says typically incur low scores in automated and human assessments of website quality. Google pointed to some types of "e-books" and "get rich schemes" in a recent overview of business models that tend to get "slapped" by low Quality Scores.[9] For the legitimate information publishers among us, let's hope Google lets that enforcement pendulum swing back a bit.

Assess Your Sales Process

Knowing that you want to reach customers through paid search marketing, unfortunately, does not automatically translate into a successful AdWords campaign that makes money for you like clockwork. Attaining decent conversion rates on targeted clicks depends on developing a solid game plan.

Most businesses today need to maximize their revenue per customer, especially as the cost of gaining a new customer in this channel rises. If you use a shotgun approach to your ad copy or landing pages, you're less likely to succeed than if you have clear, concise goals. First determine what type of customer relationship you want to establish. Equally important, think about how those relationships can be turned into additional revenues in the future. If your competitors are calibrating their bidding strategy to the lifetime value of a customer, and you're only looking at the immediate benefit, you may be underestimating the value of each click. You could wind up underbidding and letting competitors increase market share at your expense.

What's Your Goal: Retail Sales, Leads, Registrations, Buzz, Subscriptions?

Even where you have multiple goals for each customer relationship, you should make every effort to isolate a main objective for clarity of the sales process, as well as for the sake of benchmarking how well you're doing. From there you can expand to the other details and prioritize them in a sensible manner.

For example, if you know that making an immediate return of 100% or more on the ad spend through retail sales of items such as LEGO toys is your goal, that's enormously helpful to understanding what can and can't be accomplished with your AdWords campaign. A further stipulation—that dump trucks and space stations are higher-margin items and thus worth bidding more on—might be helpful here as long you don't waver from a tight focus on gaining new retail customers. Finally, in this hypothetical scenario, you might want to remind yourself not to bid any more than 20–25 cents on the lowest-margin items (such as that long-forgotten "How to Remodel Your Kitchen with LEGO" book by Bob Vila). Remember, these are initial and primary goals for your sales process. You literally cannot function if you don't pick one primary campaign metric and one primary purpose for any given landing page, and use the performance of clicks driven to that page as a yardstick of campaign performance. That does not preclude you from selling other things to these customers or other customers, or from convincing them to become a member of your frequent buyers' club, or entering your contest, or... all of the other plans you have for your business. But you can't attempt to do all of this at once.

You should engage in, at least, a formal process of narrowing down your main general goals; following that, you'll want to select campaign metrics like cost per sale or ROI and stick with them. In the informal narrowing process for the initiative, then, you might think "emphasize converting first-time visitors to buyers of high-margin products; failing that, get them to buy something else." Consider other goals as secondary. From this type of thinking, you'll probably gain valuable cues as to whether your website is suitable to attaining your goals. If pages are cluttered with other things you're asking users to do, they're likely to go away confused or perform actions that are more like browsing than entering into some kind of relationship with your company.[10]

At this point it's worth noting that strong brands don't always have to follow the rules to the letter. You can get away with some clutter and disorganization because users already accept you as a vendor; they're going to poke around your wide selection or other offers more often than they would with a niche vendor, where they'll be looking for credibility cues. A famous case is the tale of one particular Amazon.com test that showed an initiative to "radically declutter" many pages on the site resulted in *lower* sales, so the company quickly reverted to the full-featured pages users have come to expect. We'll return to these themes in Chapter 11, which discusses increasing conversion rates.

Lessons from a Seafood Company's Campaign

One of my former clients, a global conglomerate that owns a popular supermarket frozen fish line, decided to test the waters for online sales of fresh lobsters in fall 2003. At the time, they were concerned that conversion rates might be low because consumers, trained by years of seeing their displays of low-cost frozen products in supermarkets, might have trouble perceiving their products in higher-priced "fresh delivered" categories. In spite of assurances of special packaging to ensure freshness, this fear turned out to be well-founded. Conversion rates were poor. This deep-pocketed company was being outbid on AdWords by owners of small boutique fresh lobster shops. By all indications, those boutique shops were converting more sales because the more tactile and "small feel" of their operations and brands reassured customers that they were getting fresh goods right out of the ocean, worth paying extra for. Since the campaign was based in the United States, some buyers possibly liked the idea of supporting a smaller local business as opposed to a Japanese-owned conglomerate.

Despite this shortcoming, as I saw it, the fish conglomerate's fresh seafood campaign objective was pretty clear: sell specialty fish products, especially lobsters and a couple of other rare, high-margin items. If they had also tried to promote their frozen lines, build their brand, get consumers to join an email list, or enter a contest, I would have had a harder time helping them out. From an AdWords standpoint, focusing on converting visitors to buyers of identifiable products would at least translate into a campaign that could be measured and improved. As I'll discuss later in the chapter, I had to debate this with the client. Sure, I think opt-in newsletters are neat, but do they sell fish? Do they sell enough fish to make up for the cost of driving people to the site? It's unlikely, especially given customers' increasing propensity to ignore email.

While I thought the fish company's primary campaign goal was worthwhile and achievable, I ran into a snag with the retail expert who'd been brought in to provide a second opinion. I suggested a streamlined shopping cart that got the customer to place the order before filling out the shipping and billing info. Experience has shown that with complex shopping carts and preregistration procedures, shopping cart abandonment rates are very high, thus preventing the initial transaction from occurring in too many cases. Clearly, someone on the verge of shelling out $100 for fresh mussels to be shipped overnight in special packaging (something that does require quite a leap of faith) would be a potentially lucrative customer to have. Therefore, to my way of thinking, you should do everything you can to avoid turning them off just before the successful completion of their first-ever transaction, especially since clicks aren't free and it takes as many as 50 to generate a customer on the relevant keywords.

As too often happens, though, the combination of a third-party web development firm that apparently didn't care about usability or revenues unless they were paid extra to do so, and a retail expert who seemed to be living in the 1950s and believed that a good way to develop loyalty was to bombard potentially valuable customers with to-do items instead of turning them into customers quickly, the shopping cart abandonment problem wasn't solved. This shopping cart's outmoded seven steps to checkout were killing conversion rates. With each additional step to checkout, more potential customers fall by the wayside. This is simple, unwavering math. To make a sale online, reduce the number of steps wherever possible. Amazon didn't patent "one-click" ordering for nothing.

What's Going on Behind the Scenes?

In the case of the seafood merchant, something very simple was made into something complicated. This led to more questions than answers. Should we rehire the developers to fix this issue? What about a focus group? Are there any studies we can look at? Probably, but in some cases, a focus group of one or two people can tell you what's glaringly wrong. Why does the retail expert assure us that the extra step doesn't matter when it clearly does?

Budget allowing, empirical proof can be gleaned from user testing of the sort that is done by usability labs (Nielsen Norman Group are pioneers, but now these kinds of labs are widespread). But even without that, proper "funnel analysis" using a well-customized installation of Google Analytics, Omniture, or other analytics package would provide backup for early decisions about how to rebuild the cart.

With less budget, but some common sense, all that needed to be done here would have been to look at other checkout processes around the Web (some of them belonging to quite dinky-looking, but very successful, smaller businesses), and engage a web development firm that would implement a better checkout process as if usability issues and cart abandonment rates were their business, not just the client's problem. In this case, "check out without registering" should have been an obvious and easy option to implement by a qualified programmer. Some web development shops are no better than rote implementers of third-party solutions on a "white label" basis, and don't even understand the technology well enough to go out and find a different, more appropriate canned solution, let alone having the technical chops to write custom applications.

Rather than getting caught up in outdated retailer-centric moralizing about what a typical customer should or should not do, today's online marketers must attack problems pragmatically and test responses iteratively. In the earlier example, we needed to focus on lowering cart abandonment rates so that the initial transaction could take place and the fish would get to the valued customer's door. Regrettably, since it wasn't clear that that was the primary goal, it was easy to forget about this and to gradually focus more and more on other, less quantifiable priorities.

The debates about the seafood site didn't end there. Another goal was to ask people to sign up for a free newsletter. This would contain free recipes and offers, and would either help the conglomerate to build their brand or lead to an online sale (the one this consumer didn't complete in the first instance because he or she wanted something free instead).

This goal created new problems. How much is a newsletter subscriber worth? How much should we be bidding on keywords in order to attract the types of people who might not want to buy today but, based on feel-good communications including tasty recipe ideas, over time might become good customers? Which keywords should we be highlighting to attract those kinds of customers, as opposed to customers who might be expected to buy lobster today? Who do we contact to install the tracking software on the appropriate pages associated with successful newsletter sign-ups? Nobody knew right away, and answers were slow to come, since this was a secondary goal on its way to being a tertiary goal. It just sort of hung there as another thing to look at.

This opens up a much broader topic—the current cluttered state of permission marketing through email—but for the present purpose, marketers do need to clarify their customer relationship strategies. Most know in general they "need a newsletter" (because that's the conventional wisdom), but how aggressively should they pursue the effort of building up that subscriber base, and how much (if anything) should they spend on it? Many of us assume that emailing customers is a good thing, but is it? The exercise of thinking this through might lead some marketers to conclude that building this "permission asset" may not be worth the cost today. Take a hard look at the newsletter idea, which many marketers today just haphazardly fold into their thinking based on best practices that are five years out of date. Perhaps the act of asking customers if they'd like to join something like a newsletter should be reserved for the most enthusiastic subset of customers, or not undertaken at all.

Customer Relationship Strategies

For marketers looking to maintain relationships with a loyal customer base, it will pay to keep thinking about their needs in a cluttered world. Consider less intrusive formats than email, such as RSS-based news feeds, blogs, or a nonintrusive discussion group or social media platform.

If you're a real chatterbox, you can even Twitter (Obama does, why can't you?). I know that many of the current social media fads will die out, but some will thrive, so don't be afraid to experiment. (My acid test seems to be: if "real people" are finding success in leveraging such strategies for business advantage, I take it seriously; I do not put much stock in the exhortations of insider technorati types such as Robert Scoble or Steve Rubel, in the so-called "echo chamber" of the "blogosphere."[11]) Because other marketers have been abusing permission and creating a "tragedy of the online commons" situation over the past five years, you need to think ahead if you want to form lasting relationships with your customers. Don't assume that email is a must-have channel, in particular if your efforts to build out that channel are killing or confusing your online sales process.[12]

Consider this: there isn't any law against using direct mail to send good customers offers. A postcard from a sunglasses retailer won't offend anyone. Believe it or not, phone calls from the suit salesman at Harry Rosen or the service department at Downtown Acura don't offend me (while the upsell calls from Rogers Cable do). Somehow, businesses struggled through and maintained customer relationships in the days before email.

Many of the retailer websites I visit force me to use my email address at checkout, and then they send me special offers. I'm not sure I like it. More to the point, the way many of them are doing it today might not be legal next year, or the year after that. Spam filters are also getting much more sophisticated. I'm not privy to how the spam filter works in Gmail, for example, but I notice that whereas permission-based messages I actually read seem to make it into my inbox, those I don't look at get labeled eventually as spam, especially if the vendor emails me every couple of days. Tiger Direct permission emails seem to get through, but a volley of emails from an apparel vendor I recently dealt with, Everlast, were stuck in my Gmail spam folder along with the various Nigerian bank scam emails and the offers from "v*agra" vendors and purveyors of Russian brides. As they should have been. I might want to hear about a monthly special, and I might tolerate email every two weeks. Email me every day and we've got a problem.

Clean up your AdWords campaign strategy by streamlining your goals as they pertain specifically to the campaign. You're paying for every click, so you need to develop a goal that revolves around a specific success metric, whether that be cost per order, cost per lead, or cost per action.

Cost per Acquisition, Cost per Order: Two Brief Case Examples

The forthcoming example may be quirky, but we learn more from driving on rocky roads than smooth pavement anyway. Let's turn to an example of a fairly messy AdWords campaign experiment that nonetheless yielded a clear cost per acquisition (I also like to call it cost per action) metric within 60 days. Then we'll look at a case where tracking cost per order added a useful dimension to the analysis.

Brian's Buzz (Generating Newsletter Subscriptions)

At the time I worked with this client, Brian's Buzz (also called Windows Secrets) was a newsletter produced by a well-known technology author and consultant, Brian Livingston. *PC World* reviewed it and declared it good enough to be on their "best free stuff" list (one of the tags we tried out in the ad copy). But of course nothing in life is truly free. If you're paying for clicks, it had better not be!

Brian's business model was too complicated for my tastes, but I am grateful for the wealth of ideas he brought to the campaign, some of which caused us to identify key flaws in the AdWords platform itself. The business model was a mix of free newsletter subscriptions, paid subscriptions, volunteer "thank-you" tips from free subscribers, and "other income."

Going into the AdWords campaign, the goal was to increase subscriptions to the free product and then to track voluntary donations. The hope was that the cost of the clicks would be recouped within a month or so (requests are made at the end of each newsletter, every two weeks), with any additional revenues being gravy. This would require a 100% ROI within 30 days—a timetable I felt was unduly restrictive, especially considering how well the AdWords campaign went. Certain keywords attracted high volumes of clicks, and conversion rates from clickthroughs to newsletter sign-ups were consistent if not stellar (13%–15%).

After two months, we came away from the exercise with an important piece of knowledge: what it costs to generate an individual subscriber. (This is often called *cost per acquisition,* or CPA, but at times I call it *cost per action,* the measurable action being a newsletter sign-up.) The cost per subscriber of about 60 cents seemed well below industry norms for such a filtered group. More importantly, the advertiser, Brian Livingston, has full control over delivery and can assess many factors in the process of attracting these subscribers. By contrast, many lead-generation services can be mysterious as to how they generate leads or subscribers for you, and the quality can be uneven at best.

The absolute number (60 cents) on its own isn't all that telling until you can determine the long-term value of a subscriber. The ROI after 60 days, focusing solely on the voluntary thank-you payments given by some subscribers (fewer than 3% chipped in, thus identifying a hole in the model that allowed 97% of readers to free-ride on the generosity of others), was only 40%. That is to say, from about $2,000 spent on clicks, only $800 was raised from these donations. But over a one- or two-year period, if we could identify, say, an average of $3 in revenues per subscriber (through advertising, book sales, paid subscription conversions, and so forth), the ROI would probably look excellent—4× or better.

Some clients are shy about sharing their full revenue picture with me, preferring conservative disclosure to ensure we're careful about bids and budgets. Later on in discussions with Brian, I satisfied myself that his various revenue streams, which indeed included premium subscriptions, books, and speaking, would have made the average subscriber worth quite a bit more than he was letting on. Focusing on the thank-you payments only, and tying bids to the ROI on those alone, was an attempt to create a campaign that was self-funding from the beginning. But longer term, each new subscriber was clearly worth more than 60 cents—$3.00 or more is my educated guess based on further discussions with the client.

Even in the short term, the raw "60 cents per new subscriber" cost-per-acquisition metric is useful because it allows Brian to directly compare the effectiveness of the AdWords campaign with other lead-generation sources: Yahoo Search Marketing, subscriber generation services, banner ad campaigns, and so on.

One subscription generator service that we were tracking in tandem with this AdWords pay-per-click campaign charged only 30 cents per subscriber, but as long as I was watching the tracking data, these subscribers subsequently contributed $0 in revenues to Brian's Buzz.

Either these were just a bunch of recycled, infrequently checked Hotmail addresses being sold off to many other marketers, or these were the world's least responsive readers.

When you track your results carefully, you can prove or disprove a lot of claims, as we did here. The people clicking on the AdWords ads were reasonably responsive over the short term. At least we were able to identify a pulse!

Brian's campaign was a qualified success. Although ROI goals were not achieved as quickly as he had hoped, the campaign did work well on several levels. It could not have generated useful data or moved closer to achieving its goals, though, had the primary goal not been identified from the start: *generating as many well-qualified free newsletter subscribers as possible* for the lowest feasible cost per subscriber. This goal coincided well with the ad copy and keyword selection, and the custom-tailored landing page (see Figure 6-1). By being focused—by avoiding the trap of conflating a number of objectives—key metrics were established that should allow for sensible adjustments and progress towards solid profitability.

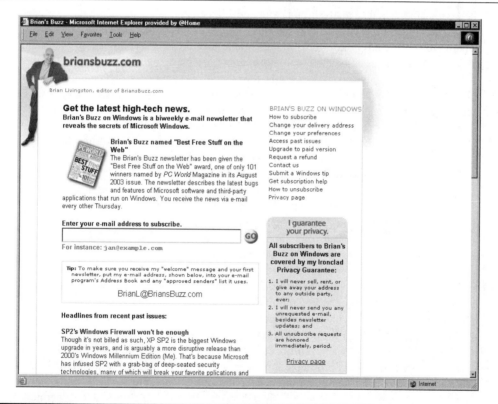

FIGURE 6-1 Brian Livingston's landing page asks you to sign up for a newsletter. Nothing complicated here, because the goal was well-established from the start.

FourOxen Corp.: Pinning Down an Allowable Cost per Order

FourOxen Corp. (not their real name) sells a commodity technology service. It's an ongoing challenge for this company to achieve decent ROI from a paid search campaign because many of the keywords are expensive. On their main keywords, large companies like Microsoft and Yahoo are bidding very high, presumably because this product is merely a loss leader in a whole suite of services these conglomerates hope to offer once they hook a new customer. By avoiding bidding wars and by tracking results, FourOxen has been able to show steady improvement in their campaign performance.

In spite of FourOxen's being a fairly recognizable brand name in their own right, and with plenty of brainpower resources at hand (over 200 employees), at first they were doing little if any meaningful post-click tracking. Because all company computing functions are centralized, I was told we could only get access to full stats reports on the 1st and 15th of every month. This makes it difficult to feel the impact of campaign adjustments. (Almost through accretion—or was it attrition?—more recently, I was able to convince FourOxen to allow me on-demand access to conversion data through Google Analytics and Google Conversion Tracker, greatly reducing the headaches associated with data analysis and campaign adjustment.)

The main bits of data that were sent to me every two weeks were the numbers of orders corresponding to specific ads or keywords in the Google AdWords and Yahoo Search Marketing campaigns, and the revenues associated with those orders. By plugging in the total cost for all clicks generated by those same ads or keywords, the spreadsheet summary I received would spit out a dollar figure for whether that part of the campaign (represented by a unique tracking URL that I created for each ad and/or important keyword in the AdWords interface) was in a "profit" or "loss" position vis-à-vis revenues associated with a keyword or ad group. This reporting seemed problematic to me, because the more popular keywords generate a lot of new business at a slight loss. It makes these keywords look like culprits in an otherwise healthy campaign, because they generate a high volume of "money-losing" orders.

If their click volume were lowered, these keywords might generate a smaller aggregate loss, and that would (possibly wrongly) be read as "improvement." Clearly, there is a point at which you may be losing too much money on each sale, but unless you know what that point is, the profit/loss methodology might cause you to abandon keywords that are excellent for acquiring new customers who will become profitable repeat customers within a year.

Therefore, I suggested that we also add *cost per order* into the reporting to give us a consistent feel for what it was costing to acquire a new customer, instead of looking only at a "loss" number that would escalate as you put more money into the campaign.

For a long time, FourOxen's management remained vague as to the allowable cost per order. At around $15, I knew that the company was making money on the average first order, so clearly, that would be a safe figure. But we haven't been able to get some high-volume keywords much below $30—territory I still feel is profitable long term and worth mining given the high volume of new customers available through this route. Given the vertical integration of this particular tech space, I suspect a well-run company in this industry might have an allowable cost per new customer acquisition of up to $50–$60. Market share, not just pure profitability, is always a consideration in any cut-throat industry.

Something fascinating happened about a year after I finally had access to their on-demand analytics. The CEO and Marketing Director of FourOxen talked with me about a radical new business model that would potentially make a lot more sense for AdWords promotion. This was based in part on recent acquisitions that refocused part of the company's resources on high-ticket "premium" items. While the "commodity" campaign runs on autopilot at low volumes, doing slightly better than break-even, we're now mapping out new ground. It's music to my ears. So often, companies conceive of "improving their campaigns" inside tight little mental boxes that hinder growth. Sometimes, new product lines, new prices, and new business models are the only things that allow them to regain some swagger in the AdWords auction.

While FourOxen's campaign objectives were not initially clear, they have become more so over time. By monitoring both the profit/loss metric and the cost-per-order metric, we gained a balanced perspective on whether any parts of the campaign were performing unacceptably. Confident that AdWords wasn't a sinkhole, we eventually dropped the confusing profit/loss metric entirely. (It was confusing because their various prices and subscription models make it pure guesswork to assign specific dollar figures to many of the sales events that occur. Some are mere low-dollar renewals by existing customers who nonetheless used Google ads as a navigational tool; others are high-ticket subscriptions from new customers who stick around for years.) It was decided that the CPO number provided a decent "read" of campaign effectiveness. In the past three months, the aggregate CPO for the "commodity" account has carried on at an unimpressive, but still acceptable, $40. But the really exciting part is the transition towards higher-margin products.

Difficulties in Forecasting

Many marketing managers charged with the task of "costing out" a Google AdWords campaign may be facing an uphill battle because the cost really is difficult to predict in advance. It isn't impossible to come up with estimates, but they may be far rougher than you might wish due to the unpredictability of the relevant variables. The aggregate cost of a campaign will be hard to pin down due to the instability of a number of factors.

Forecasting Cost per Click and Click Volume

When adding new keywords or changing bids, AdWords offers a Traffic Estimator tool that shows you how many clicks that bid level is likely to generate for you in a day, in what average ad position (see Figure 6-2). Multiplying this by 30 gives you the estimated cost for a month for a given keyword or ad group. By now it's fairly common knowledge that you can't put much stock in these estimates.

There are several reasons for this. First, AdWords tries to predict how many searches the general public will perform on a given phrase, but this tends to be volatile. Second, advertisers may enter and leave the auction. Third, the very fact that it's an auction means that prices are hard to predict, as advertisers may change their bids frequently. Fourth, your ad position is difficult to predict because it depends on how well you optimize your ads (and your competitors, theirs) for Quality Scores, which, along with your bid, affects ad position. Since ad position will affect

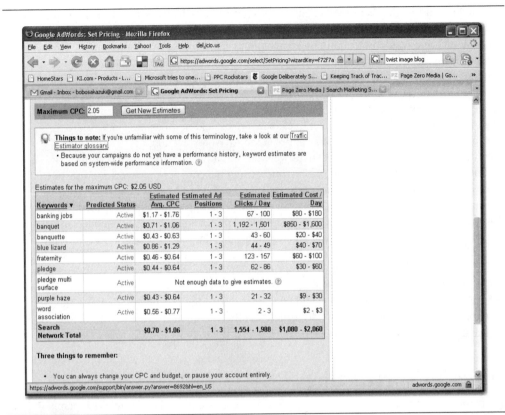

FIGURE 6-2 AdWords offers a tool to help you with spending projections, but real-world campaigns are volatile and often miss projections. Luckily, you can also adapt your budget day-to-day in the (same) real world.

visibility, and thus the volume of your clicks, this adds yet another element of unpredictability, which Google's Traffic Estimator tool is hard pressed to deal with. Finally, the Estimator likely does an even worse job of predicting patterns on partner sites and the content network. Geolocation parameters can add yet more uncertainty.

Click volume is difficult to pin down because the early stages of a campaign should involve not merely deployment of a predetermined keyword arsenal, but also ongoing keyword discovery. You need some initial data to build on, but it's often difficult to tell how your efforts will progress week to week.

A more accurate method than using the Estimator tool is to look at what actually happened (in other words, build a small test campaign, and see what happened in real time in a given week). Unfortunately, the first couple of weeks of your campaign (for reasons of editorial review, partner and content network syndication, or other undisclosed technical issues with ad delivery) will not be a particularly good bellwether. New campaigns seem to ramp up over time before stabilizing at a more predictable ad spend pattern for any given day of the week.

For these reasons, then, costs can be difficult to predict. If solid budget figures are absolutely required, you will have to budget conservatively at first, while expecting a sharp increase in your spend (and hopefully, associated revenues) as the campaign progresses.

Forecasting Clickthrough Rates and Conversion Rates

I'm more comfortable predicting CTRs than conversion rates. Developing a series of ads that will pull pretty well is not particularly difficult, so it's fine to go ahead and estimate that you will achieve 1%, 2%, or 4% CTRs, depending on how confident you are and on how ultratargeted your keywords are. Then again, even if you do hit very close to the CTR you'd been expecting, this does very little to tell you how much you'll spend.

A strange thing with CTRs is that you can have very high ones and very low ones mixed together in the same account. Content targeting might garner a paltry 0.1% CTR, for example, or it might even be ten times worse than that! Again, the rate doesn't tell you much about the bottom-line impact. Recall that with content targeting, as opposed to the search component of a Google campaign, you aren't penalized for very low CTRs.

The game of predicting how many visitors will turn into customers after they click (conversion rate) is also subject to such serious miscalculation that you probably shouldn't forecast. You can get rich quite easily on the back of an envelope. When I began selling my own information online, I had no idea how many copies I would sell, or what it would cost me to generate sales over and above word of mouth. I just hoped *someone* would buy! In reality, the patterns kept shifting. I vastly exceeded expectations early on, but after a few years, the dynamics changed, with competition, rising click costs, and the buyer's need for constant novelty in format and content. Today I suppose my ebooks' conversion rates on AdWords are between 1% and 3% depending on the day. But that could easily be raised to 6% by constraining the keyword list to only the most highly relevant (and expensive) words, or lowered to 0.1% by going really broad with keywords (and paying less for them). A raw conversion rate number doesn't tell you much. It also doesn't tell you how many "walk-ins" your initial advertising might generate down the road. Although users are cookied by most common tracking services, and tracking can accurately attribute conversions from AdWords campaigns 30, 60, or 90 days down the road, people do switch computers, clear their cookies, and so forth. Insofar as tracking is imperfect, a recorded 5% conversion rate might be a real conversion rate of 10% or higher based on "nonattributed" sales from users navigating directly to your site in any given week.

One thing is clear: once you establish your approximate conversion rate, you want it to get progressively higher. You want to know about factors that create conversions when customers are waffling. But pulling a number out of thin air in advance, as if you're entitled to this revenue, never made it happen.

An Alternative to Forecasting: A $2,000 "Testing Budget"

Simply try this: put aside at least $2,000 and 2–4 weeks for a trial run on your AdWords campaign. This will help you generate benchmarks for CTRs, conversion rates, ad position, CPC, and so forth, which will be helpful in further forecasting.

If that's too much, and you're a very small company, you can still generate 500 clicks at 40 cents per click for only $200. This will often be enough to give you a sense of where things are headed. Preferably, too, you'll make more than $200 back from the effort!

If $2,000 is too small and will make your colleagues laugh at you, forget we ever had this conversation, and up it to $10,000 or $40,000 as need be. A division of a financial institution I worked with in 2004 had a 90-day "testing" budget of about $300,000! A few companies "test" using budgets even higher than that. Based on the learning from that financial firm's successful test, the budget for the same period in 2005 was set at $1 million. The same logic applies regardless of company size.

In running your tests, try to start with very targeted terms that are more likely to lead to a sale. It's easier to build on a modest success—a few initial sales conversions—than to know which way to turn if you strike out completely.

As I discussed in Chapter 5, another good reason to target quite narrowly at first is that initial Quality Scores matter a great deal in the process of gaining early traction towards establishing a data track record in AdWords. More relevant words, higher CTRs, and so forth are always important, but particularly important in the early going. Your account history now matters, so you need to establish a strong one from the outset. That means don't test ridiculous stuff in an account you're planning to use for any serious business purpose. If you've got an old weathered boot of a failed account lying around somewhere, use that for strange tests.

As I've made clear, I prefer testing to forecasting. In many ways, the first six months of a paid search campaign is like a lab experiment gathering valuable data. Building on that initial effort, campaign management should require less ongoing effort each month, even as its budget increases.

Endnotes

1. Janis Mara, "Search-Style Ads Lift Brand Awareness, Study Says," ClickZ.com, July 15, 2004.

2. Interactive Advertising Bureau, "IAB and comScore Release New Research on the Effectiveness of Online Local, Directory and Classifieds Advertising," March 13, 2006, archived at iab.net.

3. For a brief summary of this study, released in May 2006, see http://yhoo.client.shareholder .com/press/releasedetail.cfm?releaseid=196082. The PDF of the full study is also freely available and should be findable with a brief search effort.

4. See also his recent tour de force, *Meatball Sundae: Is Your Marketing Out of Sync?* (Portfolio, 2007).

5. He also wrote "Andrew Goodman is good." You can't believe how much flak I took from the "search engine optimization establishment" for being the lucky recipient of that snippet of praise.

6. Seth Godin, *The Big Red Fez: How to Make Any Web Site Better* (Free Press, 2002).

7. I received some friendly guffaws mixed with some howls of protest for this section as it appeared in the first edition. I'm leaving it in for both entertainment and shock value. Of course some people make money as affiliates advertising on AdWords. Many others waste gobs of time and money in a losing effort. Ever heard of the expression "the house always wins"?

8. Two excellent manuals covering lead generation and related tactics are: Michael Stelzner, *Writing White Papers: How to Capture Readers and Keep Them Engaged* (WhitePaperSource Publishing, 2006); and Brian Carroll, *Lead Generation for the Complex Sale: Boost the Quality and Quantity of Leads and Increase Your ROI* (McGraw-Hill, 2006).

9. For my overview, see "AdWords Quality Score: Can Your Business Model Be Banned?", SearchEngineLand.com, September 25, 2007.

10. Helpful suggestions of this type are now becoming second nature to panelists at interactive "website clinic" sessions held during industry conferences such as SES and SMX. A site clinic panelist might ask an audience member to explain the purpose of several competing goals on a home page, and in general help the business (as manifested in its online communications) focus. For one popular panelist's written work in this area, see Larry Bailin, *Mommy, Where Do Customers Come From? How to Market to a New World of Connected Customers* (Larstan Publishing, 2007).

11. But see Rubel's *mea culpa*, "The Web 2.0 World is Skunk Drunk on Its Own Kool-Aid," Micropersuasion.com, October 29, 2007.

12. Yes, I managed to get through this paragraph without mentioning Facebook, but that doesn't mean you shouldn't investigate it.

Part III

Intermediate-Level Strategies

Chapter 7

Keyword Selection and Bidding: Tapping into Powerful AdWords Features

Keyword selection and bidding are core features of AdWords. A clear understanding of how each feature works will help you use them effectively.

At the most basic level, your keyword list is a list of words and phrases that you expect your potential customers to use in Google searches. Bidding is the process by which you indicate how much you're willing to spend each time one of your ads is clicked. Your bidding strategy is one of the determinants of how prominently your ad is displayed when a user enters one of your keywords.

We've already covered some of these ideas, but they're such important building blocks in your targeting strategy, they're worth probing in more depth.

How Matching Options Work

Before delving into the theory and mechanics of keyword lists, let's look at matching options and how they work. Matching options provide the tools to fine-tune your keyword list and ensure that it focuses on your target audience. Without a clear understanding of how matching options work, you may be wasting a significant portion of your advertising budget by casting your net either too wide or not wide enough.

Exact, Broad, and Phrase Matching

Many campaigns I've reviewed were not working well simply because the advertiser wasn't aware of the fact that the default setting of AdWords is "broad match." I've also seen plenty of campaigns hobbled by an advertiser determined to eliminate all nonproductive clicks by forcing ads to display on exact matches only.

As you can see in Figure 7-1, matching options are activated by the use of special punctuation in the keyword list. Notice that this advertiser is using two matching options within the same ad group: exact match and broad match. The exact match for the single-word query

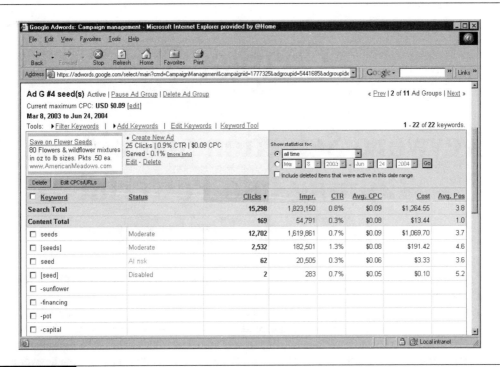

FIGURE 7-1   A short keyword list using both broad and exact match

seeds is in brackets, and the broad match is listed without punctuation. Because this advertiser set aside this ad group specifically to test the performance of a popular single word along with the plural of that word, there is no need for a phrase match in this case. (A single word within quotes actually acts the same as if it were not in quotes—since there is no word order to worry about with a single-word query, phrase match would be treated the same as broad match.) Note that the broad match for the query **seeds** generates about five times as many clicks as the exact match. This illustrates how broad matching helps you cast a wider net without doing a lot of work.

So how does this work exactly, and what is the benefit to you? We'll get to how it works in a minute. As for the benefit, it is significant, especially in terms of ease of use and improved campaign performance. Recall that in the early days of Overture advertising, everything was an exact match, which meant that advertisers' ads would not appear unless the keyword list contained the exact word or phrase typed in by the searcher. So, if you wanted to get your ad in front of the user typing **mustang gt 2002 ford**—not an unimaginable query, just a very rare one—your keyword list would have to include that exact phrase. Since anticipating every conceivable phrase a user might enter is impossible, you ended up with an enormous keyword list and still missed some potential customers.

Google's introduction of matching options has made it easier for advertisers to generate a higher volume of clicks without being forced to generate huge lists with every imaginable keyword combination in them. As discussed earlier, there might be some benefit to pursuing "The Long Tail" of unusual keyword combinations, but this benefit can be overstated. If you are pouring 50% of your time and analytical energies into 2% of your total click volume, you've got a problem.

You might find substantial differences in your cost per click, and probably in the degree of targeting, among the three major syntax forms available on AdWords:

- ■ **Exact**   The entry typed in by the user must exactly match a word or phrase appearing in your keyword list. Enclose your keyword or phrase in brackets to force exact matching.

- ■ **Broad**   Keywords and phrases entered without brackets or quotes will be interpreted as broad matching. Broad matching is designed to trigger your ad whenever all the words in your broad match keyword string appear anywhere in the user's search query.

- ■ **Phrase**   When you want a particular phrase to trigger your ad every time it appears, surround it with quotation marks. This is different from exact matching in that additional words can appear either before or after this phrase in the user's query.

NOTE   *The use of negative keywords, which can also be considered a matching option, is covered in Chapter 9.*

Exact Matching

Exact matches are useful for controlling the number of clicks generated by common words and phrases. For example, if you distribute electric drills, saws, and the like, you might include the phrase **power tool** in your keyword list. However, left on its own (broad matched), the phrase would display your ad any time both words appeared, in any order, in a user's search query. The result would be a large number of uninterested users seeing but not clicking your ad, lowering your CTR. The other alternative is equally bad—curious, but uninterested users clicking your ad with no intention of purchasing, thereby increasing your cost and reducing your ROI.

Exact matching enables you to eliminate both of these problems because your ad will display only when the user enters the words you've selected, in the order you've indicated. To create an exact matching keyword or phrase, enclose it in brackets—**[power tool]**. Keep in mind that exact matching, unlike phrase matching, does not trigger your ad if the phrase is part of a larger query. Therefore, **[power tool]** would not trigger your ad if the user entered **cordless power tool**.

NOTE   *Exact matches and phrase matches are excluded from expanded matches, which include plurals and variations. Therefore, using the previous example, the **[power tool]** entry in your keyword list would not trigger your ad if the user typed **power tools** rather than **power tool**.*

Broad Matching

The broad matching option is the least targeted and, depending on your competition, may be the hardest to make work, so you generally need to bid lower on broad matches. The other side of the coin is that broad matching offers the widest reach for the least amount of effort. For example, if you use the word **tennis** in your keyword list, your ad is going to show every time someone types a query like **ticket prices for tennis tournaments** or **history of tennis**. If you add other words but still use no quotes or brackets in your keyword list (for example, **tennis discount store**), you may capture a broader range of slight variations than you would get if you used an exact match like **[tennis discount store]**. Let's say someone types the phrase **tennis store discount** or **where do I find a store with tennis discount gear?** A broad match will still show your ad on these two searches, whereas an exact or phrase match would not.

While broad matching is not usually a good idea for common single keywords, it is great for specific terminology and names. The number of queries containing the word **tennis** is just so high, it's unlikely your clickthrough rate, or your sales conversion rates, will be sustainable if you use such an untargeted broad match. On the other hand, if you're in a niche industry selling Egyptian papyrus as a gift, your search volume on a word like **papyrus**, even used as a broad match, will be much lower, and you should be able to keep your campaign running without dropping below the minimum clickthrough rate enforced by Google, or blowing through your budget too quickly. For one word that actually means something really specific, like **aromatherapy** or **Caligula**, you might find again that the term is targeted enough that you can get away with broad matching.

Those rare advertisers who have been able to keep a one-word, popular, broad-matched term such as **tennis** alive (achieving high enough Quality Scores to make them economically feasible) have often improved their overall performance markedly. Think of the following scenario. While most advertisers can't keep their ad running on a particular term, you write an ad that's just a little more relevant. Then, you filter out a wide range of irrelevant words using negative keywords (see Chapter 9 for more on negative keywords). Between these two tactics, you manage to eke out a consistent CTR of 0.7%, and wind up paying an average of 16 cents per click on a high volume of clicks. Such a term can generate a volume so much higher than the rest of the phrases in your account that it can have a decisive impact on whether a campaign has a positive or negative ROI. And since one of the main problems with online advertising is too small a reach, many advertisers love it when they can connect with a wider range of targeted prospects while keeping the cost down.

Phrase Matching

Phrase matching is my personal favorite among matching options. When you want a certain phrase (two or more words in a specific word order) to trigger your ad, all you have to do is enclose the phrase in quotes. For example, surrounding the phrase **landscape architects** with quotes (**"landscape architects"**) triggers your ad whenever a user types those words, in that order, regardless of what else the user includes in the query. So, adding the phrase **"landscape architects"** to your keyword list means your ad will display when users type queries such as these:

seattle landscape architects
landscape architects society
east coast landscape architects who travel south for the winter

Many advertisers will discover substantial cost savings with better use of matching options even if they do nothing else to improve their campaigns. With some experimentation you will probably discover the combination of exact, broad, and phrase matching that works best for you.

CPCs on Different Matching Options

Many advertisers look at the differences in cost per click (CPC) and ROI that seem to occur with different matching options. It can be an interesting guide to user intent. Users who type three-word queries that include the words in the phrase match **"storm insurance"**, for example, might be more sophisticated on average than those who simply type the two-word query. Your bids might need to adjust upwards to reflect that, if these are better customers for you. Some advertisers seem to think that exact matching is "safer," or "more targeted," but it isn't inherently so.

Based on the assumption that exact matching is more targeted, one common question is this: are prices always higher on exact matches? If so, why? The answer is that it depends. There is nothing inherently "good" about exact match from a campaign economics standpoint. But sometimes exact matches—especially exact matches of three or more words—will perform relatively well from a CTR standpoint, perhaps because competitors using other broad and phrase matches are content with reaching a wider audience with an ad that is less relevant, on average, to any given searcher. If you really know the psychology of your user, you might find that you pull very high CTRs on long exact matches like **[research gay travel]** or **[apply for a student loan]**. Even if that exact match works great for you, you might not need to bid as high due to the CTR benefit you're receiving. There's a hole in this theory, unfortunately. Google assesses keyword Quality Score as if the keyword were an exact match—that is, in such a way as to discount match type in Quality Score calculations. So the reason you'll generally see higher prices (not lower) on exact matches is because they're more tightly targeted to user buying intent. Broad matches are not penalized for their (fully expected) lower CTR's, but their conversion rates are typically lower, so they attract lower bids to achieve equivalent ROI to the same keywords in exact match form.

In many cases, you'll be a more effective advertiser if you cast a slightly wider net with a three-word broad match like **how vc funding** as opposed to a long exact match like **[how to get vc funding]**. It's just too much work to find every long exact match phrase when you can be nearly as targeted with multiple-word broad matches.

Keyword Research

One of the most important tasks faced by an advertiser is the generation of the core list of keywords used in a campaign. While there are many keywords that are obvious, there are probably just as many that aren't. Fortunately, a number of resources are readily available to help you in your quest for the most effective keyword list.

The Google AdWords Keyword Tool

While a large number of third-party keyword-generating software packages have sprung up, the first tool you should explore is only a mouse click or two away from your AdWords campaign. The Google AdWords keyword tool is doing an increasingly better job of providing lists of suggested keywords to augment the lists that you may build yourself at the outset of your campaign. The best way to access the keyword tool is at the Ad Group level under the Keywords tab. Click on "keyword tool." Or, find the link under Tools, under the Campaign Management tab.

With the latest version of the keyword tool, you will see an interesting menu of options. For starters, you can enter a few specific phrases to get further information on those and related keywords. In Figure 7-2, you can see a list of keywords related to the phrase "disaster recovery." The monthly search frequency is included for each keyword. Note that the frequency listed will be geared to the geotargeting of your campaign, so you'll see larger numbers of searches in the stats if you're targeting many countries or all of the United States, whereas you'll see smaller numbers of searches if your campaign targets a small region.

Don't overlook the rightmost column heading, Match Type. This offers a drop-down list that quickly switches all the keywords in the list to your preferred matching option. To avoid the typical inefficiency of the average campaign that just uses the default—broad match—try

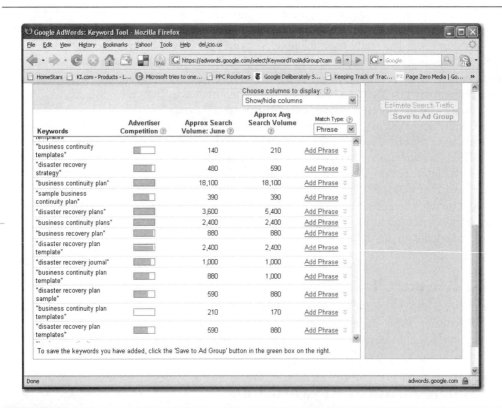

FIGURE 7-2   Google AdWords offers an increasingly robust keyword research tool, with hard data based on real monthly Google search frequencies.

switching it to phrase match. This comes in handy if you actually select any of the keywords to add to the basket of keywords you'll be importing directly into your ad group. The interface makes it easy to do this in an instant. No cutting and pasting is required. Just click on the Add Phrase link. On the far right of the screen, the keywords are added to the list, and you're offered several options, including, of course, adding them to an ad group.

The keyword tool will alert you to the many queries that might resemble your researched keywords but might be quite irrelevant to your line of business. Using the keyword tool can be a real wake-up call, reminding you of the fact that very few people typing keywords that include your word or phrase might be searching for what you offer, and that lack of targeting could be the explanation for why you are finding it difficult to keep your CTR high.

Unlike a third-party vendor, Google can't explicitly discuss keyword strategy. They're too close to the situation, with issues about their own revenues, data overload and complexity, and user satisfaction with search results to consider. So this tool has its pros and cons. The worst part is that it's rather poorly documented and won't really go the "extra mile" for you in terms of discovery.

But maybe it's all too easy to complain. The keyword tool has gotten a lot better, and many advertisers still have no idea that it's better than third-party tools that are more highly touted (and cost money). Say, wouldn't it be cool if the tool would analyze the content of your home page and related pages, and come back with a list of suggested keywords, grouped into concepts? Well, the AdWords keyword tool offers this! This is the Site Related Keywords option (one of the two main tabs at the top of the keyword tool main screen). This looks at the text on your website, or any site of your choice, and then attempts to suggest lists of related keywords, broken into themes. This requires some legwork on your part. It will give you ideas, but you'll need to incorporate those ideas into your ad group structure in a way that makes sense.

But wait, there's more! Wouldn't it be nice if you could also cut and paste chunks of text from news articles, trade magazines, marketing materials, and various places on the Web, and plug them into a keyword tool that will come up with a bunch of related words, grouped by concepts, again? Well, the AdWords tool does this too. This is a box you can enter text into, positioned just below the main Site Related Keywords section.

Perhaps it's not the lack of Google documentation that is really the issue with the keyword tool. It's a lack of motivation! Even as everything is handed to advertisers on a silver platter, most won't get past default options in the AdWords interface; many will assume third-party overlays do a better job. Yep, what's nagging at me is probably that Google is so darn low-key about their tools, they won't be on your back pushing you or instructing you to use them. I've met one of the architects of this tool, Ariel Bardin, and he and his team sound quite humble to me. Ariel probably likes the tool a lot. But he probably won't be coming to your office to play show-and-tell. So the next steps are up to you.

Keyword Research Tools and Tips

As good as the Google AdWords keyword tool is, it may not be enough for your needs. In that case you might want to consider one of the many third-party solutions that are available. In addition, you can pick up ideas simply by reading the news and watching TV.

Use Third-Party Tools: WordTracker

Every few years, about as often as I write an edition of this book, I revisit the major third-party keyword tools, to see if there's anything about them that has improved significantly.

WordTracker (www.wordtracker.com) is the best-known keyword research tool on the market. What can be confusing is to sort out whether the various add-on bells and whistles actually add anything to the core functionality of the tool, which is finding you better keywords based on what people are actually typing.

These products may be helpful, but they're far from ideal. The flawed core data collection method—search query data from Metacrawler and Dogpile, two metasearch engines with relatively low volumes—is at least comparable to getting data straight from Google, but not quite as good. Several of the add-ons are red herrings that will have you wasting your time with ponderous planning rather than just building keyword lists directly and quickly within AdWords. And a couple of the tools, such as the very sensible lateral keyword research to give you ideas about what other words and names are common for your general industry niche, seem like they'd be easier to use if you could buy them a la carte. Instead, what you get is a bloated-up package of fairly decent, but cumbersome, tools, all at a high cost.

Nonetheless, it's worth trying WordTracker to see what it does, and a free trial will keep you busy for an hour or so.

KeywordDiscovery, by Trellian

Visiting the KeywordDiscovery.com website, you're treated to a who's who of search marketing experts, including my good friends Jill Whalen, Andy Beal, and Greg Jarboe, all singing the praises of this product in the testimonials.

At the risk of not being invited to a cool Trellian party at their Australian headquarters (have a cold one for me there, Jill, Andy, and Greg!), I have to wonder if the product lives up to the hype. "Beginning at $69.95 a month" is, again, a fairly high price to pay for keyword research you could probably do somewhere else. The highlight appears to be the ability to garner keyword search frequencies from several databases, including a historical one. Does it add value beyond the Google tool? I still need convincing.

Taking It to the Next Level: Competitive Intelligence

One way to advance your keyword research, as well as your overall level of knowledge of your industry vertical, is to use tools that "spy" on what your competitors are up to.

Certainly there may be some ethical dilemmas at stake here depending on how public the information is—you should sort these out before you proceed.

AdGooroo is one among several moderate-to-low-cost offerings that offers support to paid search advertisers in the form of a suite of "power tools." One example of a report that can be generated using AdGooroo is a list of every keyword your competitors are bidding on. (How is this achieved? Possibly, by generating massive numbers of unauthorized automated search queries, and "screen scraping" to determine which ads are showing up on given keyphrases.) In practice, this seems to be less useful than you might think. I tried an apparel-related query for this competitive intelligence report, for example, and got a list of tens of thousands of terms being bid on by Victoria's Secret. Because the list isn't categorized helpfully, and includes tons of keywords that are unrelated to the products my client sells, it might actually do more harm than good. Dumping large numbers of irrelevant keywords into an account is likely to hurt the account's overall Quality Score.

Overall, the usability of AdGooroo is seriously hurting. If forced to rate the product I'd give it no better than 5 out of 10.

I've had better luck with Keyword Spy, which offers uncanny (and more usable) competitive intelligence on the keywords your competitors are advertising on, their ad copy, their organic search performance, and much else besides. It offers levels between "free trial" and reasonably priced versions priced well under $100 per month. It's particularly cost-effective if you want to track multiple competitors, or if you are working on multiple projects at once. Today, competitive intelligence has achieved a higher degree of significance in paid search strategy. Though not all the tools are reliable, and some guerrilla strategies are just plain mean or counterproductive, for most of us, it's tempting (and useful) to peek under the curtain. Spyfu is another popular and well-liked tool in this area. There are several others worth checking out.

For deeper-pocketed advertisers, Hitwise Search Intelligence offers more-reliable third-party data about user search patterns. A recent favorable review by keyword research expert Christine Churchill noted a price tag of $50,000–60,000. Depending on your needs, you may be able to scale back to purchase a less full-featured version for $10,000–20,000. Depending on your overall marketing budget, it could be worth every penny.

Read the News

As you get closer to filling out your keyword list, you'll need to search for more insights and lateral-thinking opportunities. I find that a news article on a particular industry will often contain insights into key problems facing consumers and companies in that sector. Let's say it's credit problems. Where there is a sense of urgency, you'll likely stumble across new and unusual keywords that are commonly typed by your prospects. In the credit area, for example, let's say the article is about credit bureaus and FICO scores. As you read quotes from consumers and industry players, you may find additional real-life ways of describing consumer credit problems that your more formal research has overlooked.

The nice thing is you can use a source like Google News, Topix.net, or Yahoo Finance to look up archived news on a given topic or stock symbol.

Watch TV

No, I don't mean you should sit around watching *Leave It to Beaver* reruns. (Though, if you're in the advertising business, try a personal favorite of mine—*Mad Men*.) If you come across a television ad for a company in your industry (if you're one of those increasingly rare folks who doesn't just avoid them via Tivo or flipping around), you might find certain buzzwords or promotions being mentioned that appear nowhere in your AdWords account. Picking up on these kinds of catchphrases is a perfectly legitimate way that you can leverage someone else's hefty TV advertising budget. Your competitor may be drawing attention to an issue and causing a spike in Internet searches for information related to that issue.

The Bottom Line: Use Your Own Campaign

So far, the abstract game of figuring out what people are going to search for in your industry area has a fairly unsatisfactory feel, doesn't it? It's because we're trying to generate projections based on user search behavior, which is in fact valuable data that search engine don't publish for just anyone to see. We're fumbling around and guessing. Keyword research tools can be helpful for brainstorming, but if you know your business well and build your keyword list first based on that knowledge, chances are, most of what the tools tell you will elicit a "tell me something I don't already know!" response from you.

Perhaps the most accurate and useful tools are available within the actual paid search keyword advertising interfaces themselves. The most useful projection and keyword research tools for our present purposes is the one inside Google AdWords, but you can only take this so far.

You might be forgetting that the most accurate source of keyword search frequency should be your historical, real-life campaign data! If you've built out a reasonably comprehensive account, and run the budget high enough for full delivery of your ads, you'll have a genuine sense of how many searches are being done on your keywords in a given time period. That's why it's so important to test and react to real-world data, rather than messing endlessly with projections.

Let's walk through the kind of exceptional keyword data that are available to you after you've actually been *running* an AdWords campaign. In Figure 7-3 you can see some fairly standard

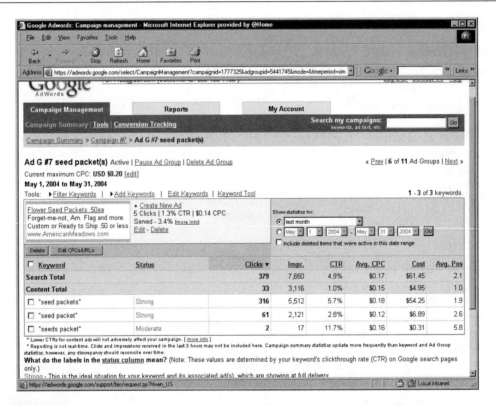

FIGURE 7-3   Ray Allen knew roughly how many people searched for the term [seed packets] in May 2004.

reporting for a typical AdWords campaign over the month of May 2004. By looking at the number of impressions of his ad on any given phrase, the advertiser, Ray Allen, now knows (assuming he kept his AdWords campaign at full delivery throughout the month) that 5,512 people in the United States searched for the phrase **seed packets** or some query including that phrase, during May. The number is slightly lower than the previous month's 6,587. That's not a projection, it's real, and it makes sense intuitively. People were more into planning for their gardens in April than they were in May. These patterns may vary from month to month, but it's a much clearer benchmark than the information provided by a third-party tool that has no way of knowing what real users are doing on Google. Moreover, this advertiser knows that 5.7% of the people typing that term into Google clicked on his ad, down slightly from the 6.7% in April. Pretty good. You'll never learn that from any "research" tool. The total cost of running that advertising to learn this? About $50. And that $50 was spent on advertising that also generated new customers.

You can get as specific in your analysis as you like once you have your campaign running. In this example, 143 people searched for **seed packets** on May 6, 2004. And 9.0% of them clicked on Ray's ad. Pretty tough to predict that without actually running a campaign.

Keywords You're Already Using

For many of my clients, especially those in retail, generating an exhaustive keyword list is a task that looks deceptively easy, because most of this material is already on their websites. Articles and sales materials may contain much of the needed jargon that would go into a successful AdWords campaign. Product pages might contain product descriptions, product names, product attributes, or brand names. Sensible categorization still eludes many companies, unfortunately. If your categories themselves aren't intuitive, then your paid search campaign will have a hard time working around that. Paid search experts can often suggest work-arounds, like custom-generated (more granular than exists on the default website) category pages. We can also take a basic keyword list, beef it up to be more robust and comprehensive, and then work on additional expansion. It's not quite as simple as it looks.

If you want to be really exhaustive, review not only your website and your competitors' websites (including any keyword or description meta tags you might be able to see in your browser by viewing the HTML source of the competitors' pages), but also your website statistics (server logs or web analytics such as Google Analytics) to see what kinds of search phrases are leading people to your site.

Examples of Unsold Keyword Inventory

Discovering new and untapped keywords can be like the proverbial ocean voyage to the new world. If you get there first, who knows what riches might await? The "new world" is getting more populated, however. To stretch the analogy a bit, there might not be much free land left, but there is still undervalued land.

As you build your keyword list, use both deductive and inductive logic to expand that list based on what you know of the demographic profile of your target customers. In other words, develop a correlation you might like to test—whether you can sell skateboards to people who type **Tony Hawk**, for example. If it hits (pulls a good CTR at high volumes with low cost, and site visitors begin performing desired actions on your site, such as buying something or signing up for your newsletter), you know you're onto something. The Tony Hawk example is cheating a bit, because it seems Tony lends his name to skateboards for sale. That means Google's Quality Score algorithm is more likely to see that name as relevant to a skateboard products page, especially one that includes Tony Hawk products. Some other famous skateboarder's name might not be as relevant and thus might incur a lower Quality Score. It's worth testing.

What about inductive logic? If an ad for sporting equipment on phrases relating to a sports figure's name performs well for you, and you don't fully understand why, back up and try to figure out why. That will give you a new theory that you can use to generate new potential correlations. For example, if you successfully sold a book on skateboard techniques to people typing **Tony Hawk** into Google, you suddenly have about 100 more names you might try adding to your campaign—assuming you're more resourceful than I am when it comes to generating the names of a hundred famous skateboarders.

A potentially clever technique is to target affinity-indicating phrases that don't attract many sellers of products. For example, pick a historical event that might be a common search phrase for people who also just happen to share the demographic characteristics that fit your offer, and bid on this phrase. How many are bidding on **Louisiana purchase**, **Gettysburg Address**, or **Battle of Versailles**?

Changing Environment for Keyword Experimentation

Well, hang on a second. Whereas back in previous versions of AdWords, it was feasible to cross over from the commercial realm to the informational realm—in other words, attempt to spark interest in your product or service among people who are searching for things like **Gettysburg Address**—in the present incarnation, AdWords is geared to allow fewer ads to show up in such situations. While the overarching challenge remains CTR, the fact that "other relevancy factors" are part of the Quality Score algorithm means that we're seeing a lot of white space in the designated ad area on noncommercial queries these days. In essence, Google is trying to tailor search results pages to user needs and expectations. This deepens the expectation that users will respond favorably to ads on commercial queries, so in some sense that helps advertisers. But it means that the notion of endless keyword inventory, there for the taking, is dying slowly as Google applies lower Quality Scores to keywords that don't seem to match up with the product being sold in a context of commercial intent. That's another way of saying they've raised prices on experiments we used to run in the hopes of paying 5–10 cents per click. (Cue sad-face emoticon!)

Still, advertiser laziness isn't completely a thing of the past, and many niche terms in the commercial realm are undervalued. Focused terms like **Louisiana travel** attract fewer advertisers than you might think, given the pool of thousands of advertisers who could stand to benefit from placing ads on this term.

The Long Tail Is about Users Being Unruly

Search frequency distribution graphs show that a lot of terms get searched only once or twice in a given year. What's most interesting is the percentage of searches that have only been performed once, ever. Search engines regularly report that their entire historical search database shows 20–25% of search phrases having been searched only a single time.

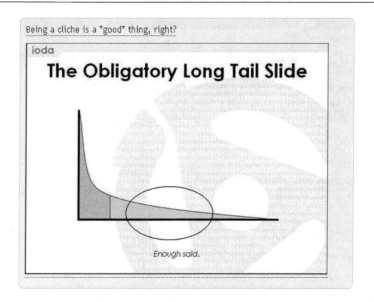

Being a cliche is a *good* thing, right?

ioda

The Obligatory Long Tail Slide

Enough said.

FIGURE 7-4 The "torso" of the Long Tail graph is the part in the middle. These are niche, semipopular terms that will often be your campaign's bread and butter.

What does this tell you about users? They're unpredictable. They want a lot of different information. Micro-niches are likely to thrive in terms of user response.

Knowing that there is a Long Tail of infrequently searched terms (I discuss the concept of the Long Tail a bit later in this chapter) is not the same as having a good strategy for tapping into the few relevant ones that will impact your business. The reality is, you can no longer jam hundreds of thousands of phrases into your account (using some kind of mass keyword mining tool, for example, to generate endless lists) hoping that some will get a response. Either Google will simply forbid it above a certain threshold or you'll run into Quality Score issues unless most of the keywords are highly relevant.

So while you'll want to research infrequently searched keywords *to a point*, don't expect to go all the way down the Long Tail, discovering every potential phrase. The middle of the search frequency graph is where a lot of the potential customers lie. This is sometimes called the "torso." (See Figure 7-4.) Advertisers should be as exhaustive as possible in discovering relatively obvious, semifrequently searched terms, rather than spending countless hours searching out the most infrequently searched terms at the skinniest part of the tail.

Benefits of Being the Only Advertiser on a Phrase

In Figures 7-5 and 7-6 you can see two examples of search engine results pages that have only a single advertiser. The most obvious benefit to this is cost: if you're the only advertiser on the screen for a given term, you'll have less competition. Of course, due to the magic of Quality

An Israeli manufacturer takes advantage of the lack of advertisers on a misspelled term.

Clever advertiser Gurneys advertised on the botanical term **verbena tenuisecta**. It would be much harder to gain high placement in organic results.

Scores, you won't necessarily pay the minimum of 1 cent, but in general, you should find some bargains. The more of these phrases you have in your account, provided they're relevant, the better your economics will look.

The best way to have more phrases that no one else can successfully advertise on is to engineer your business so it does something unique. Companies that try to drive traffic to an existing stale product lineup by interrupting people are going to have a tougher challenge on their hands than companies whose marketing is "in sync" with an evolving, responsive lineup of products and services.

The second benefit of being the sole advertiser may be branding and positioning. Be the Purple Cow! For many businesses it's not particularly desirable to have to prove that you're the best at something. The key to strong margins and customer loyalty is to have customers think that you're the *only* viable solution to their problem at a given time. When Ray Allen and I first discussed the idea of advertising on the Latin names for wildflowers, no one else was doing it. Ray has no doubt gained hundreds of new customers by showing up—in both the free search index and in Google AdWords listings—on botanical search terms that none of his competitors thought to highlight. The fact that many advertisers keep their campaigns turned off when their products are out of season might play into the hands of the advertiser Gurneys, who is showing up for a botanical term in Figure 7-6. Being the only advertiser there, a click would likely only cost a few pennies. Hardly a calamity even if some products are out of season.

Of course, it's getting harder to find that niche. If there is anyone at all out there doing what you do, chances are they're going to stumble on AdWords eventually, especially for the core terms relating to that business. Type **"pet urn"** into Google and you'll see not one, not two, but several ads for pet cremation urns.[1]

One of the big challenges for online advertisers, especially with the advent of comparison shopping services such as Shopping.com and Froogle, is to guard against declining profit margins that result from exploding consumer access to goods and comparative information about those goods. Some consumers will compare on price alone. Others may run you ragged with questions about your products and services before they buy.

One way to fend off this pressure on profit margins is to build a trusted brand by making sure you're showing up in many different places online (paying for traffic in a variety of areas), building a word-of-mouth reputation, and doing things that no other company does.

But another great way to get around the comparison shopping problem is to be smart enough to be the *only* advertiser to bother to show up on a given search term.

Keyword Brainstorming: It's about *Them*

Keyword selection is pretty much synonymous with *targeting*. Let's start a conversation with potential customers who are interested in what we have to say. And let's not waste money and precious user attention bothering everyone else. AdWords offers a certain amount of flexibility to push that envelope, but you can't completely violate the rules of relevance and common sense.

With broad keywords and broad matches, you're often targeting, well, broadly. But as you build a longer list of unusual phrases, you'll find that you're micro-targeting your ads to some very specific types of customers. You have the opportunity to get "in the face" of only a small subset of people. Therefore, one of the best investments of your time may be in brainstorming to come up with very targeted keywords and phrases.

Solve Your Target Market's Problems

Certainly, the best prospective customers are generally typing a search query that actually describes your product or service, but other searchers (and this doesn't mean they aren't potential customers) may be typing something related to the problem your product could solve for them. Let's think about problems for a second. There are many kinds of problems: broken windows, broken promises, broken relationships, broken laws, broken homes, broken legs, broken software, broken hardware, broken banks. And there are thousands upon thousands of businesses dedicated to patching up, fixing, solving, healing, or masking such problems—or just consoling or distracting people who suffer from them. People using search engines won't always type in words related to your solution, patch, consolation, or distraction, but they may have all kinds of ways of describing different aspects of their dilemma. Most will be searching for information and will not be in a buying mood. But if 2% click on your ad, you only pay for those clicks. From there, 2%, 5%, or 10% may buy. It's a numbers game.

Someone selling allergy medication might want to include **irritated nasal passage** and a host of other symptoms of someone suffering from airborne allergies, for example. (In spite of the fact that I used this example in the first edition of this book, at this time there are only seven advertisers in the United States showing up for this term, whereas there are 74,600 pages in the Google index that contain all of those words, and 136 that show that exact phrase.) If your prospective markets exhibit many *symptoms* that would predispose them to your solution, which is designed to get to the root of the problem, then you may be able to distract them (ever so slightly) from the information they *thought* they wanted. After all, people don't always know what they're looking for. People who believe that online search needs to be reinvented as some kind of product catalog, where people go in and drill down to the exact thing they need, must not have much imagination, either about what shopping is really like or about what it means to do online research.

If this dynamic applies to your business, spend a half-hour generating a long list of symptoms—be these caused by computer operating system problems, financial problems, health problems, or whatever—and think about how you might use them as keywords in your AdWords account. A computer crash could be caused by a virus. It wouldn't hurt, in this case, to try showing your ad for a personal firewall technology to people typing in very specific phrases related to computer errors and crashes they might be facing. It's nitty-gritty work, though. After you get past the obvious—**computer crash, computer infected, windows problems**—you'll have to dig deeper to come up with a more extensive vocabulary. The benefit of stopping your discovery process early is that it saves work and you'll probably be focusing on the most obvious words, words that are nicely targeted and have the best chance of creating a sale. Those of you who continue to add new groups of experimental words, though, will discover less expensive words. Some of these will *always* be less expensive because they're so offbeat and won't attract crowds.

Have you noticed that this type of keyword research is actually a bit of user-profiling research that requires empathy and reason at your end? Keyword research tools will only take you so far; they'll help point you to similar phrases that are popular with searchers. But you can discover more useful ones on your own.

It's not the specific example that matters here; it's the process. Once you've identified your target audience, the game becomes a strategic brainstorming exercise of imagining their online search behavior. You'll be asking yourself a slightly different question than a traditional media buyer might ask—"what magazines do potential buyers of our skateboards read?"—but then again, it's not so far off. What you're essentially doing with a keyword discovery process is buying exposure to a very specific target audience. Because there's never been anything quite like this in the history of advertising, you have to throw a lot of your traditional assumptions out the window.

Unless you've been dealing with search engine marketing as a full-time job, you're bound to be lulled into making the classic rookie mistake—the same mistake most of us made when we thought we were optimizing our sites for "free" search engine traffic: focusing on a limited range of keywords, obsessing about them, and trying to put all of our efforts into attracting users who search for them. While it's true that the most popular search queries are indeed valuable commodities to the advertiser, it would be foolish not to continue searching for the incremental revenue that might be generated with further testing of unusual or highly specific keyword ideas. Do this as long as it makes sense, but then, it's OK to stop. The incremental value of endless keyword research may be slim.

In some industries, especially highly technical or B2B markets, mental blocks get in the way of keyword research. After observing how dozens of client accounts went from being trapped in impossible bidding wars to being consistently profitable, I asked myself what the problem was with the first approach they had typically taken to keyword selection. The problem was often this: they were getting caught up in insider phrases and insider thinking. Insider thinking is endemic to corporate life, it seems, even if you're a small startup. Hold a meeting, even if only two people are present, and suddenly it's about "we this" and "we that." But what about *them*—the potential customers? Let's face it. Every person that might be predisposed to buy the services of a disaster recovery firm might not type the phrase **disaster recovery firm**. There is some art and some science to determining what such a person might indeed type in. If it's not **disaster recovery firm**, then what? Should we just load in words like **disaster**, **hurricane**, and **flood** and hope for the best? Of course not—too general. Millions of people use Google to search for information about disasters and hurricanes. A tiny few would want the services of a certain type of consulting firm, and Google won't show your ad if only a miniscule percentage of users click it.

Typing just about any query is good enough to show corporate arrogance in action. When I type **disaster recovery**, for example, in the advertising area on Google there is a range of IT firms screaming at me about "data disaster recovery." Indeed, for their own convenience, many appear to have talked themselves into believing that there is only one kind of disaster that can occur in the world—data loss disasters. Beam me up, Scotty... please.

We don't know, and probably won't soon know, all that much about user intention and how it breaks down among people typing ambiguous queries into search engines. But in determining what keywords to target and the likely response, it's probably worth taking a deep breath and trying to understand at a commonsense level what a user might be looking for when typing a term like **disaster recovery**. Let's say the searcher is a manager who is going to be charged with developing a disaster recovery plan for her company using a mix of in-house and outsourced expertise. She's in the preliminary research stage before having a meeting to determine the terms of reference. She wants some reading material on the main issues about disaster recovery and will also be looking around for some experts she can talk to who might be able to point her towards companies that might be helpful in an advising capacity.

The first thing this user comes across, listed first in Google's main index results, is something called *Disaster Recovery Journal.* She subscribes immediately, becoming the 60,001st subscriber. She then goes to lunch.

Luckily, you, as an advertiser, have also been reading this publication. Already, this gives you an extensive lexicon of terms that may be of interest to your target market! Hundreds, when all is said and done. Sometimes, your target reader will want to learn more about one of these subtopics and will head to, you guessed it, Google, and type in that term. If you're lucky (and yes, a certain amount of luck is surely involved), your ad, targeted to one of those nitty-gritty little industry phrases, actually appeals to her more than any of the other listings she sees on the page. If you're good at converting website visitors to leads, and leads to sales—and yes, that process can take anything from a few seconds to a year, and is a numbers game like anything else—then it will be mission accomplished. As obvious keywords become prohibitively expensive, more and more guerrilla advertisers will need to understand how to find customers through the back door by targeting secondary terms intelligently.

One of the things you immediately notice from studying the disaster recovery industry and its jargon is that there is quite a bit of talk about "business continuity" in the same breath as "disaster recovery" planning. So advertising on the phrase **business continuity** becomes a no-brainer, or at least you'd think it would. It gets better, though. If your tracking is set up right, over time you'll be able to determine the return on investment of that part of your Google AdWords campaign that focuses on **disaster recovery** and related keywords, and the part that focuses on **business continuity** and variations of that term.

You don't need to know this in advance. You simply go ahead and set it up as an experiment and let the market tell you what works best. Then you'll be able to tell people (those you trust) strange stories at cocktail parties: "We generate more disaster recovery white paper downloads on the disaster recovery words, so at first we thought it was the higher-performing keyword area, but as it turned out, the ROI on business continuity words turned out to be much higher, because web exposure in this area helped us initiate several relationships with Fortune 500 clients! We know because we track things using this cool software..." Just be prepared for the victim of your minute analysis to make an excuse and head for the veggie dip. The life of an AdWords junkie can be lonely.

That's not a bad example, actually. Two years after using this example in this book (2005 edition), my firm finally bagged a client in the disaster recovery industry (we didn't have one at the time). Because I made competitor bid prices (in 2004–2005, I checked those out on the

Overture bid tool) public then, it won't violate client confidentiality to tell you that you'll pay upwards of $14.00 for a click on the phrase **business continuity**. But, of course, many other words are less expensive; it's a matter of patiently testing to see if any of the alternatives converts to leads.

You never know who's typing what, and you never want to base your keyword selection or your bidding strategy on gut feel or limited data, especially in B2B. When you're in a business that might generate only one or two really large contracts a year while generating a steady stream of smaller service contracts and software sales, a "rational" look at the payback on certain keywords, especially if it were over a short time frame, might lead you to wildly underestimate their value—at least until that big client inks a deal, at which point you might reevaluate your suppositions about what a certain phrase is worth to your business.

In any case, there often seems to be a subtle difference between advertising on terms that represent the kind of jargon and problems that might be fodder for your target market's search queries, and the preoccupations of the people who happen to work at your company or sit on its board of directors. Think about your market. Customers don't hold the same sacred views of your industry as you do—they're searching in an area that is new to them, after all. They are in a process of discovery. If you intercept some of them early in that process, you have a much better chance of being seen as uniquely able to fulfill their needs.

As branding consultant Rob Frankel wrote in an article entitled "Why Ads Are So Stupid" (www.robfrankel.com/dumbads.html):

> The fact is that the dynamics of advertising are different for everyone, at every level, in every business. Even looking across the street at your local competitor can be dangerous. I can't tell you the number of clients who tell me they run radio spots here or banner ads there because that's what their competition does. Oh yeah? Well what made the competition such media mavens? How do you know that they didn't follow someone else's misguided notions? Do they have more or less to spend than you do?

Keyword Variations: Plurals, Verb Forms, and Misspellings

When it comes to selling ads on keyword variations that might be considered trivial, such as plural forms, the industry is at a crossroads. The instinct of many large media buyers is that bidding separately on **ski boot** and **ski boots**, for example, is too complicated. But experienced advertisers know that no two situations are the same. While plural and singular forms might connote a similar meaning on one keyword, in another keyword area the differences in meaning from an advertiser's standpoint might be substantial. Moreover, many experienced advertisers have data that show one form of a word makes them money, whereas another form does not. What exactly is the reason that **pearl earrings** seems to be a more commercially viable term than **pearl earring**? I don't know for sure, but can speculate that the first person is more likely to be a shopper, and the second person might, at least some of the time, be looking for a photo, the name of a band, or who knows what. In most garden-variety retail search situations, plurals convert better and are, consequently, worth bidding higher on.

None of this would matter so much if the advertising weren't based on an auction system, or if Google didn't create such strict rules around things like CTR. But the fact is, once you get used to the idea that you can bid less on a form of a word that converts poorly to sales, it can be tough to give up that control. Also, if Google wants advertisers to be relevant and enforces rules to that effect, it might be hypocritical if they began selling keywords in "bundles," taking away some of the granularity that advertisers have come to appreciate.

Overture was the first industry player to begin automatically using matching technology (it was called Match Driver) to save advertisers the trouble of listing both singular and plural forms in their accounts. This soon expanded into verb stems and common misspellings. If a user types **seattle hotell** by accident, wouldn't an advertiser for **seattle hotel** want to show up anyway? No doubt. But because this kind of technology is automated, there are all sorts of unforeseen outcomes. And at various junctures, Overture was pushing the envelope too far, showing ads on too many variations without regard for the advertisers' wishes. At one point, they began factoring in the ad title you'd written, along with the keywords in your account, to decide whether to show your ad on a related keyword. A ridiculous example was an old ad of mine that I'd all but forgotten about, running only on Toronto-related and Canada-related keywords such as **Toronto marketing consultant**, **canadian search marketing**, and **search engine marketing Toronto**. The ad had a frivolous title: "World-Famous Consultant... from Toronto." Apparently, based partly on my ad titles, Overture's Match Driver was showing my ad on queries that had nothing to do with the keywords in my account, such as **famous Canadians**. A lot of people type that query, it seems. Hey, my title was a joke to get local companies to read my ad, but I'm obviously not Celine Dion or Peter Jennings. The kinds of people who clicked on the ad weren't prospective clients, needless to say.

In fall 2003, Google released a similar technology called "expanded broad matching," and it immediately began causing problems with campaign performance for some unlucky advertisers. Complaints on industry discussion forums, such as WebmasterWorld.com, were rampant. Some of my clients ran into major problems with increased spending for little return.

Google has been tweaking the technology ever since. It does work better now. At first, I feared that the new technology would render many of my favorite keyword tricks obsolete. But it did not. Google has backed off the expanded broad matching initiative to the point where many small variations are still performing quite differently in the marketplace, and are worth bidding on separately. You can often save money on some odd variations by using them explicitly and bidding less on them, which frequently generates higher ad positions for less money. You can opt out of expanded broad matching by making phrases into phrase matches or exact matches. This means that advertisers will continue to have the ability to maintain control over small keyword variations if they choose.

Let me run through a few of the major keyword variations you should consider adding to your account. The list is not exhaustive.

- Plural and singular forms.
- Verb forms, related nouns, related idioms (fix, fixing, fix up, fixing up, how to fix up, fix-it, fixer upper, fixer).

- Spelling mistakes or spelling variations (address, adress; email and e-mail).

- Numbers and codes (years, product numbers, other weird uses).

- Hyphenated and unhyphenated versions (soup ladle, soup-ladle).

- One word versus two words (teacup, tea cup).

- Abbreviations and acronyms.

- Phrases with who, what, when to capture readers who type a question into the search engine. (For example, **how do I repair a kite** or **how to launch a new business** might be common queries and might convert quite well.)

I've tinkered with many other tricks, such as using punctuation marks (**U.K.**) instead of just letters (**UK**). I'm not sure if they all work, since AdWords likely disregards certain punctuation marks such as periods. At certain points in time, these methods have worked, even if by accident. All I can say is, if conventional keywords aren't giving you great performance, try these tricks and any others you can think of. Although Google's policies may change, and some are undocumented, for now, some important principles to consider may be:

- The ampersand symbol (&) is treated like the word "and." You needn't include it.

- Periods are largely ignored. So "heroiclemur.com" will be interpreted as "heroiclemur com".

- Apostrophes in "men's" may be treated as a different search term than mens. You could try both variations.

- Again, this is mostly conjecture and subject to change. Adding variations doesn't hurt. But punctuation in keywords is ignored unless it changes meaning, by and large.

Going Narrow

After achieving some success following a principle like "more specific keywords are often more profitable," many of us become complacent and stop exploring. Real estate, for example, is an increasingly competitive field. Many realtors have discovered the value of targeting home buyers and sellers in particular regional markets using phrases like **atlanta home values**. While working with one realtor, I went a step further and made a suggestion that seemed obvious to me as a resident of a well-known area (High Park) that is sought by a percentage of home buyers: people are probably typing the names of neighborhoods into Google! Heck, for all I know, they're typing streets and the names of specific condo developments. So, if you've got a small campaign that's targeting buyers of Atlanta real estate, but find the keywords are getting too pricey, simply build out your keyword list. (Of course, that's not all you have to do. Your website is going to have to display your unique positioning and personality in that niche market, or you can forget about turning those clicks into leads.) A realtor who wants more business should have no problem generating it for still-reasonable costs per click just by thinking intuitively about probable search engine user behavior in the home buying field. In a hot condo market in many urban centers around the world, I find it amazing that so few realtors are buying AdWords targeted to the names of new buildings.

Whatever your field, make it your goal to double your click volume, targeting extremely targeted searchers, on keywords that should be priced at rock-bottom levels (due to other advertisers being too lazy to do what I'm suggesting here). In most cases, the return on your investment will improve substantially.

As you move forward, you'll engage in a process of extended keyword discovery. Once you master the art of keyword brainstorming and start using uncommon phrases along with keyword variations, you'll want to look at your account every month or two and attempt to revisit your keyword expansion efforts.

But listen to that other voice of reason, too. Know when to stop.

Keyword Progression, Initial Quality Scores, and Troubleshooting

Google is always happy to advise you what to do in order to keep the keywords in your AdWords account in a healthy state of "Great" Quality Scores: you should write more relevant ads and use sound campaign organization, as I've discussed thus far, to ensure you're getting as high a CTR as possible on all keywords. But what if the keywords come out of the gate with poor Quality Scores before you've had a chance to experiment with various ads? Under Quality-Based Bidding, it's crucial to understand that keyword expansion should almost be done with a "reverse logic": generate high CTRs and high Quality Scores by establishing your ad groups with low-volume, highly specific keywords, before entering broader words and broader matching options. Few of your competitors will understand this new logic; as a result, they may establish poor initial Quality Scores and be relegated to paying through the nose for clicks. A competitor in distress? In increasingly competitive markets, that's synonymous with hope!

Proceeding with Caution to Avoid Low Initial Scores

CTRs are a vitally important factor in Quality Score, and as they are established, they tend to predominate as a factor. The worst thing you can do is to lump a bunch of questionable, irrelevant, or very broad keywords into an ad group. To be sure, you'll want to try this later, but in the initial stages, pick very specific words that are clearly only directed at users with strong intent relevant to your offering. For example: **buy ski boots**. Advertisers cannot live on super-relevant phrases alone, I know. But get some high CTRs and high Quality Scores established for a few days or even a few weeks before building the more general words into your ad groups. It's a pain to have to stage it like this, but that's Google. You are better off building confidence in your quality first, rather than having to dig yourself out of a hole later.

Disapproved Keywords

Google doesn't allow advertising on certain keywords. I've run into prohibitions on liquor advertising and certain kinds of weapons, for example. From time to time, areas like casinos and online pharmacies are off limits, and using related keywords in your account might trigger an editorial review. If you run afoul of Google's keyword policies, they likely won't refer you to an exhaustive written policy to justify it; they'll simply send you a disapproval message, and there is likely little you can do. Policies on keyword prohibitions are set by senior people in the company, including the cofounders; editorial staff simply apply the rules.

Increasingly, you won't receive any type of editorial disapproval message because Google has folded many keyword policy decisions into the black box of Quality Score. Many kinds of keywords, and some specific keywords, have lower Quality Scores by default; or they may have lower Quality Scores in relation to your ad or landing page, from a relevancy standpoint. What that means is Google isn't willing to step up and explain a particular policy to you, but rather, conceals that policy behind a formula. You can now show your ads on certain classes of words— it'll just be enormously expensive, so you probably won't. That gets Google out of having to justify every decision they make about "troublesome" or "controversial" keywords. Apparently, Google can measure the price of "trouble," and charge you approximately the amount that'll be needed to offset it from their standpoint.

As with any decision, you can appeal to Google's editorial staff to reconsider, and sometimes your request will make it to a policy specialist for review. You have nothing to lose by trying, but some of these rules may be firm, so don't get your hopes too high.

Approaches to Bidding and Ad Position

Bidding is at the heart of AdWords strategy. If it makes logical sense to bid according to the quality of targeting you get from any advertising, then each keyword, potentially, has its own "best bid point" for your particular business. What makes that more complex is that this "best bid point" fluctuates with seasons, changing economic conditions, and as competitors come and go in the auction. As I've already discussed, AdWords determines ad position by assigning a Quality Score to each keyword and then by multiplying your maximum bid by your Quality Score. When many advertisers are competing, you must either bid high or have a high Quality Score, or some combination of the two, to appear near the top of the listings. Don't bid emotionally. You need to understand what a rational bidding strategy is for your marketing objectives, and stick to that plan.

What Do We Know about Ad Position and Visibility?

An unfortunate misconception in the industry today is that ad position is utterly decisive in determining whether you'll be visible. While both heat mapping (user eye tracking) studies and studies of campaign data certainly show that a higher percentage of users click on the most prominently placed listings, they do click in decent numbers on all listings that make it onto the first page of search results. Many users are curious enough to scan down the page to look for something that interests them.

One past problem with the Google bidding system is that you couldn't lock your ad into a certain position, even if you decided you preferred it. Let's say you find that positions 8, 9, and 10 are bargains, but you prefer 10 above all. Short of using third-party bid management software, you'd have trouble staying in that slot. Google has now released an option called "position preference." While it doesn't work perfectly, this feature attempts to keep your ad in the position range you specify, as far as your max bid and Quality Score make this possible. I find that, like many picky features in the interface, I never use this. This one can lead to underdelivery, so I'd rather actively manage a campaign and let my positions float.

Be aware that on some partner sites (such as AOL Search, Ask.com, etc.), you might not be visible unless you're in the top three or four ad positions. This is one reason your volume of impressions and clicks can go up significantly when you up your bid to go from ad position 5 to 3, say.

We all have our likes and dislikes. I am partial to ad positions 2 and 3, but I also like 4 and 5. Often, but not always, ad positions 2 and 3 will get you prominent placement above the results on Google Search, with a colored background. Ad positions 4 and 5 typically put you at or very near the top of the ads in the right-hand margin—a personal favorite of mine. You pay significantly less than you would for positions 2 and 1, but you're still at the "top" of the right-hand listings, which looks good.

Others think about whether they're "above the fold" on the right-hand side of the page. Does your ad show on the user's screen, or would he need to scroll down to see it? That's not a huge worry. On a desktop monitor that's on the small side, assuming three ads make it into premium top-of-page position, I can see eight ads above the fold. On a tiny laptop you might only see six or seven ads.

It's starting to sound like lower ad positions can be a bargain, isn't it? For the small business on a limited ad budget, you can take a low-bid approach, sit in sixth or seventh position much of the time, and stay out of costly bidding wars. This reduces your risk.

Users' browsing habits vary so much that the benefits of one position over another are more a question of tendencies and averages than absolutes. On the whole, higher ad positions do generate more volume, and many "big spend" advertisers feel that they just don't get enough action in lower ad positions. Some swear that the brand cachet of a higher-position ad is better and thus converts to sales at a significantly higher rate.

CTRs are much higher in premium positions (typically 1–3) on urgent, specific queries with commercial intent. It's in these positions that my clients regularly see CTRs in the 10–20% range—not that you should expect that or consider it the norm. For the time being, depending on the query and the user, we remain in the golden age of the not entirely mythological "golden triangle" of user attention being laser focused on search results (and paid search results) at the top of the screen.[2]

Showing up in lower ad positions doesn't harm your Quality Score, due to the lower CTRs associated with those positions. Google "normalizes" CTRs to account for ad position and industry vertical, so your relative performance is what goes into calculating CTR for the purposes of Quality Score.

Thus far, I've sort of implied that your bids and preferred ad positions come down to a matter of taste. In reality, of course, they usually come down to affordability; specifically, affordability in relation to the ROI or other user response metrics generated by that keyword.

Do Your Bids Have a Sensible Purpose?

Your bidding strategy is important not only because it impacts the cost of your campaign, but also because it determines your ad positioning. When you look at the campaign summary or ad group view in your campaign management interface, you'll see the average ad position (Avg. Pos) reported over the selected time period. Since ad position fluctuates due to the nature of the auction system, the reporting tells you the average of where you showed up—say, in position 4.2 on the page—over that time period.

AdWords defaults to using one bid for an entire ad group. While this may be a real time-saver, most advertisers generally want more control over their bidding and, therefore, ad positioning. To accomplish this, they use a granular strategy of bidding on individual keywords. Fortunately, this is not an either/or scenario. Bidding individually on thousands of keywords can be counterproductive, but having the flexibility to bid and track some of your most important keywords separately is very useful.

Set and Forget? Using Goal-Based Bid Management Tools

Many advertisers are concerned about the need to monitor their accounts. The key is to consider how much it's going to cost you to monitor bids closely. For smaller accounts, it may not be cost-feasible to pay a person to watch closely, or to invest in some of the third-party bid monitoring services. But larger accounts need loving care. With growing third-party use of the AdWords Application Programming Interface (API), we'll see more rules-based bid management technology being developed.

As an individual small advertiser, you may be able to build your own custom software applications to make a certain number of changes to your accounts each day, at no cost. Typically, though, a software developer or agency using the API will pay for "non-user-based" accesses of the Google AdWords interface. Various operations performed via software (change a single bid, change an ad, etc.) are subject to small charges, based on a "token" system. If a large number of operations (say, tens of thousands of bid changes a week) are performed, this cost is not trivial.

There are dozens of bid management technology vendors on the market today. Some leaders, such as Atlas Search, are now part of large companies (in Atlas's case, Microsoft). I've run across accounts optimized using these tools, and can tell you that they are an aid, not a panacea. Many advertisers swear by them, but your decisions will have to come down to a variety of criteria—price, management credibility, ease of use, compatibility with other tools or tracking protocols you use, and so on. I'd really like to see prices on such tools continue to fall. I think a big flaw in many of them is that they encourage too many bid adjustments too frequently. This drives up token costs, and in turn seems to drive up the overall cost structure typically applied to bid management tools.

An alternative approach, followed by second-generation bid management tools such as Clickable and Adapt, is to focus on superior usability and decision support for account managers trying to manage complex sets of data. Newer-generation tools aim to provide smarter, "alert-based" approaches that suggest changes that you should consider making, in priority order based on severity. (See Figure 7-7.) This is likely to limit the degree of automated, needless tinkering, and as the resulting cost of API tokens will be lowered, we can only hope that some of the savings are passed on to the end user. Another important feature should be that you can also manage the accounts directly, hopping into AdWords and later into (say) Clickable, without disrupting anything.[3]

Remember that Google has a bid gap discounter that automatically charges you the minimum amount needed to maintain your current ad position. You can set your maximum bids fairly high and yet find that from day to day, the average actual cost may not differ very much. Some days,

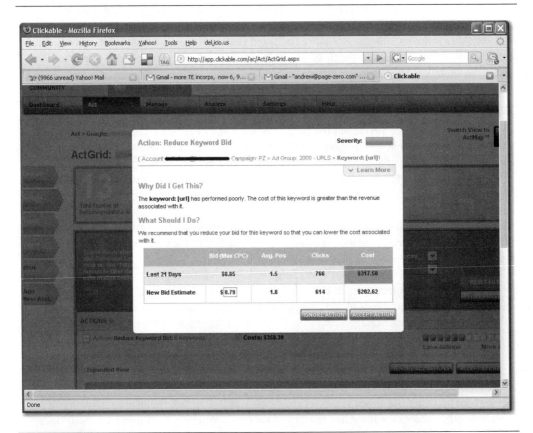

FIGURE 7-7   Clickable offers an intuitive console that assists in decisions about your AdWords account, including bid changes. As opposed to pure automation, it is automation that aids an intelligent campaign strategist's work.

one of your competitors may take a holiday and you'll suddenly be getting cheaper clicks without having done anything with your bids. Because of this, it sometimes pays to look more closely at your actual costs than at your bids.

There are additional shortcomings of bid management tools you need to be aware of. The lack of direct access to the AdWords interface can mean you lose some of the subtleties. If you're using these tools to change ad copy, you might not see an editorial warning message, for example. Sometimes, when lowering bids, you might inadvertently lower them so low that you're below the assigned minimum bid on these keywords. By attempting to simplify user interactions, the third-party apps run the risk of oversimplifying.

How to Use Powerposting to Bid at the Keyword Level

Powerposting is a handy bidding technique that allows you to go into your existing ad groups and specify a bid for a specific phrase while leaving the "global maximum bid" for the group the same as it was. Let's say your max bid for the "lizards" group is $1.50. You want to bid higher on the phrase **buy lizards** but lower on the phrase **discount lizards**.

NOTE *Google no longer highlights the term "powerposting" to describe this, but some oldtimers still use the term as a nickname for bidding on individual keywords.*

There are several ways to powerpost. The easiest is to access your list of keywords in AdWords, select the keyword(s) to modify, and click the Edit Keyword Settings button that appears just above the keyword list. This displays an easy-to-use Change CPCs and URLs form. Simply enter the maximum CPC, enter a different target URL for this keyword if so desired, and click the Save Changes button. While you're doing this, you'll see that it also gives you the ability to change your global bids for the ad group as well—at the top of the screen.

If you prefer to do your own manual editing, you can access the keyword list, click the Edit Keywords link, and enter your own notations to signify different bids. The process is fairly simple. Just enter a pair of asterisks after the keyword, followed by a bid amount (for example, **"buy lizards" ** 3.05**). When you're finished, click Save.

Let's say your global maximum CPC is set to $1.50. After you add powerposting notations to tell Google to bid something other than $1.50 on some of your phrases, the list of keywords in your ad group might look something like this:

Lizards
"buy lizards" ** 3.05
kapuskasing
"discount lizards" ** .40
iguana

In this example, the maximum CPC for **"buy lizards"** is raised to $3.05, lowered to 40 cents for **"discount lizards"**, and kept at the default ($1.50) for **lizards**, **kapuskasing**, and **iguana**.

Powerposting has become a must for some advertisers, so they wind up doing a fair bit of this after-the-fact editing. For many of your keywords, you may want to bid only enough to keep your ad in position 2, 3, or 4 as opposed to 1, but if you're bidding high enough to keep your more expensive keywords visible to searchers, you'll potentially be bidding more than you need to on your "cheaper" ones, putting them in the #1 ad position when you'd be content with #2 or #3. If you're in #1 spot too often, that can be a red flag that you're overspending and may need to either lower your bid for the whole group or edit individual bids, or do both. In fact, there will be times when you get clicks for 5 cents in second or third position, but you'll pay something like 31 cents or 50 cents to get listed first. You may not want to be first all the time, and in cases like this, it can really mess up your average cost! At the risk of belaboring a point, this brings up a third reason to be tidy and organized in setting up campaigns and groups: it is easier for you to be thrifty. For many advertisers, the use of powerposting is like housekeeping to improve the effectiveness of their bidding strategies. You can go overboard with powerposting, though. Use it judiciously so you don't create mounds of difficult-to-interpret data and a lot of additional work in managing all those different bids.

Just a reminder: if you go with more sophisticated rules-based automation, you'll be shooting for an ROI-based range for your bids, and being prompted to change bids to reflect the value of that keyword to your business.

Google's Conversion Optimizer

If you have Google Conversion Tracker enabled, and a minimum threshold of sales or other conversions in the past month in a given campaign, you may be eligible to use Google's new Conversion Optimizer tool. The principle here is the same as any rules-based conversion optimization or bid management tool. You set your target cost-per-acquisition number (say, $12), and Google will adjust your bids in that campaign in an attempt to keep your ROI within the range you've specified. Needless to say, this could increase your spend and click volume, or decrease it. The automated system, not you, is now "driving" your account.

My sense is that this tool may be OK for some users, but there is still enough offered by third parties that goes beyond Google's functionality that it's worth looking into outside bid management.

Making Bulk Changes Quickly with the AdWords Editor

I don't mind making minor edits online within AdWords, but there is absolutely no joy in making bulk edits online. Adding new ads can be a long, painstaking process, and inevitably, the phone rings or my Internet connection gets flaky right when I am on a tight deadline for a client and getting ready to head out to catch a flight.

Google's AdWords Editor is a customized take on work-offline workarounds such as Excel; you may prefer the interface because it's tailored to the task of making bulk AdWords edits. This handy desktop application downloads your AdWords campaigns, including performance statistics, to your local desktop, where you can edit them offline and then upload the changes back to AdWords when you are ready.

The AdWords Editor has a nicely designed tree-view interface that lets you drill down and edit keywords and ads, set bids, daily budgets, and geographic and placement targets, and do just about everything else you can do with the AdWords interface online. Further updates are forthcoming with the latest version of Quality Score (discussed at the end of Chapter 5); of course, as AdWords changes, so must the Editor tool. With features like global search and replace, duplicate keyword finder, and the ability to cut and paste entire sections of your account, you can overhaul an entire campaign in a fraction of the time it takes online (unless, like me, you have a fast online connection and are addicted to the online interface). Another nice feature is that you can archive a backup copy of your whole account, so that in case the major overhaul you just made doesn't work out quite the way you had expected, you can quickly roll back to the previous version.

For now, be aware that there are still some AdWords settings that can only be controlled online, such as ad serving settings (accelerated or even delivery) and ad scheduling. Google also seems to have grappled with how much advanced functionality to offer. An "advanced bid options" link leads you to a useful tool that will help you bulk-change bids in a variety of ways, including by percentage. Overall, the key advantage of the AdWords Editor is that it is faster and offline. Yet this tool is still not without its quirks and shortcomings. Third parties will still outshine Google in the area of rules-based decision support, it seems. The Editor tool particularly shines in hard-core practical areas, like bulk-editing ads, which can be super-pesky.

Software Saves Time with Keyword-Level Tracking

Third-party software does have one major advantage: keyword tracking. Even if you don't use bid management software to actively manage your bids, it can be an indispensable aid if you're going to be tracking by keyword. A major problem with bidding by keyword is making sure you have the correct tracking URLs in your AdWords account so that you're also correctly *tracking* by keyword. You'll find it prohibitively time consuming to enter unique tracking URLs (another feature of powerposting, and a second set of asterisks followed by a URL) by hand for hundreds or thousands of individual keywords.

If all you use for ROI tracking is Google Conversion Tracker or Google Analytics with autotagging enabled in your AdWords account, no special tracking URLs are required. Many third-party systems require them, however, and will append them to keyword-by-keyword destination URLs throughout your account, using the AdWords API.

Dayparting

Some software vendors emphasized early on the benefits of rapid bid changes and the need for *dayparting*—the turning on and off of ads, or adjusting bids based on prior knowledge of time periods when customers are more or less likely to buy. As you gain more experience with AdWords, you'll probably feel the need to explore such advanced bidding strategies at some point. Large retailers may have no choice but to daypart, as their razor-thin margins make it crucial to generate revenues on as many clicks as possible, and not to waste money showing ads to nonbuyers (for example, in the middle of the night).

Many advertisers can safely ignore this for the time being. You can out-think yourself. For example, it could actually hurt your company to reduce exposure with some advanced dayparting method when this exposure might actually be a cheap long-term brand-building method that compares favorably with exposure in other media.

One problem with dayparting is that ads do not always turn on and off instantly, especially on the sites of content and search network partners. So you can't be too exact with it.

Also, in an auction scenario, if everyone starts dayparting, the advertisers who remain should save money as advertisers drop out, thus canceling out the benefit of dayparting. It never hurts to consider ways of optimizing your account, such as turning the campaign off on Saturdays if you're sure that having it on is hurting your bottom line. But be careful not to be lulled into underspending based on faulty premises.

Dayparting also underestimates latency in purchases, especially between "at home" and "at work" buying. Many Monday morning purchases from a work-based computer were initiated through a search on a home computer over the weekend. Shut off your ads on weekends? You could "mysteriously" miss out on Monday sales.

Google AdWords Ad Scheduler

Because ad scheduling (including an advanced approach that lets you boost or reduce bids by time of day, on a set weekly schedule) is now available in the AdWords interface itself, I tend to set up specific scheduling regimes inside AdWords on the rare occasions I make use of dayparting.

For my purposes, it's actually proved to be a clever workaround for making wholesale seasonal bid adjustments, while keeping the original campaign in the same state, for when the season ends. Let's say I want to set a configuration that bids 130% of the default bid across the campaign on weekends, and 120% on weekdays. That's easy to set up in a snap. Rather than looking into individual bids across ad groups and keywords, changes are made across the account. So when you want to change back—or revert—to your default bid strategy, you just shut off the ad scheduling and you're back to "normal."

A colleague of mine suggested that Google could allow you to save multiple bid configurations, and name them for different seasons or purposes. In short, that would allow "bid themes" so you could use my above technique even more cleverly... if you can imagine being that clever! How about it Google?

Dealing with Foolish (or Rich) Competitors

The increasing cost of keywords is nothing new. Every month brings new waves of advertisers testing the waters. Some will muck things up for you. But there's no need to panic just because some newbie comes in with both guns blazing, badly overbidding on your best keywords. You probably shouldn't be relying that heavily on those keywords anyway.

Advertisers shouldn't be goaded into bidding wars or overly discouraged by what seem to be high costs per click. Wait until you receive a series of monthly reports with sufficient data to see a pattern. Things might not be as bad as you think! Look again at your data.

New competition entering your space is no laughing matter, though, to be sure. For many of my clients, new competition has been the #1 source of rising CPCs in the period 2006–2008. Just two new feisty competitors can raise your CPCs 50% to 100%, especially if you've come to rely on the volume generated by juicy, high ad positions. Do I have a magic bullet for this? Of course not. You have to outdo competitors in the ways available to you. Sometimes that can be with scale and persistence; other times that has to be continued testing, creativity, and laser focus on niches. The chess match here plays out in a somewhat daunting economic-Darwinist format, to a degree. Bigness is no guarantee of victory, but the advent of many big monsters entering the ad space certainly isn't making more oxygen for the little guys to breathe.[4]

As much as CPCs may be rising in some areas, in others they might be dropping as advertisers pay more attention to their ROI data. In some fields we see reverse bidding wars taking place as some advertisers take a stand that they won't bid to position, but rather, to a certain cost per click that seems reasonable. So prices can rise, but they can also fall, and by taking action in lowering your own bids, you can contribute to that fall. When two or three of the top advertisers stop beating each other's brains out, you can see significant declines in CPCs in areas that were once thought to be cost prohibitive.

Endnotes

1. With thanks to Matt Van Wagner, who has been known to use this case example—complete with prop—in his conference presentations.

2. For some further information on the so-called golden triangle, see for example "Enquiro Eye Tracking Report 1: Google," July 2005. Available at enquiroresearch.com.

3. Disclosure: in fall 2007, I began working with Clickable as a beta partner, trying out advance versions of the product and providing bug reports and feature suggestions. I did so because my initial test drive of the early beta was favorable, and I was drawn to the idea of an intuitive interface that would support human analyst decisions and shorten execution times, rather than monopolizing the process or creating an extra, cumbersome layer.

4. For more on the gruesome logic, see my piece, "Your Paid Search Performance Is Relative," *Search Engine Land: Paid Search*, May 15, 2007, archived at http://searchengineland.com/070515-075604.php.

Chapter 8

Writing Winning Ads

Since AdWords (not counting the content-targeting program, which is multifaceted) allows no graphics, colors, font styles, or other eye-catching elements, and even limits some powerful textual elements (exclamation points, symbols, caps, and more), your ad copy is the only thing you have to entice users to visit your website. Therefore, it has to catch their attention right from the start. In this chapter I'll provide pointers on writing effective Google AdWords ads.

Before delving into the mechanics of copywriting, you should be aware of two key principles of advertising on the Web, both of which target the user's experience as he or she makes the journey from a search query to a purchase on your site.

Targeting and Testing: Key Principles of Web Advertising

First, as you may have heard from various web pundits already, it's all about personalization. Regardless of whether you call it personalization, targeting, or micro-targeting, the harder you work to achieve it, the sooner you'll leave your competitors in the dust.

Imagine the "Perfect Ad"

Tongue in cheek, it's worth laying some groundwork here by pointing out that the rare ads that get the most extreme positive responses are typically those that benefit from urgency or a favorable buying situation you cannot manufacture; all you can do is be in the game to capture some of those situations. If someone were to type "my pantleg is on fire" into Google, an ad that read "Handheld Fire Extinguishers—Put out the fire now! Delivered instantly to your desktop!" would probably garner a very high CTR and an unusually high conversion rate. The pathological among you will now ask me for tips on how to set people's pants on fire.

The overarching philosophy of this chapter is to talk about principles that seem to matter in generating improved user responses. I know such principles based on long experience across a variety of campaign types. But the other part of the equation is, you have to test in order to find out what fits for your situation. Tips and tricks are just a starting point.

A reminder: uncertainty in response (as with worldly events in general) is usually greater than our brains are wired to expect. Sometimes, innovative ideas help you hit the jackpot. In other cases, your job is to deploy an ad budget effectively without embarrassing your company. The trouble is, there is no clear way of predicting whether we are in line for big jackpots (what author Nassim Nicholas Taleb calls the positive variant of black swans, or highly improbable events). As Taleb argues, sometimes we are living in Mediocristan (a relatively stable risk environment that offers little potential for catastrophic losses, but also no huge upsides), and sometimes we are living in Extremistan (a risk environment that eventually produces enormous, unexpected gains or losses).[1]

I suspect what has made Google AdWords such an object of fascination for so many around the world (myself included) is that it allows us to cheat Taleb's view of probability: because we're free to shut off our ads at anytime, and we hold no massive sunk "portfolio" of keywords in the sense of an asset we can lose; yet also, because in certain industries with certain ads, creative in certain circumstances, some rare companies can hit a "jackpot-like" sales result. We get to limit downside while staying exposed to major upside. I'm not telling you that AdWords is risk-free,[2] but rather, simply musing on how the positives and negatives of uncertain results don't seem to hurt advertisers as much as they do, say, investors in subprime mortgages, or the not-so-mythical turkey who feels like things are going along fine on the day before Thanksgiving, as they have for the past 1,000 days, until…the next day comes.

Cater to People and Keep Yourself in the Game

The fact that searchers are typing specific, interest-driven keywords into a search engine is part of an age-old phenomenon with a modern twist—the search for a solution to real or imagined problems. Advertisers who recognize this simple truth will, on the whole, enjoy better performance with their online campaigns.

In an age of heightened expectations, the user who feels catered to will be a more responsive user. As soon as an ad fails to address the user's wants, needs, or expectations, there's a good chance that a potential customer will move on to the next vendor. In Chapter 7 I mentioned Ray Allen of AmericanMeadows.com. Ray knows that it's not enough just to lure the potential buyer in. He keeps the personal touches flowing even after the user clicks through. This is why he includes things like the regularly updated, beautifully illustrated blog on his site (see Figure 8-1).

This kind of personalization combined with a passion for the subject matter can make a difference in retaining customer loyalty in a fickle world.[3] Little wonder that, along with the rest of his marketing, Ray's Google ads look different from everyone else's. As a former advertising executive, Ray likes to draw on past experience and try out a variety of hooks: up-to-date special offers, seasonal information, and so on.

The second principle to bear in mind is that testing is the key to determining the effectiveness of your ads. Empirical data (results) matter more than anyone's opinion about what kind of ad copy to write. The performance of your ads is so readily testable that your ad strategy should largely revolve around which elements to test as opposed to following some theoretical law of

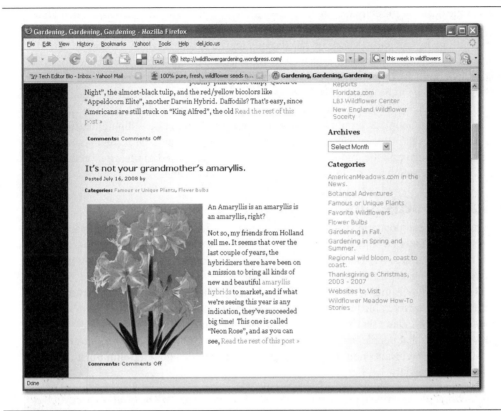

FIGURE 8-1   Ray Allen's frequently updated blog, like his frequently updated ad copy, gives web surfers the kind of customized, relevant information they seek.

ad copywriting from the experts. When testing produces unexpected results, it can be an eye opener, and this helps you take a major step forward in understanding your audience's psychology and needs.

How Your Ads Look to the User

In Chapter 3 my goal was to convey a feeling for users' reactions to search listings and ads. Remembering that you're not creating a single ad to appear in a predetermined space is vital to understanding the variations you'll likely see in user response.

Impact of Media Type and Location

In the advertising business, the choice of media type and location (where the ad is placed) has always been a decisive factor in how an ad performs. The selection of media is, as much as possible, the selection of an appropriate target audience based on what we know about audience demographics.

Since Google does not currently require users to register with personal information, we don't have direct clues about audience age, gender, income, and the like. Like everything else on the Internet, that may change in the future. (Microsoft has recently moved to offer advertisers more advanced targeting of this nature.) Even without such clues, the selection of keywords on which to advertise provides an opportunity to select an appropriate audience, albeit indirectly.

One key variable to be aware of is the placement of the same ad with different online services. A user who sees your ad as the result of a cobranded search on the Verizon DSL home page, rather than a Google Search, may respond differently. It might be a simple matter of placement, such as the ad appearing in position 4 instead of position 2. Or it might have to do with the ad showing up in the middle of a keyword search as opposed to seeing it on the page where the user is reading an article, or beside a conversation in Gmail.

Fitting Big Ideas into Small Spaces

If you're sitting there wondering how you're going to turn 95 characters (including spaces and punctuation) into killer ad copy that will sell your product or service, don't worry. Yes, it's true that the character limit is so strict some advertisers refer to Google ads as "advertising haiku," but this is not the selling stage and therefore doesn't require lengthy copy. Google ads are, or should be, qualifiers—the tools that sort, or prequalify, prospects, not sell to them, as I'll explain shortly.

After all, if you were able to write very long ads, and Google showed ten of them to a page, do you really believe that users would read them? Would you read them? Of course not. This system—short ads that people may read but can easily ignore if they wish—works well. The ad you write has to be relevant enough to induce action, but specific enough to limit that action to potential customers only.

TIP *Forget about cramming your whole sales pitch into your AdWords ad. You only have space for a clearly worded offer, plus one or two of the following: (a) a clear, concise benefit statement, value proposition, or third-party endorsement; (b) a call to action; (c) an offer; (d) special wording that might weed out inappropriate prospects.*

Remember, there will be plenty of space for detail on your landing page, after the potential customers have arrived on your website. You need to convey one or at most two concepts in your brief ad. Most importantly, the ad must be clear and unambiguous. Avoid using abbreviations, acronyms, and other devices that the target customer may not recognize. That doesn't mean you can't use them at all. If your potential customer should be familiar with them and they are relevant, by all means use them. Just make sure they're appropriate for the intended audience.

TIP *Clarity is a guiding principle of copywriting.*

Adopting the Right Tone

The correct tone for your ad is the one that best suits your audience. That may sound obvious, but depending on that audience, it may mean simple, exotic, mellow, wild, homey, sophisticated, or even technical to the point of being unintelligible to the average user. In the end, what counts is speaking the same language as your potential customer.

TIP   *Setting the right tone for your audience is a guiding principle of copywriting.*

Bearing in mind that Google users are probably savvy enough to see through high-pressure sales pitches and other intrusive advertising, you'll want to avoid ad copy that focuses more on the cleverness of the writer than it does on the product being advertised. In reflecting on the general tone of the ads I've seen working well—and their general lack of cleverness—I've come to realize that the principles for writing effective AdWords are not so far from what some of the advertising industry icons of the 20th century, like David Ogilvy, have counseled (see the upcoming sidebar, "Giving Tradition Its Due").

What is different is that we're seeing more ads being written for a much wider variety of situations than ever before, and these ads are often being written by relatively inexperienced copywriters. Inexperienced copywriters should avoid the tendency to stereotype the process of writing ads based on what they've heard about contemporary advertising trends. Writing ads is a practical task and one that's unlikely to win you a major award. (I still haven't won any Grammys or Webbys, even for that ingenious "pantleg on fire" ad.)

So if you feel a hankering for a major creative release like the one you might get in the traditional advertising industry that creates what amount to short films designed to interrupt people, you'll be disappointed in this medium, and you'll probably do wacky things with it. Your little ads play an important role, and some of what you do is creative, but you're kind of boxed in to a narrower realm. You know what? That can be liberating. To try a sports analogy: a pitcher in baseball has a "boring" life, too. He has to throw the ball over the plate, in the strike zone. But when you learn how much strategy is going on inside those narrow parameters–he can throw some pitches outside the zone; he can mix speeds, throw curveballs, and occasionally throw over to first base and check the runner–it's apparent that you can lead a pretty full life inside those constraints! Writing and testing AdWords ads is a science. Getting it right can be exhilarating. Getting it wrong will cost you. Certain principles usually hold true, and violating them will waste time and money. For the time being, major ad agencies are relatively uninterested in this science

Giving Tradition Its Due

The great copywriters of old, such as David Ogilvy, did know a thing or two. Many of Ogilvy's admonitions in *Confessions of an Advertising Man* (Southbank Publishing, 2004), particularly the section about writing headlines, still apply to search advertising. He counsels directness over cleverness and offers suggestions such as ensuring that headlines appeal to readers' self-interest, for example. He says that copywriters must resist the temptation to entertain, and that their performance ought to be measured by how quickly they can foster the adoption of new products and ideas. Ogilvy's views on such matters seem to have great foresight considering that no one could have foreseen the flexibility of the Internet, the fragmentation of media, and the demanding and highly measurable Google AdWords environment.

because those billable hours aren't as profitable as other agency activities, like creating TV commercials and purchasing TV ads. More to the point, they don't have the analytical personnel who can do it properly. Anyone who understands that this is not so much a buy as an ongoing test can thrive even if large agencies begin to run campaigns against them.

Many of those who work in the ad industry today repeatedly ignore the wisdom of pioneers such as Ogilvy, preferring to create ads that impress peers.[4] But peer recognition isn't what we're after here. As Ogilvy aptly put it in *Confessions,* "juries that bestow awards are never given enough information about the *results* of the advertisements they are called upon to judge." Instead, they fall back on "their opinions, which are always warped toward the highbrow."

Fortunately, with all the data at your disposal, your opinion is the last thing you'll be forced to rely on when it comes to writing effective Google ads.

Trying to win an award in such a small space would be difficult, wouldn't it? Let's look at a hypothetical ad by Tad, a transplanted agency type who is so bored with writing search engine ads that he comes up with this ad to sell software from a company called Reemar:

Reemar's On Ya

Devgeeks say w00t! to PrSolvR 2.0.
Yo BigCorp: we're here to destroy u </rant>

Apparently, Tad thought this ad would be "triply ironic." No one would think anything like this would be cool, so by some convoluted logic, Tad believed this ad would imprint his "signature style" and really have them talking (not customers, but ad industry people and awards juries). The only thing that would probably happen is that the ad would confound users, they wouldn't click, and the Quality Score gods would soon have their way with Tad's account.

Not only does the ad fail even to hint at what PrSolvR does, or indicate any benefit whatsoever, it violates Google's editorial guidelines. (Different versions of Tad's ad also had even weirder punctuation, in addition to the veiled threats against BigCorp.) The word *yo* would also be seen by the AdWords spell checker as a misspelling, and the author of the ad would then have to wait for Google Editorial to grant an exception. They might not grant it.

Now let's look at a non-Madison Avenue approach to Reemar's ad. Perhaps you believe that a more industry-centric ad would speak to your target audience, who, you think, are savvy in the extreme. So you try this:

Faster DWW Func in FWall?

GMUI modules 3X beat KLT security
"best pligtonferg of '07"-WRSS Mag

Well, maybe the people who read your ads are not that savvy. Or, like most average people, even savvy ones, they prefer not to read gibberish. This ad fails too. With the use of less jargon and more plain English, you can turn the previous ads into a winner:

Easy & Powerful Firewall

Reemar ProblemSolvR beats BigCorp
Terminator by 74% in industry tests

This example uses the word *easy,* which tests out better than a few other adjectives describing your software. It says you're selling a firewall, which is exactly what you're selling and what that user typing **firewall product reviews** is probably looking for. And it introduces doubt about the quality of the industry leader (you have proof on your website). They happen to have 61% market share (you only have 4%, so comparing yourself with them is inevitable), but their product is rather expensive and difficult to use. This piques the interest of real prospects—enough to click on your ad—but because it's fairly clear about what you're selling (and mentioning BigCorp Terminator makes it even clearer, as it further "marks" this territory), you don't attract the confused or the vaguely curious.

Plain and simple is often the most effective ad copy to use. While every attempt may not be a winner, as long as you hit the tone right and write a clear ad, you'll know you're on the right track if your ad is attracting a strong CTR and, ultimately, if your post-click tracking shows these clicks converting to sales, leads, and registrations. Tracking users after they click is covered in detail in Chapter 10.

Here's another example that shows the difference in performance when you do a better job of understanding your target audience. The first ad uses a generic and somewhat hyped-sounding headline, with some impressive but unverifiable claims:

Hot Stocks Uncovered

Our portfolios were up 67%, 58%, &
34% for 2003. Free trial & report.
www.FindProfit.com

The second ad uses more specific language and touts the founder's credibility:

Short-Term Trading

New site from Raging Bull founder
RT commentary. Free report & trial
www.FindProfit.com

The first ad pulled only 0.5% CTR; almost certainly too low for the Quality Score gods' taste. The second ad pulled a much healthier 1.3%.

A third ad was a hybrid of the two, using the short-term trading headline but sticking with the claims about portfolio gains. As you might expect, it performed somewhere in the middle, at 0.8%. The underperforming ads were dropped, and a couple of additional tweaks were then tried with the winning ad. Tone, directness, and credibility helped this new information service find its audience. Of course, we only know this in hindsight. No one could have predicted in advance that Bill Martin's and Matt Ragas's past experience in creating investment-related content at financial discussion site RagingBull.com would resonate so concretely with the target audience.

Bill and Matt gained some fame in the dot-com boom era as college students who founded a stock discussion site that grew rapidly from inception in 1997, attracted $22 million in investment from CMGI and CNET, and went on to be acquired by Terra Lycos in 2000. Many savvy online traders seem to know who Bill and Matt are because they remember trading stock information at Raging Bull. Based in large part on their paid search campaigns, the paying subscriber base of FindProfit.com continued grow from 2004 through December 2007, when the publication merged with another in its field, the Bull Market Report.

Credibility is a guiding principle of copywriting.

Be careful not to obsess about ad copy so much that you change it when you perceive it to be stale. Remember the maxim that you should stick with a campaign as long as your accountant likes it.[5] Who cares if you're bored by a certain phrase or angle; who cares if your friends wonder if you're ever going to put up a new ad? If it ain't broke, don't fix it! Continue to test new theories; you may find something that works better. Just don't make changes simply for the sake of making changes. One of my European colleagues regularly tries to argue that ad "freshness" degrades, hence requiring that new and "fresh" ads be actively written. I agree that seasonality and changing trends might severely affect user response to some ads (fashion and counter-obsolescence imperatives abound in some industries), but degraded ad performance doesn't occur because of "staleness" as some kind of general rule. There are many reasons for fluctuations in campaign performance, and isolating the impact of ad freshness in situations where it does seem to matter is nearly impossible.

One approach that withstands the test of time is the appeal to your customer's self-interest. Saving money, making money, winning at something, getting a deal, being able to make installment payments, alleviating an annoying headache,[6] beating a competitor, making a friend—these are all reasons for users to decide that what you have to offer may be the ideal choice for them.

It's possible to go too far in analyzing the underlying motivations (money, sex, love, beauty, simplicity) that supposedly drive every purchase. At the extreme are the ads you see from time to time in technology magazines somehow trying to convince readers that supermodels will be impressed if they would just acquire the latest in encryption technology. It would be funny if it weren't so prevalent. Surely there must be a better way to convey a product's benefits. (And yes, I'm aware that domain registrar GoDaddy has become notorious through the use of a "sex sells" strategy, but let's not assign too much causality to this in either GoDaddy's, or your, business. They're also benefiting from heavy investment in every type of media exposure, and the "winner take all" effect in new product categories devoid of household names, that used to be so prevalent in the television-industrial complex era. If Apple computer sales increase this year and its operating system gains market share, should we conclude that a folksy ad campaign that caricatures the uptight competitor, almost to the point of making the competitor seem lovable, "works"? Again, it would be tough to generalize based on this sequence of events, given that your competitor might not, like Microsoft, be a household name who released a new operating system that absolutely bombed.)

In some industries, exaggerated promises work. For a brief shining second, some golfers appear willing to believe that hitting a ball two yards farther is akin to conquering the galaxy. In almost any business, appeals to customers' rational side—to improve their communications skills by buying a book, tape, or hiring a coach, for example—often work. But what motivates someone to purchase seeds for a certain mossy perennial? They desire a beautiful garden, of course. Do we need to know why they want a beautiful garden? Probably not. I'm not sure I even want to know. Ideally, at a certain point, the process takes care of itself: users want what you have, and you sell it to them. At times, I think it may be a blessing that Google advertisers can't gather detailed demographic information on Google users. Unlike some advertisers, deep down I don't necessarily want access to the proverbial electrodes to the head that might reveal every motivation that drives purchase behavior. Having access to a narrower set of user data actually makes this job easier for the average business to deal with.

Addressing Multiple Priorities

Writing ads would be easier if you had a single goal in mind, but that isn't the case here. You must weigh a number of priorities. The two primary goals of an AdWords ad actually compete with one another. Sound confusing? It isn't really. On one hand, your goal is to encourage prospective customers to click your ad. On the other hand, you want to discourage inappropriate prospects from clicking on your ad so you don't waste money on clicks that have a low probability of ever turning into sales. But if all advertisers became extremely good at this filtering process, Google would be showing ads that got lower CTRs across the board, which would hurt them in at least a couple of ways. First, the perceived relevancy of Google ads would be in jeopardy, but more importantly, Google would make less money per page of search results served, because fewer users would be clicking on ads. As a result, as I already emphasized in Chapter 5, Google designed the system to *reward* you for a higher CTR, along with some other relevancy factors.

All else being equal, you should test your ad copy with a view towards generating higher CTRs on ads. If your highest-CTR ads turn out to perform worse from an ROI standpoint, then you'd need to revert to the one(s) that offered the optimal trade-off between CTR and ROI. That's a matter for experimentation with the help of post-click tracking data, discussed in Chapter 10.

Balancing CTR and ROI

When it comes to gauging the performance of your ads, you may be thinking that a higher ROI is the holy grail you're pursuing. But this is an oversimplification, given how vitally important CTRs are in allowing you to gain favorable ad positions with lower bids and ultimately improve ROI. Remember, you must encourage prospective customers to click your ad while discouraging inappropriate prospects from clicking your ad so that you don't waste money on clicks that have a low probability of ever turning into sales. While ROI will be the ultimate arbiter of success, realize that in the early going, you'll probably need to move CTR higher up your priority list than you might expect, or wish to, because of the strong incentive system built into AdWords that favors high-CTR ads.

Other goals for your ads might revolve around credibility or leadership. You might wish to use certain phrases or wordings to reinforce your company's brand awareness, regardless of how well the ads perform over the short term. Management has every prerogative to sacrifice short-term sales numbers for long-term strategic goals if they believe that to be their mandate. Sometimes, then, ads that aren't really about selling anything directly might make their way onto the user's radar screen. Some companies wish to increase "mindshare." One company I work with allocated $800,000 for 2008 as part of an effort to demonstrate "category leadership" for certain seasonal transactions. Such efforts are part of a multifaceted effort to shift customer perceptions of a brand over time. If turning a big company's strategy around is a little like steering an ocean liner, then so is changing deep-seated customer perceptions of such companies.

To be sure, a sampler of searches for dozens of terms will turn up few big-brand advertisers, and even large advertisers appear to be drawn to AdWords mostly as a highly measurable, direct-response medium. For the time being, most of the "presence and awareness"-style ads are from government and nonprofit organizations. On a search for **pesticides**, it's fascinating to see several nonprofits and government organizations competing for awareness against companies (such as Orkin and HengDongChem[7]) who actually sell pesticides or pest control solutions. For the time being, "awareness"-type advertising is relatively rare on AdWords, but as high-profile politicians gain ink for their savvy use of online promotional opportunities, awareness of raising awareness through AdWords is growing.

A fascinating study in opportunism comes through a search for trendy Democratic presidential nomination hopeful **Barack Obama**.[8] The top-position ad, in premium position, is from BarackObama.com, the senator's official site. The landing page, my.barackobama.com, is tailored to generate signups to be part of a list of people interested in the campaign, including notifications of rallies and events.

It doesn't stop there. Google itself, through its subsidiary, YouTube, has placed an ad suggesting that you "watch videos from each of the 2008 presidential candidates." At the time of this writing, over 14,000 people had subscribed to the Barack Obama page on YouTube that collects videos of his speeches. (Just in case you were getting your hopes up about the depth of political engagement in America: by contrast, a video by Obama Girl, a young singer professing her love for Barack Obama, had been viewed over 4 million times. Obama Girl does say "Hey B., … I was just watching you on C-SPAN" on the video, so maybe there is hope for the fusion of politics, sex, synthetic drum tracks, and geekdom after all.)

An opportunistic project, the Iowa Global Warming Campaign (supported by multiple interest groups and nonprofit organizations), weighs in with an ad exhorting users to "learn how Barack Obama proposes to solve global warming."

Finally, a retailer is promoting a "super soft Obama t-shirt" that says Obama is My Homeboy. This is also the title of the ad. The copy on the landing page says "Barack Obama is like a latter day JFK, but way more accessible."

Evidently, in the case of **Barack Obama**, direct marketing opportunities take a backseat to awareness-raising. But in the end, we see a fascinating blend of the two.[9]

Why don't big companies do more with AdWords to raise general consumer awareness of their adaptations to new trends? The effort would be far less costly than all those TV campaigns. They're starting to get it, but slowly. Some ads will have multiple roles, attempting to increase sales, but only indirectly, by changing consumer perceptions. What about a company like McDonald's, which recently underwent a successful turnaround from a declining purveyor of supersized calorie-laden meals, to a solidly profitable company that can convince people to buy $6 salads at a drive-through where they once bought a $2 burger? ("Mickey Dee's" is doing very well, financially speaking, these days. Its stock price has appreciated steadily over the past five years and it now pays a healthy dividend, still yielding 2.5% in spite of the healthy stock price).

Many customers know about the salads now, but it wouldn't cost that much to add to this awareness with a simple AdWords campaign. Online promotions by large companies have often been obsessed with complex schemes involving coupons, loyalty, contests, and so on. They require high-powered thinking. But given the low cost of a paid search campaign, a basic campaign merely alerting the public to the sea change in McDonald's product mix—for example, adding awareness of the quality and health benefits of their new salads—would be worth every penny, even if no particular tracking scheme were built on the back end. For all the money companies spend on expensive television and billboard campaigns "getting their message out," paid search seems like an incredibly cost-effective way to achieve that goal, one highly targeted customer at a time. And those kinds of avid customers create word-of-mouth advertising, which is free. A campaign of this nature wouldn't need particularly clever ads—"learn more about our delicious new salads" or "50% off coupon to try our Mandarin Chicken salad—limited time offer" would be enough. It would be the power of the salad-related keywords and the fact that the clicks were so inexpensive to reach out to salad enthusiasts that would be the real driving force behind such a campaign, not necessarily the ad copy.

To give you a better sense of the current economics on such a campaign, let's say McDonald's managed to garner a million ad impressions on their AdWords ad at ten cents per click, for a cost of $1,000. Their effective cost per thousand ad impressions, or CPM, would be $1. A million impressions for a comparable television ad would cost significantly more. According to recent press reports, CPM rates on 30-second ads on network prime time are running at about $16. Shorter commercials in off-peak hours might cost 40% of that, but ads on specialty channels can cost significantly more. At a relative "bargain" CPM of $7, a 15-second spot for McDonald's would cost $7,000, or seven times more than the AdWords ad. This doesn't factor in heavy production costs for TV advertising, nor does it measure its relative effectiveness. Search ads are significantly more effective and measurable even than other forms of *online* advertising, yet on a lot of highly targeted keyword inventory, you still don't need to pay an outrageous premium. Keep in mind that those "impressions" for a McDonald's spot are impressions of the ad by *anyone with their TV tuned to that channel.* Search ad impressions are restricted to people who have actively typed a query into a computer. The difference is difficult to quantify, but no matter how you slice it, the contrast is stark. Performance aside, the disparity in price between TV advertising and search advertising (7× in this example) is great enough that more big companies will find the opportunity worth investigating.

Some time after pondering this example, I did spot a special McDonald's promotion being tried in an AdWords ad for McDonald's Canada only (triggered by a search on the keyword **McDonald's**). The campaign didn't make much sense to me—coupons for low-end sandwich meal specials for different days of the week—but I was intrigued to see larger companies beginning to experiment in this way.

Currently, forward-thinking campaigns by large corporations concerned about protecting their brand image or sending a general message to consumers are relatively rare in the paid search ad space, which leaves many opportunities for nimble smaller companies.

Maintaining Accuracy

One of the most important pieces of advice I can offer is, be meticulous. The image of your company as a provider of quality at every level of the operation certainly won't be helped if you have misspellings in ads or use nonstandard punctuation. Some companies are willing to take small hits in short-term performance in order to maintain a certain image. For example, you might prove that capitalizing the first letter of every word in your body copy (now allowed by Google) slightly increases CTRs and ROI. Yet your CEO and/or shareholders might think this looks amateurish. So be it: there is nothing wrong with sticking to principles for long-term image purposes. (If that weren't the case, every television spot would probably end with the direct-marketing pitch, phone number information, and other calls to action favored by, well, direct marketers on late-night TV or infomercials.) Some advertisers write their Google ad copy as if no one is watching. Obviously, just the opposite is the case. Don't make spelling and grammar mistakes and don't write like a four-year-old!

TIP   *Accuracy is a guiding principle of copywriting.*

You should generally avoid false or unverifiable claims. Google Editorial might clamp down on you if you use unverifiable superlatives such as *best, cheapest,* or *longest lasting* anyway. But no matter what Google says, it's up to you to decide whether it's in your company's best interest to shade the truth, misrepresent your product, or misreport your pricing. On the other hand, if you're sincere, there is nothing particularly wrong with making true but difficult-to-verify claims, and Google doesn't prohibit them all.

Depending on the product or service you're advertising, you may be under a closer microscope, remember. "Accidentally" inserting *fresh* for a frozen shrimp delivery can land you in regulatory hot water, for example. And you aren't allowed to advertise insurance (for example) in a state where you aren't licensed to offer insurance. But your customers are probably going to be dissatisfied soonest, regardless of the looming and generally toothless threat of federal regulation. Advertising fresh shrimp when it's really frozen is literally a classic example of the improper information "scent" (discussed in Chapters 10 and 11) that can cause dissatisfaction among searchers, lower conversion rates, increase "bounce rates," and cost you money.

If you're a consultant, or work in a company with a clear chain of command that requires approval of written materials, leave new ads paused until the appropriate person approves them. For smaller companies, this offers another advantage. While the big guys are waiting for approval, you can beat them to the punch and test new ads at will.

Getting the Most Out of Your AdWords Ads

Possibly the most consistently successful copywriting tactic is to write more ads, make them more personalized, and make sure that more of your ad titles and/or body copy match (or come close to matching) the keywords the user types in. This dovetails with the admonition to "organize, organize, organize" in Chapter 4.

Clearly, if you sell a fairly diverse line of (let's say) diamond jewelry, your performance won't be as good if your whole campaign relies on a single generic ad:

Diamond Jewelry Store

Earrings, bracelets, watches, more
Check out our weekly specials!

This ad might be fine for those searchers who have specifically typed **diamond jewelry**, but if they typed **diamond bracelets**, it would probably be outdone by a more specific ad run by a competitor. As I've said before, users most often gravitate towards the ads that match more closely to what they've typed into the search box. To improve on the performance of this ad, you'd simply write ads that are more targeted, such as this one:

Designer Diamond Bracelets

Diamond bracelets by top designers
Dazzling one-of-a-kind items!

The effectiveness of an ad depends on a large variety of factors. As you ponder alternatives at the outset, don't overthink. Just plunge in and write an ad or two that you believe will attract your target audience, and test and adjust from there. In this case, I mentioned one-of-a-kind items to reinforce the image of designer jewelry so as to attract a higher-spending clientele.

A Technique for Ad Refinement in Stages

To make this process a little more systematic, I've developed a rough two-stage process that is meant to get your initial "good" ads up to "very good" (step 1), followed by a data-intensive phase that can raise "very good" performance to "even better" (step 2).

Step 1: Discover the Main Triggers

You don't want to start off aimlessly testing piddling little differences in your ad copy, just to prove to yourself that the ad rotating function does indeed work. What you'll be looking for are significantly different approaches to getting your message out to prospective customers that can teach you something you can take away as you use the winning approach as a basis for another round of refinements.

For example, you might not know in a certain context whether fast shipping, low prices, a big selection, or some other major element of your retail experience for customers is a particular trigger for them. Don't expect to do exhaustive research here. In one case, I pitted three potential triggers against one another: price, selection, and the ability to do research and access schematics on the website. Shipping offers became a permanent feature of our ads, as their efficacy had been demonstrated in separate experiments. We discovered that selection consistently (though not always, across all products) beat price and research as the best trigger, when combined with the shipping offer, which referred to the speed of shipping. Later, I tinkered with subtle wording variations: "big selection"; "huge selection"; "full selection."[10]

When you do this for your own business, try to write three or four ads that are distinctive enough to return information to you along the lines of "what are they thinking?" and "what causes the right people to click and buy?"

Step 2: Multivariate Testing

You might want to try a couple more rounds of tests based on new ideas that fit in roughly with the Step 1 type of research. Once you're armed with a lot more information about what triggers seem to be consistent, you enter the refinement stage.

Multivariate testing is a systematic approach to testing ad variations. Let's say there are four elements of the ad you want to test: the headline, a discount offer, a certain punctuation quirk, and the use of a brand name in the body copy. Let's say you've got three versions of the headline, two versions of the discount offer, yes or no to the punctuation quirk (such as a single exclamation point), and yes or no to using the brand name. Doing what math whizzes refer to as a full factorial multivariate test—that is, a test of all possible variations of your ad—would give you:

$$3 \times 2 \times 2 \times 2 = 24 \text{ ad variants}$$

Multivariate testing is becoming commonplace for landing page designs, but it's possible to do it with ads, as well. With the above method, you can often generate amazing results testing 16, 24, or 32 ads as part of a single multivariate test. Part of the power of such testing lies in discovering unexpected variable interactions. Independently, a certain headline may not perform all that much better than the other two. But in one particular combination with two other elements of your ad, you might discover that headline #2's performance is consistently better (let's say it's ad variant #19 that hit the jackpot in this way). You never find this stuff out unless you test all variants.

The drawback to a full multivariate test is that it's infeasible with limited click volume and sales volume. If you're doing a good job of organizing your ad groups to be quite specific, any individual ad will not necessarily generate enough sales volume to generate meaningful feedback in a reasonable time frame.

Enter a modified form of multivariate testing that allows you to generate results more quickly and with fewer test combinations, called fractional-factorial testing.[11] Advanced mathematicians have developed shortcuts that create meaningful results with many fewer testing variations. One method, *Taguchi testing*, is quite common. It's also quite controversial, because it might miss a truly winning combination, but I'm willing to try anything that will work reasonably well. One Taguchi-based ad-testing protocol I use takes a seven-element grid with two values for each variable (64 total variants) and provides a recipe that gives you 8 ads to test instead of 64. You can muddle through this "by hand," as it were, on a useful site called Blair Gorman's AdComparator (http://adcomparator.com).

The beauty of multivariate testing is that you can answer several questions at once, often more accurately than through serial A/B tests of different theories over time. Implemented across an account, you'll likely see patterns of performance of specific ad elements repeated time after time in different situations. That should be teaching you something.

Ad testing is both art and science, requiring creative inputs and at least a rough experimental method. While you don't need to be an advanced mathematician, the ability to apply some of the math-based tools available is a must for superior performance.

Getting Help from the Experts

Can we learn about what works from professional copywriters, for example, Bob Bly and Nick Usborne? Having reviewed their work, I'd say yes and no. Consider that many AdWords advertisers (myself included) stumbled into the process with no formal background in writing marketing copy (but plenty of general experience in thinking, writing, persuading, and testing ideas). By all means, read the works of such authors—especially Usborne's *Net Words: Creating High-Impact Online Copy* (McGraw-Hill, 2001), which is particularly accessible. But keep in mind that some of their teachings about writing for the Web only apply to websites and e-newsletters, both of which provide considerably more room to develop your message.

For other background materials that help achieve better bottom-line results from ads, more and more marketers are delving into the literature on "scientific advertising," which begins with a very old book by Claude Hopkins entitled (not surprisingly) *Scientific Advertising* (Chelsea House Publishing, 1984). It includes various split-testing practices that have been adopted by many direct marketers (direct mailers) over the years. A more recent book by Seth Godin, *Survival Is Not Enough: Zooming, Evolution, and the Future of Your Company* (Free Press, 2002), helped me understand the evolutionary process of more rapid testing and improvement that seems to be required in modern companies.

With so much material available, it's easy to get carried away. Not only have social scientists been writing about this type of thing for centuries, but since the "Total Quality Management" movement, the market has been flooded with books about testing and improvement of manufacturing processes. This carried over to other fields such as web design. More recently, buzzwords from the manufacturing world seem to be leaking into general usage to cover almost any situation, but they don't always apply. When your child's T-ball coach starts talking about Six Sigma swing improvement, it's probably time for a reality check.

In any case, writings covering the rapid technological improvements at companies like Intel and Netscape—and now, Google—have been a staple of the business bookshelves and have filled magazines like *Business 2.0, Wired,* and *Fast Company* in recent years. It's sexy to maximize performance and to "iteratively" improve your processes through a series of versions, just like chip manufacturers and software companies do. But even these companies understand that the point is not to improve on every single aspect of their operations, just the aspects that matter.

Six Rules for Better AdWords Copy

While the two-step process described a bit earlier in "A Technique for Ad Refinement in Stages" narrates a plausible, staged approach to refinement, it's also useful to keep general tips and best practices in the back of your mind.

So far, I've discussed how principles of advertising and copywriting provide a foundation for writing AdWords ads, but one problem with following standard copywriting techniques is that Google AdWords are anything but standard. Since they are out of the mainstream of copywriting experience, a specific set of rules might be helpful as a kind of shorthand applicable to this domain. Here are my six rules for writing better AdWords copy:

- Match the user's query as closely as possible.

- Send appropriate cues by speaking the same language your target customer speaks.

- Filter out inappropriate prospects.

- Get the prospect's "action motor" going by inserting a "call to action."

- Based on CTR and conversion data, pick the winning ads among several you've been testing. Occasionally, introduce new ads so the testing process never stops.

- Inject some flair or brand appeal in the process.

Pick any example ad, and these six rules should be enough to get you thinking about how to write winning copy.

Rule #1: Match Ad Titles to Searched Keywords

The example about diamond bracelets gave you an idea of the typical process of improving on a single generic ad by writing many more specific ones so the ad titles match query keywords. (The example is drawn from a client campaign, but the type of jewelry has been changed to protect the confidentiality of their data. My tests consistently proved the power of creating a large number of more specific headlines as opposed to a smaller number of general ads about the jewelry store. In most cases, the more specific headlines had significantly higher CTRs.) This isn't a rule that applies across the board, but in many cases where users are looking for a specific item that might be found in a retail catalog, such as a diamond brooch or a diamond pendant, ads that contain that exact item in the headline feel more personalized to the user, so they're more likely to click.

Working for clients like this, I'm often amazed at how well they can do against much larger competition simply because the other advertisers may have limited themselves to a generic ad covering, for example, diamonds or jewelry in general. Ads that have a "canned" feel to them— or more to the point, ads that don't seem likely to take the user to a page describing *exactly* what he's looking for—might not get clicked on quite as often.

Perhaps you're wondering if this tendency would continue if every ad on the page had exactly the same title. If everyone did this, and every ad contained "diamond brooch" in the headline for ads appearing next to searches for **diamond brooch**, it's possible that a different sort of headline might stand out and therefore be clicked more often. For the time being, this is still a strong rule, but like any user tendency, it's subject to change.

Rule #2: Send Appropriate Cues to Your Target Audience

A corollary to matching ad titles to searched keywords is *appropriateness* and sending cues to certain consumers, and that's a bit subtler. You might not consider the mention of "one-of-a-kind" jewelry items to be filtering out bad prospects so much as it is a kind of cue that you hope will resonate with a very specific type of customer because it literally speaks their language. Some car buyers will respond to "240 hp" or "6-speed manual"; others will assume the horsepower is in line with comparable vehicles and will actually respond better to "zoom, zoom." (I would like to state for the record that I am not one of those who would buy a car just because it goes "zoom, zoom.")

Consider using language and terms that will resonate with your target audience. Let's say you sell housewares and your target customer is female, moderately affluent, and seeking the latest style. You're not selling traditional dinnerware, and there's simply no better way to convey that than just to tell it like it is, by using words like *modern* and *contemporary* in your ad copy. Clearly, different demographics require subtly different wording in ads, which can be achieved with an adjective here, an expression there. For example, even though I'm a nonexpert when it comes to martinis, and I don't throw dinner parties, I knew that the ad copy "elegant martini misters for the discerning martini-meister" would work well for my client, KlinQ.com. I was speaking the *lingua franca* of the affluent, young, martini-drinking set. A light touch of tongue-twisting humor and a post-materialist (nonbasic, nondiscount) ethic were conveyed to give that demographic what they were looking for. The fact that customers quickly found what they needed, and felt that this retailer understood their needs (my ad was only a small part of that equation), quickly overcame any price sensitivity on the part of the *bon vivants* in the market for martini-ware.

Rule #3: Filter Prospects

The process of filtering out bad prospects begins with keyword selection and targeted phrasing. Make sure your keywords are not so broad as to cause your ad to appear in searches that are irrelevant to your product or service. For example, if you're offering loans for cars and title your ad "Low APR Loans," you'll get people looking for personal loans, mortgages, home equity loans, recreational vehicle loans, and student loans, most of whom are not your target customers. By adding the word *auto* ("Low APR Auto Loans") to your ad, you can eliminate a large percentage of those nonproductive clicks.

Probably the most common problem pay-per-click advertisers face is the bargain hunter who clicks on an ad seeking an inexpensive or free product. Sometimes it just doesn't pay to be subtle. One client from the UK was getting too many tenants applying for loans, even though the product was clearly targeting the home equity loan market and even though the ad made it seem reasonably clear that you'd need to be quite creditworthy. The problem was easily solved by making the first word in the ad copy: "Homeowners!" (A searcher would be hard pressed to misinterpret that.)

As paid search advertisers, we need to be mindful that there are millions of noncustomers out there clicking away on our ads. We need to be particularly careful of those who are looking for something cheap or free. Unless you rely on a strategy of upselling people from an entry-level product or free offer, you might need to filter the low end of the market. I realize that advice won't apply to all of you, but the general principle of filtering does, and the "low end" (low-budget buyers and tire-kickers) presents a formidable challenge for advertisers. Keep in mind, though, the difference between someone who is in the early phases of a normal buying cycle (just not ready yet) and someone who is simply a poor prospect for you. They won't all buy immediately.

The classic example that's been given by companies like Google at seminars on this matter is the seller of graphics software who, due to poor ad copy and indiscriminate keyword selection, is inundated with clicks from people looking for free clip art. When I refer to the low end of the market, I'm really referring to a type of behavior that is endemic to search. Most of us constitute the low end (or "no end"!) of the market for advertisers on any given day, because we might be looking for free information, shareware, and so forth. If we click on someone's ad listing when we're in the "looking for free stuff" search mode, we usually wind up costing that advertiser money. Niche advertisers are looking for a relatively rare bird: a reasonably warm prospect who is likely to convert to a customer.

Does this mean you should put your prices in your ads? You're welcome to test it, but it doesn't necessarily work. You can convey a sense of your positioning in a price range with verbal cues and brand names. Most folks have a general sense of where Pier 1, Holt Renfrew, Home Depot, Best Buy, McDonald's, Outback Steakhouse, and Target stand in the price spectrum just from their well-known brand names. If you're not well known, you can certainly choose your words carefully to convey a sense of price points. "Competitively priced data loggers" or simply "data loggers" might convey one message, whereas "industrial use data loggers" might convey another. Someone who is confused and seeking a speedometer gizmo of some sort for his bicycle, at the very least, is unlikely to be confused enough to click on the ad if you work in cues like "industrial." On popular terms, sometimes even stronger language may be required to deter the mass market from clicking on your ad for a niche product. One simple word might not be enough. Though it sounds redundant, "data loggers for business and industry" might be needed to weed out the wrong sorts of browsers if data logging for personal uses like sporting activities were suddenly very popular. When too many eyes are flitting quickly across ads, it may not hurt to hit them with a couple of really obvious prequalifying words (such as both "business" and "industry" in this example). Note too that such examples are not cast in stone, because search behavior is fluid. Spikes in search activity on certain keywords can be driven by shifting trends, news items, and consumer tastes. These spikes in the frequency of certain keyword searches can cost your business, so you need to be attuned to changing search patterns and filter more aggressively if you believe that you're paying for too many mass-market clicks that don't genuinely want what you have to offer.

I've worked with service-oriented clients, such as one in the web design business, who are upset that they receive too many low-budget inquiries from their pay-per-click ads. Unfortunately, though, shouting about a $5,000 minimum price tag up front is no answer to this dilemma. After all, why deter potentially good clients? Some relationships take time to develop. The process of sorting out qualified leads for a complex sale isn't something you can expect to take place solely in your 95-character ad. While it's sometimes useful to "cool off" nonprospects with restrictive-sounding messages, don't you need to convey initial warmth (or at least relevance and an open-for-business attitude) to actual prospects? It's all too easy to forget that there are many others competing for those customers (and advertising in the same space!), and that for these prospects, $0 is always the default amount that they plan to pay you until they get to know you a little better. When a potential customer is early in the buying cycle, you can hurt yourself by posting a price completely out of context, not least because a competitor can easily undercut you in the same space with a price that looks better than yours on the surface.

Wholesale versus retail, and business-to-business versus consumer, are two other common filtering concerns. In wholesale and business-to-business, the number of target buyers is smaller. There should be no sugar-coating the fact that filtering out all the inappropriate prospects is difficult. Mostly, this should be done with keyword selection in your AdWords account. But when it comes to ad copy, you'll want to experiment. In certain industries, terminological conventions tend to emerge, such that you can really catch people's attention if you stay current and use the most current buzzwords. For example, in web hosting, an ad title like "Reseller Hosting" or "Co-Location Servers" would be fairly well understood by your target audience. You might soothe executive decision-makers with messaging around "redundancy" and "security."

Rule #4: Insert a Call to Action

Google now recommends experimenting with calls to action, such as "download" or "shop and compare." Believe it or not, in the early days Google was inclined to reject many common calls to action—including "buy now"! Editorially, today Google only rejects a small percentage of calls to action. (As stated in their written policies, they prohibit universal calls to action such as "click here.") They've been a bit quieter about the related notion of an "offer," which is a staple of ad copywriting. But that's your job, not Google's. Invent compelling offers if they might generate a response, and see what happens.

One client, for example, tried this ad that included a bland mention of their company name along with a product benefit:

ClearTone Acne Treatment

Finnish acne cream now available!
Clearer skin in as little as 7 days
foracne.com

A second ad contained a benefit and a free offer:

Get Clear Skin in 7 Days

European Acne Treatment now in the
US. Act now & get one month free!
foracne.com

The first ad pulled a CTR of 0.8%. The second ad pulled 1.7%. By generating a higher CTR, we were able to keep more keywords enabled, and we were able to lower bids and significantly lower average CPC while maintaining a similar ad position. This did improve ROI, though ROI could have gone down in the process of attracting more clicks. This is why it's so important that Google typically rewards advertisers with higher ad position when they do increase CTR.

We are hearing more now about testing calls to action such as "buy now" in pay-per-click ads, but what is not often discussed is the wide range of calls to action that is possible.

Such call-to-action suggestions should connect closely with the nature of your offer or with a larger marketing strategy that you're pursuing. One of my clients, a popular technology journalist, established a relationship with his audience by having them subscribe to a free newsletter about the foibles of Microsoft Windows as they affect the average computer user. It was his firm belief that the word *subscribe* sounded too daunting (he thought users would worry "Would it cost money? Would it mean an arduous sign-up process?"). He was adamant that we try the word *get* instead. As it turned out, those who saw the ad containing the word *subscribe* were slightly more likely to become subscribers than those who saw the ad containing the word *get.* The word *get,* evidently, did not explain to prospects what they'd be doing as well as the word *subscribe* did. Moreover, the word *subscribe* did not result in unsustainably low CTRs. The concern over this word turned out to be much ado about nothing.

Rule #5: Run a Test, Keep the Winning Ads

Unless your marketing campaign consists of nothing more than a single AdWords ad, you'll need some method of measuring the effectiveness of your ads. With one ad, your sales either increase or stay the same. If the sales go up, your ad is effective. If the sales stay the same or go down, your ad is ineffective. If you're running a number of ads, and you should be, the only way to determine the effectiveness of your campaign is to do some testing. After running a test, you'll delete or pause the losing ads and keep the winners.

Is it really that easy? Sometimes. But wait! There's always a fun loophole or two to consider. For example, I've gone back and looked at ads a few days after I've paused them as "losing" ads, and due to latent sales that have come in after the ads were paused (but are credited to those particular ads), they are now tied with, or beating, the "winners"! The only recourse I have in those quirky cases is to unpause those ads and keep running the test.

Rule #6: Inject Some Flair

Keep in mind that copywriting flair and writing catchphrases that cement brand awareness can be overrated in a realm where targeting and testing reigns. You might require more panache if your job is to write longer copy for the sales page on the website. Here, though, I am referring solely to your AdWords ads. For example, earlier I mentioned the example ad text "elegant martini misters for the discerning martini-meister." In many contexts, this ad would be too silly, but my test identified this ad as the winner, likely due to the whimsical tone. There are many more examples, however, of attempts to inject flair, whimsy, or style into an AdWords ad that simply fall flat. First and foremost, search users are trying to find their way around, not get a chuckle. In an ad for a website-building product aimed at novices, I tried the ad title "No Web Geek? No Problem." This didn't work; the ad got low CTRs. However, the factual ad text "no programming required" did work. Flair-driven advertising is still more the exception than the rule in AdWords copywriting, but you need to incorporate it as part of your repertoire of techniques depending on the target audience.

Some Ideas for Testing Ads

The most basic form of testing Google ads is through a split-test or A/B test. The AdWords interface is set up so you can test the performance of ads "head to head." For ideas about what kinds of variables you'll want to consider testing, see the section "Ideas for What Variables to Test," a little later in the chapter. You'll typically (though not necessarily, if you use Google's tracking products) be using special tracking codes to distinguish one ad from another. The subject of tracking is covered in considerable detail in Chapter 10.

In the broader marketing world, split-testing is an advertising methodology that has been perfected over the years by direct marketers, often at considerable expense. Sending two offers randomly distributed over two segments of a mailing list is one way of testing response. The marketer varies a key variable, such as envelope color or the copy in the introductory paragraph, and tests response rates. It might take many years to learn which combination of elements is optimal.

How Split-Testing Works

Since 2002, Google AdWords has made split-testing easy and cost effective. In any given ad group, you simply use the Create New Ad feature (see Figure 8-2), and presto, you're testing two or more ads against one another. The primary metric you'll be looking at is CTR, but if you're tracking by ad (using tracking URLs or Google's conversion tracking products), you can also track conversion rates and ROI on each ad. The most detailed reports are available by running custom reports under the Reports tab in the AdWords interface, but conversions are also noted at the campaign, ad group, and ad variations levels. In some cases, at these latter three levels, you may not find all the data you need; you can add it to the display by clicking Customize Columns.

When you're running multiple ads in a single campaign, Google automatically rotates ads as evenly as possible. Therefore, if you run four ads simultaneously, each ad should be shown approximately 25% of the time. If your numbers do not show that to be the case, it might be the result of looking at a date range during which not all ads were running for the entire period. To make a reasonably accurate comparison, you'll want to wait until all ads have been running long enough, and then choose a date range during which all ads were running. Unfortunately, you cannot adjust Google's automatic rotation so that some ads appear with more (or less) frequency. There is an automatic "favor the ads with the highest CTR" (the Optimize setting) feature in the Edit Campaign Settings interface (see Figure 8-3), but for active testing I recommend this be switched to Rotate, or "show ads more evenly."

The results of split-testing can be educational. Even small changes in the ad copy can cause CTRs to vary significantly. But, as discussed above, the best practice to follow at first is to vary the ads significantly rather than testing minute differences. Test smaller differences at the refinement phase.

Ideas for What Variables to Test

The first thing to consider when planning a test is the number of variables to test. Initially, it may seem that the more variables you introduce, the better your testing. While it's true that you could introduce an almost infinite number of modifications, keep in mind that the more variables

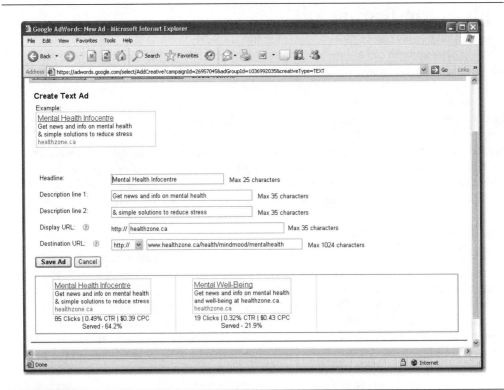

FIGURE 8-2 Click Create New Ad, and presto, you've initiated a split-test.

you have, the more difficult it is to achieve conclusive results. Minor variables will eventually test differently over long periods of time. Therefore, the best method is to test with four or five possible *objectives* (brand, ROI, CTR, clarity, credibility) for your ad copy firmly in mind, in whatever proportion feels right.

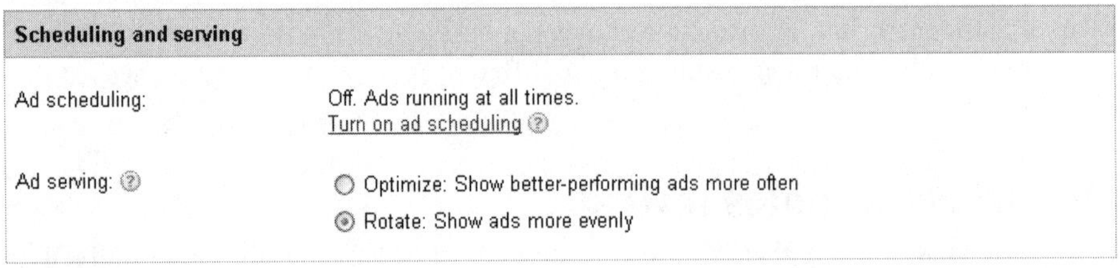

Scheduling and serving	
Ad scheduling:	Off. Ads running at all times. Turn on ad scheduling ⑦
Ad serving: ⑦	○ Optimize: Show better-performing ads more often ◉ Rotate: Show ads more evenly

FIGURE 8-3 Select Rotate, or AdWords will decide for you which ad is the "best performer."

However you choose to approach your testing, you'll probably find that your first couple of tests weed out the really poor performers from the better performers. At this stage you can either make drastic changes to the poorest ads and put them back in the mix, or just concentrate on fine-tuning the better ads in the bunch. However, there is a limit to the amount of fine-tuning you can do. Eventually, the law of diminishing returns will kick in, and it will be time to stop the tweaking and use the ads that have provided the most profitable results. Remember that other factors such as shifting tastes, randomness, timing, and so on, can affect the performance of your ads.

Testing on Calls to Action and Offers

One of the easiest things to test is the effectiveness of a simple call to action. In one ad, simply describe your product. Then create an identical ad, but include a call to action such as "Buy now!" "Download Free Trial," "Try 30 days free!" or some other variation.

Generally speaking, your call to action should connect with an action that's easily available from the landing page that the ad takes the prospect to. When testing multiple calls to action, be sure that each one takes the user to a different landing page. This is the only way you can accurately determine the effectiveness of the different calls to action.

Closely related to calls to action are offers, which typically combine a call to action with a time limit or discount. Even without a call to action, an offer *implies* a call to action (purchase before a certain date to receive a discount, for example) and typically creates a sense of urgency. This real-life example should give you an idea:

Cool Birthday Gifts

For anyone! An amazing selection
of quality products. Delivered.
Uncommonlygifted.com

Cool Birthday Gifts

For anyone. An amazing selection.
15% discount for a limited time!
Uncommonlygifted.com

These two ads were tested over a relatively high number of clicks—in excess of 2,000 for each ad. Searchers clicked on the second ad more than twice as often (1.9% to 0.9%), allowing Uncommonly Gifted to bid lower on popular gift-related terms (average CPC was reduced from 17 cents to 12 cents) while maintaining visibility with a high ad placement on the page. The benefit continued after the click, as this ad generated a higher conversion rate to sales.

One large retailer I work with was swamped with Christmas orders by simply resorting to offering "free shipping until Dec. 15" with no minimum order or restrictions. Such is consumer psychology: such offers may be worth less to people than their reactions warrant, in terms of vastly increased conversion rates. And why is free shipping, which reduces the price to a consumer by, say, 10%, more attractive to that consumer than cutting the price by 10%? Perhaps because shipping feels like an unknown, and it turns into a known, thus reducing uncertainty. Also, people are poor at making quick calculations. Whatever the psychology, these are the types of offers you should be testing.

Testing on Syntax Variations

Minor syntax variations, like plural instead of singular, can have a significant impact on the response your ads elicit. Since the ad space is so limited, you'll be tempted to use abbreviations and symbols where possible. Remember that Google policy limits the use of symbols to their true meaning. Whatever you use, try testing both—the abbreviation and the full word or phrase, or the symbol and the word. For example, try using *and* in one version of an ad, and an ampersand (&) in another. See if it makes a difference. But doing this should generally only make a difference if the saved space allows you to write a significantly better ad overall.

Some small differences in wordings actually have a deeper meaning, so I don't always consider these trivial. "Ships same day" might actually ring more true than "same day shipping," so the consumer sees the former as more credible. Or, it might be the other way around—the second variant sounds more natural, and faster. I'll leave it to you to test for yourself.

Differentiation of Ad Copy from Other Ads on the Page

Many of the ads that appear for a given search will have very similar titles and copy (see Figure 8-4). If you find that to be the case, try setting your ad apart by using different copy or a totally different approach. The traditional approach to differentiation is to communicate your

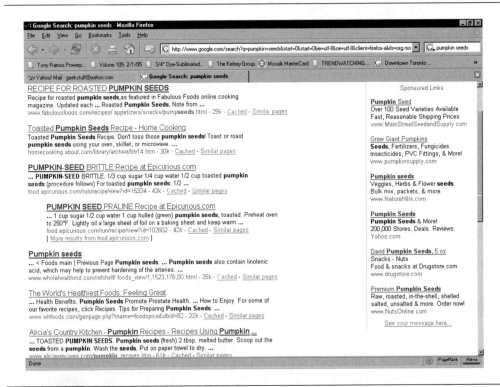

FIGURE 8-4   If all the ad titles look similar, try making yours different.

company's unique selling proposition or points of difference and focus on them; I'm referring to something a bit narrower here. As many advertisers will begin thinking alike about what creates an effective ad, you could try creative, unusual ad titles that might boost your CTR relative to the others. If seven ads say "pumpkin seeds" and yours says "premium pumpkin seeds" or "grow giant pumpkins," you might stand out just a bit.

Sell a Solution, Not a Product or Service, and Test It

If you were selling knee braces, you could have "Knee Braces" in your ad title, of course. But why not test an ad with "Knee Problems?" as the title and "knee braces" in the body copy? In general, ads that remind the consumer of their fears, problems, or concerns—"scary" ads—can be effective if the product or service being offered in the ad resolves the prospect's perceived problem or fear. This approach is particularly effective in certain industries such as computer network security, tax law, and insurance.

Differentiation, Period

In a related vein to both making an ad different and selling a solution, depending on your audience, you'll need to be addressing them with differentiation rather than a bland introduction. It's fair to say, for example, that someone seeking liposuction or facial surgery has done a decent amount of research already. Saying that you offer these services isn't going to be much of a differentiator, obviously. Why should they choose you and not the next plastic surgeon on the page? It's tough to explain in a short ad, of course, and in a world populated by tens of thousands of similarly qualified professionals, being told to "come up with a unique selling proposition" for your website and ad copy may feel like an insult to the intelligence. Sure, but if you want anyone to click and convert, it'll help to have a hook, whether that be testimonials, famous clients, your upscale facility, your blue-chip medical training, a new piece of equipment or technique, a white paper battling myths, a free gift, financing, or something else. Some of your clients may be attracted by an enticing description of the end result, much like they are by exercise-equipment ads that tout "a flatter stomach in 30 days." How about "a flatter stomach in zero days"?

The long and short of it is, for increasingly savvy consumers, closely matching their query and saying you "have that" may not be enough in 2010 and beyond. We're getting a long way from the old Sears Roebuck or Eaton's catalogs circa 1910. Consumers have choices and have done research, and in this age of e-commerce, they know they can easily buy things. So for example, the headline "Is Your Family Safe?" might galvanize more buying interest than "Carbon Monoxide Sensor." However, it might attract people looking for locks, alarm systems, and smoke detectors as well. The only way to know if it produces the desired results (higher ROI) is to test it.

Flair vs. Flat

As I've already pointed out, plain ads often work well in Google AdWords, but depending on your business, light humor and flair can help connect with the audience. For one client (KlinQ.com, a seller of designer housewares), I tested a fairly plain ad for teakettles against one for "whistling teakettles" that concluded with the hokey phrase "just whistle." The latter won out, much as the "discerning martini-meister" ad had performed well for another one of their products. This surprised me because such flair does not usually make a significant difference. The target audience in this case is obviously looking for the psychological lift that comes from purchasing "fun" kitchen items; they are seeking style, not merely basic need satisfaction or the best price.

In the realm of style, identifying a product with a celebrity might also be worth testing. Drawing attention to someone who endorses a product (a baseball player who wears an Indian Motorcycle jacket, an actor who wears a certain type of jewelry in a movie, a celebrity who has learned to drive a go-kart at a training facility) can provide context that reminds searchers of hot trends and also hints that the celebrity's glamour might rub off on them. If you use this technique, the content on your website needs to be factual in such cases to avoid potential liability issues.

The third-party endorsement falls under the general rubric of credibility. Rather than seeing this as merely a dimension to test, I believe that advertisers should always be thinking about credibility of this nature. "Voted best free content by PC World" or "USA Today recommends" are excellent endorsements that would stand out from other, similar ads on the page. However, it must be clear that the endorsement is real, as proven by the content on your landing page, or Google Editorial may reject it.

Brand Impact and Story-Telling

Consumers will look at the display URL before they decide to click. They'll also look for cues in the ad to decide if you're full of hype. So does this mean that you're facing an uphill battle if you're not a big company with a recognizable URL? Not really. To be sure, in some industries consumers will outclick a "familiar" ad by a factor of 4 to 1 over an ad from a company they've never heard of. But you can overcome the familiarity factor by capitalizing on your unique position in the marketplace.

Using familiar phrases, features, and benefits associated with your company, or emphasizing your long history, are things that should help you stand out from a crowd of wannabes. But if you don't have these, you need to invent something. You need to begin telling your own story and writing your own history. That doesn't mean misleading people! But your buyers often respond well to imagery and mythology. They want *you* to *create* this. "Diamonds are forever" isn't just a cheap slogan. Marketing campaigns by de Beers repositioned diamonds completely in the marketplace. They went from being just another precious gemstone, to the standard for engagement rings, with a suggested "two months' salary" dollar value attached.

Seth Godin reminds us that in the wider world of marketing, you don't get much time to tell a story. But if told consistently, encountering just a tiny sliver of the story later on can remind people of what you're all about. Godin shows an image of two-and-a-half letters of the Starbucks logo, and he's right: by viewing just a couple of letters and a single pointed shape from the logo, I immediately began to feel myself walking into the familiar Starbucks store layout. The other image he shows is a tiny drawing of the tip of an elephant's trunk. Just by glancing at a couple of circles and lines, the mind begins to evoke the majesty and beauty of this hulking beast.[12]

So you might consider your AdWords ad the "tip of the elephant's trunk." It can work in your favor whether you're a large company or a small one. But not if you haven't made the effort to invent a mythology to help your customers convince themselves about the experience of buying from you.

Some categories lend themselves particularly well to smaller players. A maker of fresh pastry shipped overnight—let's call her "Little Old Pastry Chef"—may do better than a large company whose brand name has already been associated with lower-priced products selling in supermarkets. Sometimes consumers are captivated by "small." Supermarket products aren't remarkable, but custom-made items are. If the smaller retailer seems dedicated to a niche like fresh pastry, consumers will be open to buying from it. Small companies with focused ads can beat large companies who run ho-hum, me-too ads. In some cases, it's the big guys, not the little guys, who look out of place. Unless you're really sure the recipient would like it, for example, you're probably not going to order a box of Dunkin' Donuts as a birthday gift.

The increasing consumer appetite for customization, and the growing adoption of local search, also gives smaller firms a potential advantage. Such trends at least don't appear to put the niche player at a significant *disadvantage,* as long as they're content to stay small. Larger retailers can also capitalize on such trends if they understand the psychology of their customers. A great example is Zingerman's (www.zingermans.com), which began as a deli in 1982 and today is one of the most successful online food retailers in the world. The remarkable thing is how few of their competitors are currently taking advantage of the wide-open keyword inventory on keyphrases like **online deli**, **cheeses**, and **specialty vinegar**. Zingerman's today advertises on some deli-related searches; they didn't seem to be doing so in 2005 when I first wrote about them here. Their competitors would be wise to follow suit: the market and word-of-mouth potential surely makes it worth taking a shot with some low-cost search marketing.

As people search more nowadays with local intent, a sense of physical place can be the biggest advantage going for the smaller retailer. A Canadian boutique called The Added Touch evolved into a mail-order (and now, online) sales leader. The company's brand was built largely around the Oakville, Ontario location of the original physical store, and customers are well aware of this. If Martha Stewart found herself in the Toronto area, you can imagine her making a beeline for tony Oakville (wouldn't that spice things up).

Many online sellers today have a great story to tell, but they aren't telling it. Why not test ad copy—and website copy—that refers heavily to your physical location and humble origins against copy that emphasizes only product features and benefits?

Testing the Display URL

Speaking of the display URL, recall that this is prominently displayed at the bottom of every ad. Users may look at this for some cue as to the identity of the company they're dealing with. Some URLs, particularly short, readable ones, may inspire a more positive response than others. If your company name is two words, a typical thing to test is whether an all-lowercase URL gets a higher CTR than one with a capital letter at the beginning of each word—dolphinzone.com versus DolphinZone.com. You shouldn't uncover major differences in user response, but it's worth a look.

Because Google may allow you to include a subdirectory name in your display URL, you may find that a keyword-rich subdirectory name helps. For example, if you worked for Apple, you might test www.apple.com versus www.apple.com/ipod-nano. For some time now, Google hasn't required that the display URL containing a keyword-rich subdirectory name take a user to a page that matches that exact URL, as long as the root URL is accurate. Incorporate this trick into your testing.

Some companies set up dedicated URLs to capitalize on their brand name while focusing the user's attention on a hot new product. For example, on a U.S.-based query for "Blackberry 8820," Research in Motion is sending me to a site called Blackberry8800Series.com. Cool. Microsites like this often offer tighter testing opportunities for the marketing team, and the combination of the beloved brand with the specific product name makes for an interesting experiment. Granted, many users will opt to buy that device in an offline store or through their wireless carrier, so tying these revenues back to the AdWords campaign isn't easy.

Beware of the microsite strategy if it drops your trusted brand out of the picture. In general, a well-respected brand should strive to garner the benefit of that brand in the display URL. A financial conglomerate I worked with tried (generic examples given for confidentiality reasons) www.FinCon.com against a more generic site with the URL www.home-finance-savings.com. A second test pitted a longer but more targeted URL against the brand-name URL: www .FinConHomeFinance.com against the original www.FinCon.com. Run your own test if you like, but if I had to guess, I'd bet your generic microsite will see significantly worse performance than the one that incorporates your brand name into the URL—including the display URL.

It's Not What You Say, but How You Say It

As we've all discovered at one time or another, your choice of words does matter. There's a big difference between *happy* and *ecstatic,* even though both describe the same basic emotion. Therefore, as you test your ads, try using different words and phrases with similar meanings. If you're looking for a catalog of suggestions for word variations to try, see Richard Bayan's book *More Words That Sell* (McGraw-Hill, 2003).

Tracking Results

The best way to track the performance of your ads is to tag each ad with a unique tracking URL, usually using parameters dictated by your web analytics software, and a naming system that you find helpful. For example, you might refer to campaign 2, ad group 23, with the numerical code "0223," and to denote each successive ad you test in that group, you might use a letter of the alphabet. So a typical tracking URL for the first ad might be http://www.qvack-qvack.com/shirts .asp?source=adwords&ad=**0223a**. The next ad in that same group would have the same URL, but end in the letter *b,* and so on.

To make sure you also get keyword-level data (without excluding the ad-level performance data), you can enable autotagging in AdWords and use a special parameter that will dynamically append whatever keyword triggered the ad, right on the end of your own tracking string. To do so:

1. Go to Account Preferences.
2. Select Auto-Tagging.
3. Add the variable, **kw={keyword}**, to your ad destination URL like this:
   http://www.qvack-qvack.com/shirts.asp?source=adwords&ad=0223a**&kw={keyword}**

Statistical Significance in Testing

Advertisers often wonder if there ever comes a point at which you can be confident that one ad will outperform another over the long term. Some statistical experts will say that as few as seven occurrences of the desired outcome (clicks or sales, in this case) provide enough information to be confident. While such claims are based on raw math, they assume that no other influences are at work in the experiment. In the real world, I have found it necessary to run tests longer than some experts suggest. Unevenness in ad delivery across different sources, different user behavior at different times of day, changing ad positions, comparison behavior by users seeing different competitors' ads at different times on different keywords, and numerous other factors make it difficult to trust the orthodox statistician's approach. Without a better way to describe it (I'm no math PhD), allow me to suggest that patterns can be "wonky" over the short term, but become very reliable over a longer period of time. That does not, of course, explain why previously solid patterns begin to reverse themselves so that black becomes white and up becomes down. But often you can chalk that up to changing market conditions, shifting consumer demands, and strategic behavior by competitors.

Since AdWords clicks are generally pretty inexpensive, I suggest that my clients run ad tests for a relatively long period to ensure the results are accurate. "Relatively long" plays out differently for different ad campaigns.

Practical experience has shown that ads may even out in performance, even though probability theory would have given them a 95% chance of continuing their gap in performance. It is beyond the scope of this book to fully explain why this is so, except to say that conditions change rapidly in this environment, and there is more randomness and volatility in small samples than there might be if you were flipping coins. Clicks and buying interest might flow in from one region all at once, for example, skewing results towards one particular ad, but only temporarily. Probability theory doesn't account for consumer enthusiasm, which might flood into this process and then vanish as quickly as it came.

So, as long as a campaign is within the normal range of attracting a steady number of impressions and clicks, I make sure not to jump the gun on interpreting split-tests or multivariate tests. Instead of thinking in terms of numbers of clicks or sales, I often think in terms of a representative time period, such as two days or a week. My rule of thumb is to give tests time to play out fully. If I'm looking at CTRs primarily, I'll look for 100 or even 1,000 or more clicks on each ad, if I can get away with holding the test that long. As shown in the example for UncommonlyGifted.com, we generated over 2,000 clicks for an ad containing a time-limited discount offer to compare it with an ad that did not contain the offer. Our findings form the foundation for a long-term campaign strategy. We are surely not going to plan such a strategy based on some statistician's views (not directly suited to this complex medium) that seven clicks are enough to compare ad performance. After generating over 2,000 clicks on each ad, at 17 cents per click, we're rock solid in our belief that the ad with the offer works better. The $680 spent on that test is an inexpensive piece of market research, especially considering that they are making sales while conducting the test.

Looking at conversions and ROI is even more fraught with uncertainty, because the frequencies of sales can be low and big-dollar sales can be "spiky" and skew results. You can wing it and make sure you don't make any decisions based on fewer than 20–30 sales, or use any of the generic tools you can easily search online that will give you statistical confidence levels for picking long-term winners based on your inputs. These models incorporate the degree of separation between the two results (if you have ads with conversion rates of 2% and 8%, versus ads with conversion rates of 2% and 3.2%, the latter pair will require considerably more data to reach the same confidence level) as part of the calculation. After some practice, assuming you have decent sales volumes, you get better at picking out the winning ads after an appropriate period of testing.

Moving from Ad Content to Campaign

So far in this book, I've addressed the short history of paid search and how it fits in with other forms of marketing. I've shown you the basics of how the AdWords interface works and introduced you to some intermediate-level campaign management concepts that should help you succeed over the long haul. And you've now gotten a taste of how easy it is to tweak your ad copy to improve performance. It's the world's fastest and cheapest market research!

Speaking of testing and market research, a lot of companies get a bit gun-shy when it comes to actually launching their AdWords campaigns, because of the difficulty in forecasting results. Not uncommonly, paid search will have an advocate within a company, but this advocate may lack the support of senior management. Whether your company employs two people or two thousand, it's worth taking an in-depth look at how this kind of marketing campaign fits into your overall corporate strategy. Some corporate cultures still resist innovative marketing methods because they feel they're too unpredictable. If you glossed over Chapter 6, you may want to revisit it now. There, I explored ways of convincing the boss (and yourself) that AdWords is a relatively low-risk, if unpredictable, marketing opportunity. I also explained how to shape your campaign from the beginning by identifying key campaign goals, carefully assessing your sales process from clickthrough to revenue generation, and asking where your business model fits in the context of other successful online business models.

Let's move onto the challenge of squeezing out more volume from a campaign that is already working well.

Endnotes

1. Nassim Nicholas Taleb, *The Black Swan: The Impact of the Highly Improbable* (Random House, 2007—no the publisher info is not an April Fool's joke). Taleb's work illustrates so well for the layperson how apparently simple math problems reach incredible complexity with the addition of a greater number of highly uncertain variables. He gives the example of predicting the location of a billiard ball as it bounces around a real-world (not theoretical, two-dimensional) pool table. AdWords is at least as complex as that. Educated readers may wish to arm themselves with Taleb's wisdom in this and his previous volume, *Fooled by Randomness: The Hidden Role of Chance in Life and in the Markets* (Random House, 2005). Among other things he offers a critique of over-interpretation of data and an exaggerated sense of causality that is wired into our brains—or what he refers to as the

Baconian "narrative fallacy." Empirical skepticism is a mentally tiring habit, according to Taleb, but it seems like one we'll need to adopt if we're to avoid making major errors in judgment in important situations. Perhaps more to the point, in a climate of big potential upside, you should be open to possibility and bullish about the future, in spite of the many layers of uncertainty that face the would-be "planner."

2. You need to be particularly aware of the "spiky" nature of episodes of "bad" clicks, which can cause you to have the mother of all bad days. Whether it's daily budgeting, an alert-based bid management system, or a high degree of rapport with your AdWords rep in cases of click fraud, avoiding or reversing catastrophic events can be (as in many situations in Extremistan) financially more important to you than frequently squeezing out a tiny bit of extra performance from a "tweak," especially if you overinterpret and assign too much causality to such "tweaks." A lesser version of the catastrophic day of nonconverting clicks is the Post-Christmas Problem: many retail advertisers fail to lower bids or pause campaigns in the four weeks following December 25, during which, quite predictably, in many sectors, conversion rates drop to their lowest points of the year. This is exacerbated by the fact that many advertisers have (often belatedly) raised bids to capture sales volume during a period of unusually strong conversion rates. Giving back all your holiday profits based on predictable events isn't random or improbable, though: it's just stupid.

3. Matt Ragas explores this phenomenon nicely in his book *The Power of Cult Branding: How 9 Magnetic Brands Turned Customers into Loyal Followers (and Yours Can, Too!)* (Crown Business, 2002).

4. For a recent critique that makes this point, see Bob Garfield's *And Now a Few Words from Me: Advertising's Leading Critic Lays Down the Law, Once and For All* (McGraw-Hill, 2004).

5. Jay Conrad Levinson, *Guerrilla Marketing: Secrets for Making Big Profits from Your Small Business* (Houghton Mifflin, 1998).

6. OK, maybe not that. To quote Seth Godin, the marketing guru who is so influential he has his own action figure (as well as being cited too often in this book), "I solved my headache problem twenty years ago."

7. When I clicked their ad, HengDongChem.com's site was down. More recently, they seem to have disappeared from the page. Another weak player weeded out by the AdWords environment.

8. Date of query: December 30, 2007.

9. After the dust had settled on June 3, 2008, Obama became the Democratic nominee for President, although it took Hillary Clinton some time to concede. Shortly thereafter, final numbers on each candidate's Google ad spend came in, showing Obama's $2.08 million spend in 2008 far outstripping Clinton's. The strategic nature of the Obama campaign's ad buy is further emphasized by the fact that $1.7 million of it was deployed in February 2008 alone. See Kate Kaye, "Clinton Spent Far Less Online Than Obama," *ClickZ*, June 16, 2008; Kate Kaye, "Obama Spent Most of $3 Million on Google," *ClickZ*, May 29, 2008.

10. Appropriate thanks are due here to Mona Elesseily, account director on this client account, with whom I collaborated on the copywriting and testing efforts.

11. On the ins and outs of different types of multivariate testing, the counsel and writings of Scott Miller of Vertster and Tom Leung of Google have been very helpful.

12. Seth Godin, *All Marketers Are Liars* (Portfolio, 2005), 70. For the counterpoint, which criticizes large companies and their advertising agencies for being propagandists, see Laura Penny, *Your Call Is Important to Us: The Truth About Bullshit* (Crown, 2005). Penny is an enemy of phoniness, especially phoniness in the pursuit of profit, but never makes it clear what authenticity would look like.

Chapter 9

Expanding Your Ad Distribution: Opportunities and Pitfalls

Probably the most common challenge I face in helping out "mature" AdWords accounts—either those that my company has been overseeing for some time, or new clients who come to us having reached an impasse in their efforts—is insufficient click volume. The problem is easy to describe: the advertiser loves the results so far and just wants more of them! "Great. We're at $28 a lead, comparing favorably with the $74 per lead generated by offline advertising. Now we need more leads!" might be a typical directive.

This can lead to some interesting judgment calls. Do we increase the average cost per lead of the whole campaign in order to generate additional volume (by, say, increasing bids to improve ad position)? Or do we hold firm on the cost per lead and search harder for ways to increase targeted clickthroughs at low cost? (The latter, obviously, is the bigger challenge. It's pretty easy just to go in and increase all your bids.)

Conventional wisdom suggests that when you've found the low-hanging fruit of inexpensive customer acquisition methods, you're forced to pay more for incremental customers. As discussed previously, there are tactical and philosophical considerations that determine whether a company wishes to pursue market share or profitability at a given juncture. Marketers typically use terms like "aggressive" as shorthand for pursuing more leads or customers by raising average CPC and ad position. Those who can't afford to raise their cost per new customer too high, and want to squeeze the maximum ROI out of every click (or not incur that click at all), might refer to themselves as pure direct marketers, conservative or cautious, slow growth oriented, or ROI focused.

Even if you leave bids where they are, you can push your ads out in front of more prospects by using AdWords. This chapter offers some suggestions for the most likely avenues to accomplish that, so you can implement an expansion plan with a minimum of fuss. This chapter also covers a couple of advanced topics in ad distribution: local targeting, new types of content targeting, and new developments with content targeting (such as new reporting capabilities that might give you more confidence in bidding on content).

I'll assume that you've already selected the check box that shows your ads on search partner sites, a first step in expanding distribution beyond Google Search, and that you've already thought about which countries are good places to show your ads and selected them accordingly in your campaign settings.

Getting the Most Out of the Keywords You Know

You may be tempted to think that generating lists of additional keywords and throwing them into your AdWords account is a good way to make more money with your campaign. I'll cover that, but first, are you getting the best performance out of the keywords that are already there?

Deal with Your Lowest-Quality Keywords

If some of your keywords have gathered poor quality history, they may be shown in lower ad positions, or they might even fail to meet the "bid requirement" on many queries, and therefore in those cases not show at all. No keyword is technically inactive today under the new regime I've called AdWords 2.7, so there is no urgent need to "rescue" any given keyword from "deactivated" status. That means your task here is less urgent, but also harder, because your poor quality keywords still stay active. So overall, the process of improving your account and raising volume is going to be subtler than ever before.

In the old days, prior to Quality-Based Bidding, Google never had consistent advice for reactivating keywords deactivated by low CTRs. Yes, there was boilerplate advice for those suffering from "deactivated keywords syndrome," but it tended to be ineffective. The complexity of the task of cleaning up a low-quality account has grown more complex with the advent of Quality-Based Bidding. You'll have to make some judgment calls about how well you've built your account so far, and consider pausing, moving, or deleting some keywords or groups to improve quality. The usual advice about continuing to test ads, and sending users to appropriate landing pages, certainly applies in spades.

First, go back to some of the fundamental advice shared previously. You should have started your account with highly relevant and narrow terms, and gradually built campaigns with broader, less targeted terms as you established a strong account history. If you didn't do that, and your account is in tatters with poor Quality Scores all over the place, you may have difficulty digging out of this hole, because some aspect of the Quality Score formula includes an account-wide Quality Score that acts as an "overlay"—either helping to "green light" or "red light" new keywords. I recommend you contact your Google rep and ask them whether the account is worth fixing, or whether its poor start makes it unlikely that your actions will fix an intractable situation. Ask them if it makes more sense to delete the current account and start again with a new one. Generally speaking, accounts with histories are better than fresh accounts, even if some of that history is poor. But some might be lost causes.

In doing this, you are possibly accomplishing two goals. The first is getting more information out of Google as to the best recommended course. Make it clear to them that you want more clicks and are eager to learn (beyond pabulum boilerplate-type advice) how you might expand your click volume. The second goal, though, is tied to the hope that they're listening to your troubles and willing to take a look at some of the stats associated with your account. If you're lucky, maybe someone will see that your account-wide Quality Score is an undue hindrance to you, and manually adjust it. This is a gray area. No one really knows how often such manual overrides are done, and how much they actually help in relation to improving the actual signals and stats that go into your Quality Score in an automated way.

At one time, there seemed to be no harm to having unsuccessful or ill-chosen keywords in your account. At other times, Google has alluded to "account-wide" calculations that can hinder full delivery of your ads. Today, it seems wise to sweep through accounts periodically, looking for keywords deemed to be poor quality. You can even get a bit more specific than that, now that Google is making available detail that will show Quality on a scale of 1 to 10. You should study the very poor quality keywords even more closely than borderline OK keywords. Don't delete keywords if they seem relevant to you, but do be ruthless if the meanings of those keywords don't really quite sync up with the product or service the associated ads are leading the searcher to. For example, in a campaign for a company that facilitates the buying and selling of businesses (a broad-based B2B campaign that is still quite different from similar B2C campaigns), a subtle difference in the searcher's query (**arby's franchise** as opposed to **arby's outlet**) seemed to be indicative as to whether the search was most often from a consumer (who would be dissatisfied with the results if they visited the landing page on the query **arby's outlet**) or a prospective business buyer, who might search for something like **arby's franchise information**, but is certainly somewhat likely to search for **arby's franchise**. Using predictive tools and then machine learning, Google's Quality Score algorithm attempts to first predict, and then confirm, which keywords are irrelevant to your target customers. Tossing unrelated keyphrases into your account doesn't help searchers, and ultimately, doesn't help you. In this day and age, you have to tighten things up. Delete poor-performing keywords that are obviously irrelevant (such as **arby's outlet** here), to insulate yourself against Quality Score woes down the road. This will have the indirect effect of allowing you to expand your overall click volume, because the offending keywords won't have a polluting effect on account-wide quality measures.

The bottom line? Any keyword that shows up as poor in your account for an extended period of time is a symptom of deeper problems. In some cases you may want to keep them running and take the chance that they won't be hurting your overall account. But in many cases you should fix the underlying problems (poor relevance, lack of ad testing, insufficient granularity, irrelevant or poor landing pages) or delete those keywords, rather than soldiering on with them. In the example of **arby's outlet**, Google's machine learning can actually measure the dissatisfaction consumers feel when they go to a page thinking it might provide a map or business information, and stumble instead on a niche, B2B site trying to attract franchise investors. The angry consumer hits the back button immediately (or in rare cases conveys their dissatisfaction to Google through a form or email). Such behavior will tend to lower Quality Scores on particular keywords, and also lead Google to begin slapping predictive low Quality Scores on words in new accounts that have a high probability of dissatisfying users in a similar way.

So at this point, I am actually offering you a warning. It seems tempting to expand your account willy-nilly. Just give me more, more, more! cries your brain. But if "more" means throwing a pile of keywords into ad groups without regard to searcher intent, the strategy is actually stupid. And Google AdWords, as sure as the day is long, will punish you for reckless kinds of expansion.

So far, it doesn't sound like it will be easy to expand your ad distribution, does it? Well, that's a curious thing. Google's bias towards tight targeting creates an even bigger paradox than ever before. One way to finesse this is to choose ads that do well in CTR terms, and take a short-term hit on ROI in some cases. If you build an account with industry-leading CTRs, Google AdWords will begin to love you on the whole, and this might give you leeway down the road to expand your account. Another way to think of it is that you need to think tight and precise, even as you expand. If you want to undertake experiments in looser targeting and experimental expansion, consider keeping those experiments (campaigns and ad groups) separate from the rest of your account, for ease of decision-making going forward.

Two-Word Broad Matching

Many conservative AdWords advertisers prefer to use phrase match and exact match rather than go broad with their keywords. But this can limit your distribution. To expand your distribution cautiously, choose one popular word and then enter 20–30 two-word broad-match combinations that include that word. This will show your ad to more users but at the same time will allow you considerable control over the types of queries that show your ad. The fact that the second word will typically need to appear in the user's query will reduce the potential distribution enough to make the ad highly targeted, without ruling out users who type in long, unpredictable queries that include any number of other words. This is not entirely precise, given that Google has made broad match a ground for semantic experimentation; as discussed in Chapter 7, the broad match method is not literally rules-based and may vary somewhat as Google experiments with what it calls expanded broad matching.

The additional advantage of the two-word broad match is that it can be fairly specific, so you'll probably generate healthy CTRs. As such, you can afford to bid less and generate a strong ROI. The same general logic applies to three-word broad matches.

Four-word broad matches are rarely worth bothering with. It's generally too much effort to use long strings of words in your campaign, except perhaps in special situations. For example, you might find that a fair number of users put questions to the search engine, such as **how to sell my timeshare**. Even here, a three-word broad match—**how sell timeshare**—would handle many possible combinations, as would the two-word broad match omitting the word *how*.

Expanded Broad Matching: Disable Only if Necessary

An additional benefit of broad matching is that it invokes Google's expanded broad matching feature, which may selectively show your add on similar phrases that include plurals, verb stems, and other close variations without making you do all the work of discovering them. Although at first, many advertisers saw expanded broad matching as worrisome when it was rolled out, Google has been careful to test the technology and to calibrate it conservatively enough that ads are not showing on all kinds of unrelated search queries. A good rule of thumb is, if you are bidding particularly high, you need to be more concerned about the potential of the expanded broad matching technology to show your ad on less relevant searches. The only simple way to disable expanded broad matching is not to use broad matching at all. But if you've been overly dependent on phrase and exact matching and are looking for more volume, you should strongly consider broad matching to achieve fuller coverage.

One-Word Broad Matching + Negative Keywords

Many advertisers ignore the potential of the one-word broad match with good reason. It can cast too broad a net, and paradoxically, because uncreative or deep-pocketed advertisers may be drawn to such words, prices can be too high.

The other reason that many ignore the potential of one-word broad matches is, it must be said, slavish adherence to conventional wisdom. Google does its part on this one. If you ask staff for advice on your campaign, they'll often recommend against such "untargeted" keywords.

As the imagination of the average advertiser is increasingly captivated by more targeted keyword choices, one-word broad matches may now be a relative bargain. The other important benefit here is that they can provide your campaign with huge additional volume! And for most experienced advertisers, volume is where it's at. As long as the conversion rates generated by such words are keeping the cost of an order or lead in line with what you're getting from other parts of your campaign, you'll be fine.

There's a danger that these words will run into Quality Score problems, because your customers come from a small subset of phrases that include the word in question; so only a few people click on the ad. One effective way of keeping one-word broad matches in a healthy state (higher CTRs) is to enter long lists of *negative keywords* to ensure that the ad isn't showing on any popular queries that are irrelevant to your business. You can continue to discover and add negatives to solidify your CTR on the broad-matched term.

Another way to guard against single-word broad matches triggering too many irrelevant matches is to use the little-known technique of making them "one-word phrase matches" by enclosing them in quotes. Logically, these should actually be the same as one-word broad matches, but the key difference is that broad match allows Google's "expanded broad matching" whereas phrase match does not. The single-word phrase match will therefore often provide a more reliable matching experience for single-word keywords. This treatment of one-word keywords is an undocumented aspect of AdWords but is informally confirmed by Google reps.

To discover what phrases that include that word are popular of late, you can use the keyword tool, as we saw in Chapter 7 (see Figure 7-2), but with a twist. Select your keyword—let's say it's a broad keyword such as **nuts**. Go to the Match Type drop-down list box and set it to Negative (see Figure 9-1). Depending on what keyword you've selected, Google's smart technology is going to show you a variety of popular matches on that keyword. Some will be words like "organic" that are still in the realm of relevancy. Others may be more like shots in the dark ("bolts") that could be shown by Google's matching technology on expanded broad matching, as the matching technology grasps at straws. If you're broad matching, you can't do without negatives. Add as many negative keywords as you can in order to exclude those searches that are clearly not relevant. Of course, keep the relevant ones. This means you may need to scan the list of several hundred potential negatives "by hand" (or by eye and brain, anyway). If you over-automate this part, all you'll do is reduce your click volume to near nothing, by stopping your ad from showing on many relevant queries as well as irrelevant ones.

As you can see from Figure 9-1, each potential negative keyword is easy to add to the keyword list by clicking on Add Negative. This is a lot of work, but it allows you to employ broad matching with confidence, which can help you outdo other advertisers in competitive

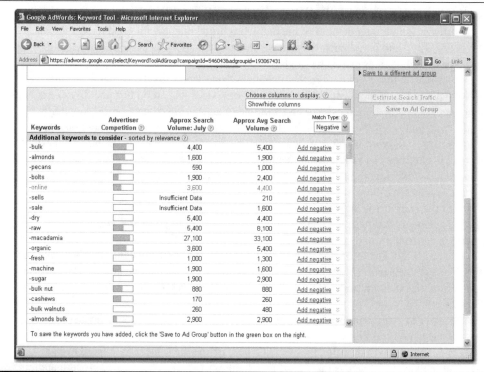

FIGURE 9-1   Google is experimenting with the best way of suggesting negative keywords to power users. Their current, coy method is one you should stay on top of.

fields and increase volume on a stalled campaign. It can be well worth the few minutes a week you spend doing it. If you're wondering what is the maximum amount of negative keywords I've added to a campaign… it's 8,500. I'm not proud of that, or anything. Stuff happens! (It turned out that was too many, and we cut it back to 500 in that case.)

Beware: some third-party vendors are accessing all of Google's suggested negatives through the AdWords API and then passing off the list as their own proprietary list. The list is valuable, but the price of access is generally free or close to it if you get the information right from Google. And as I mentioned, if the list of potential negatives is particularly long, you do need a set of eyes and a brain to pick and choose the truly irrelevant words.

Advanced Technique: "Go for the Tail"

Lately, software and service companies have been moving aggressively into the paid search advertising game, some armed with ambitious business plans and fueled by venture capital.

It's now fairly common to hear such companies advocating the benefits of bidding on 50,000, 100,000, and even a million keywords and phrases. Although this strategy might make sense for large retailers with broad-based catalogs, I'm always surprised when I hear this strategy being recommended for small to midsized companies, or companies with a relatively narrow offering.

The logic goes something like this. Most advertisers are ignoring the huge numbers of highly specific phrases that are typed by search engine users. By examining server logs for referral phrases coming from the regular (or organic) Google Search results, we can see that in some industries, obscure phrases with only one or two referrals per month might make up 50% or more of overall visits to a website. By entering as many as possible of these phrases into a campaign, the argument goes, the average CPC will come down, and ROI will increase markedly. If the most obvious, frequently searched keywords form the "fat part of the curve" on a search frequency distribution graph, then the large number of infrequently searched terms can be called the tail; hence, to focus on these is called "going for the tail." I also call this the "keyword dump methodology."

One problem with the tail chase is simply factual. If your "tail words" only make up 5%, rather than 50%, of your commercially viable search queries, then the attempt to find all of them can be overrated.

I agree with the premise—indeed, the fact that a high number of unique queries are typed in by search engine users has been fundamental to my approach to AdWords since day one. But I don't necessarily think it follows that the average advertiser will see a significant improvement in performance by aggressively going for the tail using word-generation software. I believe such overkill can be a distraction from a healthy focus on a variety of determinants of success or failure of a campaign. At the end of the day, it depends on the nature of your business, and the resources you have at hand.

The first thing to remember is that by using phrase and broad match, advertisers are reaching much of the tail anyway. That's the whole purpose of matching options. What proponents of the keyword dump methodology will now say is that the bidding process on AdWords may allow you to reach that tail *more inexpensively* than if you used phrase match. Perhaps this is true to some small extent, but it is all too often exaggerated. Advertising on exact phrases like **find me a good hotel near Houston**, because it showed up in your server logs as a search referral, or because some software generated this as one of a million variations, is certainly an option. But you'll still be competing for position with others in the hotel industry (for example, advertisers using a two-word broad match including the words *hotel* and *Houston),* and you'll still find the CPC expensive.

A real drawback to going for the tail so aggressively emerges in your tracking and post-click analytics process. If you decide to track everything by keyword, you'll be left looking through sheaves of results that show numbers of impressions and clicks in the single digits. Worse still, if you use an automated method that determines how long to keep a phrase running, you could be overanalyzing and turning good phrases off based on random user behavior on phrases with tiny sample sizes. The typical revenue associated with one of these phrases will be zero; every so often, there will be a purchase, possibly a large one, on a highly specific phrase. Who is to say that this highly specific phrase was actually the *cause* of this purchase? One purchase could lead you to overestimate the value of a certain phrase for months or years to come. That's why I think it's safer to think in terms of groups of related words.

Clearly one of the real drawbacks to using the keyword dump methodology is that the task of interpreting and acting on such fragmented results is too unwieldy for even a hard-working analyst. To this argument, tail-chasers will respond that they facilitate analysis by ensuring that similar keywords are grouped. Some will refer to patent-pending linguistic technology that helps them group words—without mentioning that Google's own technology in this area is likely to be offered to advertisers within a year or two (and already is, to the extent that the keyword suggestion tool shows related words that you might want to consider); being thorough in the "torso"; and making smart use of matching options.

Final consideration: going for the tail too early can hurt account-wide Quality Score. Hardly the low-risk proposition it's often billed as.

So we've really come full circle. By grouping keywords, and tracking based on those groups (assuming the software that attempts to automate these "groupings" actually works), we're back to the methodology I've been recommending all along: developing an AdWords strategy that revolves around groups of like keywords.

Building on Success: Hypothesize, Extrapolate, and Profit

One of the easiest things you can do to increase profitable click volume is to look again at your successes and try to build on them. It's easier to do this if you've made discoveries that are based on testing a particular theory.

I hope a couple of brief examples will give you the flavor of this kind of "determine what works, then do more of it" method of experimenting. FourOxen and I are always pinpointing which types of online searchers are likely to be their most profitable customers. We don't have all the answers, but we have been able to make a couple of interesting discoveries using common sense first, followed by data analysis.

Recall from Chapter 6 that FourOxen is in a hotly competitive Internet-related service business. One of the few differentiators we could identify with FourOxen's service offering amid a sea of competitors was that they pride themselves on superior customer service. (Notwithstanding the fact that my colleagues at Future Now rightly point out that customer service is generally a pretty weak fallback in an otherwise-undifferentiated product strategy.) Since many advanced users view the service as a commodity to be bought as cheaply as possible, it was becoming rapidly evident that targeting these savvier customers—at least when we were paying a lot per click to do so—was a money-losing proposition. I proposed that newbies seem like FourOxen's best AdWords prospects. These customers would be attracted by advertisements that promised integrity and more hand-holding as opposed to ads promising rock-bottom pricing.

To give that theory a solid test, I added more and more phrases that were the types of things that a confused, "unhip," new person to the particular technology in question might type into Google. I even tried certain very broad phrases indicating an interest in starting up a new web venture, such as **new web**, and many others besides. Some of the terms, as advanced users might see them, would be considered mistakes or at least very awkward ways of expressing the "correct" idea. No matter. If a newbie typed it in, I wanted to show them this ad.

The theory proved correct. The cost per new order for these kinds of keywords was significantly lower than the cost per new order on the rest of the campaign. That meant our work wasn't done. Since we had strong evidence that the newbie theory was correct, the trick was to go out and find more of them. Keyword discovery in this particular realm—"newbie words"—is ongoing.

Another area that we tested was various relevant brand names and trade names ("industry words" or "competitor words"). In spite of the ongoing legal controversies over the use of such keywords to trigger relevant ads near search results, we do know that they're often effective lead generators. Here again, the effectiveness of this group proved itself quite readily, so our job is to continue with keyword discovery as long as we can find new ones of this type.

If we find that performance begins to degrade in either of these groups, we'll take a hard look at recently added words that might be the culprit. As the groups get very large, it makes sense to subdivide them to test further distinctions and microtheories about what works even within this narrow realm. Keep in mind, this doesn't mean you have to track each and every keyword.

Upping the Bid and Movin' On Up

Certainly, it is likely going to cost you more to up your bids as a means of gaining more click volume. Many business owners reject the strategy out of hand. But at a certain point it's time to take a harder look at your allowable cost per acquisition, and other assumptions. If you're thinking of moving up into a new 'hood, you might need to change a few things—better haircut, new clothes, finer wines, etc. But seriously: if you can make fundamental changes to your business so that higher CPCs are now palatable to you, the "bid higher" strategy is not to be discounted. Let's start with the less drastic changes, and then touch on some more advanced considerations.

If some of your ad groups are performing at a significantly lower cost per acquisition than others, it doesn't make sense to keep the bids low on such groups just for the sake of frugality. If your average ad position is, say, 3.3 on one of these successful groups, you might want to find out how much more you need to bid to push it to 2.8, or 2.1, and whether raising the average position creates an unacceptably high cost per acquisition.

To keep bids too low means you're generating too few potentially profitable clicks. But at some juncture, you will have raised bids to the point where the additional clicks cost too much. There is no hard-and-fast rule for how to approach this, and results may fluctuate from month to month. But clearly, leaving one part of your campaign with very low bids if its ROI is particularly strong makes little sense. Generally speaking there shouldn't be vast disparities in ROI across a campaign. An ad group's ROI can indeed be too good. An ROI of 400% might simply be an indicator that your volume is too low in that part of the campaign and that you need to bid more to increase clicks. Remember, *total profit* can go up even if your ROI goes down, if sales volume increases enough.

Let's get into a couple of considerations that will help you move your bids up so that you're in ad positions 1–3 for your core keywords, even though this currently seems unaffordable. We'll go into these points in more depth later, in Chapter 11, which covers increasing conversion rates.

Launch a Conversion Improvement Program

Short of changing jobs or changing your whole business model, the best way to be able to afford the higher CPCs associated with higher ad positions is to raise conversion rates (the ratio of clicks to sales or leads). This process isn't magic—it's mostly science. But a good degree of creativity and testing will be required to improve landing pages. Even sophisticated multivariate testing is open to the average advertiser, now that Google offers a free tool called Website Optimizer. Simple A/B testing can be effective, too, especially if you have lower sales volumes.

Focus on Web Credibility, Online Reputation, and Repeat Business

Strict conversion improvement testing on particular landing pages is one thing, but you need to be thinking about related user dynamics and customer interactions as well. Especially when selling higher-ticket items, you need to disclose more about your company and soothe user concerns about security and trust issues. Go beyond your own site to research your online reputation to make sure rumors aren't creating unseen objections in consumers' minds. Work on your upsell and repeat sales channels and tactics. The baseline fact is: click costs will continue to rise. Tweaking bids and such will do little to keep you in the race if you don't also take multiple steps to increase your average revenues per customer.

Content-Targeted, or Contextual, Ads: Take a Second Look

As I explained in Chapter 2, at one time, online advertising brokers (or "networks") such as DoubleClick played an important role on the Web, allowing advertisers to place large banner ad buys without having to approach individual publishers and giving publishers access to more advertisers. Today, these first-generation online ad brokers are rapidly being displaced by the second wave: programs like Google AdWords, Yahoo Search Marketing, Quigo, ContextWeb, and several smaller players. (Google has acquired DoubleClick, to put an exclamation point on the story of this trend.)

Ads Appearing near Content

Having regularly insisted they'd stay "laser-focused on search," Google surprised some observers in March 2003 by launching an ad network that pays publishers for displaying ads that look very similar to standard Google AdWords ads. If you're an advertiser, the option to display your ad on these publishers' sites appears as the Content Network check box in your campaign settings area; you'll be asked if you want content targeting turned on or off (see Figure 9-2). The content targeting program came under a lot of fire early on due to its spotty quality, but today it has reached a new stage of refinement and many of the old problems are a thing of the past.

How does content targeting work? As with many things that Google does, the exact formula is proprietary. One thing's clear: it doesn't work the same as the ads appearing next to search results. The key thing to understand is you're essentially going through a stripped-down media buying process to buy online display ads (often but not always in text format) at various publisher sites around the Web.

With content targeting (sometimes called contextual advertising), the keywords in your account still serve a purpose. Google's semantic matching technology uses these keywords, along with the amount you bid, to decide whether or not your ad is relevant enough to show on a particular page. The semantic matching technology "reads" pages for meaning; it isn't just pure algorithmic keyword matching. Ads are selected on the fly as the code on the publisher's page loads the Google AdSense ad creative. These *ad creatives* (*creative* is an online ad industry term for the size and shape of an advertising unit) can vary in size, but they take up the same screen

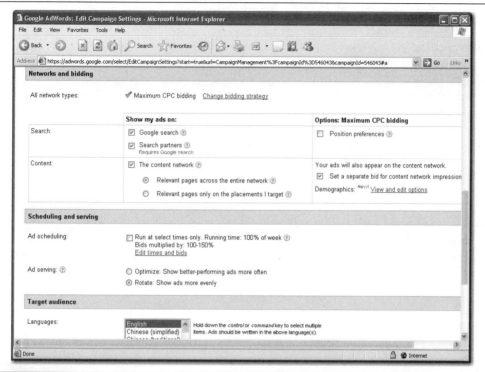

FIGURE 9-2   Campaign settings with content targeting across the network turned on

real estate as the graphical ad banners that were once ubiquitous online. Other units, such as banners, animated banners, and interactive banners that operate using JavaScript code (called Google Gadgets, or generically in the industry, widgets), are now also available through the same Google AdWords platform. Under Create New Ad in the Ads tab of your ad group, Google lists several options, including text ads, image ads (also known as banner ads), video ads, local business ads, and mobile ads. Under image ads, just as an example, Google offers eight banner sizes and allows you to upload files in any of four file formats (see Figure 9-3).

Google has now rolled out a new twist that helps you control your placements more precisely: placement targeting. Essentially, you are able to use both keywords and your own specific site choices to plan where your ads show up. In selecting placements, Google offers a menu of sites that you can choose to show up on, and will allow you to enter a maximum bid for each of those placements. Note that in the campaign settings you'll be asked to choose to show your ads either "on sites from the entire network" or "only on sites I select." Personally, I've grown fond of the wider reach of the "entire network" approach of classic content targeting, since it contains a smart, keyword-matching element. But more precise targeting is the only thing that will work for some companies.

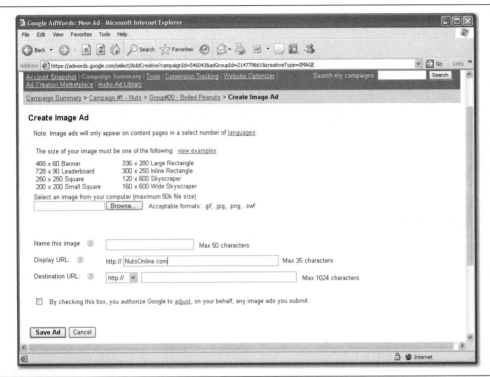

FIGURE 9-3   Setup screen for Google image ads, a format allowable under content targeting

Online content is not restricted to any particular format. So-called contextual ads can be placed near discussion forum content, email messages, articles, or, as the example from the online photo sharing site Flickr (see Figure 9-4) shows, thematically tagged images. As an advertiser, you'll need to be flexible in how you think about content, because chances are you'll have the opportunity to show your AdWords ads in a lot of different places in the coming years.

The price you pay for any given click isn't easy to pin down, but your average costs are reported clearly in the main ad group views; more detailed breakdowns are available under the Reporting tab. It's not an auction in the same sense as the search ad program. You won't pay more than your maximum bid, but how much less than your bid you wind up paying can be determined by another proprietary Google formula. Essentially, Google has improved the quality of its ad network by firing some publishers, and simply reducing payouts to other publishers whose inventory has tended to convert poorly for advertisers.

Google has also begun disclosing more about the types of content your ads appear near. If you're using Google Conversion Tracker, the "content types" report will show you CTRs, spend, and conversion rates on parked domain pages, error pages, and other offbeat forms of content. Google also shows you whether your ads are showing near news stories on sensitive topics, like

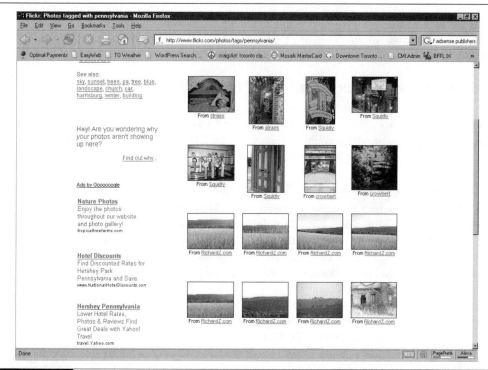

FIGURE 9-4   Ads by Google appearing near photos on Yahoo-owned Flickr

death and tragedy, or adult or suggestive content. You can now opt out of showing ads on any of these subsets of content. Control is at the campaign level.

After having experimented extensively with contextual ads, I can confirm that these ads do provide many advertisers significant opportunities to increase the profitable click volume in their AdWords accounts. But the big *if* here is this: it will likely prove profitable for many of you *if* you're able to bid lower on content targeting than you do on your ads that appear near search listings. As discussed previously, Google now offers content bidding, enabled within Campaign Settings. Don't forget to bid separately on all of your content-targeted placements, and measure and monitor their performance separately.

Even more effective, if you have the time, is to mirror your search campaigns with entirely separate content-targeted campaigns. This facilitates separate tracking, but another thing this does is allow you to experiment with different ad creative than you use in search. Because a user's intent is far different in a contextual ad (often you are interrupting users rather than being searched for), often the psychology is different. To be frank, search is a medium to be treated as kind of sacred ground, because that's how Google's users (and algorithms) see it. Content, rightly or wrongly, is more amenable to gimmickry and salesmanship in ad copy. It's not right for every brand, but you may want to try a variety of styles of text copy. You might also want to dip your toe into the world of animated banners and other creative formats, including larger ones. The tragedy of the commons is that this "scorched earth" treatment of online display ad spaces by advertisers means users have developed banner blindness. But for your purposes, you'll need to consider strategies to break through this blindness.

Low CTRs on Content Placements Don't Impact Quality Score

Another thing to keep in mind with content targeting is that CTRs will typically be much lower than with your search ads. Do not panic! AdWords does not count CTRs from content targeting against the performance of your account. So you won't rank lower on your keywords because of these low CTRs. Google uses only search ads to calculate CTRs for ranking purposes.

Special Case: Ads in Gmail and Other Google Properties

Did someone say Google isn't just about search anymore? They now offer Gmail, a fast, innovative, web-based email service that offers virtually unlimited storage. In exchange for a free account, users accept that Google will show ads in the right-hand margin of the interface and sometimes at the top of the page. While some observers fret about privacy issues inherent in customizing ads to the content of email discussions, many users find the ads to be nonintrusive, similar to the familiar AdWords ads near search results.

Ads appearing in Gmail are part of the overall content targeting program. Undoubtedly, Google will beef up its reporting and opt-out capabilities in this area, as they've done with parked domains and sensitive content. Like the contextual ads discussed previously, ads in Gmail are matched with the content of emails based on a semantic matching technology Google doesn't disclose. One handy feature of Gmail is the threading of conversations, which makes it easier to refer back to previous emails in a series. I've noticed that as a conversation gets longer—as more emails back and forth start to pile up—the matching technology is more precise. Ads seem to get more relevant by the third or fourth email in the exchange.

What I've said about ads in Gmail also applies to various Google-owned properties, such as YouTube. For the most part, they are simply part of the content targeting program, but there seem to be ongoing mysteries in how Google handles them. How Google handles placement and reporting on your ads showing up on Google-owned properties outside of Google Search seems to change regularly. I expect more disclosure and control to be added in the future. For more on Google's ever-expanding list of products and services, see Chapter 12.

Advanced Uses of Content Targeting: Current Affairs

In certain cases, content targeting proves to be more suitable than search targeting. A case study presented by TV cable network Comedy Central at the Search Engine Strategies conferences in 2007 points to an example of an innovative use of content targeting. This media company was trying to promote its television content—for example, *The Daily Show* with Jon Stewart—in innovative ways. Comedy Central believed that timely current affairs topics would be excellent complements to *The Daily Show*'s newsy focus. The problem with focusing only on search targeting is that the related keywords might be prohibitively expensive. In addition, such terms might be deemed "irrelevant" by Google's Quality Score algorithm, making it less likely that such ads will be visible next to search results. An exciting workaround was to enable content targeting for such topics. Suddenly, witty ads for *The Daily Show* appeared on news sites, current affairs forums, and all kinds of hard-to-predict locations around the Web. The exposure was gained for very reasonable CPCs (below 20 cents), and helped *The Daily Show* build its audience by targeting relevant viewers.

If that doesn't work for you, you can always call Yahoo or Microsoft. Being in second and third place in the search wars, they must try harder. So they might find you more favorable terms for search targeting on current affairs terms.

Trademarks as Keywords ("Competitor Words")

There has been ongoing debate about whether it's legal to use a competitor's trade name as a keyword in your AdWords account in order to trigger your ad near search results on that keyword. But the status of this tactic is clearer today than it was a couple of years ago. GEICO lost a landmark case, *GEICO v. Google,* a lawsuit launched to stop competitors' ads from appearing near search results when users typed queries including the trademarked word GEICO. I see the judgment in this case as a vindication of the principle that AdWords—even when triggered by trademarked words as long as there is no reasonable likelihood of consumer confusion—can foster legitimate forms of comparative advertising similar to those that have long been legal in the United States. Most U.S. trademark experts agree that there is such a thing as fair use, and that whether the use of a trademark in advertising is illegal hinges on whether it causes consumer confusion. Google has, however, lost similar cases in France and is likely to lose them in some other jurisdictions. Eric Goldman, an expert in this field and a member of the law faculty at Santa Clara University, maintains an extensive blog on the subject of marketing and technology law. He is the author of a paper specifically dealing with recent cases like *GEICO v. Google* and *American Blind v. Google.* Goldman takes Google's side, marshaling considerable evidence in the attempt. Formerly the general counsel for Epinions.com, he has also defended WhenU.com, a company that uses pop-up ads to trigger comparative contextual ads. See http://blog.ericgoldman.org for a collection of resources. Several cases since *GEICO v. Google* have confirmed the general trend; most have been addressed on Goldman's blog.

Remember, you aren't typically using that competitor's name in your ad or intending to cause confusion, you're just using it inside your AdWords account to see to it that your ad appears in the advertising-earmarked area on Google Search should a consumer type in that term.

I've watched the debate closely and have watched the performance of campaigns that experiment with brand names and company names. For several years, these types of words typically outperformed other keywords, especially in a competitive industry with expensive keywords. Unfortunately, Google has chosen to profit from this situation, and to head off potential controversies, by setting Quality Scores lower on such words. The specifics aren't disclosed, but the costs of these keywords are on the rise. That's a shame for enterprising advertisers.

In any case, don't take my word for it. If you're uncertain about the legality of what you're doing, seek legal counsel. Also remember that trademark law in North America may be different from laws in Europe and other parts of the world.

If you try this tactic, you might want to create a separate ad group or campaign for such words (or even two or three for different subtypes) to facilitate tracking. You might use the names of companies, people, and publications, as well as product names, domain names, and so on.

Exporting Your Successful AdWords Campaign

Some observers have argued that AdWords works like a focus group, giving you valuable insight into your market. Once you've tested an AdWords campaign and achieved some success with it, there's no reason not to put some of that knowledge to work.

Google's Main Competitors

What works on Google AdWords is likely to work on at least two other major competing services: Yahoo Search Marketing and Microsoft adCenter. It may or may not work on other such services. The question you'll need to ask yourself is whether it's worth the effort. In practice, after Google AdWords and their two largest competitors, it often isn't worth your time to set up accounts with second-tier services, with the possible exception of Miva, Business.com, and Ask.com. Internationally, you'll need to research the competitive landscape in different countries.

Shopping engines are a separate subject. They also operate on a pay-per-click basis in many cases and are a must for retailers to investigate.

Yahoo Search Marketing and Beyond

You could take a few different approaches to using the knowledge you've gained on AdWords and transferring it to Yahoo Search Marketing, but in recent times the process has become much smoother.

With the release of its new search advertising platform, nicknamed Panama, in September 2007, Yahoo took moves towards standardization of formats with Google AdWords. There are some picky differences remaining in allowable title and description lengths, but much of the logic is consistent. The names for the account elements are now identical: Accounts, Campaigns, and Ad Groups. Among other things, this facilitates the migration of an AdWords campaign to a Yahoo campaign.

There are still glitches that may occur in transition, however. Google seems to have taken steps to confound the migration process by frequently changing their account export format. You may need to bring in a specialist to clean up a migrated AdWords campaign in the Panama platform. Larger advertisers and agencies may take advantage of Yahoo's support in migrating campaigns, but this is case by case. A similar situation exists with Microsoft.

Another completely new development with Yahoo is that they now rank ads based on a quality index, similar to Google's Quality Score. However, the formulas remain distinct, and here there may lie optimization opportunities that differ from platform to platform. Like Google, Yahoo offers contextual advertising. Their network and platform are less developed, but we should see improvements coming.

Industry consolidation seems to mean that we'll see plenty of good news coming from all of Microsoft, Yahoo, and Google going forward. The process of buying more volume will get easier, and I hold out the hope that the marketplace between buyers and sellers of ads will continue to gain efficiency. ContextWeb is one company that advocates a true "exchange" model (ADSDAQ), where advertisers set "bid" prices and publishers can set their "ask." Worth a look.

Second-Tier Players

My clients rarely want to experiment with lesser-known ad providers, and I'm happy to accommodate their indifference. It's a matter of volume, trust, and focus. In most cases, it just isn't worth the trouble it might take to investigate the foibles of lesser providers. However, with recurring opportunities to make their cases in conference sessions or on the exhibit floor at search marketing trade shows, it is worth occasionally catching up with companies like Marchex, LookSmart, and Miva. Some of the second-tier players have ripped off so many advertisers with low-quality traffic, it's hard to assess their credibility. I believe in second chances. Fifth and sixth chances? Maybe not.

Google Ad Planner

According to Google's announcement on the Inside AdWords blog, Google Ad Planner is a "research and media planning tool that connects advertisers and publishers." The idea is, you enter demographic information and sites your audience is associated with, and the Ad Planner tool will return a list of relevant sites your audience is likely to visit, complete with stats like audience size and "fit" with your target. The tool got a big reaction when it was launched. To me, it didn't seem all that surprising. Then I realized why the process seems so familiar.

The logic and visual impact of how you use Google Ad Planner is essentially the same as building a Placement Targeting campaign in Google AdWords. Based on your criteria, the app shows you a list of relevant sites, with data to help you decide whether to place ads on these sites. The key difference is that AdWords Placement Targeting, of course, only provides background audience information on sites that are participants in the Google Content Network (put another way, Google AdSense Publishers). The Ad Planner provides information on pretty much every other significant web property out there, as well. It provides icons and additional information for Google Content Network sites, and leaves that blank for nonparticipating sites.

Audience segmentation is a snap with this intuitive tool. To take an example, let's say I want to get my ad in front of women of a certain age and income. I checked only the snobbiest boxes (the highest incomes, education, and ages 35–64) and this whittled down the available sites in the menu. From there, I'm free to select promising sites and export them to an Excel file if I wish.

As you can see in Figure 9-5, from an initially massive universe of U.S.-based websites, I am now down to a smaller universe comprising a total country reach of 2.5%—and still, a long list of sites to consider.

From there, you could ask a number of further questions about the sites; questions that are definitively not asked or answered by Google's tool. Is this site accepting advertising? Is it easy

FIGURE 9-5   Narrowing down appropriate publisher sites using Google Ad Planner

to buy from them? What are the prices, visibility, desirability, user intents on the sites, etc.? As a planning tool, it is a great starting point, but no more.

A note on the demographics: these are rough guides to the types of visitors that are seen as coming to the site. They are not accurate counts by any means. It's merely a question of how a particular site "skews": Ad Planner, no doubt accurately, reports that potterybarn.com skews female, affluent, etc. But there is nothing to suggest very accurately how much it skews that way, nor is it implied that you could limit advertising impressions to just the selected demographic. All we have learned is: in the event that the site in question indeed turns out to accept your type of advertising, potterybarn.com is probably a pretty decent place to show your banner ad, all else being equal.

One current caveat is that the tool only gives the illusion of providing data across many countries. For nearly every country outside the United States, including relatively developed online advertising markets like the United Kingdom and Canada, the demographic information is spotty once you drill down even one level. For these countries, you may be using the tool to find sites related to or similar to a site you specifically enter into the tool, but you'll be hard pressed to do any comprehensive planning based on demographic segmentation here.

Some observers believe that Google Ad Planner is shaking up the technology ecosystem much as Google Analytics did. The free tool and open approach to data encroaches on the business models of companies like comScore and Hitwise who typically sell this data for higher prices. But of course, there is not total overlap. This is closer to what Compete.com and Quantcast do: provide background information on website visitation stats, much of it for free. These services use a variety of data sources (including, perhaps, panel-based measurement, installed toolbars or tracking code, user data sold to them by ISPs, etc.) to arrive at educated guesstimates about the audience composition of websites. Before long, Google's product is likely to outshine these services in terms of accuracy. From a variety of angles, Google simply has the most data about users and websites.

Beware of bias: should you trust the seller of ads to be your media planning "advisor"? Well, no. But here, Google isn't selling but a small portion of the total reach addressed by Google Ad Planner. So it looks like the situation was similar to what happened with Analytics and Conversion Optimizer, among other products. Google saw a hole in marketers' and advertisers' arsenals and wished to fill that need, in part to position Google as the ultimate service provider in online advertising. Google became increasingly impatient as various existing providers in the space kept advanced functionality out of the reach of all but a handful of deep-pocketed advertisers.

The "cloud computing mentality" pervades Google's thinking with regard to every new field the company considers breaking into: the analogy will always be with the IT services and bandwidth costs that have plummeted in the past decade, allowing innovative businesses of all sizes to thrive in the information economy. Instead of: "wow, that data is worth a bundle, you should charge a lot for it," as usual, Google's thought is: "would providing this tool to businesses reduce friction in the marketplace?" In general, Google wants advertisers and publishers to thrive, and they believe that more transparency and bridging activities will facilitate that. The online media planning and online measurement industries have been moving too slowly in the direction of transparency and ease of use. This is a step in the right direction.[1]

Offline Marketing

The strange thing about search engine marketing is that it's a bit like "anti-marketing." You don't bother people—they find you when they're ready to look into a subject. Finding customers this way can help teach you a lot about what those customers actually want. Listen to them, and keep giving it to them, or develop new products and services to fill those needs.

So under the heading of "expanding your marketing offline," I'm going to tread a bit cautiously. Seth Godin, in two recent books (*Purple Cow* and *Free Prize Inside*), trashes most modern marketing, insisting that the product or service offering itself is what wins over savvy consumers. Marketing is ideally built into the product from day one. The idea that marketing professionals can simply be brought in at will to "put lipstick on pigs" and create demand for a new product is a myth. If your market is growing at a solid pace, or if it's really taking off, chances are that some underlying forces (the merits of the product, your personal reputation, changing market trends) are at work, not just the fact that you decided to shout louder.

Telling you how offline marketing works is outside the scope of this book in any case. But one (admittedly radical) approach to the subject of advertising and marketing offline is, do less of it, and plow the proceeds back into innovative products and features that will delight customers and make you stand out in the marketplace. Amazon.com, for example, slashed their television ad budget so they could offer free shipping. Great move. Your company might be better off investing in design software, customer relationship management solutions, or other forms of automation that boost productivity than it would be to invest in ads that create top-line growth of new customers who enter into the same old inefficient relationship with you. You must weigh your priorities.

For the less radically inclined, you can certainly transfer some AdWords learning over to your offline campaigns, but you'll probably need to retest. If certain ad text or sales copy on landing pages works well for you online, it can't hurt to try it offline. But these things don't always translate. In a perfect world, the direct mail people would talk over their findings with the online marketers. By sharing insights, marketing projects might proceed more quickly through the early learning phases, with fewer failed experiments at the outset. Time will tell if the integration of direct marketing agencies and online marketing consultancies will lead to a productive synthesis that can help more companies reach their marketing goals more quickly.

Above all, marketers need to be open to unorthodox ways of persuading consumers to try their products and services. Infomercials, for example, caught the marketing world by surprise just as AdWords is now doing. One unsolicited endorsement from a leading author, athlete, or celebrity could mean more to your business than a year's worth of magazine ads. Don't assume that because large brand advertisers are spending heavily on traditional television, billboard, or radio ads that you ought to do the same. Look before you leap.

Many advertisers try to generate traffic from a wide range of sources, making for an unwieldy and chaotic marketing strategy. I've tried to argue here that you may be best served by taking simple steps to increase profitable click volume from your existing AdWords campaign before troubling yourself with a host of other online marketing experiments.

Endnote

1. A version of this section appeared as my column in July 2008 at Search Engine Land. Repurposed with permission. Thanks to Danny Sullivan.

Part IV

Winning the AdWords Game:
Advanced Issues

Chapter 10

Measuring Success: A "What's Changed" Report

The plain-language name for web analytics these days, "measuring success," is apt. It's as simple as it sounds, and yet not as easy as it sounds. Your boss's or client's reaction to a campaign depends heavily on defining the terms of campaign success, and then attempting to use tools and techniques that will actually put accurate and actionable reports into your hands. Sometimes it's relatively straightforward, sometimes not. If you're the business owner, theoretically it's a bit easier. You know that the bottom line is what matters the most. But many arbitrary decisions, judgment calls, and unstated strategies come into play in attempting to attribute a value to paid search clicks—so much so that even after this chapter is completed, you'll need to continue your learning elsewhere on an ongoing basis. Consider this chapter a rather advanced introduction to the field; also, apologies in advance if I don't make it into a purely technical manual. The ins and outs of getting Google Analytics properly linked to your AdWords account, of using a particularly persnickety goal customization in Omniture, and much more, are matters that give me as much of a headache as anyone. Sometimes I plow through them myself, sometimes we can find a vendor or a customer support person to help. Enough said on that.[1]

This chapter is divided into roughly three parts. To kick things off, I provide a summary approach to the very basic steps anyone should take to get their house in order to track AdWords clicks "after the click," condensed in the extreme from the first edition of this book. This, in essence, is the "What Hasn't Changed" report.

From there I go on to talk about some of the eye-opening new developments that have taken hold in our field, making it more likely that any given advertiser—including you—will be implementing basic tracking more seamlessly with less additional cost, as well as exploring more sophisticated add-ons to your routine. The name of this chapter pays homage to (or if you prefer, is shamelessly borrowed from) analytics vendor ClickTracks. One of their nice features has always been a "What's Changed" report that helps you discover action items more quickly than you would otherwise, poring through the large amount of available data in monthly statistical reports. Likewise, I assume many of you don't need a rehash of the basics, but would like a bit of a roadmap to what is truly significant and what's actually different today as compared with the state of the art in 2005.

And finally, I briefly outline a long list of foibles, errors, quirks, and self-indulgences that seem to hinder many marketers as much today as they did in 2005. This part looks at what hasn't changed, but the message is: I hope it will.

What to Measure, How to Manage: Skinny Summary

Not to belabor the obvious, but there are a few key approaches to measuring success that don't vary much from year to year. I reported on most of these in the last edition. Here is a concise summary of how smart advertisers are making use of key metrics to improve their bottom-line profitability with paid search.

To succeed, you must understand your business objectives, know what key campaign metrics you need to pay attention to, and decide what tracking methods and tools are best for you. There is a plethora of web analytics and tracking systems available in the market today, including the free conversion tracking tools within AdWords, and the more extensive Google Analytics, which I cover in this chapter. Most of the popular analytics tools require you to place some JavaScript tracking codes on your website pages, although there are still some pure weblog analyzers that don't.

How Tracking Works

No matter what tracking system you decide to use, they all require two essential bits of information in order to track post-click actions. First, they need to know where the clicks came from, and second, they need to know what action on your site you want to track.

The information about where the clicks originated involves appending some tracking codes to your destination landing-page URL, a process known as tagging. For example, if your landing page is http://www.woolscarves.com, the same landing-page URL tagged with tracking codes might look something like this:

    www.woolscarves.com?source=google&kw=alpaca_scarves&ad=summer

The parameters, *source*, *kw*, and *ad*, inform your analytics tool how to associate clicks from your campaigns with visitors on your website. These may be arbitrary parameters you choose, or parameters dictated by your tracking software. Or, the tracking software might even *auto-tag* your landing URLs by plugging into Google AdWords through the API. It varies. Just choose a method you're comfortable you understand. If Google Analytics is correctly linked to your AdWords campaign, theoretically you should not need to do anything specific to tag your landing URLs.

In the preceding example, we are tracking by network, keyword, and ad, but you can track at other levels as well, depending on your analytics tool. I generally like to start by tracking at the ad and ad group level and then selectively track a handful of specific keywords, typically those that are most popular or most expensive.

The second part of tracking post-click activity is to identify the pages on your site that you want to track by placing a snippet of JavaScript code on those pages. This script is provided by your tracking tool and is usually placed on the "thank you" page after a visitor completes a download, completes a form, or orders from your online shopping cart.

When a visitor from a paid search campaign gets to one of these pages, the JavaScript communicates that fact to your analytics package, essentially completing the feedback loop so that you can associate a click to an eventual conversion activity.

The World Isn't Perfect, and Neither Is Web Analytics

In earlier chapters, I told you that one of the biggest advantages of paid search advertising is that you can track and measure how every part of your campaign is performing, from the price you pay for clicks to the effectiveness of your ad messages and your keywords.

Compared with other forms of advertising, this is absolutely true, but that doesn't mean that it is perfect. Just as Heisenberg famously described uncertainty at the subatomic level, it is also true that the more granularly you examine your PPC campaign metrics, the less certain your data become. You need to avoid the delusion that you can track every sale back to the specific keyword that triggered a specific ad in a specific ad position at a certain time on a certain day of week.

Here are some situations, for example, that make tracking imperfect. Let's say a person shops online for wool scarves on her home computer, clicks on a paid search ad, and finds the perfect website. On her lunch hour the next day, she types the website URL into her browser and buys a scarf. Paid search drove the sale, but it's impossible to track this sale back to a PPC campaign. The same could be true if she had picked up the phone and ordered. And even if she had ordered from her home computer, it is possible that she searched on a variety of terms, and clicked on several ads, before reaching your offer. Google Analytics and Google Conversion Tracker, discussed later in this chapter, assign credit only to the last ad and the last keyword clicked.

In spite of, or perhaps because of, these limitations, it is important to realize that insights gleaned from your tracking data accumulate over time and give you a relative idea of how your campaigns are doing. It is the accumulated trends that give you the actionable data you need.

What You Need to Track: Metrics to Consider

When in doubt, simplify. Many of my clients do very well with a simple measuring stick such as cost per acquisition (CPA) or cost per order. Even though these may not take into account the dollar amounts spent by the customer, they can be reliable measures with a history in any given line of business. Comparing these metrics among various ad sources, keywords, and ads will give you a sense of your relative performance trends.

These metrics are the ones that tie together the performance of your campaigns (clicks, costs) with your business objectives. Here are a few of the metrics that will get you (or any analyst or manager) to the heart of the matter:

- **Rough ROI or ROAS**   No one is going to be able to prove exactly how well an advertisement paid off, and profit margins can vary from sale to sale and from product to product, making an ROI a challenge to calculate. What many companies do, instead, is use a "dollars in divided by dollars out" (that is, revenue divided by ad spend) calculation as a working measure of the return on ad spend (ROAS). As with all metrics like this, it is useful as a relative, rather than absolute, yardstick.

■ **Cost per acquisition**   CPA is a generic metric that could cover any type of conversion activity, such as newsletter signups, new customers, or any other goal you can measure, including offline actions such as phone calls or visitors to your open house. Even if this metric can't be calculated by your online tracking tools, it is a very easy hand calculation to make by simply taking your ad spend and dividing it by the number of actions registered that you can attribute to your Google ad groups or campaigns. If you spent $420 and got 10 newsletter signups, your CPA is $42.

■ **Cost per order**   Retailers will probably want to keep track of the cost per order related to any particular referral source, keyword, ad, or ad group, since different product lines have different gross profit margins, some high and some very tight. If order values vary wildly, you will want to use this measure in combination with ROAS.

■ **Revenue per click**   Another way to measure ROI, revenue per click, is again a relative measure that can be easily compared to determine whether a bid is too high or too low for a given keyword or ad group.

Once you've put your tracking systems in place, and you are collecting all this data, don't be afraid to make changes based on your data. Unfortunately, it's not always easy to interpret your metrics, and the differences in performance may not be big enough to make big changes, but the simple act of tracking these metrics will give you an idea of when you have ads, ad groups, and keywords that are underperforming or not performing at all.

Measuring Success: "What's Changed" Report

In no particular order, here are some of the developments in web analytics and AdWords performance that you should take account of.

Analytics as an "Industry" Has Exploded

Even in the past three years, the number of individuals who consider web analytics to constitute all or much of their job description has exploded. Jim Sterne's E-Metrics Summit conferences and related events have grown by leaps and bounds, and membership in the Web Analytics Association has mushroomed.

How much this does or should affect you, however, is worth questioning. Much as you may not have the time, resources, or vendor selection smarts to hire a usability consultant or search engine optimization specialist, an analytics focus can only run so deep in many companies. If the effort is not tightly integrated with what you do, then it may be misapplied anyway. So your task, likely, will be to increase your analytical savvy without making a whole career out of it.

The name of Avinash Kaushik's blog, Occam's Razor, is promising. Kaushik is one of the leading web analytics experts today. Formerly with Intuit and now a consultant to Google and sought-after global speaker, Kaushik backs his assertions with a meaty 443-page book entitled *Web Analytics: An Hour a Day* (Wiley, 2007). I've been delighted and inspired by Kaushik's work—but Occam's razor, it is not! The book contains just four pages on measuring "PPC effectiveness," including a single mention of ROAS (just mentioning that it is a metric that exists), and, well, 439 pages about everything else. We're left aching for a lot more of that paid search part. Like Jim Sterne, Kaushik does yeoman's work encouraging large, slow organizations to be crisper and nimbler in their use of web user data. But if your job requires you to be radically crisp and nimble, you'll want to set much of Kaushik's excellent book aside as a comprehensive desk reference to be accessed as needed. Us AdWords folks need to *really* cut to the chase; we need Occam's Razor, Mach IV edition.

Urchin Rules the High Seas

Once upon a time, if we are to think of website statistics vendors like ships, a great diversity of crafts roamed the analytical waters. There were big boats, little boats, ugly boats, and pretty ones. Expensive, cheap, and sometimes free ones. Some of the "boats" required you to install a JavaScript tag across your site, or on conversion pages, to record visitor activity. Others used a "captain's logfile," analyzing it in retrospect to create more accurate, but sometimes more cumbersome, reporting. The best ones, like SeaTrends, used both methods. The big boats sometimes got into skirmishes, and the odd one went down, but relative peace prevailed.

Rather than this competition providing a stimulus for innovation, just as often, it led to confusion among investors and passengers. These folks, collectively known as "customers," found they were wasting too much time at boat shows debating the technical merits of the various crafts. The act of taking a piece of many different boating companies, and riding in a lot of different kinds of boats, was getting exhausting for the marketplace. The Boat Captains' Union didn't much like it, either. While it was a bit of a barrier to entry to outsiders, the effort required to master the controls and quirks of so many different types of boats was more trouble than it was worth. All collectively sighed: "If only there was a Standard. One Big Boat Type that

Google Analytics vs. Urchin

For ease of navigating this section, which is intended to be a lighthearted look at the difficult problem of web analytics vendor selection, keep the following in mind. Google acquired an analytics software company called Urchin, and made the basic product free, renaming it Google Analytics. You can use Google Analytics in a relatively seamless way to measure results from your Google AdWords campaigns. Today, the offering is far from "basic"—in other words, it's amazingly powerful for a free product. Still, Google has continued to sell more advanced versions of Urchin, and this product will cost you money. It comes with more features and more dedicated customer support, and therefore competes with full-featured analytics packages such as Omniture, WebTrends, and Coremetrics. The majority of my clients use Google Analytics, and many use more than one analytics package at the same time.

we could all ride on, invest in, and pilot, and just a few other boats on the side for playboys and hobbyists that we could pretty much ignore." None thought the day would come anytime soon.

Little did the captains of all these ships know that the captain of one unassuming midsized vessel (Urchin was its name) full of engineers—a captain who would later become known as The Urchinator[2]—was concocting a diabolical plan. The Urchinator observed that one seafaring organization, SeaTrends, had grown by leaps and bounds by making side deals with the port owners (also known as "web hosting providers"). Port owners would recommend SeaTrends' boats to anyone who would listen. They began acting as distributors, too. "Aha!" thought The Urchinator. "The devil is in the distribution!"

And so The Urchinator concocted his diabolical plan. He would sell his midsized company to the granddaddy distributor of them all: Google and their 1,000,000 advertisers, and 20,000,000 attentive owners of businesses vying for better online results. The plan with Google would give away the now-Universal, now-Massive Urchin Boat for free, as a gift, to advertisers! (Like a Trojan horse. The Urchinator, and Googlers, study their classics.) Google would wish to subsidize the giveaway in order to funnel even more advertisers into their system, and to gain access to a goldmine of data. Google would then invest in massive computing power to keep the product free and useful, and would then add features that The Urchinator highly approved of, to make the product even better without charging a dime.

And so the deal was done. Google Analytics now rules the high seas. And while some playboys and hobbyists may have their reasons to invest in the other expensive toys and cheaper cool hacks that are available, everyone can agree on the convenience of using one Big Boat Type, and linking it up with an AdWords account. A few holdouts, wary of the Trojan connotation, choose to look this gift horse in the mouth. Seeing his evil grin and diamond-encrusted bling, they vow to "never!" acquiesce to the Google Analytics standard. But most are hypnotized by the grin, and sign right up, linking Google Analytics to their AdWords accounts. Another standard is born.

Horses! Boats! Captains! The remainder of this chapter will be mercifully much lighter on the tortured metaphors and bumbling allegories. And no puns, either. I hope you took your allegory medication before reading this section.

So sign up for Google Analytics if you're brave (or is it cowardly?), and follow the help files to ensure proper installation of code on every page of your site.

Setting Up Goals in Google Analytics

At least a dozen current, high-quality books are available just about Google Analytics and web analytics in general. Analytics offers a wealth of reports about user behavior and can be customized in many ways. But for AdWords purposes, you'll be looking to tune it so you can read and react to the performance of visitors that is tied back to specific keywords or ads.

To lay the foundation for this, you can establish Goals in Analytics. As with Google Conversion Tracker, you're essentially going to be telling the software what a "conversion" means for your business. Like many computing tasks, this is quite technical and literal. To tell Analytics about your email signup goal page, you'll be entering the URL of the thank-you page for successful email signups. A slightly more technical variation on this theme will be required for you to establish an e-commerce checkout completion.

And there are even more nuanced goal setups that may require you to work around problems with your site. For example, if your pages always include dynamic ID strings, you can instruct Analytics to use a match type that disregards the changing strings, so that it recognizes the same basic page as your success page. If you have Ajax presentation in a checkout or multistage form-completion process, your "goal funnel analysis" may not work, so you can't set goal pages for somewhere in the middle of the process, and you may not be able to correctly assess abandonment rates. I'll leave it to you, your development team, and a bottle of ibuprofen to figure out.

The Substance of Goals in Analytics

I discuss this elsewhere as well, but just a quick reminder of what you might do with the information you see. You're going to be trolling through reports to look at the performance (dollar or conversion rate wise) of particular keywords or segments such as ad groups. You can also do this for ads.

One example involved an "arbitrary" goal for a financial site that had deferred revenue and a third-party page that we didn't have access to. For Analytics to help us assess user behavior day to day, we considered "reached the application page" as a goal. We had the arbitrary goal value as a few dollars, and we decided that any keyword that had a value of over $1.00 was worth further investigation. Those below that were suspect, and those below $0.50 were red flags and might be paused.

Two issues arise from this example. First, the arbitrary goal value itself proved highly arbitrary; a poor predictor of real revenues. Users merely reaching the application page helped us with quick assessments of which traffic was at least sentient and reasonably targeted, to be sure. Very low values were associated with confused users misinterpreting ad copy, weakly targeted keywords, and so forth. But many of the high-value words did not ultimately translate into back-end revenues. In some financial areas, many users will show brief interest but ultimately not qualify for the product.

Bounce Rates, Time Spent, and Pages Viewed Are Core Metrics in Analytics

Bounce rates, by the way, were always strongly negatively correlated with the dollar values of the keywords. A variety of "you done good" metrics tend to show you about the same thing, just expressed in different ways, but this depends on your sales process.

The bounce rate for a keyword (or any segment, such as a page, a campaign, a geo-segment, of your site in the aggregate) is the percentage of users who get to your website and do not click even one more time. A bounce is not the same as a "very short visit," though it usually is that, too. Some users who "bounce" may stay on the site for several minutes, just on the first page, without clicking a link. In some cases, websites with Ajax presentations that do not take interacting users to a new page on a click may be seeing very misleading bounce rates.

Time spent and number of pages viewed speak for themselves, and based on the preceding comment, it would seem that even more detailed user tracking might be beneficial to websites that want to go beyond these sometimes uninformative metrics. Check out analytics tools like GetClicky, CrazyEgg, and Robot Replay; they provide visual information about mouse click patterns and even replays of whole user sessions so you can literally get a better picture of what is going on. Do people always go for the search box? Do they ever click the links below the fold? Are too many people clicking on an insignificant link?

High bounce rates are red flags that your traffic is untargeted or unsatisfied. Unfortunately, on broad terms in paid search, you're going to see a lot of bounce rates in the 50% range. Don't panic at this level, although 15–30% should be your comfort level. Above 70%, it's a bright red flag that something is amiss.

Bounce rates are doubly important because they are likely being used in Google's assessment of website quality for Quality Score, and in predictive quality assessments in the early going. Google might even look at how quickly users hit the Back button to return to Google Search; 3–6 seconds might be a huge red flag for Quality Score (and yes, even organic search algorithms are looking at user clickstream data), whereas just a little bit longer, like 20 seconds, might be treated much more leniently. For the purposes of evaluating you as an advertiser, there is likely no substantial difference between a user time spent on site of 20 seconds and 5 minutes. More may be better for you, but a bit less isn't getting you in hot water with AdWords.

But Don't Forget to Install Google Conversion Tracker

It's helpful and fun to "troll through" these reports, as I put it above. But Google Conversion Tracker and other numbers right inside AdWords are what really put actionable analysis into high gear.

Because Google Analytics is getting so much ink, newer advertisers put a lot of stock in it and actually aren't aware of how plodding their routine is. The available reporting is comprehensive, but in fact, the paid search specific reports are not always as handy as they could be. To really motor through your routine, you want to be working right inside the AdWords interface. To do this, you'll need to install Google Conversion Tracker JavaScript code as well.

Conversion Tracker, as discussed earlier, allows you to adjust bids on keywords, adopt winning ads from an ROI or goal standpoint, and determine the relative effectiveness of segments such as content targeting. When the numbers look really bad, you'll need to pause keywords or even re-evaluate entire campaigns, including your targeting and website effectiveness. What's so handy is that you get to look at these numbers and adjust your bid strategy right there in the AdWords interface.

AdWords Conversion Optimizer

So how, exactly, do you adjust bids to ensure you're staying within range of your target ROAS or CPA goals? There's no universal method, believe it or not.

As mentioned in previous chapters, you might want to tweak your bids on individual keywords, but on mid- to lower-volume keywords, you'll probably need to measure ROI and manage bids for the entire group as a whole; in other words, consider keywords in "buckets." How convenient that Google designed AdWords' powerful logic around the ad group level, not solely at the keyword level.

Without having the space to prove it here, I'll assert that some makers of third-party bid management software are working with flawed assumptions or flawed technology. At best, it is fair to say that the primary sweet spot for such solutions is high-volume e-commerce that absolutely requires intraday bid changes to avoid overpaying for product sales with razor-thin margins.

Bear in mind, as well, that high-volume, frequent bid changes cost money if they're done through a third-party application that accesses AdWords through the API. That's why those solutions cost a lot, or pass costs directly onto you. If you have specific automation needs, you could build your own app and maybe get a break from Google on API token costs, but unless your application is really one-dimensional, you're talking $40,000 to $200,000 in development costs. Automation that costs 3–5% of your monthly spend leaves very little in your budget for human analysis. That could be a costly budget mistake.

A low-tech way to automate some of your bidding—or at least, to guide your bids to slot your ads into a specific range of ad positions on the page—is to enable Position Preferences in Campaign Settings. If you always want your ads to show up in positions 3 through 7, and to not show up if Google's automation deems it impossible to show up in that range, you can set that range of favored ad positions. I've never found this to be particularly advantageous as I have limited proof that I'll make less money if I occasionally spike up to (say) position 2 or down to 8. This setting may put you where you want to be, but generally speaking, your own bid strategy can do the same, without cutting into volume as the Position Preferences setting typically does.

I am still hearing many marketers on a regular basis making assumptions that bid adjustments are needed frequently or that human analysts are inferior to "sophisticated" computers. Certainly, computers are better than us humans at handling rote tasks on high volumes. However, many of those who adopt third-party bid management solutions are wasting money and possibly handing over too much of their process (sometimes requiring more code, privacy intrusions, upsells to expensive services, and so forth) for account work that could be accomplished by (and which, indeed, may require) a qualified human analyst. Many accounts do well with bid adjustments no more frequent than a "round" of bid adjustments weekly. Some bids remain valid for months at a time. In other cases, bid gamesmanship may be warranted, but in the new complex auction, most legacy software is obsolete when it comes to the bid environment.

Still, there is a certain attraction to "set and forget." Similar to the benefit of Google Analytics, Google's free feature, AdWords Conversion Optimizer, will adjust your bids in an attempt to keep you within a target CPA range that you set. You can set this feature at the campaign level; 100 monthly conversions are required by a campaign to qualify for this feature. My experience is that it works fairly well for certain kinds of accounts, but you may suffer from decreasing volume. The availability of this free, integrated tool (that Google engineers are working to perfect) prompts me to further question the benefit of third-party bid management.

It's notable that Google sets a hard minimum of 100 conversions per campaign to qualify for this intelligent bid automation. To be blunt, those who seem to believe that bid management solutions are going to make an appreciable difference in performance on low-volume campaigns— or worse, on poorly performing campaigns with low conversion rates—either deeply misunderstand the math involved or don't understand the factors that combine to achieve high e-commerce performance. You should not adjust a bid until performance on a keyword or segment achieves statistical significance, and a "smart" bid does very little to rescue a dismal campaign; in many cases, the smartest bid may be zero, and you shouldn't need a computer to tell you that.

I like alert-based bid solutions that assist human analysis by letting you know about the bids that are farthest out of your target range, or identifying keywords that are at zero ROI for a significant period of time. This way, you get the best of both worlds: the advantages of automation with the control and judgment of a human analyst. Two comprehensive campaign management solutions that take this approach are Clickable and Adapt. You might say I'm a fan.[3]

Quality-Based Bidding and Instability

There are enough variables in the Quality Score formula, and they are sufficiently dynamic (gathering significance and certainty over time), that our ability to "read and react" is affected. Sometimes, our ad positions may rise or fall significantly as we gain or lose favor with the algorithm, but this process is even less predictable than it was in the past. In the past, the system was semitransparent at least: we could see our bids and our CTRs and know that some assessment of these was pretty much the only thing affecting our ad rank.

The system is also sophisticated enough that it may be moving you up in ad position and giving you more search volume as a result *because* you're more likely to convert to a sale. Don't take the "because" literally here; conversion rates aren't included in Quality Score calculations. But many of the signals that give Google a strong indicator of quality are the exact same factors that go into creating strong user experiences and thus higher conversion rates.

The takeaway? Don't be biased against certain ad positions. Keep reevaluating where you stand—be open to more volume, and don't short-change yourself.

Marketers Are Using Analytics to Test Sophisticated Theories

I alluded earlier in the chapter to the usefulness of using statistics like bounce rates, pages viewed, and time spent to diagnose problems with your campaign. These are the deeper forms of analysis that take you beyond simply bidding to ROI, into a more thoughtful analysis of targeting and technical issues.

There's plenty more you can do in Analytics.

A favorite of mine is the Ad Position report. If your Analytics account is properly linked to AdWords, you can pull up an AdWords ad position report with multiple views that you can toggle. One view just shows you how many clicks you got on any given keyword, by ad position. This is shown visually so you can see exactly how many clicks (over a given date range) occurred in the top premium spots or in the right-side margin spots. From there, if you have Goals enabled, you can go so far as to examine your conversion rates in various ad positions. If conversion rates are not significantly higher, or are in fact lower, on higher ad positions, then you'll want to consider whether it's better value to go for lower volume in a less visible ad position.

More than anything, this excellent report is a fine way to overcome myths in the industry perpetrated by similar reports that aggregate data across the entire industry. Who cares what someone else's account did in various ad positions, for keywords unknown to you? This is your conversion behavior, for your account, for the keywords you select. This is extremely powerful information, and Google has seen to it that you get it for free with nearly no customization effort or expense.

It's fool's gold, of course, if you don't look at a large enough chunk of data to get statistical significance. Also, if you haven't experimented with different ad positions (we sometimes call this a "volume test," when we bid much higher for a week or so to secure an average ad position of 2.5 or higher), you don't learn as much from the report.

You can test dozens of other kinds of theories using Analytics data—you can, for example, assess user sophistication levels and behavior by looking at screen sizes or browser choices. You can inform usability debates, again by looking at typical monitor resolutions. You can look at conversion rates varying by geography, and decide to exclude certain areas in the geo-location settings in AdWords campaign settings. There's not much you can get on user demographics yet; for this, you might want to check out Microsoft's rival analytics product, code-named Gatineau. I have no doubt that if you study hard, you'll gain enough insight to not only become conversant with the metrics shared by presenters at E-Metrics Summit—you could very well be up there on the podium yourself.

Marketers Understand That "Analytics" (Relevant Statistics) Live Right Inside AdWords

People who frequent the big ol' Professional Analytics world sometimes seem to have an awfully narrow view of where to get relevant statistics. For particularly unimaginative members of this crew, analytics is something that happens within Google Analytics, or preferably, within WebTrends or Omniture, or some other third-party vendor product that they can get reseller revenue (or subsidized travel to industry powwows) out of.

Analytics? How 'bout Ad Positions, CPCs, CTRs, and ROAS?

Friends, you can get the majority of the numbers you need right within the AdWords interface. As we reviewed in the first part of this chapter, all of your keyword-specific, group-specific, and ad-specific data are pretty much right there in front of you inside AdWords. And yes, usually that conversion data (CPA, ROAS) is what really rules, though clients and bosses also like to hear peripheral numbers about spend, CPC, and CTR trends.

Quality Score Is a Stat

Did you consider that Quality Score is actually a statistic? When you see a keyword Quality Score of 3 or 1, as opposed to 9 or 10, that should be speaking volumes about your status as a good/bad guy in Google's eyes, and as to whether you've managed to deal well with Google's obsession with tight targeting for new accounts, and leniency on looser targeting once strong account history has been established. High minimum bids on mature accounts likely mean that your CTR relative to competitors is still lagging, which means you'll need to redouble your efforts to test ads.

Segmentation, Segmentation, Segmentation

Marketing analysts use generic terminology to discuss *segments* of the target audience. In our world, the most important segments are keywords and ad groups; in some cases geography is also key.

Over on the content-targeting side, the AdWords interface offers increasingly sophisticated choices. You can choose specific publications you want to show up in, or you can let the system match content around the Web for you.

Of particular interest is the excellent reports available in the Reporting tab in AdWords. You can run a report on the performance of ad placements broken down by domain, to identify poor converters. You can respond to these by entering site exclusions at the campaign level (or "negativing out") those sites.

Again, in content targeting, AdWords now breaks out content types, such as parked domains, or tragedy & destruction content. You can opt out of these, or at least see that they are performing up to par, in order to combat industry stereotypes about performance.

CPCs Have Increased and Competition Has Intensified

Going over the past four or five years, it's not uncommon that a typical CPA number has tripled or quadrupled for any given company using AdWords. Multiple factors are at play here. First, Google has developed increasingly sophisticated means of monetization to bump up CPCs, including making it harder to bid at the absolute minimum on "long tail" terms. Second, many of the individual "micro-auctions" going on in the overall AdWords marketplace have reached a tipping point. With sufficient advertisers in the race for the top five or so ad positions, bid prices simply go up; sometimes, dramatically. Third, other advertisers are also testing and improving their copy and other aspects of their targeting, so they can afford to bid more. Fourth, other advertisers are improving their conversion rates, improving their offerings, offering discounts or free shipping, and so forth, so again, they achieve relatively attractive offerings at the expense of others' conversion rates. Fifth, opaquely buried in Quality Score algorithms is a punitive minimum bid regime on clever keywords we used to thrive on, including brand names and people's names. Google admits that *ceteris parabus*, "certain" keywords such as large company words that are potential trademark issues, and people's names, are going to give you Quality Score headaches more often, and cost you a lot more. My experience has been that this essentially cripples the better-performing 5–10% of some accounts.

The end result of all these factors? It's a Darwinian environment, but also one that is tilted to favor the intelligent designer of that environment. If you stood still in the past four years, you probably saw your ROAS fall sharply, or your CPA number quadruple. If you improved steadily, it's not uncommon that your CPA might have doubled. Everyone else feels the same pain. The big winner in all of this? Look at the annual financial statements! Look at Google's revenues and profit margins. The winner is Google. The consumer also wins, as advertisers are forced to become more relevant and as Google actually removes ads from users' field of view while making more money from the remaining ads.

How does this affect your reading of trends? It's tough to say, but I'm willing to go out on a limb and suggest that it's unfair to expect CPAs to improve in absolute terms over any given four-year period. Prices on targeted clicks in our industry began at rock bottom in 1998–2002, and rose from there.

Sound process, relentless testing efforts, and localized improvements need to be given due credit, and businesses need to look hard at strategy. In other words, judging a long-term testing effort solely on the CPA/ROAS statistic is misleading. The environment has deteriorated for all advertisers. So, unfortunately for those who like to think in absolutes, we are left to speculate on "this is how bad our campaign would have looked had we sat still and done nothing."

Remember, many AdWords success stories are that way because a certain company was virtually the only serious one in its industry segment. The frontier is no more; it's bound to get harder to compete as others climb whatever barriers to entry may exist, and begin going after your customers.

What Hasn't Changed (But There Is Always Hope)

Given how specialized the AdWords task is, it's unsurprising that many myths and clumsy practices still prevail among companies in the first stages of coming to grips with it. Specifically with reference to data and measurement, I've only gained secure beliefs and insights after years of double-checking assumptions and watching real-world performance. It's not hard to see why someone would come to the table with certain off-the-cuff assumptions. But unfortunately many of these assumptions are wrong. Here's a list of some of the things advertisers (I may broaden the term to call them "marketers" in this section) are still messing up.[4]

Marketers Must Set Objectives, but Fail to Do So   Some advertisers come forth with a media "buy" mentality only: can we get *x* number of clicks this month for 20 cents a click? Sure. But then eventually the recriminations about the quality of the traffic, and the ROI on that spend, kick in. Even where such advertisers are just promoting something in general, management needs to engage in some kind of planning process—such as setting arbitrary goal values, placing values on impressions that may be accruing from quasi-arbitrage activities such as ad sales, or supporting existing ad listing clients—in the beginning. Asking the lower-downs in the organization to buy a lot of traffic and then questioning the value of the traffic out of the blue is, unfortunately, commonplace management practice to this day. It takes some time to defend or define ROI contributions on campaigns of this nature. This is ideally done early in the process, not after spending money for two years.

Marketers Fail to Appreciate Complex System Math   Let's just take one example. CEOs of e-commerce companies are notorious for making wild claims about the "free" or inexpensive forms of online exposure they can achieve based on their "brand," or "direct navigation," at "no cost" or "low cost." A manager at a major consumer electronics company once told me they get most of their "web traffic" from "direct navigation," and implied that this was without cost. (That direct navigation, of course, spikes after TV spots and full-page color weekend newspaper ads and flyers.) In other words: in planning online campaigns, many organizations act as if their lavish offline (print, television, and so on) campaigns are done at zero cost, while assigning full cost or more to their web divisions in their efforts to gain direct response online. One organization we worked with cut its web marketing budget abruptly because a production crew for their lavish television ad shoot in Africa exceeded its budget. (Keep in mind, this company sells tents and barbecues back here in North America.) I can only assume that some of this type of behavior is more tied to internal politics and inefficient nest-feathering than to a true bottom-line concern.

The investment in offline advertising has long been largely a "faith-based initiative."[5] Online has been moving in the opposite direction. But in a world of complex customer behavior, a little faith is not a bad idea. Pure direct response isn't feasible at every moment of every campaign.

Marketers Fail to Appreciate Randomness   As I've mentioned previously in deference to Nassim Taleb's excellent work in the field, not every event can or should be explained or narrated. A brief spike upwards in campaign performance does not constitute a new benchmark for expected performance that you can deposit in the bank. Nor does an unexplained pause in sales flow mean much if patterns are looked at with a zoom lens. The explanation may simply be that randomness and, occasionally, highly improbable events are built-in features of the natural and social worlds.

Marketers Only Pay Lip Service to Volume and Statistical Significance Issues but Do Not Understand the Math   Try this exercise. Design a multivariate landing page test with 16 page permutations, with 50% of the impressions going to the test pages and 50% going to the control. Jot down your current conversion rate—say, 2%. And project your expected improvement in that rate as a result of a test—say, 25%. Now jot down how many clicks you'll be getting to that page, per day (let's say 500). This is a test you could run using Google Website Optimizer. The projection of how long it will take this test to achieve statistical significance is something you can figure out with a projection tool Google provides in their Google Analytics help files (at https://www.google .com/analytics/siteopt/siteopt/help/calculator.html). OK, now it's time to guess how long the preceding test would need to run to achieve statistical significance. Done?[6] And yet a quick guess might produce a "let's rock and roll" type of prediction, such as that it would take about a month, or "we should be seeing solid improvements in a couple of weeks." It simply doesn't work that way when the math is this complex and your volume is low. There is hope, however. Change the test up a bit. Get to driving 1,000 clicks per day to that page. Send 85% of the traffic to the test and only 15% to the control. Chop the permutations down to 12. And hope to do better: project a conversion rate improvement of 40% over your baseline of 2%. Now you're down to 87 days. That's more than 12 weeks, but at least you won't be racing against your own life expectancy getting to a completed test. This is why I'd recommend an A/B/C test for this particular example. Putting the clicks back down to 500 a day, we can still project the A/B/C test will pick a significant winner within 23 days. Nice.

There Are Still Data Discrepancies   Analytics experts agree that total accuracy in tracking conversions is impossible. Different tools differ even on the definition of a click. Conversions are "attributed" to the source that caused a conversion, but what does causation mean? Typically, that means the last click before the sale. Sophisticated industry research indicates that prior research may influence final sales, and choices of search terms may be narrowed as users get closer to certainty. With short cookie lengths, latent conversions may not be credited. These nuances are important to take into account, not to nitpick, but to realize that many of our points of analysis are intended to be relative and heuristic, rather than absolute and "true."

We're Still Poor at Measuring Offline Conversions   While it is rare to find a company that has mastered a "silver bullet" solution to attributing offline and phone conversions back to their

AdWords campaign, one thing anyone could do would be to assign a dedicated 800 number or numbers to landing pages created solely for the AdWords campaign. This and other "broad brush" attempts to give AdWords credit for sales that do not take place online are helpful in assessing the value of the investment. Yet few companies take the trouble. Some business owners prefer to hide high-ticket special order sales from marketing staff, perhaps in an attempt to downplay the website's contribution, as a motivation for said staff to work harder. Again, the definition of a profitable campaign is up for debate, and a little faith helps lubricate operations for most any growth-oriented company.

Marketers Don't Keep Tasks in Proportion   What's probably more important to the bottom line: a killer ad headline, or many across an account, or adding 20 more negative keywords to each campaign, or 10 more negative keywords to each ad group? I'm thinking the former. Ad positions, conversion improvement, changing business contexts, and a host of other drivers are important to watch and execute on, as well. It's easy to dwell on seemingly "overlooked" tasks, and it's pretty tempting to believe that flashy "look busy" marketer or Google staff member is helping your business with the appearance of hustle. Sure, I think it's important to "look alive out there," as your Little League coach might have said. But let's be clear: some account actions nibble at the margins whereas others are fundamental to the bottom line.

Marketers Try to Sell People What They Don't Want   Perhaps this is most fundamental. Most of the mistakes in AdWords are made by trying to put your ads in front of people who just aren't interested. So much so that Google has taken away your ability to do that by setting low initial Quality Scores on advertisers who seem like they're probably bothering uninterested searchers. Before concluding that there is a problem with a bid, some kind of discrepancy in Analytics, a change in the "trend," or the need for a "more timely" report, have you asked yourself whether your performance woes may be related to a real lack of demand for a particular product or service, by the people at whom you've targeted your ads in an attempt to attract them to your website? If your definition of "analysis" also includes "brutal honesty," you're ahead of the pack.

Somewhere in between avid consumer interest and a complete lack of demand usually lies a middle ground. You'll be led to a number of opportunities for additional segmentation and refinement to filter out uninterested prospects. Moving from analytics to action in paid search is often about such careful refinement over time.

Endnotes

1. Google's Matt Cutts, in his generous (and extremely accurate) review of the first edition of this book, wrote: "The cover of this book looks like your typical 'How to use Adobe Elements/Microsoft Word/3D Studio Max' book. I normally hate those books. Do I really need a book to walk me through what the File menu does in an application? Do I need a chapter devoted to simple things that anyone could figure out in five minutes just using the software application? No! Personally, I hate that 60% of the bookstore space is filled with books that tell you how to use a software application. Where are the books such as *Hackers and Painters* or *The Mythical Man-Month* or Tufte?" Thus exempted by the dude from Google, I'll continue on with a view to giving you insight into the landscape

and concepts, rather than explaining how to drill into menus which may have changed by press time.

2. This book's technical editor suggested several alternative names, such as Urchinoficles, Urchinedes the Great, or Urchinias. Sticking with Urchinator, I must point out that in this chapter as with the rest of the book, responsibility for all errors, omissions, and stubborn refusal to take suggestions, lies solely with the author.

3. Disclosure: I have been an early beta tester and adviser to Clickable. I have no stake in the company.

4. Due to space limitations, I make little effort to defend my assertions in this section. If you're interested in deeper discussion, I'll buy you a venti green tea and we can have it out.

5. Thanks to Avinash Kaushik for the turn of phrase.

6. The answer is 952.64 days, or getting on for three years!!!

Chapter 11

Increasing
Online Conversion Rates

Online conversion science, which attempts to define those factors most critical to turning a casual click into a profitable action, is one of the hottest trends in Internet marketing today. But it hasn't been an overnight success. Earlier generations of web marketers often threw together websites hastily, optimistic that they'd get rich as long as they could find visitors. Such a strategy might have worked then, but certainly not in today's competitive marketplace. Competition aside, the cost of paid clicks continues to rise. Achieving higher conversion rates is a must if you expect sustained profitability from paid search campaigns.

> **NOTE**
> *Online conversion science is an emerging field, so some terminology used in this chapter will be new. I am coining the terms* conversion science *and* conversion scientist *in an attempt to describe a particular group of Internet marketers—those who specialize in increasing clients' online conversion rates. I consider online conversion science as a subset of the broader field of web analytics. Conversion scientists are not only interested in measurement issues per se; they are engaged in "doing something about it."*

There are few famous *conversion scientists* yet. Many have toiled behind the scenes in marketing positions, improving the ROI on online marketing campaigns for their employers by testing various online buying processes. Much of the work has been experimental and based on trial and error.

Testing response online started primarily with email marketing, which is why the first wave of conversion scientists cut their teeth on email. Many marketing publications still devote a large (often disproportionate) amount of space to the subject of testing response to so-called email "blasts." But email-offer testing protocols, often inherited from direct mail methodologies, don't begin to scratch the surface of user interface testing that's made possible on the Web. For our purposes, users will be arriving at some page on your site from a search—but a very specific kind of search: a paid search click whose messaging and path you have some control over.

A typical unsung hero in the early going of online conversion science is Marc Stockman, an email marketing consultant who was formerly a marketing VP with TheStreet.com. As a publicly traded online content company in the financial field, TheStreet.com was suffering from regular quarterly losses. In 2001, TheStreet.com only generated $15.2 million in revenues for the entire year, posting an operating loss of $31 million. To come closer to breakeven, the company wanted to dramatically increase the conversion rate of its free email newsletter subscribers to paying subscribers. Under Stockman's tutelage, the layout and sales copy in emails, as well as the layout, copy, and checkout process on the website, were all tested and improved. This resulted in a surge in paid subscriptions and a material improvement in TheStreet.com's profit picture. The company generated $9.5 million in revenues, and a slight profit, in the final quarter of 2004. By 2007, the company's annual revenues were $65 million; net income was a very healthy $17 million (excluding a one-time tax benefit). Subscription revenue makes up about half the company's total revenues. The profit picture is now so consistent that TheStreet.com pays a small quarterly dividend.

There are few better examples of the power of conversion science to make or break a company. Did Stockman's work literally mean the difference between delisting and bankruptcy, and the $235 million market capitalization TSCM enjoys today? We'll never know for sure. But it's safe to say that testing online response towards higher subscription rates played a large role in the company's survival, and then, profitability. Testing key conversion pages for a high-volume marketing program may cost $5,000, $10,000, or $100,000. But the expense pays for itself many times over. The added revenue, especially for digital products, comes with negligible additional cost or overhead. And confidence rises that it's possible to expand marketing efforts so that profitability comes with growth.

Stories like TheStreet.com's are not uncommon. Many online content companies needed to replace lost ad revenues that had put a serious hole in their business model. Many promised investors that they'd make a transition to paying subscribers, but many did a poor job of converting free readerships into paying subscribers. The rate at which prospects convert into paying customers can make or break companies of all sizes. The low conversion rate pinch has been acute of late among the proliferation of Web 2.0 companies who relied on "freemium" business models without ever figuring out whether they could convert users to paid services. If only more of them would try, rather than deferring the inevitable! Web 2.0 companies that refuse to test for profitable conversions all but resign themselves to the need for quick acquisition. They also weaken their position vis-à-vis subsequent rounds of investment; by contrast, hot companies with some provable revenue streams can afford to take less money at a better valuation. Why do some venture capitalists salivate over the Web 2.0 "free services" model? Because hot companies crash and burn without revenue, and the early-round VCs can swoop in and vastly increase their ownership stakes before figuring out whether to flip the companies or inject better business practices to turn them around. But that's neither here nor there.

In this chapter I'll focus on the impact of website and landing page design, copywriting, and layout on conversion rates. Experience has taught us that conversion science has a number of elements, each of which plays an important part in moving an online visitor from curiosity to action. These elements include, in addition to your actual offering, the aesthetics of the user interface, ease of use, content, and credibility of your website.

I'll review a few elements in the overall recipe of what to test, before turning to more textured discussions of how case study information has bubbled up to create useful principles that are becoming more widely adopted across the online marketing professions today. Even Google support staff, who once were only versed in the language of clicks and traffic, are keenly aware of user experiences all the way through to goal completion. This goes hand in hand with widespread adoption of Google Analytics and Google Conversion Tracker, and the general interest Google has developed in the user experience.

Conversion Science Isn't a Beauty Contest

Before we delve into the meat of conversion science, I want to cover a couple of general principles. To begin with, conversion science isn't about turning water into wine, or putting "lipstick on a pig." Trying to sell a blah product or a poorly conceived service on a great website is generally a prescription for failure. Therefore, make sure your offering is solid before assuming that problems converting sales are the fault of the usability specialists, data analysts, or web developers who are advising you.

Great user experiences aren't purely a function of the attractiveness of your website. You might have long-term image and revenue goals that require a consistent, contemporary design. If so, great. But many plain (Craigslist) or even ugly (PlentyOfFish.com) sites are notorious for making their founders boatloads of money while eschewing fancy designers or even usability studies! According to legend, Google's own plain home page was conceived because the company founders "weren't designers and didn't do HTML." A lucky accident indeed.

Today, Google is possibly the best living example of a company that merely pretends to be laid-back about user testing and interface design, while in reality placing enormous weight on certain key factors. User response testing at a massive site like Google played an important role in the company's overall growth. Of course, the quality of search results and the clean interface would be right up there among the key factors that have kept users coming back. Certain fanatics have held Google to its original (accidental) principles; one Google supporter is famous for sending in the number of bytes in the weight of Google's home page, as a reminder not to "bloat" that all-important page. Google has also set a gold standard for page load times in the most complex of large database searches in the world, putting other, slower websites on the defensive.

Google is also a reminder, though, of the power of the familiar. Arguably, many large companies' sites have many "imperfect" elements if you go by the book. So, some of the current links and layout elements on any Google page are not "by the book" perfect. Usability experts can easily point to principles and practices that, on the average website, would improve the "flow." But how about the cost-benefit of making further tweaks to a familiar experience that is making tons of money for a leading company? As part of the cultural experience expected by millions of users, leaving "imperfect" but beloved elements unchanged isn't always rational, but it may be wise.

The task facing a conversion improvement exercise, then, varies widely by the stage of business and the type of business. Unless you're a real kamikaze visionary with very deep pockets, you'll probably be looking to build design, copy, and interface elements that "reference" or "look like" something an Internet user already knows about. Jakob Nielsen once humorously referred to "Jakob's Law of the Web User Experience"; namely: "users spend most of their time on other sites."[1] If you monkey with web standards and conventions, tinkering with the meanings of known icons, design cues, word choices, and so forth, you'll make people's brains hurt. Don't make folks drive through hedges and over parking barriers to get to the entrance of the drive-thru. And by all means show them "conventional" photos of burgers, salads, and drinks when they get there. They're hungry.

Recently, Bryan Eisenberg solicited his blog readers to comment and advise on usability tests for the online presence of Canadian housewares store Home Outfitters. Amidst the wide variety of voluntary comments proffered by expert observers, the one that came up the most often was "please test whether replacing 'Add to Bag' with 'Add to Cart' has an impact." The site designers had just decided to rename "Add to Cart" to "Add to Bag" in an attempt to reflect something slightly cutesy about the brand, or to place their own stamp on the exercise. I sympathize with the ennui they may be feeling in building yet another site, but it's also our professional responsibility to generate profit unless instructed otherwise.

Heck, "Add to Bag" might work out fine. On another site I've visited recently, the Zegari laptop bag site, I notice "Add to Shopping Bag" and don't feel as leery about it. That's probably because of the super-clean design of that site, and the limited choices that make it pretty clear what the user would do in this case. At the time of this writing, Zegari offers only two products: two different models of laptop bag; one of them, fittingly, is called The Minimalist.

It's OK to test innovations occasionally—Seth Godin might say that introducing a meme mutation (or mDNA) into your company's processes gives you a better chance of evolving ahead of competitors.[2] But let's not confuse system conventions with fashion and product innovation. Sure, you need to innovate, but if you want to make money this year with a better checkout interface, my money's on intelligent design, and sticking with Add to Cart—until proven otherwise.

These principles apply to user experiences at all levels, including, of course, the design of everyday things and a variety of technology products, online or offline.[3] To minimize the cost and cognitive strain of rediscovering useful conventions, we generally want the milk carton to pour in one or two standard ways. We want the Back button on our web browser to keep working like a Back button should (and we'll hit it really quickly if we think we've landed on the wrong web page!).

What and How to Test Depends on Business Type

Debates on what is the "best" home page, category page, offer page, product page, and overall interface design will never be definitively solved. Nor will the question of how much brute force testing is warranted, as opposed to how much "borrowing from leaders" and "best practices" will need to be built into your assumptions from the start. There are probably several hundred significantly different business types when it comes to conversion improvement. Just breaking down into categories such as B2B vs. B2C, small volume vs. high volume, several demographic segments, degree of content or community possible or required, and so forth, we could arrive at a few hundred types of businesses that elicit different user responses in general.

To get to a correct overview of your audience and probable user responses, a full-service approach might be to begin with "persona research," and to construct offers on your site based on the known psychology of the typical visitor. That's going to require a significant amount of organizational continuity, and a significant investment.

AdWords advertisers working with modest budgets, though, can do a kind of "skinny research" on their own without as much fuss. They can test responses to a variety of landing pages, connected to relevant keywords, very rapidly. More importantly, the process of testing ads and landing pages will—I bet you—lead to a confirmation of at least one high-level principle that can simplify most of the rest of what you do.

> **TIP**   *Just a friendly reminder: when testing landing pages, be careful not to "orphan" them. Google's landing page and website quality guidelines want you to make it easy for users to figure out where they are and who you are, so include at least some elements of your global site navigation on any page or you may risk a credibility gap and lower Quality Scores.*

The Discovery of Scent: God's Gift to Interface Designers?

That high-level principle is now widely known in the industry as "information scent." I won't waste our time attempting to sort out exactly who coined the concept; whether it was Jared Spool, whether it has descended from research findings originally shared by Jakob Nielsen, or whether Bryan Eisenberg has been its leading popularizer, although all of the above are no doubt true.[4]

"I like a man who knows what he wants," so say a surprising percentage of personal ads. The folks who run search engines and usability labs today often see confused people stumbling around, but still assume "that man" is buried in there somewhere, and that it is the fault of marketers, interface designers, and so on for not giving "that man" what he "wants." True enough, the subset of individuals who really do know what they're looking for online is significant, and our effort as conversion scientists is to make sure we don't do anything silly that prevents "that man" from getting to what he (or she) wants.

Researchers noticed early on (putting aside, for the moment, that users in these studies are usually *supplied* with tasks and strong intent that fuels "scent") that a common pattern holds for users seeking relevant information and products. They keep going forward, drilling down from a search result or web referral link, into the conversion funnel or conversation interface of a website, until such time as they either complete a desired action or encounter something off topic, bewildering, or contrary to the exact thing they were seeking. With the latter, they typically leave immediately, hitting the Back button. Web users are fickle and impatient. In the inimitable words of web analytics expert Avinash Kaushik, users who leave your site immediately without clicking on a single link (known as "bounces") are basically saying to you: "I came, I saw, I puked." (Or maybe "that man" wasn't in the chair that day, and the weak-willed, bored, or ambiguous person stumbled on your site. So maybe the reaction isn't always as severe as Kaushik lets on. Maybe some users—rather than puking—just lose the scent, and wander off, like suddenly uninterested or confused bloodhounds. Or maybe some of them aren't bloodhounds at all, but are, rather, butterflies.)

As an AdWords guy, I can summarize this scent concept in a tiny nutshell. In large part, this take on it is shared by the designers of the ad ranking formulas at Google, Yahoo, and Microsoft. Let's say you run an ad that shows up whenever a user types **bag of hockey pucks** into Google. Ideally, your ad would reference the availability of a bag of hockey pucks at your store. The user would be taken to a page showing a bag of hockey pucks, and that page would allow them to easily add the bag of hockey pucks to their shopping cart. They then have no problem making that purchase. From there, you rapidly ship them said bag of hockey pucks. That's a successful transaction based on relevance and continuity of purpose throughout the path to purchase—in other words, a strong and persistent scent.

There are many complications to this oversimplification, of course. A user searching for a 2004 Reserve Cabernet from Chile might be far enough down the path of consideration that it makes sense to think of the Web as a simple store shelf. But we also know that users are often in research mode. In other cases, their queries are ambiguous—maybe even to themselves. If someone types **wine**, or even a more specific query about wine, it's pretty presumptuous to show an ad like:

Wine
Get wine here! Free shipping on wine.
Buy now.
www.vino.com/yeah-baby-yeah

From the standpoint of connoisseurs, wine is something you research, savor, and consider carefully—it's not a commodity. And yet how do you develop the expertise to know enough to type in a more advanced query? That's something that rule-bound folks who have newly discovered the concept of information scent don't have a very good answer for. Web search cannot, surely, be merely an ordering mechanism for predetermined tastes.[5] It also needs to be a discovery mechanism for the cultivation of tastes, framing of debates, and asking and answering of questions. So search engines' role in leading users from general interest into more refined or specific needs and wants is pivotal. And corporate websites may need to play a dual role, enlightening consumers through a forum approach, building content and community while somewhere else on the site running a tight catalog. Public relations firm Thornley Fallis, for example, has focused much of its efforts for client Cuisinart Canada on creating a more vibrant corporate website that brings customer voices and brand ambassadors to the fore. Scent orthodoxy and the building of an accurate catalog-type mechanism will come into play later, when the company invests more in the e-commerce division. Both are valid objectives.

It is safe to say that on broader queries, Google may want to show users fewer paid results (because they're less likely to be what users are looking for), and may attempt to rank pages high in the organic search results that could be considered definitive, or at least very useful starting points, for users looking for information on general topics. They do this in a number of ways: by suggesting popular or related queries to broad queries, by ranking highly definitive content sites in a category, and more. In this process it is pedantic to expect designers, marketers, or anyone else to adhere to "the" principles of "the" scent, because in many cases users are *not* "informavores."

In some cases, they have yet to discover themselves, and don't know exactly what they want. Any number of human "guides" who offer overviews of "where to begin" on a topic might be at least as helpful as machine-driven search results pointing to particularly "granular" or "accurate" pages on a particular site. (Hence the role of human-driven quasi-search services such as Squidoo, About, Mahalo, and more, as alternatives to literal-minded scent-obsessed search paradigms.)

All told, then, the concept of scent is helpful, but not to the point where it's gospel; not to the point where we should accept one-dimensional lectures or examples (like my bag of hockey pucks one) as valid for every possible user's intent. As we've seen time and again, also implicit in many users' information queries is an unspoken plea: I'm looking for someone who will help me to figure out what I really think! (Anyone who is a highly followed Twitter member can attest to that.)

Common Errors That Kill Conversions

These may become obvious as we study the subject in more detail, but at this point it may be useful to catalog some of the key errors made in online navigation and design that make it difficult to achieve a positive ROI on a paid search campaign.

Error #1: Not Understanding What a Landing Page Is

A landing page, of course, is the destination URL that users "land on" after they've clicked on your paid search listing. Landing pages are a fundamental variable that can make or break your numbers, but so many businesses neglect them.

Here are some things to keep in mind concerning landing pages, especially if you subscribe to more literal versions of the scent theory:

- Virtually the entire goal of the landing page must be to induce users to take a particular action, such as making a purchase or requesting information.
- Some landing pages are better than others at achieving that goal. (Cha-ching!)
- Designing your landing page with an understanding of what is likely to work will get you reasonably close to optimal performance from the start.
- Testing in real time, using a valid testing protocol, is ultimately the only way to determine what kind of landing page converts best.

While it is true that both your site navigation and design as a whole, and the layout and message of a particular landing page, influence user behavior, it pays to focus primarily on the landing page. Yes, your "site" is important. But excessive focus on "the site" does not necessarily help you understand how to create results. Isolating the user's experience with the page she is actually on is always helpful to understanding your task at hand.

Error #2: Overloading the Landing Page with Information

One of the most common mistakes site designers make is to try to cram too much information on the landing page. The impulse to get everything in front of the potential customer while you've got his or her attention can be irresistible.

However, when you're paying for traffic, you need to be very clearly focused on what you'd like the user to do, and avoid wavering from that goal. A good approach is to limit your landing page to one primary goal, plus a secondary, fallback goal. The possibility of the user finding another part of your site through an easy-to-understand navigation interface might be the third priority. Keep your options open without overwhelming the user.

Landing pages that present the user with too many options rarely perform well. For example, if you're thinking that flag animation or a "site counter" somehow enhances your credibility, think again. Eliminate what isn't necessary. If users are particularly interested in researching your company, they can and will navigate to your About Us page.

Most businesses don't put cheesy stuff like that in the user's face anymore, though. A more common error, at least from the standpoint of a paid click from a particular keyword, would be to add vaguely related, but still distracting, offers. So a page that is supposed to be about a particular camera accessory might also show users the featured offers that top management has decided to "unload" to consumers, for some reason making it a priority to add (say) refurbished printers to the template for the entire site. So somebody (the guy who kept too much refurbished printer inventory on hand?) gets to save face, while the clicks expressly purchased to convert buyers of a lens accessory "don't perform." The only solution is to empower those running paid search campaigns to test different versions of product pages, including versions with less clutter.

Often, all that is accomplished by asking users to pay attention to "something else" is that you squander or divide the attention you've paid 20 cents, 50 cents, or $4.00 to purchase. Why ask them to pay attention to something else (see Figures 11-1 and 11-2), especially if they barely know who you are or what your main offer is?

In the case of Urban Challenge Online, you can see that all of the ideas competing for attention on the page shown in Figure 11-2 are good ideas. It's certainly not a bad idea to indicate who your charitable and corporate partners are, for example. As a page whose sole goal should be to convert visitors to registered players of a game, however, it's cluttered both in a visual sense and in the sense of priorities facing the user. Most users have no idea what this is all about, and most have no intention yet of registering as players, but the page seems intent on changing the subject by referring to distracting issues such as an entirely different contest they could enter. At the very bottom of the page, the user is asked to "send this page to a friend." How about converting that user to a registered contestant first? (By the way, it's worth noting that Urban Challenge has since revamped their site significantly, and many of the early problems are now corrected.)

Offer pages need to be thought of differently from content pages that users may navigate through in high volumes. These latter might contain conventional sharing icons and a variety of navigational options in a dashboard-like setting. But when you're paying to get someone to respond to an offer, they're arriving fresh. Narrowing their options is likely the best approach.

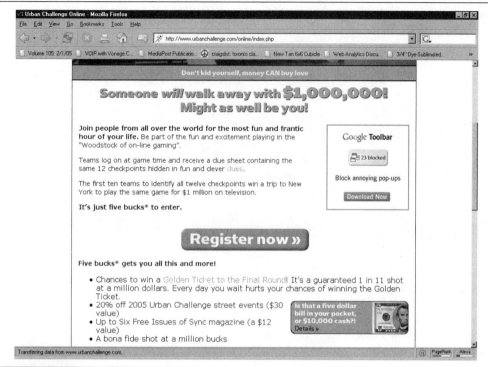

FIGURE 11-1   The user's precious attention is divided three ways.

Error #3: Assuming That the Best Landing Page Is the Home Page

Many site owners have the attitude that "the site has all kinds of stuff on it, so we'd better let them come to our home page and discover what we have to offer." This works sometimes. Most times it does not. Typically, this leads to users browsing around indecisively, or worse, leads to their simply not caring that they are on "your company page" and promptly leaving. If you got them there to look at an offer, especially if that offer is related to a niche keyword, give them an offer. Depending on the type of business you're in, you'll be better off bringing the searcher to a tailored lead-generation-oriented landing page, a product description page, or a product category page. Don't be coy.

Requiring just one additional click at the beginning of your sales process could result in a significant drop in goal conversion rates: 30–40% lower conversion rates may be typical when the thought process towards attempting that first click on the site is particularly annoying or confusing. Don't lose *persuasive momentum* by taking users to an introductory page (see Figure 11-3) that makes them decide, for example, which division of your company they want to deal with.[6] If you

FIGURE 11-2   A fourth contest detail competes with six corporate logos.

have a carefully targeted AdWords campaign, you should already know who you're targeting, so you should be able to lead users to exactly the page that contains the information you want to show them. Don't risk even a single extra click if you don't have to. (Segmenting buyers into types is another matter: a clean process that sorts out small business buyers from corporate buyers may be absolutely appropriate.)

Failure to prioritize basic information scent and navigational conventions can be particularly damaging in some situations, such as large retail organizations juggling regional priorities, infighting from franchisees, and other internal company politics. Requiring users to specify languages or postal codes prior to arriving at the desired landing page will absolutely murder conversion rates. Do whatever you can to send users to the correct page for them, even if this means making some assumptions about users or providing uniform web pricing instead of "regional" pricing. (On the language issue, you can set languages inside AdWords, and run separate campaigns for Google users searching in any language, so if you have a lot of Spanish-speaking customers and separate campaigns for Spanish language inside AdWords, there is no reason not to show that user a Spanish-language page immediately.) In high-complexity fields like insurance, users may expect to fill out forms that ask them a lot of information, and they

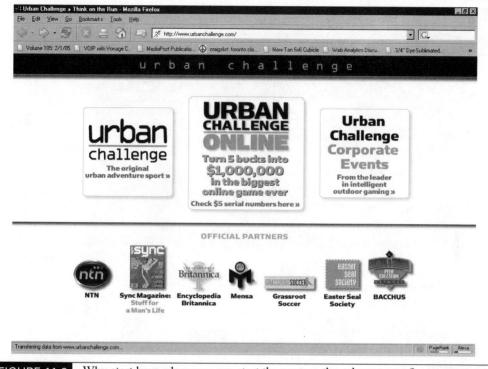

FIGURE 11-3   Why start here when you can start the user on the relevant page?

understand that pricing depends on many factors, including location. In retail, consumers figure the store is uniform—it's on "the Web," and want you to show them the product, with the price, immediately. Don't make them puke with a blank-looking splash screen or rude information request too early in the process—not if you can help it.

Error #4: Assuming That the Best Landing Page Is a Bare Contact Form

If you're in the lead-generation business, don't expect users to be so excited by your offer that they immediately give you their contact info. For example, I clicked on a banner ad on Yahoo for a specialized service by Gomez Advisors, a consulting firm. The ad took me to a raw contact page with no accompanying copy. I had absolutely no incentive to fill out the form. A better approach would be to offer a few paragraphs of information, followed by the contact form.

Another example I ran across is in the competitive credit counseling industry. Although the landing page (see Figure 11-4) has some info in the form, a few bullets, and looks like it's been

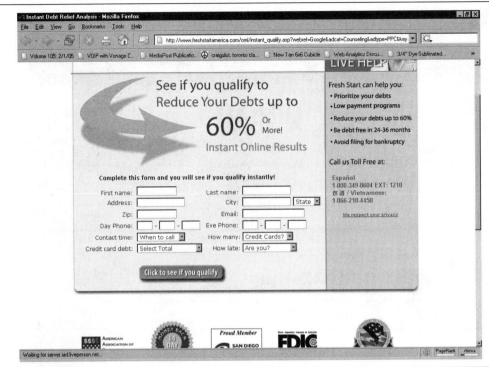

optimized for visual appeal and credibility, it still doesn't offer enough to encourage the casual
visitor to take action. In a highly competitive industry, your visitor has plenty of alternatives
if your landing page doesn't do the job. Your goal is to grab each prospect when you have the
chance—you may not get another.

Error #5: Assuming That the Best Copy Is Brief Copy

If clutter is bad, some may reason that six paragraphs should be chopped to three. But that is
not always the case. The more abbreviated some companies seem to get with their copy, the
more they appear to be talking in industry gibberish that only makes sense at internal company
meetings. If you're Apple and there have been 40,000 news stories written about the iPod, you
can get away with any length of sales copy. But if you're a relative unknown, it often helps to tell
a story.

Check out the big car companies' sites. While sometimes difficult to navigate, they generally
contain a lot of material describing every facet of their vehicles, right down to the characteristics

FIGURE 11-5   This product page provides rich detail for shoppers to sink their teeth into.

of their new All-Wheel-Drive system, braking, airbags, and so on. Imagine that you made or sold the airbags, or the brakes, since you probably don't make cars. It might help to have more than a couple of words on your site to describe the features and benefits of the product, or the reason other customers like to buy it from you.

As you can see in Figure 11-5, this telecommunications equipment vendor has proper descriptions on some of its product pages, but not on others (see Figure 11-6). An early version of the site had many such omissions. Conversion rates were low. Costly clicks were not translating into buyer interest because the site seemed inhospitable and uninformative.

TIP   *Having proper, full-length product descriptions on your website will help you attract more "stumble-in" search engine traffic as well (often at no cost to you). Without words, search engines have nothing to index.*

FIGURE 11-6   Inconsistency in adding product copy to each page has a tangible result: poor conversion rates and wasted ad dollars.

Insights Leading to Principles: How Case Study Data Leads Us to Conversion "Schools of Thought"

There are some pretty complex formulas floating around to help the average decision-maker make sense of the task facing them as a marketer. A few take things to an extreme of simplicity, such as the title of Steve Krug's classic usability text *Don't Make Me Think*. Others are very simple devices to help us remember key principles of user interface design, implicitly backed by much research—the concept of information scent is foremost among these.

Unlike most of us, the biggest websites in the world have a lot of data to back up their assumptions about how users act online. But we aren't always in a position to copy them. What we need to do is to combine our own user data and specific audience research with broader laws of behavior that we can learn about—and sometimes learn from—as gleaned from broader case-driven principles, plus the conventions and imperatives that the world's largest sites (such as Amazon and Google) force us to consider implementing because, as Nielsen argued, your users spend most of their time on "other websites."

Case Approaches: Tinkering for Dollars—It Worked!

Even a large, high-traffic website can make fatal errors that drop sales conversions by more than half, losing a company millions in the process. Bryan Eisenberg refers in presentations to a change his firm recommended to client Overstock.com. A promotional banner on a key page referred to a great new deal on DVDs for kids. Unfortunately, for the great many users who were arriving on that page looking for other things, this eye-catching promotion made it look like the whole site was about that, so they left immediately. A change to the page removed the single-issue promotion and focused on the huge DVD selection. Based on this single change, the ROI on this high-traffic page skyrocketed, with a revenue improvement impact well into six figures.

We can relate little case studies like this all day long. What is at least as interesting, though, is the high-level thinking that has emerged out of a large volume of such studies. By combining data and research from many sources, great thinkers in the business have started to refer to some processes with consistent terminology. This emerging lexicon of conversion science can help us figure out why something happened, and provide us with an agenda for testing.

Are We Plumbers or Persuaders?

In the popular film *Michael Clayton*, the lead character, an underachieving but "useful" attorney played by George Clooney, wishes to dispel any assumptions about his magical powers to make problems disappear. A wealthy client facing hit-and-run charges refuses to cooperate with Clayton's initial efforts at damage control. Clayton responds: "I'm not a miracle worker, I'm a janitor. The math on this is simple. The smaller the mess, the easier it is for me to clean up."

As an online marketer, you're probably not a miracle worker, either. So it might be instructive (if not inspirational) to view yourself as more "plumber" than "persuader." The more relevant your offer, the fewer miracles will be required to complete a sale.

The proprietary term Persuasion Architecture—used in particular consulting contexts by Eisenberg's firm, FutureNow—may be a bit of a misnomer. My take on it is that there is less "persuasion" going on than the term would have us believe. But yes, the path itself—the website architecture—is persuasive. I'm pretty sure a lot of beginners will misinterpret the concept of persuasive architecture as meaning talking people into buying something they otherwise wouldn't buy. It's far from that, in most cases.

In the first edition of this book, I tried the following terminology out to classify major schools of thought in conversion science:

- **Economists**   These are the conversion experts who promote removal of undue barriers to commerce as the way to increase conversion rates.

- **Ideologues**   Conversion gurus in this camp are convinced that you need to convince or persuade users to buy your product through sales copy, pricing, psychological triggers, limited-time offers, comparisons, and other emotional elements.

But a more informal-sounding way of classifying our major tasks is to substitute *plumbers* for economists and *persuaders* for ideologues. No matter which terminology you care to use, I'd like to make the counterintuitive point that it's mostly by getting the website's "plumbing" right that we become persuasive. The lowest-hanging fruit—the big mistakes most companies fail to correct—is generally related to making the path to purchase smooth and uncomplicated. It's been that way for years.

Seth Godin, in *The Big Red Fez: How to Make Any Website Better,* falls into the "economist" or "plumbing" camp. At one point in this short beginner's guide to usability, Godin compares a website to a Japanese game of chance, pachinko. In pachinko, disks are dropped into the top of a wooden box that contains pegs and "scoring holes" at the bottom. Whether or not you win depends on whether the disks bounce crazily off the pegs in such a way that they land in the right scoring area. It's an interesting analogy and, along with other examples given in the book, falls into the economist camp. Godin rightly reminds readers that the business owner needs to be working with a clear endpoint in mind when designing a site and particularly when designing a landing page. Any site may require users (disks) to "bounce off a few pegs" (navigate around a bit), but the amount of bouncing around should be minimized to heighten the probability that the user winds up in the scoring area (buys your stuff or signs up for something).

Is an effective "pachinko machine offer page" a "persuasive" type of architecture? Yes, but mainly due to the architecture itself, as opposed to some kind of mind control.

The most extreme ideologues (or persuaders) are the ones who want you to believe that if you just adopt the right design elements and, in particular, choose the right words to "hypnotize" prospects, you'll create an audience of automatons willing to lap up your wisdom and buy your stuff. Some even delve into neurolinguistic programming to add scientific cachet to their advice and training. But if you can achieve your goals without consulting experts at that extreme, I'm not sure these theories are much more than interesting curiosities. At the very least, they're not appropriate for everyone.

Eisenberg (along with his team at FutureNow) is one of the best-known conversion scientists in the world today, and he seems to marry elements from both camps. As anyone gets more experience in the web marketing field, and as we develop a larger database of results, we tend to gain a more holistic point of view. On one hand, Persuasion Architecture principles (or, for that matter, the "radical decluttering" philosophy from Godin's *Red Fez* book) can easily lead to common-sense testing points to help us fix what is glaringly broken or unduly distracting on a web page. But on the other hand, a long-haul perspective on the data we see can lead to an ongoing exercise in theory construction and debate among a variety of experts.

In that sense, there are no right or wrong answers in a given usability debate, but a lot of great food for thought. Ever thought of the issue of shopping cart "abandonment," for example? Your knee-jerk response to people frequently abandoning the process at stage 3 or 4 might be that there is something wrong with stage 3 or 4. Why? Poorly targeted traffic, rampant comparison shopping, a weak brand, and any number of reasons might mean that an abandonment is predetermined by the user in a high percentage of cases, as they enter the process. They are the quintessential tire-kickers. Or, they may well be interested, but are just budget conscious. They become a latent conversion a year later, smoothly sailing through a checkout process that you wrongly assume is "broken." As Eisenberg brilliantly argues: if only data mining and web analytics were as easy as eyeballing a predigested stat like "cart abandonment rates." It isn't always so.[7]

As an antidote to uninformed hand-wringing about a "bad cart experience" (presumably, you will fix such problems, too, without expecting a smooth cart to be a panacea), if you "focus on providing relevant and persuasive content based on understanding visitor intent, easily inferred from keywords (or ad copy, or the e-mail they arrived from), you'll have a much higher overall conversion rate."[8]

Plumbing aside, your most targeted prospects will be looking for more, not less, content. So lowering the rates of abandonment is a good start, but the next step will be to satisfy the information requirements of those who want to stick around your site awhile. (This is where a well-intentioned interest in creating a "smooth" and "uncluttered" page can lead site developers to fail to test long copy, and lead companies to undercommunicate in general.) Eisenberg wants us to understand who's coming to our site and to create content tailored for them. That's where plumbing stops, and persuasion takes center stage. It's logical to work harder on providing this relevant content to visitors, considering that it's often you, with your carefully written ad triggered by carefully chosen keywords, who induced the user to visit the site in the first place!

Eisenberg's theories are easy to corroborate by looking at your own web stats. Some time ago, by looking at data generated by web analytics service ClickTracks Optimizer, I learned something significant about the users on one of my sites. Those who bought something or filled out a quote request form stayed on the site for an average of seven minutes. Many of them not only read the long copy on one landing page, but also looked at the About Us and other background pages to ensure that they felt comfortable with me and my business. By contrast, those who didn't take action—those who stumbled in from search engines, for example, but quickly found they weren't interested—lasted only an average of 15 seconds on the site. Those users who spent seven precious minutes of their time reading through my material are the most interesting to me. Experiences like these bear out Eisenberg's theories about persuasion. Although I contend that there is more "architecture" in Persuasion Architecture than people realize, Eisenberg brings a truly holistic view to the task, reminding us that clean and simple doesn't mean empty or vacant.

Remove Barriers to Conversion (Unclog the Plumbing)

Think of all the reasons you didn't buy something online this year because it was difficult to do so:

- The site was too slow to load.
- The page was broken somehow.
- The site wasn't optimized to properly display in your browser.
- The site wanted you to install a plug-in.
- The checkout process was lengthy.
- You had to become a member before you could buy (or read) anything.
- There were so many options, you got confused and left.

- There was a form that you needed to fill out that didn't include "District of Columbia" as one of the available states, or Canadian provinces, or in some other way made it impossible for you to "exist."

- The credit card security system didn't like the fact that you were traveling, so your purchase was declined, but there was no alternative means of purchasing.

These and countless more issues are the worst kinds of problems because they deter even eager prospects from completing a transaction or forming a relationship with you. If there are serious barriers to people doing business with you, they usually won't. As Amazon.com chief Jeff Bezos frequently stated on his way to becoming a billionaire: "We're trying to make it easy for people to buy." It helps to know what business you're in, a degree of self-awareness Bezos always brought to his task. Gas stations, I've found, generally don't make it hard for you to pump the stuff into your tank.

Extending the analogy to your business, since you're not Amazon.com, you can't create "1-click ordering." You probably don't have the user's credit card already on file. You may be constrained in how much free shipping you can offer. You might not be able to create a site that is quite as smooth as Amazon's. But by making people really want to buy from you (by persuading them mainly through the relevance of the offer to what they searched for, and through the smoothness of the path, with just the right touches of info-candy and brand image to seal the deal), you reduce the need to be 100% perfect in your site architecture, shopping cart, or other elements of the sales process.

Given the sorry state of so many websites today, pure plumbing will lead to most of the significant increases in ROI. People will be far less likely to buy from you if your site is hard to use or literally broken. There are probably already people who want to do business with you. If you do nothing else, at least don't put roadblocks in their way. That means taking users to appropriate landing pages (instead of the wrong ones). It means ensuring that your web hosting is adequate, that your shopping cart works, that your pages load into all major browsers, and so on. Unclog. Renovate. Declutter. Then, improve your overall level of communication where appropriate, if you have additional budget. You don't have to do it in the middle of the buying process, but somewhere underpinning your marketing (maybe in a lot of places), it helps if you have a "story" to help your customers make sense of why they are buying.

Persuade, Convince, Use Psychology (Persuasion and Storytelling)

Getting rid of barriers to commerce may not be enough. In a sea of conflicting commercial messages, the one that inspires may be the one that gets the sale. To use a dating analogy, sure, removing major barriers is the first step, since getting a date is nearly impossible if, say, you never get out of the house to meet anyone. Removing the obvious impediment of hermit-hood (with online dating, even that barrier is reduced) might be a first and necessary step to getting a date, but it doesn't change the fact that at some point, somebody has to like or be inspired by you. You have to convince! You need to make an attractive offer, even if that's only making sure you have fresh breath when you say, "I know a great coffee shop near here."

The same goes for your business. The fact that you sell jewelry, and that your shopping cart isn't broken, is definitely not going to be enough to convince a high percentage of prospects to buy jewelry from you. There are a lot of jewelers. Why should prospective buyers buy a particular product? Why should they buy from you? If your landing page or site as a whole doesn't provide the answer to that question, then only a small percentage of prospects—those in an enormous hurry, for example—are going to take the plunge and buy.

Let's put it in terms that your ego will hate. But they're important terms, because it's what I and every other prospective customer is probably thinking. "So you're another jewelry store online. I don't give a @#$@!"

There are two primary elements to persuasion online: copywriting and design. Writing good copy is the most obvious of these. Beyond that, web credibility and brand cues are indirect persuaders.

Copywriting

Great sales copy doesn't grow on trees. Like anyone else in this business, I've tried to mix and match a variety of areas of expertise, grabbing insights wherever possible. If you don't have the budget to hire an experienced sales copywriter for your site, you're going to have to develop a little bit of expertise yourself.

The most basic requirement (don't laugh) is that you have copy. I've seen far too many sites with basic three-word product names and pictures of products and little else. Some amateur sellers appear to believe the Web is just an order-taking system, a big catalog that will attract plenty of eager buyers no matter what.

I've come across some mind-bogglers: for example, a successful offline sports apparel business from near Kalamazoo, Michigan, that set up shop online under an entirely different name. They chose a domain name that evoked nothing more than that they were some kind of generic online seller of sports apparel. The site, too, was generic. They had terse product descriptions and little else. No mention was made of their successful bricks-and-mortar presence. What if they had chosen a catchy name like Kalamazoo Sportswear and populated the site with not only full-fledged product descriptions, but an engaging story about the business, including the positive local PR they'd received in newspaper articles?

So don't be shocked when I tell you that the worst kind of copywriting is no copywriting. There are tens of thousands of online businesses out there with virtually no copy on their sites. As a result, they have virtually no online presence. Is a lack of copy also bad for organic search referrals? Don't even get me started.

Believe it or not, some of the advice that is useful for writing small AdWords ads also comes in handy for pages of sales copy that might go on for many paragraphs. It seems to be something of a universal law that in spite of wide variation in industry-specific terminologies, most readers—even prospects of a complicated niche business—get turned off by jargon. Sure, you do have to pay some attention to your prospects' reading level and degree of expertise to avoid talking down to them. But even for the niche reader, wading through jargon-laden presentations can be tedious. Moreover, copy that is too dry can actually suck the enthusiasm out of a prospect. Not every line of business can be "fun," but your potential customer shouldn't approach her relationship with you as if it will be pure drudgery, either.

Don't hesitate to tell a bit of a story, provided the story quickly turns to focus on the benefits of your product or service to the customer and, above all, to the offer you're making and the action you hope the prospect will take.

Be clear and direct in your language. Inject emotional appeal and even sex appeal into your copy wherever that's appropriate. For a software product, you'll want to talk about ROI (money is emotional) and problem solving (alleviating headaches is very emotional). For a motorcycle jacket, referring to a celebrity that once bought one from you would add sex appeal. Certain adjectives like *racy, heavy-duty,* or *vintage* would also add sex appeal, for those who wanted to infer it, or at the very least a sense of status or authenticity.

Let me give you an example from my own portfolio. An enterprise software company was experiencing poor conversion rates on their AdWords campaign, even though they were an industry leader in their human-resources-related field. What was needed was a rescue operation on the landing page copy.

The rescue required two steps. First we eliminated the landing page list of cold, unemotional bulleted points. Next we tackled the industry jargon. In the end we turned a sterile, confusing landing page into an appealing and informative tool to motivate visitors to take action.

Here are a few brief "clips," if you will, of before-and-after copywriting from that landing page:

Before: "performing regular talent inventory gap analysis of your human capital assets"
After: "identifying talent gaps in your current workforce"

Before: "unparalleled level of domain expertise"
After: We eliminated this, along with a variety of other empty boasts, replacing them with concrete information.

Before: "largest group of customer references in the industry"
After: Here, we asked either that they provide a list of testimonials or delete this boast. At first, the only testimonial that appeared on the site was jargon-laden and lukewarm, which was inconsistent with this claim of customer satisfaction.

Before: "...facilitates the end-to-end process of identifying..."
After: "facilitates the process of identifying..." (eliminated redundant buzzword)

Over time, the longer, more detailed sales presentation is likely to hold more interest than bulleted points would for serious buyers. Moreover, the clearer version should convert better than the initial pass with the jargon-laden long copy.

Writing product descriptions that appeal to a target audience in retail is often driven by demographic research or persona research. It might be difficult to prove that one adjective beats another in writing descriptions for Chanel purses, but it's probably safe to say that experienced fashion writers would do a better job at injecting flair into copy for such products than the average person off the street. In a small business, the owner or owners must absolutely become directly involved in communicating with customers and writing sales copy. If you sell designer purses or complicated home renovations, is it realistic to expect your 21-year-old webmaster (for example) to feel the necessary intimate connection with the audience? Yet I've seen businesspeople delegating the task of writing website copy to just such an uninformed person. It depends on your budget, but at some point, customer profiles need to be researched, and someone's going to have to put words on some pages.

Target, but Don't Stereotype

Overprofiling is a pet peeve of mine, and I tend to rant a bit against persona research when it is misused.[9] Marketing is about real customers, not stereotypes; that's why keyword-based search marketing is so powerful. We can remain a little more neutral in our assumptions and tone while leaning heavily on the keyword search itself to segment users.

Think of all the money that's wasted in media that can't lean on search keywords. The Holy Grail of the young male is pursued to foolish extents by old-school ad execs and their clients, pitching the product to the "mode" (statistically the single highest-buying age and sex) rather than figuring out how to reach disparate customers across the entire distribution graph. Ever seen a 50-year-old woman driving a "guy" car like an Infiniti G37? Ever seen a young male financial adviser scooting around in a "chick" car like a BMW 1-series, a well-used Miata, or a "vintage" Fiero? Sure you have!

In your online marketing, do a gut check to ensure that while targeting appropriate audiences, you're not using imagery and wording that alienates prospects who fall outside the "mode." Sure, marketing to "everyone" is a classic rookie mistake. Then again, you can't possibly be marketing to everyone if you sent people to an appropriate landing page from their initial search for **BMW 128i reviews** or **tax consultant Arizona**. By definition, much of what you do with search marketing is already narrow. Is there a need to splinter that market by making silly additional assumptions? (Perhaps that's why less presumptuous page images, such as the androgynous couple appearing on the Skype offer page discussed later in the chapter, can outperform stereotypical images in landing page tests.)

Design Cues: It's about Communication, Not "Hidden Persuasion"

In large part, persuasive design comes back to the improved focus, reduced clutter, standards-based design, brand cues, and other elements I address in this chapter. As entertaining as I find hypnotism as a spectacle, subtle responses to design aren't necessarily "hypnotic" or "creepy." Human cognition and emotion are part of direct response—always have been. Testing can turn up a lot of interesting responses, but your tests will likely stop somewhere short of magic.

Many conversion enthusiasts like to experiment to discover emotional responses to certain layouts, colors, shapes, images, and much more. The complex and allegedly subliminal psychology of design has long been studied by a few experts. Especially in an offline environment, for larger companies with a lot of capital investment at stake, like mall owners and store designers, such studies are indispensable.[10]

Be wary of overestimating the hidden benefits of details such as punctuation, font color, button shape, and imagery. Some of these matters, indeed, could be summed up in a key credo offered by researchers on web credibility: get a site that "looks professionally designed." Unless you have very high sales volumes, you won't be able to test "red versus blue," "triangle vs. oval," for every few pixels on the screen of your landing page. You'll often be working with a professional who can offer you a holistic page concept, and your test will have to be among two or three versions, each of which sort of hangs together with its own internal logic.

And speaking of coherent design logic, sometimes a site wins because it looks "folksy"—or *not* quite professionally designed. That's something you have to test. One client I recall had a terrible-looking site. He said it was on purpose, because a "tactile" site was soothing to his customers in that it seemed to belong to a "real person and not a big company." Then again, he refused to prove it through testing.

Although imperfect, it's often pretty effective to test two completely different versions of an important landing page, each with a distinct design "logic." One of my clients, FourOxen Corp., tested their main landing page by completely overhauling it, stripping out clutter, changing many visual elements, adding a person's face, and more. This was A/B tested against the old page; no complex multivariate testing was tried. The new page converted significantly better (most of the time), but FourOxen didn't come up with that page by studying every variable over a three-year period. The design team put together a new page that would best be described as "completely different" from the old page.

Many elements of the new design probably counted as basic professional competence in the field of landing page design; FourOxen was just staying contemporary and appropriate to their industry vertical. Professional competence and emerging standards that are shared among professionals can frequently offer useful shortcuts that allow us to achieve the results we need without starting from square one in the lab. That said, FourOxen has enough volume that they should now test versions of the winning page with more involved multivariate testing, in order to refine and improve conversion rates even more.

To sum up, your site designs and landing page tests will be built around an appropriately holistic combination of plumbing and persuasion. No need to take hypnosis courses or to hire the "world's best copywriter, Dr. Evil." Unless you're in some niche direct-response area, you can't win with "hypnotic writing" alone. The cartoonish image of advertising and marketing as somehow being able to force or hypnotize intelligent consumers into doing things they wouldn't normally do has persisted since the original advertising critiques came down the pike in the 1950s. But remember what the real leaders were saying in those days. David Ogilvy was telling you to "test the headline," and make it sell! Test the headline. How tricky is that?

So I side with Bob Garfield, a critic of many modern ad campaigns. Garfield insists that many campaigns are so poorly executed that advertising is often not persuasive at all.[11] If you can't get your overt message out there, what value could there possibly be in contemplating subliminal techniques?

Testing Protocols: Best Practice; A/B/C; Multivariate

Most companies design and redesign their sites and important pages based on a wide range of implicit assumptions. Most do not pay much heed to the art and science of response testing.

Extensive user testing experiments (such as focus groups and other laboratory studies) are outside the scope of this chapter, but are recommended for those considering pursuing more advanced paths to insight about user behavior. Here, I'll summarize some prominent approaches to testing that are being used successfully by many response-oriented online companies today.

To begin with, we know that any data collection process requires you to have an eye for statistical significance and validity issues. Most of us in this field are not professional statisticians, and the accuracy of our efforts may not be 100%. But we can do much better if we just stop making silly, unfounded assumptions, and go out seeking really obvious, provable differences in response to different versions of our pages.

"Testing" Method #1: Be a Lot Better from the Start

Web professionals of various stripes, and interactive shops that specialize in user-centered design, should get you part of the way along the path towards constructing higher-response landing pages just based on their past experience, conscientious approach to keeping current with user experience trends, and data about response they may have collected in their firms. Any professional approach to site design and landing page design needs to integrate top-level architectural and brand feel concerns with nitty-gritty layout and copywriting issues. Iteration from "ground zero" will take a very long time if you don't start with something reasonably compelling in the first place. Unfortunately, many design shops and so-called marketing agencies still trade in trends and fads, or are bent on selling you on a particular gizmo or two based on a strong conviction they have about some element of user engagement.

A minority of conversion-focused agencies take revenues and testing protocols more seriously. You can either hire them or learn from them (us) to attempt to incorporate smart principles into your page tests. A good place to start is to ask yourself what kind of offer page, and what kind of targeting, you are dealing with. Should it be:

- A lead-generation page? Will it offer an incentive or white paper?

- A standalone product page? Should it offer related products?

- A product category page?

- A compelling "long copy" information page? How long is long?

- An introductory page, such as a home page, that neatly segments prospects into the correct category?

Depending on which type of page it is, and what other supporting elements are already built into the site, you'll want to begin with a compelling layout. A web producer or web product manager certainly has enough expertise to provide direction, but a qualified design pro might do a better job of creating the layout for the offer page.

There's nothing wrong with looking for strong examples around the Web as a starting point, as long as the tone and objective-setting are appropriate to your business. Let's say you settle on the fact that you're designing a page around a single product but that it is important to increase conversions to the most expensive version of the product. Consider how you will incorporate:

- A relevant headline (and assume that relevance may trump "salesiness").

- A product description (brief but not too brief).

- A brief (but not too brief) statement that differentiates your company.
- Benefit statements (more, or fewer, and where on the page).
- Testimonials, if appropriate.
- Pricing strategy—plan the best psychology, or whether trial offers are preferred.
- Image or images. Consider whether you need high-quality, high-impact, human, or product-based images. Have a designer consider the "flow."
- White space. Is the page too busy?
- Navigation. Is the page "orphaned"? It shouldn't be. But nor should the navigational elements be excessive.
- Call to action, and how it is worded.
- The shape and look of your action buttons or links.

This isn't a test yet. It's just one page. Most companies won't be able to test very well at all, because they're not even working smart enough to plan that single, first page.[12]

A/B, or A/B/C, Testing

If you want to make some major advances or test key differences in page layouts, but don't have enough sales or lead volume to reach statistical significance in a hurry, you should still test something: two or three different versions of a key landing page, for example.

Only five years ago, A/B testing of landing pages online was still new enough that it blew people's minds when a test worked. A few entrepreneurial-minded web professionals managed to lead such processes in their organizations rather than sitting back and leaving it to a few experts at larger companies to reap all the benefit. One such professional was Lee Mills.

Mills, a marketing consultant who has alternated between independent consulting through his firm Beyond Clicks and in-house marketing roles, has conducted a number of landing page tests for clients seeking improved conversion rates. One such test, for Anonymizer.com, showed surprising results. The first landing page (see Figure 11-7) had fairly brief sales copy, a clear offer, and was attractively laid out. Mills and the client didn't believe that the conversion rate of 3.2% could be improved upon very much.

Indeed, this does seem to be a nice page, and 3.2% was a fine result. Nonetheless, a much longer page was also tried (see Figure 11-8). It included more sales copy, more education about the dangers of spyware and threats to Internet privacy, and more information about the benefits of the product. It even included screen shots. This page did far better than the first attempt—it converted at a rate of 9.6%!

In his presentation at a conference in August 2004, Mills said he and his team were surprised by the result because they'd always assumed it was important to minimize scrolling—to keep all the vital information "above the fold." The result doesn't surprise me. We often hear nonsense about the fact that people don't like to read a lot of information—"Keep it simple, stupid"—that sort of thing. Obviously, with a result more than three times better than the short page, this longer

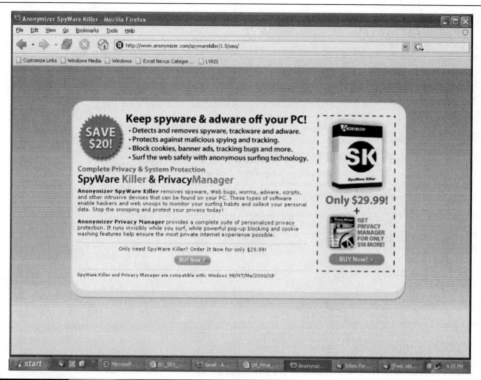

FIGURE 11-7 Good landing page: 3.2% conversion rate

page had something going for it. Having extensive sales copy does not necessarily conflict with the need to maintain a singular focus on converting the prospect into a buyer.

You can do this, too. What will you be testing for? First, of course, you need to decide on which outcome you'll count as a conversion: an order, a lead, or even a soft goal such as reaching the beginning of a signup process.

You'll then need to decide how pages will be rotated and identified so that you have a method for measuring which page led to which conversion rates.

A handy, but slightly imperfect, way of doing this in the past would have been to use Google AdWords itself. Set up an ad group with two identical ads (which, as you know, should rotate evenly if you have ads set to "rotate"), but send traffic to two different landing pages. If you had AdWords Conversion Tracker installed, you might even be able to read the results right in AdWords. According to some analysts, such as Scott Miller of Vertster, a vendor of multivariate landing page testing solutions, this methodology can lead to skewed results. Long story short, returning visitors are not always shown the same page recipe they were shown on a first visit. They may be seeing two or more versions of the page. It's a complicated argument and Miller doesn't prove his point with hard data, but the upshot is, this is a rough and imperfect method to split traffic.

FIGURE 11-8   Great landing page: 9.6% conversion rate

Today, with the available third-party tools, it seems awfully tempting to use tools tailor-made for testing and reporting on the outcomes of tests. Yes, you can relatively easily custom-design a split-testing protocol in-house with the right programming and/or the right attention to your analytics stats. But the available solutions make it easier. I'll discuss these more in the "Multivariate Testing" section.

To run an A/B test, think in terms of two or three major theories you'd like to test, and test them all at once. This is far from a statistically perfect way to do it, but remember, you're trying to get better, not be perfect. It's an absolute myth to believe that you can make meaningful progress by isolating two page elements and testing those, then two more, and testing those, over time. Variable interactions mean that as you pick winners in some areas, you have changed the playing field for the next test. And running all of these small, sequential tests may take forever, because the impact can be so minimal on some test elements as to be trivial. It's better, in most cases, to think in terms of big drivers, and layout approaches—almost like a composite sketch of two or three different "page types."

A perfect example is put forward by Avinash Kaushik in his admonitions to marketers to "just start testing."[13] Skype wanted to test an offer page. Two major kinds of pages were tested.

One, a stylish-looking page with a slightly cheeseball image concept: a hopeful-looking male chatting in proximity to an attractive female. The second page tested showed a female with a slightly obscured friend who might be female, talking in a café-like setting. (Subsequently, I've noticed Skype testing a similar couple hanging out on a boardwalk. Sometimes, one of the partners wears rollerskates. I'd have to guess that they're trying to give us cues of "fun" and "freedom," smart thinking that runs counter to the first instincts of a typical software or telecommunications equipment company.) The key was to determine if the typical cheeseball telecommunications-company sales pitch page would perform better or worse than the understated, but still image-rich, San Francisco-café-chic page.

To offer some added perspective, a new page idea entirely, with much more white space, a bold blue-and-white "paint splash" design, and less imagery, was also tested. Reaching statistical significance on a high volume of sales, the verdict came in: the pleasing white-space page (the upcoming Figure 11-10 shows an example) didn't convert as well as the image-rich pages. And by a significant margin, androgynous freedom-loving friends (see Figure 11-9) beat the earlier-generation cheeseball telco guy-meets-girl trapped in a less evocative white-space layout. The bottom line improvement for Skype, in the form of tangible sales revenue increases, would soon run into six figures. A simple, elegant, and yet reasonably scientific example of an A/B/C test in action.

Take note: the specific outcome in the Skype example is not what is important. The process is something that any qualified designer and marketer, working in tandem, can try. Nothing ventured, nothing gained. In Figures 11-9 and 11-10, you can see that Skype is clearly continuing the testing process they began some time ago. Even after ruling out hackneyed telco imagery, they carry on with new tests. Here, they appear to be segmenting tests by nation and language,

FIGURE 11-9   This image-rich offer page moved the needle for Skype. This advertiser looks to be testing small refinements at this stage, such as heart balloons and a "no adware" benefit statement.

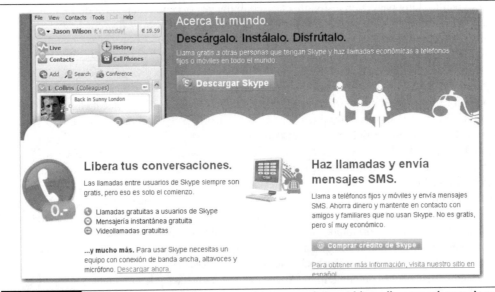

FIGURE 11-10 Anecdotally, the "white space plus screen shots and icons" approach wasn't as successful. But it looks like the advertiser is still keeping it in their testing mix for the time being.

and may well be testing smaller variations in an advanced multivariate test, as they should. For example, does the image sell more or less with the green rainbow or heart-shaped balloons? Which version of the buy or try button works best? Does a mention of "no spyware or adware" help or hurt?

On Statistical Validity

If you run a major e-commerce site or are sending high volumes of traffic to a page, you can test and retest frequently. However, I believe that it's possible to oversell the notion of rapid experimentation. Many companies generate too little traffic—especially if they have multiple low-volume landing pages—to test in the ways that some experts advise.

Several other factors make split-testing more complicated than some would let on. To be sure, understanding basic principles of statistical reliability is helpful, and simple tools like the Vertster Clickthrough Rate Validity Checker (see www.vertster.com/adwords-tool/default.asp) can help you get a feel for this (see Figure 11-11). Using the tool, I told it I had received 28 clicks from ad A and a CTR of 3.0% (which means that I must have had, according to the tool, 933 impressions). For ad B, I told it I got 39 clicks for a CTR of 4.3%, which means that I must have had 906 impressions of that ad. One of the things these tools are good at demonstrating is how you reach a high level of reliability in a split-test sooner when there is a wider gap in CTR performance. In this case, the gap is fairly wide—4.3% to 3.0%. Vertster's statistical analysis tells me that 80% of the time, the current winner will continue to be the winner in the future.

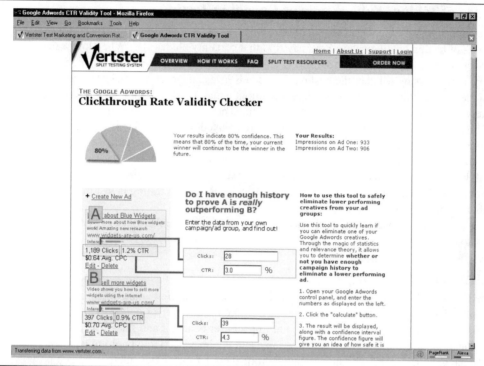

FIGURE 11-11 Vertster's Clickthrough Rate Validity Checker (GWO is more powerful)

A better tool, though, is not ad-focused but landing-page focused. Google's Website Optimizer (GWO) tool (discussed in more detail later in the chapter) has a more sophisticated wizard that will offer projections of how long it will take for your A/B landing page tests—or even complex multivariate landing page tests—to reach a high statistical confidence level. Just punch in your particulars, and GWO will offer you some projections. It will update those projections, and statistical confidence measures, on the fly as you run your tests, too.

Unfortunately, the reality here is complicated. What if your CTRs or conversion rates don't diverge as much as this example? Given the wide variety of user motivations and mind-sets as they arrive on your site, how can you know that a conversion rate of 0.70% is really significantly better than 0.63%? It might take you quite a while to find out. This suggests to me that you are often better off gaining a deeper understanding of your marketplace and of web persuasion theories that will ultimately allow you to create new landing pages with *vastly* improved performance. If you go from 3% to 9%, you won't have a tough decision as to which page performs better. Unless you have very high volumes, beware the myth that testing landing pages is about making dozens of minute tweaks. It's about rethinking your communications strategy so that you're making big leaps forward in performance. Those leaps are the ones that make you feel confident about making permanent changes.

Beware of Taking "Soft" Events as Gospel in Testing

If you happen to be using a lead or other nonrevenue event as your conversion event for the purposes of testing landing pages, you may find that certainty eludes you. When long sales cycles are in play, you'll need to go through more complex processes of ensuring high lead quality, and assessing whether the best page for leads is also the best for total revenue generation down the road, all things being equal. Again, without a massive data mining operation, you're unlikely to get right answers to the toughest questions here. Just be aware that you may be fumbling around in a fog if your revenue events are delayed. Beware of leads that are too easy to generate. Many businesses, for all their efforts to improve their measurement protocols, will also need to sift through leads and sales to get a qualitative sense of issues like lead quality and overall business improvement. Not every business is set up to give instant answers as to which page or site design leads to the best *long-term* response. Response testing is just that: it's most suitable for direct-response businesses.

Let's move on to discuss more advanced testing of a larger number of page "permutations": multivariate testing.

Multivariate Testing

In Chapter 8, in discussing ad testing, I provided an overview of how multivariate testing works. The principles are similar for landing pages as they are for ads. Let's say you identify four important page elements that you think might impact user behavior and sales conversions: the left navigation area, the headline, the body copy, and the imagery (large photo of a person, say). For the navigation on the left, you feel that additional clutter may be distracting, so you propose two versions: the current one, plus a cleaner version with the same links but not the additional promotional boxes. You want to try two new versions of the headline, and test those against the current headline. Body-copy-wise, you might want to test a relatively simple theory—long vs. short copy, for example—or something substantive, like adding or subtracting a second (redundant) call to action statement, or adding or subtracting a free bonus offer. Finally, you have two versions of the large image that you'd like to test against the current image, and no image. The total number of page permutations, varying these four elements, comes to:

$$2 \times 3 \times 2 \times 4 = 48$$

Sound silly to test 48 versions of a page? Well, it isn't feasible in many cases because of low volume, so you may need to employ simpler 8-, 16-, 24-, or 32-permutation tests. But it definitely isn't silly. Out of 48 page permutations, it's not uncommon that one or two versions combine the elements in a way that gets things just right from the user's perspective. The whole, here, really can turn out to be more than the sum of the parts.

With the correct kind of reporting, you get information not only about which is the winning "recipe," but about which elements contributed the most to better or worse performance. Strategically and mathematically, experts advise that you should continue running the entire test until it reaches statistical significance, even if one element (say, the headline) can be declared a clear winner earlier than the rest. The second-best headline, for example, may wind up being in the winning overall recipe, when combined with certain other variables on the page, due to a phenomenon known as "variable interactions." This is like saying: this is only the second-best sermon, but when delivered in a stone church with a flower garden, by a bald pastor, on a sunny day in April, the second-best sermon is part of an overall winning recipe (for "best overall experience" leading to, say, higher donations) that beats out several recipes that include the "best" sermon, such as the best sermon being delivered by a blond pastor on a sunny day in a wood-and-glass church with a flower garden in August. It's all about how things hang together.

Recently, Google developed a fantastic tool for multivariate testing called Google Website Optimizer. It requires Google Analytics to be installed, and for your techie to install additional code on the landing page. In addition to a certain amount of technical competence, GWO relies on you to have sound thinking and strategy, solid creative inputs (images, copy, and so on), and a structure for planning and evaluating results. Because GWO does such a great job of managing, monitoring, and reporting on the tests, I'll focus on Google's product and provide a case study to really hammer home the potential benefit.

Which Pages Should You Test?

Testing sounds easy, but it's a fair bit more resource-intensive than it sounds, so consider focusing on one or two key pages to start. The page with the most impact on conversions, especially from paid search campaigns, will be one reasonably close to the end of a transaction. This might be a lead-generation page, a product page, or a category page.

On the flip side, though, low-volume pages don't lend themselves well to testing. Some small businesses can do pretty well by just improving a mediocre home page, even though there will be additional intermediate steps beyond that before the user initiates a purchase. If your home page has by far and away the most traffic, you should probably be testing its independent impact on conversion events.

Quick reminder: GWO will measure conversion rates from all traffic sources, including direct referrals, direct visits, and organic traffic—not just paid search traffic. Whereas paid search clicks often go to targeted, internal pages, the rest of your traffic might quite often be coming to the home page. So testing the home page is a good move for a lot of sites.

If you're concerned about messing with success, you can also set GWO to show test pages only to a portion (whatever percentage you like) of visitors, while showing the majority of users the default or current page.

As you run a test, the power of the interface becomes evident. Several helpful screens show you how your apparently simple testing ideas are contributing to a complex testing process (for an example, see Figure 11-12).

Quick Case Study: Planning and Executing a Multivariate Test with GWO

"Big money goes around the world." Or so says a song title by Rush, a band adored by the clients who own Rex Art, the art store and e-commerce site I'll be using for this case study. Since the client and I like to trade Rush references, expect me to work a few into the mix here. This is not intended to be an exhaustive study of the GWO product,[14] but I'll show you how a typical small business can benefit from using Google's tool for multivariate landing page testing.

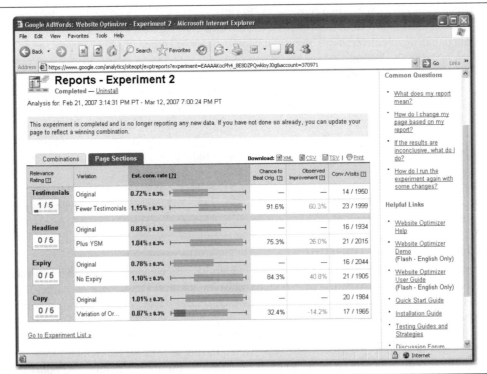

FIGURE 11-12 A glimpse at one of my own early GWO tests. It involved four page elements of my e-book offer page, totaling 16 page combinations.

The planning phase, bringing background and expertise, or at least hypotheses, into the process, is what separates real testing from random tinkering. Not only does the test improve business results, we hope it will help to educate the client on what makes their customers tick, and what kinds of considerations might inform future tests. Our high-level goal here was to improve response to the home page. In collaboration with the client, Page Zero's role would include contributing some design elements, headline copy, body copy, and so forth, as well as an accelerated yet sophisticated (we think!) usability analysis.

Beware the Sounds of Salesmen

I hope this account serves as a realistic but optimistic antidote to the breathless "we increased conversion rates 500%!!" case studies so often seen out there, that don't tell you that they did so by removing obvious nonperforming keywords from a paid search account or by fixing obvious shopping cart problems. Starting from a low base certainly makes any improvement story sound more impressive, but I assume most of you are looking to pick the middle-hanging fruit, not that easy-to-reach low-hanging variety.

Methodology Basics

Although our methodology was based on a wealth of experience and a study of relevant theory, the roadmap we created was practical. The goal was to plunge in quickly to create a properly diverse set of page combinations, while also fixing glaring problems with the home page.

- After a brief initial cleanup comprised of "must do, can't test everything" edicts from Page Zero, the existing (slightly modified) home page would serve as the control for the experiment. (The slight modification proved its mettle in short order, in a brief A/B test.)

- We identified four strong potential influencers on performance, and generated creative alternatives for each page element to be tested. The test would have two values for three of the elements, and three values for the fourth, so 2×2×2×3 = 24 permutations.

- Our developer used GWO to install the correct code snippets on the page, and to point to the location from which the various creative elements would be served. A visitor to the page is cookied, to maintain the accuracy of the test in case of latent sales or repeat visits.

Assumptions

Among other things, we assumed:

- The home page is an important page on this site. A high proportion of the company's sales still comes from "core" paid search words, and while it's important to discuss the whole keyword portfolio, economic performance is definitely dependent on making such core words work. The home page served as a good landing page for this core keyword inventory, such as "art supplies," but it had to improve.

- Low volume of overall traffic would require a long test period, but related to the preceding point, being relatively high volume, the home page is an excellent candidate for a test.

- We agreed to live with a variety of extraneous influences on the test, such as seasonality, shifting proportions of paid and unpaid clicks, and so forth.

- The math of a higher-converting home page made this worth the time, effort, and consulting cost—even for a small business. Significantly higher profit margins carry over for the long term and also make total profit go up faster than expected in many cases, because it becomes economically feasible to buy a higher volume of paid clicks.

- We used our background in the industry to zero in on what to test, funneled through the lenses of "better plumbing" and "better persuasion." Thinking deeply about customers and their mindset is one thing we tried to do. The easier work was drilling in on elements of the page we thought clearly sucked.

Page Elements Chosen

After arbitrarily eliminating some page clutter and moving some other things to reorient priorities, we selected four page elements to test. Depending on your site's traffic volumes, you can't test everything, unfortunately.

- **Headline** If you have any kind of core message, headline, tagline, or other element at the top of an offer page or home page, this seems to be a perennial influencer of results. It's telling the user what you are, but it's here that you can also introduce doubts in the user's mind. You can unwittingly plant negative or misleading thoughts that lead to an aversion to doing business with you. The three headlines tested could be summarized as follows: (a) the original, a long headline alluding to discounts and a free shipping offer; (b) a shorter headline eliminating the free shipping offer and alluding to a wide selection as well as the discounts; (c) a shorter headline alluding to trust and the company's history selling online since 1995.

- **Body copy** This is a company proud of its dedication to its niche and its long tenure online. But we simply wondered about the time-honored long-copy vs. short-copy conundrum. I rewrote the fairly compelling long copy to reduce the number of benefits and information points, while hopefully conveying the same message. At this stage, I feel like the test isn't quite right because the short copy doesn't get a fair shot; it seems to unduly change the whole feel of the page by being so short. Body copy, too, falls squarely within the range of persuasion and getting a message sharply across to the target customer, but it's potentially a navigational issue also. Do people scroll and read? Do they scan? The beauty of multivariate testing is that we don't need a theory to tell us what is right—we just need the theory to prod us into testing something. The test can prove or disprove the theory that long copy is too long, but it does so more conclusively when the test also takes into account variables in other page elements (a perfect recipe overall).

- **Clutter-muck #1** We thought the whole site was too cluttered. There were four small boxes with different product promotions and other info at the top of the body copy. Small is still annoying if there is too much stuff. This element was tested as a simple present or absent element: yes or no to the promo boxes. It's mainly about plumbing, in the sense that we're looking for the statistical rationale to go ahead and declutter what we felt was a cluttered interface. Test, don't guess.

- **Clutter-muck #2** Yet another clutter element, there was a box for a rotating featured special that pushed other info boxes, such as the shipping offer, farther down the page in the right navigation. Could this element alone contribute to lower conversion rates? We went with the present or absent test here, too, and we did it for the exact same reason as the other test: we thought the home page was too cluttered, but we needed proof.

Early Feedback: Bad Plumbing Hurts, and Better Persuasion Doesn't Help

At first, we were getting some pretty mixed results from our testing. This first test ran over many weeks, and the numbers were somewhat conclusive, and sobering. Three of our four testing elements got no better, and sometimes worse, results. But all was not as it seemed.

Read on and you'll see that persisting to test our hypotheses for a second round was the key to truly translating concepts into action. But for the first go-round, here's what we found:

- "Short copy" was the biggest loser. The original converted much better.

- Eliminating three cluttery product promo boxes above the body text did not hurt conversions, but it didn't help, either. It seems that "clean design" has its limits.

- Two new headlines we tried were pretty big losers, also. The longer (original) one was the winner. We believe this was because it contained the shipping offer, which is a real driver to conversions and user behavior throughout the process of filling the cart. At this point the belief that I am smarter than the client is starting to wane. I'm thinking "any escape might help to smooth the unattractive truth."

- The decision to remove the "rotating special" promo box in the upper-right margin was a good one. Given what a small part this played in the overall page layout, the modest improvement in conversions here was proof of our hypothesis. This eliminated clutter, but also moved (yet another) mention of the shipping offer up into view.

- We settled on the winning combination (not exactly the same as the winner of each variable showdown, but close) as our base new home page. At this point, the winning combination was only 33.7% better in terms of conversion rates than the original, with only a 36% chance of beating all combinations. An OK result, but not too conclusive.

So far, you're underwhelmed. In the first test, the winning combination eked out only a slight victory over the original. Many of the contending combinations were so much worse than the original that the ensuing graph of competing combos showed so much "red" it was embarrassing. (Or as Geddy Lee sang in 1984, "I see red, and it hurts my head.")

What We Did for Test #2

Test #2 was much better. In debating what to include in the second test, we had to shelve several test ideas, or simply implement additional changes arbitrarily, because too many combinations hinders the effort to reach statistical significance in a reasonable time frame. We wanted to limit it to 8 or 12 page permutations this time. You don't want to be testing for months on end.

I carried over some nagging concerns about the winners and losers from before. I felt that the "short copy" I'd contributed wasn't implemented too well. In some page combinations, the short copy came out looking weird. I decided the solution would be to write "medium-length copy" while continuing to attempt to improve the messaging. I also tried to exercise some control over visual layout. Finally, I experimented with signing it more personably—the Rex Art Family—as the family-owned business aspect is touted in other parts of the messaging but for some reason, in the original copy, that signature said "staff" rather than "family."

I also thought the "original" headline still wasn't optimal. But rather than tinker with it again, I tested a font and color change.

Finally, we decided to learn more about the "clutter boxes" above the text. Conversion rates were about the same when we eliminated them. What if we added three more of the pesky little critters? My wife looked at this in action before we ran the test and exclaimed "yikes, that's just wrong. I'd leave the site immediately." Her concern proved to be more or less warranted.

Testing copy variations, headline font, and clutter boxes gave us eight combos this time around, a relatively simple 2×2×2 test.

The Consumer Response

This time around, the test reached statistical significance ahead of the expected schedule. GWO (rather than the familiar "you have an estimated 29 days to go…") shouted "Congratulations! Combination #4 is the winner!" a mere ten days into the test. Ah, the payoff.

So what exactly happened here?

My persistence in trying to improve the sales copy was rewarded. The first time out, we didn't prove that "short copy worked" but we also didn't prove the original copy was optimal. As it turns out, my medium-length copy worked well with other page elements. It included a revamp of the H1 level headings and a change of the heading fonts, but also another extensive copy rewrite. This was a big winner, proving that clarity and persuasion are integral to the customer experience. It also proves that iteration is important in copywriting. As superstitious as it sounds, your subsequent drafts always seem to get better when you allow the first version to age on the page (really, in your mind) like a fine wine.

The new, crisper font and color for the headline grabbed an early lead, but convergence set in and it didn't make any difference in the end. Bear in mind, different *wordings* for the headlines had been clear losers in test #1. People were reading and noticing what was being said, the first time around.

And what about the clutter boxes? Having three boxes above the text wasn't a negative, but six boxes was a slight conversion killer. A no-brainer? Maybe so. But now we know. I doubt we'll be going to nine boxes.

As we concluded the test, the winning combination was converting 106% better than the winning combo from the first test, and the second- and third-place combos, 63% and 51% better. After two tests, we were clearly doubling conversion rates from the original.

The changes pursued here stop well short of a full site redesign, multichannel branding campaign, or business plan changes, which could have a more dramatic effect. But a doubling of conversions from mostly organic referral traffic, and broad paid terms like "art supply" arriving at the home page, is no small victory.

Despite the increasing accessibility of complex testing to the average business, the multivariate nature of the interactions makes this process more complex than one-dimensional, haphazard hackers and tweakers often let on. As for practitioners of the "old ways" of testing response—to close out with another lyric from Rush's Neil Peart—can they "face the knowledge that the truth is not the truth"? Can you say "obsolete"?

Will This Testing Potentially Harm Organic Rankings?

For a small company to so ruthlessly test its home page, especially when it's responsible for more than 50% of the company's overall traffic due to favorable organic rankings, seems reckless.

Jamie Roche has advocated such testing,[15] and GWO spokespeople have stated that such tests won't harm search rankings. But where's the proof? Is it a question of appetite for risk? A question of whether the conversion rate improvement offsets any disruption to rankings that leads to a decline in organic traffic? Or are rankings left largely unaffected? Are there cases where organic search rankings might actually improve, as in the decluttering effort that leads to potentially quicker page load times and more user time spent on site, which are quality signals that might increase organic and paid search standing? I'm afraid this elephant in the room is so complicated that I'll have to mix that metaphor in a future publication, perhaps titled *The Complicated Elephant on the Home Page*. But clearly there is enough doubt here to suggest that no one should just plunge into arbitrarily testing important pages, without understanding the risks and rewards.

GWO Does A/B Tests Too

Good news! If you want to run a simpler, A/B test, GWO is a handy interface to run one of these as well. It has specific setup options for A/B testing. In using GWO for this, you'll benefit from the quality of the reporting interface, and fantastic features like showing the test page to a smaller proportion of incoming visitors, to minimize the potential negative impact of testing on your business results.

More Advanced Testing Services

GWO isn't geared to handle every complex application. Some leading third-party testing software/services are available and well respected for allowing large businesses to conduct advanced multivariate or A/B testing. These include Vertster, Optimost, Test&Target by Omniture, and SiteSpect. SiteTuners.com is a well-known leader in the service end of this business, marrying advanced mathematical analysis and consulting with proprietary software.

A Few Things to Consider Testing

In retail, it's customary to spend time testing the actual content of your offer. What is your customer getting, for what price? You can always test to see if highlighting the following elements improves your conversion rates:

- Free shipping (and how that benefit is conveyed)
- Free gift or add-on
- Time-limited discount
- Bulk discount
- Price increase or decrease

The last element is one that many sellers overlook. Sellers of software and information often underprice their material. Unless you test the total revenue potential of different price points, you may be leaving money on the table. You might also be projecting a discount image that could hurt you long term. On the other hand, your goal might actually be to increase your customer base quickly, if you calculate that lifetime value is potentially high. In that case, you might consider lowering prices if you can see a significant volume increase at that lower price point.

If They Don't Buy, Get Them to Do Something

Many businesses sell products and services with a price point that is just so high, the conversion rate is too low to gain any measurable feedback for many months. If your business is like this, you need to create *proxy* metrics. If a potential customer of Cubicles, Etc., requests a fabric sample, for example, this generates zero revenue at first. But if fabric sample requests tend to convert into sales at a consistent rate, then the conversion rate from clicks to fabric sample requests becomes a valuable metric, one that occurs with more frequency than sales.

When you're measuring conversion rates, then, keep in mind that in looking at final sales, you might not be measuring the most *appropriate* or *helpful* conversion rate. By helpful, I mean the conversion rate that will help you analyze data and quickly adjust your campaign to respond to it. An early client of mine, Brookbend Outdoor Furniture, considered distribution of a color catalog to be an important metric even in the absence of an immediate sale. Similarly, another small company, Bruce Baird's California Golf Schools, considers a brochure request as an important metric, along with an online information request (a lead, if you will). Many service businesses capture leads or other "weak" expressions of interest given the infrequency of, and delay in completing, sales. The goal is that you organize your sales process such that you're measuring *something,* so that you can take the feedback on that conversion rate and improve from there, for example by adjusting bids, deleting ad groups, or turning off content targeting.

Earlier in the chapter, I warned about taking "weak" or "soft" conversions as gospel in testing. True, they don't equate 100% to revenue. But many businesses feel strongly that customers converting to these soft actions are consistent in their behavior down the sales cycle, so they're willing to highlight the soft conversions in their response tests on the site. In fact, without using these, they wouldn't be testing at all. If you are one of those businesses that has a long sales cycle, don't put off testing; instead, build a system that allows you to test some kind of a response. You might be amazed at what you find. Without real testing, you'll be relegated to looking woefully at web analytics stats like high bounce rates. Seeing that a lot of users "puke" when they arrive at a page is not only uninspiring, it's relatively uninformative.

What Are Typical Conversion Rates?

Just a few of the examples in this chapter indicate the wide variety in conversion rates. As I discussed earlier in this chapter, two Anonymizer.com landing pages tested by Lee Mills were widely disparate at 3.2% and 9.6%, respectively.

My advice is, don't try to guess what others in your industry are "converting at." These numbers can be artificial anyway. If your AdWords account is restricted to only very highly targeted words, you might convert at a very high rate. But that might mean your volume is too low. The more words you add in an attempt to increase volume, the greater the chances that your average conversion rate will fall. But if these new words were quite inexpensive, they'd perform well from an ROI standpoint regardless of the actual conversion rate number.

If you read reports on typical industry conversion rates, take them with a grain of salt. Conversions are highly dependent on what type of listing users clicked on, what type of search they did, and so on. Conversions also might vary from product to product.

For companies generating certain types of leads, conversion rates could be higher or lower depending on how much effort is required of users filling out a contact form or survey. On its core (most targeted) keywords, an insurance-related campaign I worked on saw 20% of the visitors who clicked on an ad beginning to fill out a survey that would ultimately generate a lead for the sales force to follow up on. Only about half that number—10%—completed the survey, thus counting as a "lead." That might have indicated problems with the usability and smoothness of the survey process, but some of the drop-off could be attributed to a normal filtering process, where inappropriate prospects dropped off as they discovered they did not qualify. There is always something to improve in any online sales process, but by and large, this result was satisfactory. What wasn't so easy to take was the escalating prices on clicks for those core keywords! Once generated, only about 10% of the leads turned into sales. Because 10% of clicks had turned into leads, only about 1% (10% of 10%) of the clicks on these core words ultimately turned into sales, meaning that 100 clicks were required for each sale. So in this case, at a hypothetical cost of $5 per click, the cost per sale was $500.

Depending on how you look at it, this could indicate a problem with the sales force, but it also could have been attributed to the quality of the leads. Or, it might simply have been normal for the industry. The horrible secret (though it should come as no surprise to anyone with empathy for consumers) is that products and services that aren't in demand generate conversion rates close to zero. Confused visitors clicking on misleading ads convert at rates near zero. And inappropriate, poorly thought-out landing pages convert at rates near zero. No matter whether your industry benchmark is 0.5%, 1%, or 10%, you're clearly getting nowhere and likely losing money quickly when your conversion rate is zero. I wish I could say that never happened. In reality it does, because in a competitive marketplace there are often too many sellers of goods and services, and not enough buyers.

Retail Landing Page Design: Focus vs. Selection

One of the key dilemmas in landing page design is whether to be highly focused on a particular product or to also provide related product suggestions or similar products in a category, to evoke selection or to trigger a Goldilocks effect.

Category Page vs. Single-Product Page

If you run a site with a catalog involving a lot of individual products, what converts better, a category page listing a variety of products under a given heading or a product-specific page? For starters, that depends on the ad. For example, a specific brand name attached to a wristwatch wouldn't take potential customers to a huge selection of all watches. At the same time, they probably wouldn't take them to the page for a single watch unless their selection was small or that watch was a particularly hot item. They usually wouldn't get more specific than a category page for, say, a variety of Timex watches, simply because most watch makers have hundreds of individual models and it would usually be impractical to build a campaign with several thousand ads all going to separate landing pages.

Most of the experts I've talked to lean towards category pages, but none of them rely exclusively on them. A category page, as long as it looks inviting (such as the nicely designed "coffee, tea, & espresso" page at KlinQ.com in Figure 11-13), offers an interesting happy medium between the home page and a single product page.

Keep in mind that if everyone already knew that they wanted a "Beacon Hill Sugar Bowl with Spoon," there would be no need for search! Consumers, at least those who are shopping for gifts or housewares to upgrade their current lifestyle, want to browse various designs, brands, and sizes. A category page is often a great place to start. This can be enhanced with "featured suggestions" to give the user a sense of the breadth of the site's selection.

The thing about rules, such as "minimize clicks at all costs" or "reduce the number of items on the page," is that you need to have enough flexibility to violate them for a good reason. By all accounts, there is absolutely nothing wrong with showing the shopper images of several related products in a category. If a brand is strong enough, or if the site makes a lasting enough impression on users, they may return later to buy one or more products, or they may decide to buy something they weren't considering when they first performed a search.

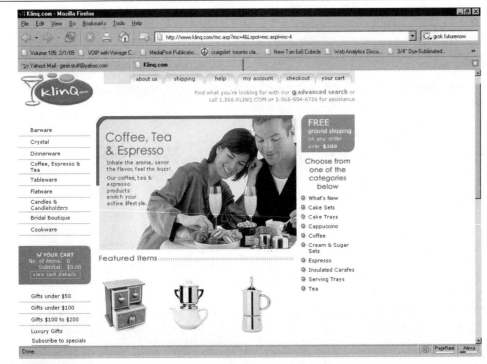

FIGURE 11-13   A nice category page with custom photography and cosmopolitan flair. The text probably should be tested further.

Your site may not have an obvious category that relates to every popular keyword that you're bidding on, but you can still take the user to a dynamically generated "site search results URL." The Pier 1 Imports site has no category page for "director's chairs," for example, but users are still taken to a page full of director's chairs by way of the URL for a site search. (Depending on your situation, you may want to work with your site developer to hard-code such results pages and make them into shorter URLs, or indeed turn them into category pages.) Misty Locke of Range Online Media, who works on Pier 1's campaign, has stated that pages like this selection of director's chairs in Figure 11-14 do quite well in terms of conversions from click to sale.

Locke has also found that successful results came as a result of testing the search advertising copy. She found that an ad with flair, including the phrase "lights, camera, action," produced higher conversion rates on director's chairs. She believes this may be partly as a result of Pier 1's strong brand and its middle-class target audience, who already know basically what type of product they want.

Advanced shopping cart functionality (or even more advanced personalization technology at leading destination e-commerce sites like Amazon) will do a good job of suggesting related items

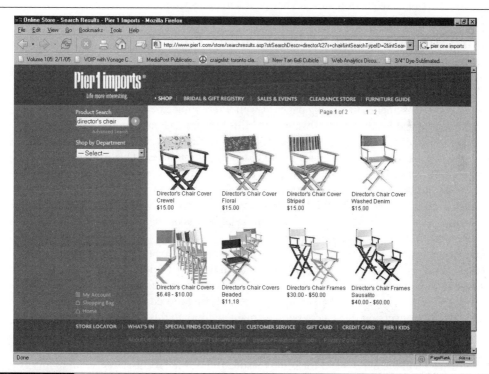

FIGURE 11-14 While singular in focus, this page offers the shopper an easily navigated selection of director's chairs.

Goldilocks and the Three Soup Ladles

Consider a "good, better, best" attitude when working on related product layouts, to encourage users to opt for the "middle" or "top end" product depending on their psychological inclination. Moving more buyers to the middle category ("Goldilocks approach") can be achieved by putting the high-end product slightly out of reach, moving the midpriced item up in price, and positioning the lower-end product as too basic, or somewhat deficient. Need anyone remind you that even a soup ladle can be "aspirational"?

that the searcher might also want to look at. While that may appear to violate my rule of thumb "don't suggest other things until they've become a customer," some retail environments are more amenable to users browsing among various items. Indeed, some sales of lower-priced items may have virtually zero profit margins, so it's incumbent on retailers to make potentially well-heeled customers aware of a couple of related higher-priced items as well.

Ensure Keywords Are on the Landing Page

We've discussed scent. Let's reinforce the point, perhaps ad nauseam. (If you're puking, skip ahead. There is no Back button in a book.) In search, consistency is key. You already know that ads often receive a higher CTR when you include the searched-for keywords in your ad title and/or ad copy. This applies to landing pages as well. Presenting case studies on his clients Anonymizer.com and St. Bernard Software, Lee Mills has stressed on several occasions that taking care to add core keywords to the landing page will almost always raise conversion rates. (It's pretty cool that Lee made this point before Google ever introduced Quality-Based Bidding, and before folks started "harping on that stuff.") This is why many companies will write several dedicated landing pages to improve conversion rates. For example, if you're running ads on **car insurance** as well as **personal watercraft insurance**, you'd probably get better response if you had a separate landing page for each including those keywords on the page, rather than taking all searchers to the same generic **vehicle insurance** page.

One of my former clients, a financial institution, wanted to focus heavily on home mortgage refinancing, but during the AdWords campaign, their IT department was slow in creating a tailored landing page for that product line. Instead, those who clicked on the ad for mortgage refinancing were taken to an application form tailored to new homeowners! Needless to say, conversion rates were poor, as many visitors to this page immediately left. When a more targeted landing page was finally developed, conversion rates doubled. Should be obvious, but until recently, the "get me bottom line results, but I have no control over the website" crowd had the upper hand for some reason. Today, the "scent-savvy" community is gaining the upper hand.

Web Credibility

The state of mind of many new visitors to your site can probably be summed up in one word: incredulous. Who are you? Why should they believe you? Will you deliver on your promises? Will you rip them off?

When I go through the swift process of buying a book on Amazon.com, I'm 99.9% certain that the information I see is reliable and that my order will be fulfilled to my satisfaction. That degree of certainty drops significantly if a site is less familiar to me.

Unless you are a major brand or are dealing with a repeat customer, you have a fair bit of work to do to ensure that the visitor is "in your camp," taking your word for what you claim on the site.

I'm convinced that if everyone took the various principles of web credibility seriously, starting with a deep understanding of the fact that online interaction can still feel distant and unfeeling to many, most of the other pieces of the puzzle of creating better conversion rates would fall into place relatively easily. Do yourself a favor and pick up a copy of B. J. Fogg's book, *Persuasive Technology,* and focus on Chapter 7, "Credibility and the World Wide Web."

B. J. Fogg and Stanford Research on Web Credibility

Web surfers face an ongoing challenge: to "determine what information is credible." Web designers, to connect businesses and organizations with potential clients, must "create highly credible sites."[16]

Do we actually know what increases or decreases web users' perception that the information they find on a site is credible? Thanks to studies carried out by the Stanford Persuasive Technology Lab, we actually have a very good idea. Between 1999 and 2002, Fogg's team conducted large-scale studies as well as some smaller pilot studies involving over 6,000 participants in total. The 1999 study involved 1,409 participants, and the 2002 study involved 1,649. The average age in the first study was 32.6 years; in the second, 35.5. More than half the participants were Finnish; most of the rest were American. Gender was about 45% female and 55% male in both studies. Participants were typically middle-income college graduates with extensive Internet experience.[17]

By and large, the findings do not contradict the investigators' hunches about what factors increase and decrease credibility scores. According to the Stanford studies, the following are some key factors that increase credibility:

- The site gives the organization's physical address.
- The site gives a contact phone number.
- The site looks professionally designed.
- The site lets you search for past content.
- The site is linked to by a site you think is believable.
- The site has articles containing citations and references.

- The site lists authors' credentials for each article.
- The site provides a quick response to customer service questions.
- The site was recommended by a friend.
- The site represents an organization you respect or a news organization.

Want to blow your credibility? The following seem to be no-no's:

- The site is sometimes unexpectedly unavailable.
- The site makes it hard to distinguish ads from content.
- The site is rarely updated with new content.
- The site is difficult to navigate.
- The site has a typographical error.
- The site's domain name does not match the company name.
- The site links to a site you think is not credible.
- The site has a link that doesn't work.
- The site automatically pops up new windows with ads.
- The site takes a long time to download.

The people—at least those in this study—have spoken, and the preceding are the factors they say most influence their perceptions. In the real world, some of these mistakes can be even more damaging than the study might indicate. And some of the "must-haves," like providing contact information, are becoming more important all the time.

Bear in mind that Fogg and his researchers believe that credibility is made up of two dimensions: perceived trustworthiness (unbiased, fair, honest) and perceived expertise (knowledgeable, experienced, intelligent).[18]

TIP   *For a handy summary of web credibility guidelines, visit http://credibility.stanford.edu/ guidelines/index.html.*

Don't Neglect Site Search

Recall that an element of web credibility is the ability to search for archived material. On an e-commerce site, people are looking for products, not articles. It's vital that there be a search box to help consumers who are having trouble navigating through your categories to find the item they're looking for. Site search has become increasingly sophisticated. Successful e-commerce site developers know which options are available and whether they are built into the shopping cart package you're using, or whether a customized version of a third-party solution might be required.

Be wary if your developer seeks to reinvent the wheel by throwing together his own "homemade" search engine. Product search and the ability of a site search tool to suggest related items can be a complex matter.

> **NOTE** *Amazon.com is one of the world's top search technology companies. The ability for users to browse their huge catalog without getting lost is an important driver of Amazon's current profitability, since this increases the average order size.*

If you want to maximize your conversion rates and you have more than a few pages on your site, you need quality site search. Some low-cost and free site search options are offered by companies like Atomz and Google, but make sure that you investigate fully. The lowest-end products might not be sufficient for your needs. Unfortunately, Google's dominance in search makes the average manager think that site search is easy. A strong domain-specific vendor or developer (someone well versed in e-commerce) can build good site search relatively easily. But as you stray into open source platforms and custom programming for a variety of more complex types of website, don't underestimate the complexity you may face. Search is a cost, and searching a large database well may require programming resources as well as a budget for improving site performance, database performance, and server capacity.

Factors Outside Your Control

Don't confuse luck with brains. Sometimes, you don't have total control of how users will behave from day to day. However, while you may not be able to control these factors, you can plan for them.

Seasonality

Every market has up and down seasons. Housing, taxation, and retail gifts are three of the most obvious examples. Unless you have at least two years' worth of conversion data at your disposal, it can be difficult to know whether your site is converting well or not, adjusted for season. What appears to be a drop-off or an increase might simply be normal activity. How well do you understand your own business?

Hot Sectors

If you've begun working on a campaign for a product that is just hitting the market and is hard to find, you could wind up reaping windfall profits, because that's what search is really good for: connecting users with niche areas quickly. GPS phones were hard to find not long ago. One site owner in this area reaped windfall profits as a result. The design of the site had very little to do with the high conversion rates, and the drop-off in ROI that will inevitably occur as more competitors move in can't be blamed on AdWords campaign techniques or site design.

Hot sectors will eventually cool off. Users in more mature industries know that they can comparison shop. You need to allow for that. The reason people don't comparison shop when something is brand new is likely because early adopters come to the table with a status-driven "must have" mentality. If the iPod cost $1,500 and sold out very quickly from retail stores, you can bet that there would be a few bleeding-edgers who would buy from the site that could promise them fast delivery regardless of price.

360-Degree View: Create a Good Conversion Environment

The popularity of the TV show *What Not to Wear* has convinced a certain segment of the population that no matter how comfortable you may be in ripped jeans and a 30-year-old hairstyle, your career could suffer if you wear these to work. I wish more site owners—especially smaller businesses— understood that principle as it relates to the conversion rate on their paid traffic.

Online, more than anywhere else, you suffer from a need to prove yourself to skeptical prospects in an environment that feels very "cold" to those prospects. They haven't met you face-to-face. They may not have heard the positive word of mouth that you've generated. They haven't sampled the quality of your products. They can't see the line of customers outside your store. In short, unless you take particular steps to position yourself as a business with some kind of status, prospects may assume you're third rate.

A large part of how status is conveyed online is visual. Recall that in the studies by Fogg's Stanford Persuasive Technology Lab, a "site that looks professionally designed" scores as one of the strongest means to increase "surface web credibility" for an online business or organization.[19]

That's obviously a very general goal. "Professionally designed" means different things to different people. In *Selling the Invisible,* Harry Beckwith argues, "Prospects look for visual clues about a service. If they find none, they often look to services that do have them. So provide clues."[20] Beckwith's examples include visible company "front men," which can be real men such as Joel Hyatt (Hyatt Legal Services) and Dave Thomas (late founder of Wendy's Restaurants), or the pillars at law offices, an accountant's conservative attire, or a financial adviser's prosperous-looking leather portfolio. I'd prefer it if we didn't stick with the dated examples of Beckwith's choosing, so let's add the late Anita Roddick of The Body Shop to the example list. Online, though, what people see is not just images, but how those images are presented. They see your design. Good design isn't cheap, but you should buy as much as you can afford, rather than as little as you can get away with.

Leveraging Feel and Brand in Small Retail Operations

Let's look at an example of how small companies can create a brand with a quality feel, in spite of not having a nationwide chain of retail stores or the budget to hire a top ad agency.

Jeff Braverman is a savvy businessperson. His site does very well, and has become a leading online provider of nuts, confections, and specialty snack items. There are two primary reasons.

First, Braverman has humanized his site and injected web credibility into it. NutsOnline is "real." The site contains not only contact information, but a whole history of the family business, a roasted nut stand in New Jersey (Figure 11-15). "In 1929, on the brink of the Depression," begins Braverman's heartfelt sales copy, "my grandfather Sol took a bold step." There's even a picture of Sol in front of the shop in the 1930s. It would be hard to say that the Braverman family doesn't care about nuts.

Braverman also obsesses about the quality of his site. The checkout process and other details are important to him. If you're lost and use the site search box to look for **almonds**, you'll be served a page with a couple dozen product options. Everything on this website seems to work the way it's supposed to.

Perhaps the most impressive detail Braverman has obsessed over is the look and feel. It looks simple and straightforward, but that doesn't mean it was easy to put together. Rather than posting stock photos of nuts, he hired a food photographer to take proper photos of the products the Bravermans actually deliver to their customers (an example is shown in Figure 11-16). Nothing keeps it more real than accurate photographic images. But more than that, a professional food photographer knows how to make food look appealing.

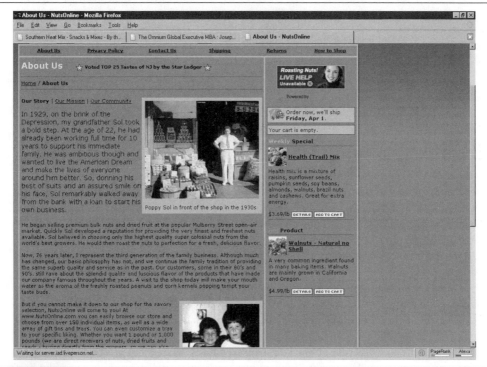

FIGURE 11-15   Web credibility and personal accountability create a good backdrop for customer loyalty.

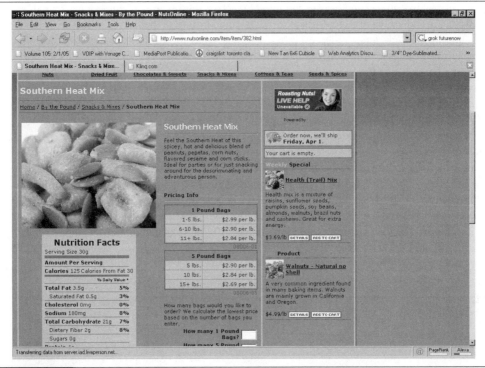

FIGURE 11-16   Jeff Braverman employed a food photographer to convey the quality of his products.

Summing Up

To improve conversion rates, think in terms of four broad priorities. First, make it smooth. Remove the most obvious barriers getting in the way of the user performing a desired action. Clutter and lack of focus are the subtlest, most insidious barriers. Broken links and nonworking checkout processes will literally kill any chance of a sale.

Second, test copy and layout elements that may serve to persuade a skeptical prospect that you deserve her business—but do so with a valid testing protocol. That includes overall page feel; matters as basic as improving product descriptions on a retail site; testing different sizes of "purchase now" or "add to cart" buttons; or expanding on and clarifying too-brief, jargon-laden sales copy on a business-to-business site. Don't use the "aimless tinkering" method. Rather, employ powerful methods: best practices or A/B/C to start, and multivariate testing only if you have high volumes of sales.

Third, make sure that you don't blow your web credibility when a hot prospect starts to scrutinize you more closely. Have contact information available; spell everything correctly; don't look desperate by hitting him with pop-ups; keep the material fresh; and so on. This whole area is now part of Google's Quality Scoring algorithm, so stay in tune with the zeitgeist on areas such as disclosure and privacy policies.

Fourth, be image conscious in the broadest sense: heed Harry Beckwith's advice in *Selling the Invisible.* In business, companies have always been judged on superficial matters. Beyond mere web credibility, the visual impact and basic architecture of your site can make the difference between becoming a real player with brand appeal, or just another peddler with a story to tell and stuff to unload. If taking control of your image means you need professional design or professional information architecture advice, you'll need to go out and find some. Don't let your business suffer just because you're afraid of offending your loyal "web person." There is always someone local, or in your family, willing to give you "web" advice. But are they bona fide professionals?

Conversion science can't fix it if your product or service stinks. At a certain point, your marketing will fail if you don't deliver the goods. If people don't seem to embrace your sales pitch or your page layout, it may be time to stop worrying so much about pitching and formatting, and "get better reality."[21]

Endnotes

1. Jakob Nielsen, "Do Interface Standards Stifle Design Creativity?" *Alertbox*, August 22, 1999, archived at http://www.useit.com/alertbox/990822.html.

2. In *Survival Is Not Enough* (Free Press, 2002), mDNA is Godin's term for the makeup of ideas in your company; he is following scientists in the tradition of Richard Dawkins (*The Selfish Gene*, 1976) positing cultural ideas or "memes" as similar to genes, in that they are "replicators." Memetic (similar to genetic) mutations are seen as a positive by Godin insofar as they prevent companies from stagnating, and closed, hidebound, or hierarchical corporate cultures don't produce enough mutations.

3. For background try Don Norman, *The Design of Everyday Things* (Doubleday, 1999).

4. The real answer seems to be that it was discovered and developed by researchers at Xerox's Palo Alto Research Center. According to Spool et al., these researchers hypothesized and proved several elements of a theory that posited searchers in "a large information space" such as a website as "'informavores' on the hunt for information." See Jared Spool, Christine Perfetti, and David Brittan, *Designing for the Scent of Information* (User Interface Engineering, white paper, 2004), 1, available at www.uie.com.

5. A grandiose economic philosopher might at this point attempt to caution against the diminution of national potential that might accompany any reduction of the marketing and web production communities to a mere "nation of shopkeepers," given the growth potential associated with the full capabilities possessed by creative classes of our ilk. Or to state it another way, the danger of putting snobs in charge of marketing, design, and online experience production is that the snobs will dismiss the task of marketing

to consumers as "creating a big ol' catalogue, and making it more accurate," precisely because they think of marketing and consumers as afterthoughts, and do not much care for them. If snobs work on complicated things, then it must follow that they rule over lesser beings and require those lesser beings to work on things less complicated and less sublime.

6. *Persuasive momentum* is a term coined by Bryan Eisenberg et al.

7. Bryan Eisenberg and Jeffrey Eisenberg, *Call to Action: Secret Formulas to Improve Online Results* (Wizard Academy Press, 2005), 175.

8. Eisenberg and Eisenberg, *Call to Action,* 175.

9. For some interesting perspectives, see Holly Buchanan and Michelle Miller, *The Soccer Mom Myth* (Wizard Academy Press, 2008).

10. Paco Underhill, *Why We Buy: The Science of Shopping* (Simon & Schuster, 1999).

11. In *And Now a Few Words From Me* (McGraw-Hill, 2003), Garfield writes: "In the ordinary course of events, the effect of advertising falls smack between Vance Packard's *The Hidden Persuaders* and Randy Rothenberg's scenario of extraneousness; it influences our buying decisions but by no means dictates them. For every 'Where's the beef?' deployment of poison gas there is a benign bicarbonate like Alka-Seltzer, which provided campaign after delightful, memorable, hilarious campaign and lost market share the entire way" (p. 191). Although the discussion in this chapter considers your landing pages and website as a whole, rather than just your ad, the argument seems fair to apply to your entire sales process. The original and current (lazy) critics of advertising, from Vance Packard to *Adbusters* magazine, probably should have been considering the entire sales process, too. When I see an ad for Harry Rosen's menswear in the newspaper or on TV, no matter how bamboozled I am by the promotion, I still need to go into the shop and interact with a suit salesman, find a garment that fits, and budget enough money to make a purchase. By rights, then, the "hidden persuaders" critics ought to be going far beyond looking at the ads. They should be following me into the store and watching as I take a follow-up sales call on my home phone six months later. By that time, though, they might have to conclude that I actually like the suit I bought and appreciate the service provided to me by this retailer, including the time the sales rep offered to drive to the airport to deliver my recently altered overcoat.

12. Thanks to Mona Elesseily for contributing to this pocket summary of landing page planning.

13. "Web Analytics 2.0: Putting the Marketer Back Into Marketing," keynote address to the Canadian Marketing Association National Convention, May 12, 2008.

14. For this, see Bryan Eisenberg and John Quarto-vonTivadar, *Always Be Testing: The Complete Guide to Google Website Optimizer* (Sybex, 2008).

15. Jamie Roche, "A Redesign Worthy of Google De-listing," *iMedia Connection*, March 13, 2007.

16. B. J. Fogg, *Persuasive Technology: Using Computers to Change What We Think and Do* (Morgan Kaufmann, 2003), 149.

17. *Persuasive Technology,* 152. Fogg notes that the 2002 study was a "snapshot," conducted in collaboration with a private research lab. He is not as clear as he could be about the methodologies or sample sizes of various studies. This area cries out for more funding and more definitive, up-to-date research.

18. *Persuasive Technology,* 156.

19. *Persuasive Technology,* 168.

20. Harry Beckwith, *Selling the Invisible: A Field Guide to Modern Marketing* (Warner Books, 1997), 187.

21. Harry Beckwith, *Selling the Invisible,* 3. "Get better reality" is attributed to Guy Kawasaki. For a deep exploration of this theme, see Seth Godin, *Free Prize Inside: The Next Big Marketing Idea* (Portfolio, 2004); Seth Godin, *All Marketers Are Liars: The Power of Telling Authentic Stories in a Low-Trust World* (Portfolio, 2005).

Chapter 12

Online Targeting 1995–2015: Fast Start, Exciting Future

In recent years, the practice of "futurism" has inspired oft-deserved derision. An IBM commercial, wherein the consultant has supplied the cantankerous CEO with "business goggles" that require the user to "put in another quarter" if he wants to see the future, comes to mind. My personal favorite is *The Simpsons*' portrayal of the Epcot Center as how "people in 1965 thought things would look in 1987."

In this chapter I'll be trying to take a look at Google's future, in particular. Given the size of the company and the pace of their innovation, this is a little bit like trying to film a speedboat race by running after the boats with a Flip video camera around your neck. On one hand, you can only run about 29.7 miles per hour before your quadriceps muscle tears off the knee tendon; on the other, you'll sink before you even get going that fast. Given the lightweight nature of the video camera, at least you'll be able to swim back to shore.

The only phenomenon that regularly attracts as much scorn as futurism is futurism coupled with bullishness about the contributions the Internet will make to the economy. It is indeed possible to oversell the contributions made by the Internet as compared with progress in other fields. Because I don't work in those industries, I find the ability of BMW to use more and more robots to build cars with fewer and fewer design flaws more mind-boggling than I find a client's ability to find a customer. I'm more impressed by the huge increases in the survival rates for some types of cancer than I am in an e-commerce site's ability to sell a tooth whitening system.

But let's not underestimate the contribution of online functionality to the global economy, either. Internet models can either add layers to the economy or remove them, making it possible for a buyer to work through an intermediary or an aggregated form of information if they choose, or to gain more direct access to information related to a transaction than they might have had 20 years ago. The Internet offers a postmodern form of choice, which means we needn't feel trapped by a particular unidirectional macrotrend in any given industry (getting rid of intermediaries versus the rise of new intermediaries, for example). Increasingly, we can actually choose more or less of a given attribute (such as how "raw" or "packaged" we want information to be).

Halfway into the writing of this second edition, I became deeply involved in HomeStars, a website that offers user reviews of home improvement companies. In this process, which involved far more in-depth planning than my usual routine of marketing project implementation, it became evident to me just how radical the shift is in the way that consumers access information. Those of us who participate in actually shaping new ways of accessing trusted information, and new ways of completing transactions, hold just a piece of the online future in the palms of our hands.

It's all too easy to trivialize the shift in how we spend our leisure time and our workdays, and changes in the forces and communications media that shape our beliefs and choices. Isn't it all just killing time? Of course not. Frankly, it's mind-blowing to think about the rapid growth in usage of something like Facebook. The joy of creation is what drives innovators like Facebook founder Mark Zuckerberg to dream up entirely new patterns of interaction that will transform social patterns and information retrieval and advertising as we know them. It's been a long time since Marshall McLuhan was quoted as saying the medium is the message. We know that's not literally true, perhaps, but we downplay the rapid shifts in communication patterns at our peril.

The focused intellectual curiosity that leads developers like Zuckerberg to build new ways of disseminating and sharing knowledge is no less revolutionary than the innovations in developing a computer operating system and taskflow environment by Apple and Microsoft in the 1980s; no less worthy than the invention of the "back and forward button" dashboard design of the Netscape web browser in the 1990s; and no less economically powerful (potentially) than the laser focus on clean, fast, accurate search and targeted ads perfected by the Google guys in the period 1998 to date.

Zuckerberg didn't need maverick cartoonist Hugh McLeod to tell him how to be creative.[1] He just built a system he thought would be interesting for Harvard and other college students to use. But for those of us a fair bit older than Zuckerberg (he's 24 as I write this), McLeod's reminder is worth listening to. If you have a vision and it's something you truly feel strongly about, you can make it come alive. You. You can do it. You don't need a million dollars or the most elaborate tools or the flashy lifestyle of a Soho artist or Web 2.0 hipster. You can build something that changes the world—by just getting started, and continuing to pursue it.

What world-changing stuff am I talking about? In my state of heightened awareness honed by investor pitches for HomeStars, I've come across a lot of interesting statistics. Citizen trust in the information found in mainstream media is at an all-time low. Nearly more Americans believe in UFOs than believe that CNN and the *Washington Post* provide unbiased information. Part of the reason for this is that for all of the admirable big media investment in investigative reporting and thoughtful analysis, the "professionalization" of journalism feels to the public like the media elite talking among themselves or siding with the subjects of their stories.[2]

Even online "influencers" like "well-known bloggers" are losing their luster. Survey data also shows us turning more to peer groups and trusted sources that we can really verify, to access opinions, hard data, and experiences. Some of the subject matter is of a political or medical nature. Other times, it's more practical, relating to getting things done, or making a purchase. Some of the buzzwords for describing these phenomena include the "Wisdom of Crowds" (James Surowiecki), or the "pro-am movement" (Chris Anderson).

It's purely reactionary to claim that the rapid shift in information retrieval and knowledge sharing methods in our Wikipedia era are leading to a dramatic increase in the noise-to-signal ratio. Rather, there has been a massive increase in both noise and signal. This will lead to new challenges in information retrieval that will require, on one hand, ever more powerful and scalable technologies and, on the other, innovative social and organizational solutions, open standards, and new kinds of communities.

Dr. Andrew Tomkins, Yahoo's Chief Scientist, includes in his speeches data about the exponential increases in potentially findable user-generated content (UGC) online. Already, we see glimpses of the enormity of the growth in Google's search product designs, which integrate ordinary web search with attempts to search all kinds of separate and distinct databases. These include your computer desktop, your instant message chats, and your email. Eventually, voice communications and video pattern recognition will be part of that searchable universe; today, one startup is already using voice-to-text technology to annotate some YouTube videos with textual metadata. Your car trips and air travel will perhaps be logged in detail, and much more besides. The zeitgeist of "what's my status now?" currently embodied in the unreliable but popular microblogging service Twitter, is going to be built into our lives from a variety of angles. You won't have to Twitter to tell your "followers" what you're up to now. A variety of technologies may well do that for you—with or without your knowledge or permission.

Tomkins remarked in one recent speech that the total amount of UGC being produced today is not that far removed, in order-of-magnitude terms, from the maximum possible amount of UCG that could be logged if everyone on the planet sat in front of their computer and just typed away, 24 hours a day. (Sort of feels like what I'm doing right now.) I believe Dr. Tomkins! There has been an explosion in the production of information that is feasibly findable and classifiable.

When Google says their mission is to make the "world's information" universally accessible, they're not kidding. That will open up new opportunities for marketers, and lead to serious privacy debates. A real value will come to be placed on sharing data with just your immediate circle, your wider trusted circle, or the public at large. As an Internet user, and as a user of various applications and technologies, marketers will want to pay you for your willingness to share more of your personal information.

Survey-based data mining and database marketing is old-school and well known to many marketers, but in a new era of surveillance-style data mining, will companies like Google be able to draw a line in the sand and resist the general trend towards deeper snooping? Marketing companies that failed in part because they were out of step with the respectful anti-intrusion ethos championed by companies like Google—spyware firms such as Gator/Claria, for example—may come to seem nearly quaint by comparison with the full-scale surveillance capabilities of the larger communications and media companies, from Google, to Microsoft, to Facebook. But depending on how things evolve, these big companies might be able to find a way to thrive precisely by enacting systems of respectful "permissions," attempting to balance profitability with users' willingness to share only with those they trust.

While the past decade or so has seen many innovators focus on finding what you need online, the coming decade will feature a growing focus on how to verify and productively use that information, and how to connect with trusted peers and virtual friends whose opinions we truly value. The first wave of this trend was clumsily called "peer to peer" (or P2P) search, but we weren't quite ready for it yet. The next wave will tackle the peering and sharing issue with renewed vigor. The old media will let out a few remaining squawks about the dangers of trusting "online information," but by and large, they'll continue to diversify their holdings into the kinds of media they once feared and attacked.

No, online innovation isn't always rocket science, but it can create cracks in old armor that eventually transform whole industries. Online stock trading precipitated huge changes in the retail securities brokerages, for example, driving commissions way down on routine transactions.

Online marketplaces using a variety of exchange models have put significant pressure on old models. It isn't just people's used junk anymore, or even just ordinary retail. Did you know that eBay Motors is perennially one of the top two revenue-generating product categories on eBay? That's because folks hate dealing with traditional face-to-face automotive purchase processes. And that trend has only just begun. You can look at such developments any way you like. You can yawn, cringe, or just try to adapt and profit.

The growth in e-commerce surely can't be hurt by the backwardness of offline retail. More often than not, consumers come to a store ready to buy, armed with product information. Because many interactions with both the salespeople and the categorization systems in retail stores are often an information-poor embarrassment compared with (at least a well produced) website, the vanguard of hybrid retailers who welcome digital search and persuasion right into their offline spaces will be poised to "keep it real" with a new, information-hungry breed of consumer.

Businesses that don't get the Web—and even those that don't understand how consumers' hunger for information, transparency, and context is being driven by their ability to search online—are going to face a lot more dissatisfied customers in the coming years. Inertia can be costly.

As entrepreneurs create new ways of putting buyers and sellers together online, thousands of new business practices are emerging today that will need to be studied by economists decades hence. Revolutions in fields like high finance, where pioneers invented ways of packaging and pooling almost any financial asset or risk category to be bought and sold, have unleashed massive efficiencies on the global economy, and are duly studied. Massive losses in wealth brought about by over-eager application of "sound" financial maneuvers will no doubt lead to checks and balances that ought to have been in place in the first place. It seems that painful reckoning episodes are a prerequisite for coming to grips with the potential for any powerful multiplier of wealth and efficiency to turn sour.

Many of the changes wrought by Internet entrepreneurs are humbler than the big trades overseen by Wall Street Masters of the Universe. But when you add them all up, some powerful math is lurking behind what seem to be modest changes in how consumers behave and how businesses interact. The improvements in our ability to communicate, target, and transact business are far reaching. Reductions in "economic friction" predicted by writers in then-avant-garde publications like *Wired* and *Business 2.0* in the mid-to-late 1990s are now coming to pass. The real challenge becomes how to manage these surges in economic productivity so that they don't consume us. Many have already arrived at the point where "always on" is more of a curse than a badge of honor. In other words, if a little bit more information or a little bit more efficiency is helpful, how do we know when to stop? Is it OK if I get the third-best price on a printer, or the fourth-best available mortgage rate? Might there be some more, just a few more, profitable keywords lurking in the nearly infinite dictionary of AdWords inventory? Or should we strive for balance in our pursuit of business growth?

More than the economy, these changes are about widespread access to specialized communities and freedom of information. Citizens and consumers have unprecedented access to information and sources of enlightenment that were once the province of a few. Many will not have the initiative or the educational background to take advantage of those opportunities. Someday, proponents of Internet community, Internet research, and Internet business will need to take a breath and go back over the knowledge utilization literature to remind themselves that the availability of information effects change in less than obvious ways, and sometimes not at all. Experts argue that rather than directly informing decisions, a growing body of evidence is often brought to bear on a specialized field over a period of years or decades and informs decisions in the background by replacing what was once thought of as common sense with a new kind of common sense.[3]

The Internet has become synonymous with sweeping economic change. And so should it be.

As you read in Chapter 2, search-centric companies like Google and Yahoo—and the pay-per-click model—have surged ahead of traditional online advertising brokers. Things may look quite different in a couple of years, but for now, the proportion of Google's revenues derived from advertising is closer to 100% than it is to, well, 95%. The world's leading search company is the world's leading online advertising vendor.

While the successes of these new leaders aren't possible to be ephemeral, it is likely that the dominance of a relatively narrow form of online advertising—Google AdWords and Yahoo paid search results charged "by the click"—will give way once again to a wider variety of targeting methods. Just as email, banners, and other forms of online targeting lost ground and suffered bumps and bruises, paid search faces key challenges such as click fraud, bidding wars, and low volume. As a result, the leaders will be forced to innovate.

The exciting thing for companies like Google is that they've made a name for themselves by providing a highly efficient platform within which advertisers can manage targeted, measurable campaigns. As the search metaphor insinuates itself into various aspects of people's lives—online and off—advertisers will be able to reach more customers in more ways using an AdWords-like bidding platform. Thus your efforts to learn the ins and outs of AdWords will be applicable to future developments in marketing and advertising generally.

Google AdWords: Emerging Trends

While it's interesting to speculate on longer-term transformations in the marketing landscape, from a practical standpoint, most of us need to keep an eye on near-term developments that may affect our campaign strategy. What lie directly ahead for Google AdWords advertisers are advances in campaign management and ROI tracking.

There have been subtle shifts in Google's philosophy on providing advertisers with additional tools to manage their campaigns. In the early days of AdWords, I was told that Google believed strongly that in certain areas, especially reporting and tracking ROI, third parties were better suited to help their advertisers. Over time, this shifted to "we'll try to offer our advertisers more tools that will help them manage their campaigns in less time."

The advent of an increasingly integrated, ever-more-powerful (and free) Google Analytics platform ushered in an era of a "total Google marketing experience." Google's main competitors, Microsoft and Yahoo, have followed suit. Yahoo, which already offered conversion tracking and analytics following their acquisitions of companies like KeyLime Software, recently acquired another analytics and bid management platform it is bent on integrating: IndexTools. For their part, Microsoft has begun to roll out their own Google Analytics competitor, code-named Gatineau, which will help paid search advertisers access demographic campaign performance information, among other things.

As noted in Chapter 10, the "bid to ROI" goal automation previously only supported by third-party players may now be addressed adequately for many retail advertisers by Google's CPA Bidding tool, which attempts to set your bids to keep your cost per acquisition in line with your target dollar figure.

Google Projects to Watch

Since they're a primary supplier of traffic to your business, it probably wouldn't hurt to be curious about Google's future direction. For search advertisers and searchers alike, Google Search has become a primary obsession. In the parlance of advertising guru Kevin Roberts, Google both inspires love and commands respect, making it a "lovemark."[4] Google's size and power seem destined to erode some of the "love" from that designation, as is seemingly inevitable in the lifecycle of technology companies, with notable exceptions like Apple. Let's take a moment to speculate on how some of Google's various projects could affect advertisers down the road, and on how they might affect Google's competitive position in the race for online user loyalty (what were quaintly referred to as "the portal wars" back in the 1998–2001 era). The immense breadth of Google's engineering and product development teams means it's an exercise in futility to attempt laser accuracy here. Projects will take on shifting degrees of significance, of course.

Google Chrome

To date, Google arguably had only one major shoe left to drop in the creation of software representing foundational elements of home and office computing. They already had a search engine, a blog platform, an office suite, instant messaging, and web-based email, to name just a few. But no browser. Many assumed their financial and moral support for the Mozilla Foundation and the Firefox browser would be as far as Google went.

Instead, Google rolled out a powerful new web browser called Chrome. It offers several interface innovations and functionality improvements such as tabs that are shielded from malfunctions in other open tabs, but what is probably most important about it is the "guts" of its architecture.[5] First of all, it contains new code elements that had grown tired in rival browsers Firefox, Safari, and Internet Explorer. Second, it offered a more comprehensive architecture that resembled a whole operating system, in that a wide variety of web or desktop applications can be operated within the Chrome environment. Third, its updated code base is compatible with Android, Google's new operating system for mobile devices. Finally, Chrome's code is open source! Google has welcomed other browser developers to make use of its code to improve their products.

Geeky stuff aside, what's the main motivation to switch? Chrome's engineered for speed. Power users are particularly impatient with slow-loading web pages, so they'll likely be the first adopters. To date, Google Chrome's market share has failed to crack 0.75%, though it enjoyed over 1% market share in the first few days of widespread tire-kicking by new users. Time will tell whether Chrome gains share, and how it will fit in with Google's overall strategy. But insofar as it is built for the future, it is a powerful force to be reckoned with, and the best proof yet that Google plans to trade blows with Microsoft for as many rounds as it takes. In the browser wars, of course, the only cost to the user is a few seconds of download time, and a brief learning period. Accessing a superior product's speed doesn't come with the same financial tradeoffs as, say, considering a new Porsche.

Google Product Search and Google Checkout

Despite a slow start, Google's shopping engine, Froogle, brought many retailers on board to upload listings through a feed service. However, the service never reached rampant popularity, and it seems that Google has revamped the overall strategy for product search, renaming Froogle to Google Product Search. Google Product Search is integrally related to Google's growth in merchant services through Google Checkout, and judging by the home page navigation, a grander "giant database" project called Google Base is considered the granddaddy of Google Product Search. Google Product Search is billed as being "in beta," which forebodes considerable testing and tweaking going forward. Google Product Search results continue to be integrated into some search results. The significance for retailers should not be lost: don't expect to rank product pages in the organic results. Buy paid clicks, and participate in Google Product Search by uploading your feeds.

Feed management is a technical task that should be taken on by a qualified developer or even a third-party consultant. To manage competing feed engines, retailers may need an ongoing bid strategy, among other things.

Orkut: The Cool Kids Moved On?

Named after Orkut Buyukkokten, the Google engineer who spearheaded its development, Orkut is a social networking site that allows friends and "friends of friends" to communicate, form groups of interest, and much more. In that regard, it resembles similar sites like Friendster, LinkedIn, and Facebook. The reality is, many folks kicked the tires on Orkut when it first came out, but in North America it simply doesn't have a critical mass of users. Like many, I haven't logged into my Orkut account in ages. I consider Facebook and LinkedIn to be vibrant, current platforms—I use one or the other almost daily.

In principle, Orkut is separate from other Google initiatives. When it rolled out, though, observers believed that the extensive personal information Orkut collects could be part of the trend towards Google developing a large "user base" like the one Yahoo has built. Microsoft, we know, uses Hotmail and Passport user data to offer demographic targeting options to its advertisers. For example, a Microsoft adCenter advertiser can elect to bid 25% higher than their base bid on paid search traffic that appears to be coming from (say) women between the ages of 25 and 34. At present, the demographic targeting options in Google AdWords are relatively weak (they are based on some reported data from some content partners in the content targeting programs), but given Google's increasing diversity of demographically rich properties, it wouldn't be a surprise if Google approached or surpassed Microsoft and Yahoo on this front. To date, they have been cautious about how they collect data, and how much of it is handed over to advertisers.

In any case, it seems likely that Google will someday offer advertisers access to deeper demographic targeting options. Projects like Orkut not only create a potential revenue stream for Google, they give Google "users," along with all that entails. Google is stealthily increasing its global footprint. But it has to be unsatisfied with its current lack of traction in the social space. I'd expect all of Google, Yahoo, and Microsoft to make bold moves in this space, including acquisitions, in 2009. Friendster (independent), LinkedIn (independent), and Bebo (part of AOL) seem like major acquisition targets as of this writing.

In October 2007, Google spearheaded an Open Social alliance to create a commonly shareable application framework that would allow third-party developers to create applications that would work across any participating social network. (In Open Social speak, an "application" is called an "application," and a "social networking site" like Facebook or Orkut is called a "container.") This has potentially explosive implications. As is so often the case, Google appears to be looking ahead in the chess match, building something bigger and just as open source friendly as Facebook, while leaving the door for it to take sides in which proprietary version of open source (that's an oxymoron that has a long history in technology) gains ascendancy. Particularly galvanizing to observers, but potentially troubling to Google competitors, must be the similarity in philosophies between Google's Open Social alliance and the open social networking system created by Marc Andreessen's Ning. Andreessen, cofounder of the Netscape browser, sided with Google in its launch of the initiative, taking nonparticipating sites to task for not joining.[6] (MySpace, Bebo, and Six Apart joined in November, Yahoo, mentioned directly by Andreessen in his post, finally joined in March 2008.) Recently, Ning raised $60 million in a fourth round of funding, placing the company's value at $500 million. A startup valued so highly at a relatively early stage? It makes you wonder if continued growth in Ning's own "applications and containers" means that it is expecting an acquisition for billions by Google or its closest competitors. To date, Ning users have created over 300,000 "containers." In essence that means 300,000 developers have rolled their own "mini-Facebooks" to create custom social networking sites of their own.

The "social graph" is a snazzy term that refers to the deep demographic data that can potentially be gleaned from observation of user social behavior. Owners of social networks can collect a vast amount of data about not only likes and dislikes, but about the propensity of one's behavior to be affected by the behavior of friends and contacts at different levels of intimacy. While the research is in its infancy, the potential goldmine of data has not been lost on Silicon Valley and investors in technology startups. It's a certainty that Google will be among the companies aggressively pushing into this space.

YouTube

A more clear-cut case of Google owning a popular website with engaged "users" is YouTube. YouTube is by far the top streaming video site in the world, and in many markets is in the top five of all websites.

Google acquired YouTube in October 2006 for $1.65 billion in an all-stock transaction. Its own offering, Google Video, was well behind in the race for user eyeballs in the online video streaming category.

At the time, the acquisition was controversial. As with a number of today's most popular Internet brands, the mainstream press hurled a steady volley of accusations of wrongdoing and illegality at the popular site. (PayPal, for example—now a division of eBay—was painted as a dodgy scheme destined to be shut down at the hands of financial regulators.) Because of the large number of unauthorized copies of proprietary video content posted on the site, many observers speculated that Google overpaid for a business that would be reduced to a fraction of its present size when YouTube became more aggressive in removing pirated video clips. Mark Cuban, owner of a library of video content, was among the pundits predicting legal doom for YouTube.[7]

As so often happens in the technology business, size and scale rule. YouTube's popularity combined with Google's resources left it in the driver's seat as the "go-to" place to post video content, an activity that began to take off in many circles. The fact that blogs, social networks, and large-scale publishers used YouTube to embed streaming video into their published content helped YouTube grow by leaps and bounds. The resulting explosion in archived video content meant that an aggressive policy to remove unauthorized material still left YouTube with massive amounts of content. In January 2008, 78.5 million viewers watched a mind-boggling 3.25 billion videos through YouTube.[8] Google owns about 34% market share in streaming video, far ahead of the #2 player.

At $1.65 billion, Google had itself a bargain, especially when compared with Yahoo's $5 billion acquisition of Broadcast.com in 1999, a deal which should be characterized as "right idea, wrong technology, wrong time." As always, Google proves that it's better to be lucky than good; it has been both lucky and good too many times for it to be just luck.

Google Labs

An interesting repository of half-baked Google experiments is Google Labs (labs.google.com). They certainly don't share everything they're working on, but it's refreshing that they do sometimes show off "not yet ready for prime time" features.

Some of Google's most important features, such as Google Maps and Google Scholar, are listed under (or got their initial introduction to the public through) Google Labs. Google continues to play the game of downplaying major initiatives by calling them "beta" or "experimental," but no one is fooled. A lot of the "experiments" listed under Google Labs will play a big part in the future of search.

Google maintains a record of which applications "graduated" from Google Labs, and currently displays it on the home page of Google Labs (see Figure 12-1). As of this writing, there are 17 graduates, including GOOG-411, a free, voice-activated directory assistance service that went from "labs to live" in record time.

Google Maps was one of the graduates. Only recently a mere upstart challenging leaders like MapQuest, Google Maps is now a staple of many Internet users. It's also very much integrated into search results, depending on the user's query. Google's pace of development of Maps has been admirable. They've integrated "pedestrian-friendly" or "public-transit-friendly" estimates

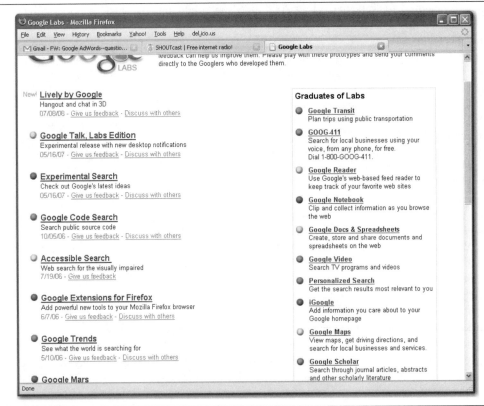

Many projects that lurk quietly in Google Labs ultimately become important Google services.

of travel times in some cities, for example (see Figure 12-2). And they've integrated the satellite view from Google Earth, if you prefer to view that.

Google Suggest is a feature that displays more specific phrases as you type, based on search frequency data. This is operational, for example, in the Google Toolbar Extension for Firefox. Marketers can actually use Google Suggest as a keyword research tool. Curious about the most popular three-word phrases that begin with "mortgage application"? Google Suggest can tell you. Savvy developers customize their research by accessing Google Suggest through the Google Search API, which allows a "data dump" of a certain number of Google Suggest results. This might allow you to do custom keyword research and organize the information in a usable format. Keep in mind that large-scale use of any Google API is likely to cost you "tokens," which cost money above a certain number of free tokens allotted for ordinary research use. Google Suggest is not particularly robust for research purposes, in any case. For users, it may be of some interest, but it is not hugely beneficial in my opinion. Google doesn't make any claims about the accuracy or completeness of Google Suggest—hence the term "suggest," I suppose.

I suggest that you check back into Google Labs from time to time, just to see what they're up to.

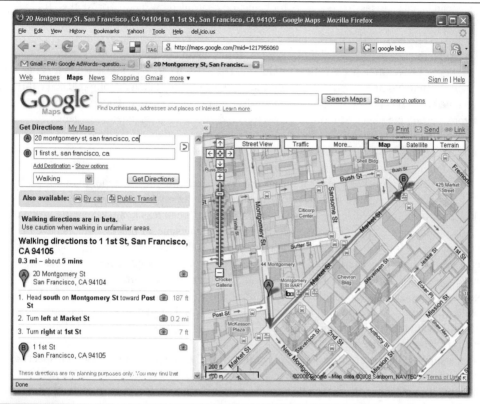

FIGURE 12-2   For some places, Google Maps lets you choose whether you want directions "by car," "by public transit," or "on foot."

The Ecosystem: Google's Competitors and Partners

Advertisers go where the customers are. Today, Google and a couple of other companies are leading options for your online ad campaigns. Relative stability in Google's immediate ecosystem makes it easier on most of us. But that stability can't be counted on. Google's ability to compete as well as cooperate will affect your relationship with them in the coming years.

Google vs. Everybody Else

It wasn't long ago that a "party" connected with a technology company was a sedate beer bash on-site, conducted among hardworking, nerdy engineers, on a Friday afternoon. Dot-com bubbles I and II created a whole new image for the technology sector: $150 haircuts, exotic cocktails consumed with celebrities in trendy nightclubs, and other such fleeting trappings of fame. Such imagery has proved to be a distraction for many of the sector's weakest startups, but it's also created irrelevant new informal standards of conduct for technology companies. Somehow, paradoxically, technology companies can be taken to task by outsiders for being too controlled by "nerds" or "dorks." If blogs like *Valleywag* had their way, every software developer would be as trendy and socially confident as semi-employed bloggers. Perish the thought.

If you read the news, you see a lot of negative stories about any new, brash company. Google is no exception. I have often been critical of Google, but I also try to give praise when it is due, which is also often. No matter what any analyst says, the decisions taken at companies like this may often be based on careful thought processes that aren't shared with outsiders. We might misinterpret certain messages. If Google seems too cold, aloof, and "maddeningly geeky" in some cases, it's probably because top management cares passionately about developing the next great product.

Google's mantra has been "serve the user." They've made powerful statements that their focus is on the user experience even if it means not always maximizing revenue. In that regard, Google has had the foresight to build a beloved online destination with staying power.

Their relationship with advertisers and other partners has been less cozy. Like parts of Yahoo in its early days, Google's youth and (sometimes) arrogance has meant that customers haven't always been dealt with as professionally and consistently as they could have been. Google took years to develop more consistent billing practices, for example; financial background checks for invoicing relationships sometimes got caught in the bureaucratic shuffle. More recently, the "geeked-out" Quality-Based Bidding algorithm seems to downplay the urgency faced by seasonal advertisers. Campaigns that take weeks to ramp up and to start working normally don't fit well either with the "up in minutes" image of Google AdWords or with the media buying objectives of large advertisers.

What's supposed to be exciting about AdWords is that the system treats you with respect even if you run a niche business that only receives a handful of clicks for a high-ticket item. But in reality, "small" advertisers (small in quotes because even a large, prestigious company or organization counts as small in some Googlers' minds until its AdWords spend reaches a certain level) may get less personalized attention than big spenders.

From such indications, it's hard not to conclude that Google is a search engine company in the same vein as those that came before it. The revenue stream is seen as just that: a tap that flows and keeps the lab running. Advertisers are a necessary evil. Isn't that a strange way to feel about a client base that makes up 99% of your annual revenues? Maybe, but advertisers have an awesome platform to work with, in spite of the power imbalance that has arisen as Google approaches monopoly status.

At its heart, Google remains a traditional Silicon Valley powerhouse with an engineering culture. Many of the eye-opening tales that have leaked out into the press appear to have been reported reasonably faithfully.[9] Empathy for paying advertisers can be cultivated over time, but there are questions to be asked as to whether Larry Page and Sergey Brin can foster this kind of deep empathy with consumers and partners. We know little of their management style or personal interactions with employees, but it seems erratic, introverted, and aloof by contrast with visionary leaders like Apple's Steve Jobs, or even Microsoft's Bill Gates. Yahoo's Jerry Yang long ago developed the sort of rounded edges and steadiness that has kept that company pointing in the right direction. None of these billionaires needs to go into work every day, so their motivations must come from somewhere—either the internal drive to dominate a market or external feedback from customers and partners.

Can the paradox persist? Google as one of the world's leading brands, yet their leaders remaining so enigmatic? Whatever might happen, we know that Larry Page, Sergey Brin, and Eric Schmidt are likely to remain firmly in control. In spite of the appearance of a democratic culture, power at Google is concentrated in the upper ranks, a state of affairs sealed by a dual share structure that gives ordinary shareholders little control over the company's direction.

Top management and investors in more traditional firms likely would have blanched at some of Google's experiments. Aspects of the initial public offering and other aspects of Google's relationships with economic power structures have been treated as more opportunities for innovation. Some, me included, feel that a company like Google can make important contributions by challenging conventions in areas like investment banking. But when every area of the company's operations, including billing and clickthrough reporting, seem to be treated as "cool hacks" rather than mission-critical bedrocks of client relations, it's not hard to imagine future crises of confidence if and when tales of the most gravity-defying inventions leak out.

As with Apple and Microsoft, future performance can't depend on top management alone. These companies maintain high standards in hiring across the board, and make frequent bets on recruiting top technical, management, and sales talent. How Yahoo and Google grapple with their hiring and organizational decisions will be part of what determines their financial fate. Yahoo, for its part, has struggled with title inflation and an excess of unproductive management positions. Google has been notable for a nearly pathological obsession with raw test scores and raw intellect. Yahoo's recent mediocre financial performance and relatively slow pace of innovation have been part of a rather traditional story of bloat and complacency leading to corporate stagnation.

By contrast, Google has yet to stagnate, and its most marked HR characteristic—hiring people with genius-level IQs—has yet to be proved as an Achilles' heel, in spite of dire predictions by observers. Perhaps we are all aware of the studies that show that people with very high IQs have social adjustment problems and even financial difficulties in comparison with ordinary people with merely above-average intelligence, and we expect that phenomenon writ large to afflict Google in some way. But perhaps such scenarios were more applicable to a time and environment where charm and persuasion were at least as economically important as creating outstanding technology products. Perhaps being charming and persuasive oneself is not highly correlated with the abstract thinking abilities needed to write the code to create the platforms in which users can themselves express their charm and powers of persuasion (while, hopefully, becoming more informed as a side effect). Perhaps it's no coincidence that one of the top current architects of Google AdWords quietly boasts of his "$10 haircuts"—less trendy, even, than the "expensive" haircuts available from Google's in-house barbershop.

From the standpoint of economic progress and quality products, we can all hope that the parties thrown by companies like Google, Microsoft, Yahoo, and Apple will continue to be equally boring. They should be at work creating the frameworks so the rest of us can enjoy better parties. Hopefully, like it's 1999.

eBay and Amazon

eBay and Amazon are the two largest e-commerce companies in the world. Unsurprisingly, their fortunes are deeply intertwined with Google's.

eBay advertises heavily on Google, both directly and indirectly through affiliates. But it also competes with Google, and future product development by both companies threatens to create even hotter competition. Take online classifieds. eBay has bought a 25% stake in popular classifieds site Craigslist and has also created Kijiji, its own international local classifieds service, now growing quickly in North America.

In June 2005, Google acknowledged that it was working on a new offering: a payment processing service that competes with eBay's PayPal service. At the time, Eric Schmidt denied that the payment processing service would compete directly with PayPal, but that depends on how you define "directly." Google Checkout directly competes with PayPal as a merchant processing service, but not for other kinds of user-to-user money transfers. Google's pricing on the service undercuts PayPal's.

eBay completed an acquisition of Skype, the IP-based voice calling and text chat service that has grown to become one of a handful of widely adopted "standards" among users, in October 2005. (Although the quality is not equivalent, Skype allows companies to set up multiuser conference calls for prices as low as free, as compared with five to ten cents per user per minute, for traditional conference calling. Because more and more users have Skype installed, customizing and initiating calls becomes quicker and quicker.) Although revenue generation has lagged, Skype has made fantastic progress since the acquisition. In the first quarter of 2008, Skype added 33 million new users, bringing its user base to over 300 million.

All of Google, Yahoo, AOL, and Microsoft offer instant messaging and some variation on IP-based voice chat. Google Talk now allows multiple-user voice chats, for example. But Skype is much farther along.

Skype's recent success almost makes it less likely to be snapped up by a company like Google, because it would be nearly impossible to set a mutually agreeable valuation on a company whose installed base approaches half a billion users. Aside from the erroneous media and Wall Street stereotype that the Skype acquisition was a failure for eBay, there is nothing to indicate that eBay will in fact divest itself of this killer app and emerging standard. There has been some speculation of a Skype IPO, which would enrich eBay and keep Skype growing at a fast enough pace to challenge telecommunications companies and Internet technology firms like Google for global telecommunications leadership.

eBay versus Google seems to be a moderately competitive relationship. But until the telecommunications and payment processing battles heat up further, both sides have more reasons to work for one another than they do to work against one another.

Amazon and Google appear to have a strong relationship. Even here, though, both have launched initiatives that could threaten one another.

In the world of books, Google has gone through several experiments with projects called Google Print and now Google Book Search. One promising element of Google Book Search is My Library: the ability to create your own personalized library (see Figure 12-3). You can annotate books with reviews, and share your favorites with friends. Google Book Search offers

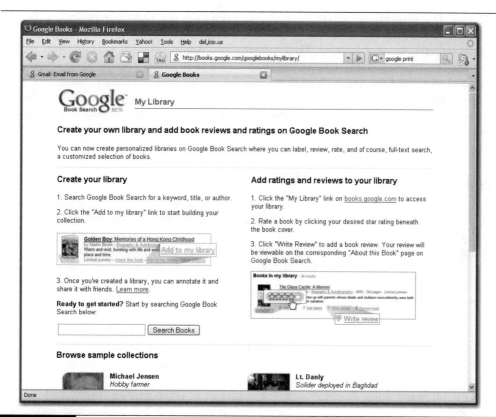

FIGURE 12-3   My Library in Google Book Search

a comprehensive approach to finding material. Some public domain information is available fully digitized; otherwise, Google Book Search can tell you where to buy it or borrow it. Authors may gain exposure for their work by voluntarily submitting their copyright material to be archived here, also. Combine these elements with a new payment processing technology, and it's not a huge stretch to imagine a world in which Google goes into the "book business." Indeed, many of the existing e-book and print-on-demand publishing facilitators such as ClickBank, CafePress, and Lulu are pretty cumbersome for authors. Surely, like Amazon, Google can do better.

Amazon has some of the most sophisticated search technology in the world. It uses this to help users navigate its site and to find related products. With a brief effort in the form of its A9 search engine, Amazon showcased its search expertise for a general audience. Users never embraced A9, however. Its market share never reached any significant level. To cement that insignificance while taking Google's VP headcount up another notch, the creator of A9, Udi Manber, left Amazon for Google in February 2006. Because A9's ranking technology actually ran on Google's index, consider it a showcase effort in a fairly elaborate job application process that had the intended effect: getting Manber a top job at Google.

Reading these particular tea leaves, I don't sense much animosity between these two companies. It seems most likely that both will keep a hands-off attitude towards any initiative that would seriously threaten the other. They currently have many interests in common. Google AdWords derives revenues from Amazon Associates affiliate advertisers who run ads promoting products and books on Amazon. Since affiliates take the risk of running the ads, Amazon gets free referrals for nothing. Google Search also ranks many Amazon.com pages well for free. Both companies derive ad revenue by showing AdWords ads on many pages throughout the Amazon site and on Amazon-owned Alexa.com. Google versus Amazon seems to be more a story of cooperation than competition, then.

Portal Wars: AOL, Yahoo, MSN, IAC

Third-party observers generally get it right when describing Google's battle for supremacy in their key markets: on one hand Google has emerged as the dominant brand in search, and repeatedly makes it to the top of the list of the most valuable brands in the world in any field; yet Google has stiff competition for leadership in online media, technology, and "everything else it does."

No one will dispute, for example, that AOL is now a shadow of its former self. But in terms of "web property" measures in the United States, AOL—with 111 million unique visitors to at least one of their properties—remains at #4, not too far back of Google, at #2 with 137 million.[10] (Including Time Warner properties, AOL Time Warner would be closer to #1.) Yahoo is still nominally in the lead, with 139 million unique visitors to its properties. High-level measures of "unique visitors" per month certainly don't speak to pages viewed, time spent, or revenues generated, but the point is that these Google competitors are very large, and have proprietary content and technology as well as a huge number of direct relationships with users and advertisers. Although Google is a clear winner in its core areas, and is gaining strength on many fronts globally, there's still some healthy competition left in search, online content, and online applications.

Google's closest competitor is Yahoo. They compete as the top two players in paid search. They also hold down the top two spots in terms of search market share, which isn't unrelated to their positions as leaders in revenue derived from search. Increasingly, though, as Google attempts to "take over the world," they compete with Yahoo on many fronts, as portals that want to attract as many users as possible to their brand and their network of online services. Predicting where things will wind up or where the new hot product category or feature will take us is difficult, but it seems clear that due to the presence of the other, neither company can get too comfortable.

In online email, Google entered the space boldly and continues to give Yahoo fits by offering more features and more storage. Advantage? Still a strong advantage to Yahoo, as the incumbent that still has a product that integrates well with calendars, address books, instant messaging, and personalized home pages. Gmail appears to have the cool factor nailed: most of my colleagues and technophile associates use it as a backup or primary email account. But make no mistake: audience measurement services such as Hitwise show Yahoo Mail still holding a commanding lead, more than double the market share of Microsoft's Hotmail and more than ten times the market share of Gmail. Google's Calendar product was released in due course to sync up with

Gmail; it's cool, too. The battle continues for users to adopt one company or the other as their day-to-day standard for these interrelated services, much as they once (largely) settled for the dominant Microsoft-based solutions. Relationships with wireless carriers and device vendors will be part of this ongoing battle for user attention.

In desktop search, Google seems to have grabbed user attention. The product is best in category and installs easily, making slow, inefficient Windows desktop searches a thing of the past. Yahoo and several other companies have released similar products, but none are getting the same attention as Google's.

Believe it or not, social media was only in its infancy in 2005. At this point, none of Yahoo, Google, or Microsoft owns any critical mass of the leading social networking properties outright. I take Facebook, MySpace, LinkedIn, and perhaps a handful of others to be the leaders. Facebook is still majority-owned by its founders and early investors, with Microsoft and some others coming on board later to take small (and extremely expensive) stakes. Fox (News Corp.) owns MySpace outright. LinkedIn remains independent of any of the majors. And Bebo was recently bought by AOL.

Popular microblogging service Twitter (founded by Evan Williams, the founder of Google-owned Blogger) is still a well-funded startup with no revenue model but a huge, engaged user base. Any prediction here will look stale by the time you read about this, but the trajectory is clear enough: low revenues, many users, and strong ties with the technology and investing communities probably translate into Twitter becoming an acquisition target for one of the majors. In the worst-case scenario, its recent performance problems would hamper it sufficiently that it has to take a buyout offer (mostly in stock) from a complementary startup, such as Facebook or Ning.

The current situation is unlikely to remain stable. Google, Yahoo, and Microsoft are all likely to develop leadership in social networking independently, via further development of their existing properties (instant messaging, photo and video sharing, email, group discussions, search) and through knitting those properties together. They'll also be motivated to make major acquisitions, if the math seems favorable.

In industry shorthand, Google came to be known as a technology company trying to expand into media; relative to Google, Yahoo is viewed as a "lifestyle-focused" technology and media company that all too often doesn't measure up on pure technology. Google CEO Eric Schmidt led two major technology companies before taking the Google post; Terry Semel, Yahoo's previous CEO, reportedly didn't even use email before taking the digital helm at Yahoo.

More recently, Yahoo—under the uneven but deeply grounded leadership of cofounder and now-CEO-again Jerry Yang—has begun to give more space to contemporary software development and emerging technology in its vision. Under the stewardship of new CTO Ari Balogh, a commonality of vision is emerging among Yahoo engineers. An embrace of open formats and interoperability with the developer community and users is putting a fresh new spin on the company. This capability was arguably always there. The departure of "don't-get-the-web" executives like Semel and Lloyd Braun is a breath of fresh air for Yahoo; the openness of the new vision should help them attract new talent and fresh respect from the ecosystem.

An enormously influential player is Microsoft, also a technology company if you had to reduce the description to a single word. It is their turf that Google is now stepping into on many fronts, so the spotlight battle has shifted from "Google vs. Yahoo" to "Google vs. Microsoft" now that Microsoft is investing on many fronts in order to strike back against massive Google encroachments on its territory. It's not so much that Google may steal market share away from Microsoft in the area of office software, through the release of Google Docs and Spreadsheets, for example; it's a matter of a war for talent and partnerships. Google has graduated to young adulthood, and is moving towards a status of becoming the "it" company boasting ownership of infrastructure and relationships on a scale once dominated by Microsoft.

Ultimately, despite all the background noise of new features, hacks, and promotions, observers of the search scene will want to know which company is leading in terms of paid search revenue and in terms of search usage. And that's where Google, for now, seems likely to hang onto its lead in what is fast racing towards becoming a $50 billion global market.

Competition has not been kind to fifth-place portal wannabe IAC Interactive, the Barry Diller–led holding company that has been buying and selling assets and changing its name frequently since its Shopping Channel days. Some of IAC's major properties, such as LendingTree, stumbled badly in the face of the subprime lending crisis and the associated economic slowdown. Ask.com couldn't gain search market share and has been rebranded to a search service focusing on women's lifestyle topics. As its competitors have grown in size and clout, much of IAC has actually shrunk. Even within its core categories, it risks being reduced to a rump.

At the time of this writing, Yahoo and Microsoft have called off merger negotiations following a drawn-out process that saw Microsoft placing a formal bid for Yahoo that rose as high as a $48 billion valuation. At Yahoo's annual board meeting August 1, 2008, the status-quo board, including CEO Jerry Yang, were resoundingly confirmed by a strong majority of shareholders. Maverick investor Carl Icahn, who had threatened to launch a proxy fight to unseat the existing board, could not muster the support of other disgruntled shareholders; nor could he count on Microsoft renewing its appetite for a full takeover. Prior to the board elections, Microsoft tried one final offer that involved a complicated but piecemeal attempt to acquire just the search portion of Yahoo's business, an offer Yahoo summarily rejected. Icahn, finally, more or less fell in line, promising to press for renewed attention to hiring a CEO with more operations savvy than Yang. Around the same time, oilman T. Boone Pickens—a major shareholder—sold his shares, declaring Yahoo's board to be "pathetic." Were a blockbuster full takeover to go through, we would open a new chapter in web history; fortunately for me, it's one I don't have to write at the moment. Yahoo is still Yahoo. The sun still rises in Sunnyvale.

Think Small to Get Big: What Search Marketing Will Look Like in 2015

Throughout this book, I've emphasized the features of search marketing that give businesses of all sizes unprecedented access to niche markets. Large businesses will need to adapt to think more about micromarkets. This is a trend they've been following anyway. The number of products and choices has exploded in most industries over the past 30 years. In that respect, search marketing has blossomed in tandem with the postmodern global economy. Increasingly, consumers and businesses want products, services, and information to be available on demand. Conducting a search is the quintessential form of expression of such increasingly impatient demands.

As large businesses adapt—sometimes too slowly—to emerging demands, small-growth businesses can get big fast. Many will grow faster than their ability to manage that growth.

Today, most of us think of a search in terms of a fairly consistent practice: typing keywords into a box, using a search engine site like Google.com, within an operating system like Windows or Macintosh, on a browser like Internet Explorer, Mozilla Firefox, Safari, or now, Google Chrome.

Of course, the present-day reality isn't that narrow. Many consumers are becoming adept at shopping search, news search, local search, and other forms of specialized searching. Some install toolbars in their browsers. Many consumers are searching on mobile devices, reading commands into their cell phones, and getting information from voice-recognition services provided by companies like Google. Luxury cars now come with navigation systems. Within five years, most new vehicles are likely to come with sophisticated local search capabilities.

The availability of new forms of targeting will give advertisers new access to a variety of new forms of "searcher" behavior. Don't be too restrictive in your definition of a searcher. It's unlikely that the next generation of searchers will restrict themselves to the forms of information retrieval that are most recognizable to us today.

The Revolution in Media Buying

I've argued in this book that the automated advertising auction systems developed by Overture and Google put significant pressure on online media buying. Yet traditional media buying has yet to be revolutionized. As AdWords-like methods spill over into offline advertising buys, advertisers will likely be able to bid on a variety of targeting options in late-night cable TV, product placements, billboards, newspaper ads, and more. This will change some of the skill sets required of those in the advertising business, but it will likely benefit both publishers and advertisers. Just as Google Search can monetize less-desirable ad inventory by making it available at sell-off prices, offline advertisers might benefit from an automated system that creates more bidding wars on (let's say) desirable billboard locations, while allowing them to command at least some minimum amount for less-desirable properties. Advertisers could simply log on and bid for the inventory they desired, provided of course that they had already fed in their graphics and were a trusted paid-up member of some sort of ad buying program.

Google has launched some new targeting options that make it clear they're bent on expanding their role in the world of online advertising. The content targeting programs have been expanded to allow advertisers and publishers to transact on a variety of ad formats. Notably, the flexibility of the targeting is improving. Advertisers have the option to target their ad placements and bids to specific websites (such as www.nytimes.com), rather than being purely at the mercy of Google's matching technology that up until now has decided which pages (not sites) make the best match for your ads. Forms of demographic targeting are gradually inching their way into the AdWords system. The footprint of this measurable, accountable digital advertising auction continues to grow.

A Transparent World

As the search metaphor bleeds into other realms, particularly into the commercial realm, consumers will grow increasingly impatient with artificial impediments to enlightenment.

I used to think it was normal not to know where to find a particular item in a supermarket. Now, it makes me impatient. I think a supermarket should act like a search engine. Before too long, many of them will.

Before the last round of the 2005 Masters golf tournament, commentators on the Golf Channel sat around the table responding to a deluge of emails on the subject of why no televised coverage was available of "leftover" Sunday morning play from the rain-delayed third round. These defenders of the status quo sided with the powers that be at CBS, making it clear that "full 18-hole coverage" means coverage of the leaders only, and plenty of gaps in coverage of players a bit farther behind in the pack. Since the leaders had not completed their Saturday round due to poor weather earlier in the tournament, they played as many as nine holes of their third round on Sunday morning before the fourth and final round began. CBS golf analyst Peter Oosterhuis—who, according to his bio, led the 1984 PGA tour in sand saves—told the Golf Channel team that "it's simply not possible to show every hole of every tournament." Yet viewers were obviously dismayed by the fact that they didn't have the chance to view live coverage of Tiger Woods overtaking Chris DiMarco for the Masters lead on Sunday morning. That morning, Woods turned a five-shot deficit into a three-shot lead on the strength of a record-tying charge of seven consecutive birdies. This was hardly "every hole of every tournament." It was the sort of drama golf fans spend all year waiting for, and years reminiscing about—if they get to watch it live, that is.[11]

In the short term, it's no doubt true that neither the Augusta National Golf Club nor a network like CBS (nor cable networks for that matter) will bend over backwards to address logistical problems that result in disappointed viewers. In that sense, it will continue to be "impossible" to watch what they find inconvenient to show us. But to hear that making such adjustments is impossible rings hollow in this day and age. Just a few days before, after all, I'd been able to access a satellite photo of my street using Google Maps, absolutely free of charge. In a context where information and images of all types seem readily available on demand, expectations go up accordingly.

Augusta National is a private club, and the networks remain powerful organizations that have every intention of playing by Augusta's rules. That rules out, say, placing low-cost cameras in various spots around the course, or placing small cameras around the necks of caddies and various patrons so that enthusiasts could access coverage of any shot of any player in the final round of the tournament. But the principle here is that it's less and less credible to claim that information and digital content are impossible to access. For better or for worse, in a full-disclosure world, you really cannot hide. And you come off looking silly and defensive when you try to.[12]

More recently, Google teamed with the International Olympic Committee to provide a dedicated channel for coverage of the Beijing Summer Games on YouTube, for countries that don't have sponsored television broadcasts.[13] As usual, Google finds itself in the center of the action. YouTube was allowed to sell ads around the content, but only ads from Olympic sponsors. Ironically, the channel was not viewable in China, underscoring Google's delicate situation vis-à-vis its Chinese operations, where human rights issues and Internet censorship practices generate still-simmering global debate. With the YouTube Olympics deal, in any case, we see the continuation of a trend towards Google making information available to parts of the world that were previously in the dark.

Beyond mere sporting spectacles, wired observers of global happenings are uploading the news in text and video form to any number of blogs and platforms, including YouTube, NowPublic, Blogger, and Twitter. It's been two generations since a famous photojournalist exposed the reality on the ground in Vietnam. Today, with a billion cellphones in our hands, the crowdsourcing of photojournalism diffuses the risk and increases the immediacy of media, with all of the positives and negatives that may entail. Notable examples include Generacion Y, a blog posted largely by a youthful Cuban blogger disguised as a tourist, from Havana hotels; and the case of James Karl Buck, a UC Berkeley graduate journalism student who may have precipitated his release from Egyptian prison by Twittering "Alive and OK, but still in jail," following his arrest for photographing a demonstration. His 48 "followers" passed the news onto the U.S. Embassy and press organizations.

In keeping with the transparency and immediacy of online search and information sharing, the fields of corporate online reputation monitoring and online public relations have emerged as rapid growth areas. Organizing the world's information and making it universally accessible—whether that is accomplished by a single company or by a billion users working on a multitude of platforms—changes the way we live and work.

The availability of data takes on truly mind-boggling proportions, providing answers to questions we didn't even have ten years ago. It's not only Google that is opening up these new worlds. Real estate search engine Trulia is just one among hundreds of startups that is creating a rich new database of information—backed by existing databases and user input—that didn't previously exist at all.

It is far from out of the question that these trends will deeply alter the way that public policy is made. Today, for example, measures of inflation might be based on an arbitrary government-led data-gathering process. With enough committed members, a measure of "true" inflation as experienced by peers would not be that difficult to arrive at based on a willing constituency of participants willing to log purchases over the long haul. It's not a matter of whether such data revolutions are possible—they are, in nearly every field—but more a matter of how they will be implemented, by whom, and how they might be used to help better our lives.

The New Geography

My maternal grandparents, and their parents before them, lived and worked on a farm near Seaforth, Ontario. In such tight-knit communities, especially for those who were lucky enough to live off the land in a fertile region, life was comfortable. A restricted set of choices was part and parcel of this relative prosperity, though. Banks, suppliers, and distributors could dictate the terms of doing business. Searching for different options meant nothing less than packing up lock, stock, and barrel and moving somewhere else. Business was transacted in places like Wingham, Blyth, Monkton, Goderich, and Mitchell, no more than 20 miles from home. It was an hour's drive to the largest city in the region, London. They'd get there about once a year.

Life in farm country has changed fairly dramatically in spite of outward appearances. With the advent of e-commerce and online search, farmers do have the ability to compare banks, insurance companies, and other financial services. There is growing use of computer technology to monitor crops and animals. Families can investigate options for their children's postsecondary education years in advance. The small, cash-based craft businesses or bed-and-breakfast operations that many rural residents run on the side, or as retirement projects, can be widely publicized online at low cost. Some will dabble in eBay transactions, making a few dollars here or there. Others will hit a rich vein of market demand and find themselves facing the challenge of running a growing business.

My parents and I have lived in a variety of urban and suburban settings, much different from life on the farm. Even though we're only 24 years apart in age, my work habits—and, perhaps, whole concept of professional geographic reach—are already considerably different from my dad's. For a significant proportion of his life, he was fortunate enough to walk to his office only a few blocks away. His bailiwick, Burlington, Ontario, was local by definition. (Since my father is an urban planner by profession, though, it would be bad news if I were to write here that he didn't have an advanced grasp of shifting concepts of work and geography!) He had the opportunity to travel to professional conferences in various North American cities, but it was nothing like the frequent airline travel of today's business road warriors.

From 1999–2004, after a long stint in graduate school got me used to the habit, I worked solely from home, while reaching a global audience of clients and professional contacts. (This flowed nicely from the precedent set in universities, where professors and graduate students were some of the first people to use email to communicate systematically and cheaply, and sometimes eloquently, with global colleagues. The main reason for this is that until the early 1990s, few outside of government, military, and university circles had free access to email.) Now, I divide time between home and a downtown office. In addition, a considerable amount of work gets done on airplanes and in hotels, or in the homes of family members I may be visiting for days at a stretch.

Office space is used in increasingly flexible ways, and is more and more cost-effective for companies. In some companies, employees need only come in two days a week, and don't even have regular desks (a practice known as "hoteling"). Wireless Internet connections, cheaper hosting, and increasingly flexible telecommunications technology are among the many shifts that allow companies to base office space decisions more around image and lifestyle concerns than around the old imperatives of productivity in a single place.

Larger companies can get even more creative. Senior engineers for one technology company I know had their time earmarked for an 18-month project of immense importance, but they didn't want to relocate to the new campus location near Los Angeles. They "commuted" by airplane for long one-day sessions on-site, once or twice a week. They worked remotely from their homes for another two or three days a week, hundreds of miles away.

Unlike my grandparents' farm (or my other grandfather's machine shop), the business we do could theoretically be transacted anywhere, but it isn't quite that simple. It feels like we have a choice as to the most advantageous way to "set up shop." But these trends don't diminish the importance of face-to-face contact. We are, in fact, face to face with more and more business associates all the time, both online (virtual but increasingly lifelike social networks) and offline (face-to-face for real). And as Professor Richard Florida has shown, "creative clusters" in cities do matter, and there are greater challenges to remotely working in a Tofflerian "wired cottage" than many realize. The logic shouldn't be too hard to follow. That hip plumber with the Blackberry still has to unclog your drain. And when that semiretired consultant calls me in the middle of the week from his second home near the lake (that has now become his primary address), let's just say I'd feel a little more comfortable if he pretended to also have an office in a big city.

The choices people have mean that talent does seem to gravitate towards certain kinds of cities today. In the old days, factories and buildings seemed to hire people. Today, a lot more workers choose a lifestyle, then find a job. That has translated into growth for wired fresh-air locales such as Bend, Oregon, and Victoria, British Columbia. It's also meant a concentration of high-tech talent in places that have the best restaurants, neighborhoods, and culture: the usual suspects such as San Francisco, New York, Boston, and Toronto.[14]

Another habit I've picked up is that I work late. Not as bad as some hackers and scribblers who still can't kick the 4 A.M. habit, but pretty different from my ancestors who had to get up to milk the cows. It's anyone's guess how rampant the practice of working odd hours is, but gauging from the habits of clients and colleagues, it's not easy to pin down when someone is available. And more often than not, it's important to get to know someone well enough to understand when they'll be groggy and out-of-sorts on the phone, and when they'll be primed for a productive meeting. For those uncomfortable with 9–5, the flexibility of working life today offers a variety of devices and excuses for behavior that might have been written off as bizarre 20 years ago. But by adjusting to different work styles, progressive companies might well be fostering a significant increase in productivity.

All in all, businesspeople today need to take a flexible approach to their concept of geography. When one's geographic focus broadens, one also becomes accustomed to a shifting concept of time, yet another development that presents both an opportunity and a burden to knowledge workers. I'm not here to argue that no one relies on local communities anymore or that no one punches a clock; in many cases, the ability to dominate a local market is a great advantage, and work schedules are more flexible for skilled freelancers and those in senior positions. But growth companies today will do well to re-evaluate preconceived notions of where or how employees should work, or where their best customers and best suppliers are likely to be located.

Business Is Global

Google is a great example of a company that operates globally and that facilitates the efforts of customers who want to operate globally. It's perhaps trite to say it, but your company is going to find it imperative to explore international opportunities in the coming years. From the standpoint of AdWords, targeting searchers anywhere in the world is relatively easy. The flip side of that growth potential is that many businesses are not ready for it. A sales presentation for an Asian audience might require more than just verbal translation, for example. It might require credible imagery of local customers and other relevant cultural references.

Business Is Local

Meanwhile, millions of businesses just want to operate in a single locale, or in a few cities. If you were to travel ahead five years, I think you'd be amazed at how many new ways you'd have to access information about local businesses. People's habits will change, gradually at first, but eventually radically. The supposed decline of flesh-and-blood interaction is the supposed drawback of online culture. That myth will be turned upside down. Store clerks who mumble and condescend will be treated with increasing degrees of contempt from device-wielding information junkies. The visitor to Ikea will be able to access all sorts of comparative information while right in the store, including user reviews of the products.

On the way to some of this advanced functionality, niche players who find a middle ground, providing relatively uncomplicated means of connecting customers with vendors, will thrive.

Craigslist today is a simple, friendly online classifieds site that has enough following in several cities that users feel a sense of community and see enough listings that they keep coming back. Want a funky office space to sublet? Need a ride? That's the type of thing you can get on Craigslist. This should probably be called Local Commerce 1.0. By the time we hit 3.0, we'll wonder what we did without it. Whatever 3.0 means! For now, the crown for best local search site in the Web 2.0 era surely goes to Yelp, a startup that seems to get it.

Considerable wealth has been amassed by the publishers of modest offline classified publications such as *Auto Trader* and *The Buy and Sell Newspaper*. When similar principles are applied more widely by more online entrepreneurs, the increase in economic productivity will be significant, and that next generation of "classifieds entrepreneurs" stands to become an order of magnitude or two wealthier than the previous generation.

Work Is Decentralized

Work-wise, we don't live in a small town any more. I don't see any particular evidence of a true loss of intimacy in people's personal relationships, but what has been widely documented is the younger generation's growing comfort level with weak ties to an ever-expanding social network. Online relationships, in particular, make it possible to have shallow relationships with a broad range of folks, while deepening and reinvigorating relationships with old friends and like-minded enthusiasts of one sort or another.

Remote working relationships are, by now, commonplace, and the strange question of whether you really "know" someone you haven't met face-to-face (or don't see often) should be treated as something of a curiosity.

Still, the pendulum definitely seems like it can overswing in some people's work habits. There is a strange wisdom lurking in the methodologies of those of us who take extra trouble to pick up the phone and talk to someone, or to seek out face-to-face contact.

I don't see the rise of weak ties or the increase in dispersed project teams—and other contemporary habits—as mutually exclusive to the wisdom of focusing appropriately on "real" personalized attention.

Discussion Groups for AdWords Addicts

You may find the following communities useful for discussion and networking on the topic of Google AdWords and related areas. The terrain shifts often, so there may be others worth a mention that don't appear here. URLs also change too frequently to publish.

- SEM 2.0, a not-for-profit discussion group for search engine marketers that I created and currently co-moderate, with Adam Audette, on the Google Groups platform

- WebmasterWorld, privately owned by Brett Tabke

- Search Engine Watch Forums, privately owned by Incisive Interactive Marketing LLC

Communications + Mobility + Interoperability + Community = Productivity

The Internet itself offered a common platform that could be used from virtually anywhere to contact like-minded individuals to collaborate or bond. The original discussion groups and text email messages had all of these characteristics. The explosion of those principles into all walks of life didn't take place overnight. What has happened has been a recurrence of increasingly complex and powerful forms of collaboration, impossible to sum up in a catchphrase ("global brain" might sound trendy, but it might also miss the mark). No one format or channel reigns supreme, but the principles that make new formats and channels particularly powerful keep recurring. To this day, "letters to the editor" writers of the old-school variety fail to grasp these drivers of economic productivity. Well-intentioned critics mistakenly harp on the supposed "mania" to "make workers more productive." This isn't what it's about. Rather, it's about harnessing friction-reducing, iterative, learning systems that achieve goals faster.

It's also about the rise of "post-material" values even amidst much material global deprivation.[15] In relatively wealthy societies, people have a strong compulsion towards choice and self-expression. This is unlikely to change; indeed, even relatively poor societies have adopted such values. In a subtle way not always communicated to the outside world, people who work in Silicon Valley at companies like Google believe that by constructing powerful engines of economic productivity, they can sweep away outmoded methodologies that have kept much of the planet impoverished, much as advances in agriculture led to giant leaps in the standards of living in societies that enjoyed them.

Investment in information technology over the past 30 years has reduced the costs of doing business, sometimes dramatically. As forms of information retrieval and communication (like search and email) get cheaper and cheaper to operate, the cost to start up a new business falls. (Google CEO Eric Schmidt is a noted advocate of this overall environment of lower-cost, on-demand web-based IT services, which he refers to as "cloud computing.") The cost to find and retain customers, the cost of searching for employees, the cost of running a wireless network, the cost of hosting a website, the low cost of creating custom programming with the LAMP Stack[16] and beyond; these trends seem to offer a great deal of flexibility for new businesses to grow at much lower cost than previously. One outcome, for example, is that innovation and change are emphasized over continuity for its own sake. When it is much less expensive to shut down a mediocre business in favor of a new initiative, businesses won't cling as long to unproductive units. As this occurs, the balance of power shifts. Many traditional monopolists lose their hold over entrepreneurs. But new power brokers will emerge.

Google is one of those power brokers. You don't really get to choose how history unfolds. Which types of companies become powerful (new media companies, say) and which lose their power (downtown office tower developers and local phone service providers, for example) is completely out of your hands and mine. But it can be fun to watch some traditional monopolies topple. Even more fun can be attempting to benefit from the new environment by exploiting new niches quickly and avoiding the same old ruts that used to force businesses to devote outsized amounts of their capital to basic infrastructure.

Conclusion: What about Peanut Butter?

At age four, I began a love affair with peanut butter that carries on to this day. Fairly early on, I discovered that I liked crunchy better than smooth. I also found that adding processed cheese slices to my peanut butter on toast horrified adults and tasted pretty good to boot. I credit the constant flow of protein with helping me get decent grades in high school while coming at least third in several regional cross-country ski races. (Unfortunately, I also liked potato chips, which, along with too much joke telling and book reading, got me bounced from the team.) I later upped the ante by adding dill pickles to the peanut-butter-and-cheese recipe. But there's more to the story, much more.

What kind of relationship do you have with peanut butter? If you're young or relatively affluent, chances are you know a bit about what's "good" for you and what's "bad."

Growing up, we didn't know anything. Peanut butter came with hydrogenated vegetable oil and plenty of salt and sugar, and that was that. Weird professors' children ate that natural stuff and drank skim milk from powder. We just assumed it was because they were poor. I consumed brands like Kraft and Squirrel, and some store brands.

In the 1980s, I was introduced to Skippy. "Super Chunk" was surely sublime. It was also loaded with the same old hydrogenated vegetable oil. And icing sugar. Icing sugar!

For the past ten years or so, I've been on relatively high moral and nutritional ground... or so I thought. I've been eating nothing but store-label "natural" peanut butter. Because I thought this was healthy (no hydrogenated oil, no sugar), I ate a lot of it... until I began to hear rumors that peanuts are loaded with pesticides. I began paying far too much for tiny jars of organic peanut butter, until further Internet research convinced me that regular natural peanut butter is perfectly fine and subject to regular government testing.

You see a lot of rumors flying around and little in the way of solid facts. Sites like peanutbutterlovers.com are actually run by peanut farmers' marketing boards. The state of information on peanut butter does seem to be relatively undeveloped. It has been a long time since anyone as great as George Washington Carver has turned his attention to the peanut.

What we have here, I believe, is merely one example of an emerging market demand: a demand for better, healthier, more interesting peanut butter, and preferably not in a tiny overpriced jar.[17] It's a relative micromarket for now, but it could be a lucrative one. (Think pinot noir, zinfandel, syrah, or some other once-obscure wine variety.) It's a demand, moreover, that some large companies have had an interest in resisting. But the tide is turning.

As recently as 2004, this peanut butter connoisseur felt himself hitting a wall. Sure, he was a bit more educated about the gooey brown paste than he was a year earlier. But he still didn't have access to a wide product selection. He didn't have access to discussions and debates about peanut butter. There were seemingly no clubs. Seemingly no tastings to attend. Few if any awards to be won. No Hollywood blockbusters about yuppies making their way through "peanut country."

The ensuing four-year period in peanut butter history proved Dr. Tomkins'[18] point about the explosion of user-generated content just about as well as anything else you can imagine. A vast Long Tail of peanut butter information mushroomed out of nowhere, and coincidentally, I began noticing peanut butter references in a way I hadn't before.

From my vantage point, peanut butter references started popping up everywhere. I realized that the planet wasn't short on variations on peanut butter, or peanut butter metaphors. By sharp contrast with the exploding, chaotic world of grassroots peanut butter references, corporate and industry sites devoted to peanut butter often seem grotesquely uninformative. Even when they aren't, they feel like they're hiding something. And in a way, they are. They wish you didn't have access to huge amounts of information about their product and their industry. But you do. How are you going to make use of it?

Peanut butter, hauntingly, found its way into the daily discourse of the industry press and the search blogosphere. A now-famous memo by Yahoo VP Brad Garlinghouse criticized the company for spreading its efforts too thinly, "like peanut butter." He also said that he hated peanut butter.

I discovered that a search engine optimization expert and author named Aaron Wall was such a lover of this food staple that he has many times referred to himself (not hater Garlinghouse) as "peanut butter man."

For Christmas in 2007, Page Zero staffer Scott Perry was kind enough to send me eight jars of specialty peanut butter from Minnesota-based gourmet peanut butter retailer P.B.Loco.

I realized that in my quest for better peanut butter, and for a peanut butter community, I was not alone. But I also realized that my half-hearted quest of 2004 had been—to use T. Boone Pickens' term—pathetic. Instead of ferreting out all the peanut butter information and community I could find, I just sort of sat back and waited for 2008 to come. I admit it: I've been conditioned to accept "reactive" research and community provision as the norm. Bring me the info, and bring me like-minded people, Mr. Internet! I'll be here, waiting impatiently. Not only is "Google making us stupid,"[19] it appears the trajectory of constantly improving information retrieval, and easily accessible community, is getting me connected without me having to lift a finger. Is the social media world also making me socially lazy? Or can I have it both ways? Can I enjoy the benefit of increased information flow while avoiding the atrophy of research and human rapport skills that could come with the reduced burden on me? And how will I avoid a descent into trivial pursuits if I let the Long Tail into my formerly truncated worldview?

Today (see Figure 12-4), you can perform a search for YouTube videos related to "peanut butter," right from the Google Search interface if that's the way you prefer to search. Here, you'll find around half a million peanut-butter-related videos. Yep, 500,000! If you search the same term from the YouTube interface, the count is only 16,000. Perhaps an issue I'll have to take up with the Google/YouTube product teams at some point.

It appears that not a single person has uploaded a video of themselves rubbing peanut butter on their bald head, as I encouraged in the first edition of the book. One video appears of a woman rubbing peanut butter into her navel. She has a number of fans. (Combined, the terms "navel" and "belly button" account for about 7,000 available videos on YouTube.)

> *Fact: Even natural peanut butter will keep for two to three months without being refrigerated. But it does need to be kept in a relatively cool, dry place. If you put your peanut butter in a wine fridge to ensure that you get the temperature just right, you're well on your way to yuppie peanut butter connoisseur status.*

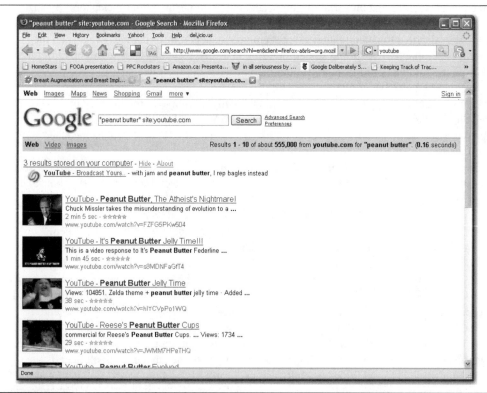

FIGURE 12-4   Searching for "peanut butter" videos archived on YouTube, from the Google Search interface

The future of peanut butter—I hope—will be fascinating. Big brands and industry groups will fight the tide of increasingly informed and demanding consumers. Niche brands will rise, and sometimes be acquired by the big guys. Enthusiasts and communities of enthusiasts will be frustrated by the gulf between forms of online gratification and old-school advertising, brand control, and shelf space domination.

Speaking of shelf space, old-school ad agencies types have, of late, desperately equated search results pages and other targeted online venues with "shelf space," counseling their clients that their goal is to "dominate the digital shelf." While the advice to buy additional exposure in targeted online media is certainly sound, the analogy is misplaced. There is no way to monopolize the search universe, and no way to block out undesirable information.

To close on a philosophical note, it may be fair to say that two guiding principles have driven the politics and economics of modernity: respect for persons (Kant), and the elimination, insofar as it is possible, of distorted and manipulated communications (Habermas) on the long road towards an "ideal speech situation." Fighting those powerful forces can be very costly indeed, especially in an era where you can go from 0 to 500,000 publicly available videos about "peanut butter" in the space of four years. Companies that hope to freeze time and keep consumers in the *Mad Men* era of Madison Avenue circa 1961 will, to enlightened searchers, possess all the credibility of Burma's[20] generals.

For smart companies, the opportunity remains vast. Some marketers may remain liars, but best to pursue that in its most positive, playful connotation.

Endnotes

1. Hugh McLeod, "How to Be Creative," Manifesto at ChangeThis.com, October 19, 2004, at http://www.changethis.com/6.HowToBeCreative. McLeod recommends creative types avoid bohemian ghettos and full-time immersion in their art; in other words, you can still "go for it" while sticking to your day job, or school, thus greatly reducing risk and servitude.

2. For more, see Eric Alterman, "Out of Print: The Death and Life of the American Newspaper," *The New Yorker*, March 31, 2008.

3. Carol H. Weiss, "Knowledge Creep and Decision Accretion," *Knowledge: Creation, Diffusion, Utilization,* 1(3): 381–404.

4. In the words of one copywriter from Turkey: "Google is my best friend! Google is my best friend! Google is my best friend! Google is my best friend! Google is my best friend!" From Kevin Roberts and A. G. Lafley, *Lovemarks: The Future Beyond Brands* (Powerhouse Books, 2004), 182.

5. For Google's announcement, see Sundar Pichai, "A fresh take on the browser," Official Google Blog, September 1, 2008. Archived at http://googleblog.blogspot.com/2008/09/fresh-take-on-browser.html.

6. Marc Andreessen, "Open Social, a New Universe of Social Applications All Over the Web," October 31, 2007, http://blog.pmarca.com.

7. I took a slightly different view, asking what the company would be worth if it faced significant litigation and were forced to pull 70% of its content offline. My take was that Google was quietly valuing YouTube at $5 billion or more, while getting a bargain price from the founders using the "potential litigation discount" as a bargaining tactic. See Traffick.com, "Meet Google, World's Largest VC," October 9, 2006.

8. Source: comScore.

9. John Heilemann, "Journey to the (Revolutionary, Evil-Hating, Cash Crazy, and Possibly Self-Destructive) Center of Google," *GQ,* March 2005.

10. Source: comScore, Top 50 Web Properties in the U.S., March 2008.

11. Anti-CBS opinion from competing news organizations was easy enough to find with a couple of mouse clicks over to Google News; viz., Kevin Scarbinsky, "CBS Needs More Journalism, Less Genuflecting," *The Birmingham News,* April 11, 2005; Bob Harig, "Ratings Soar, Not Coverage," *St. Petersburg Times,* April 12, 2005.

12. For a deeper exploration of this theme, see Don Tapscott and David Ticoll, *The Naked Corporation: How the Age of Transparency Will Revolutionize Business* (Free Press, 2003).

13. Loretta Chao and Jessica E. Vascellaro, "YouTube Strikes Online Olympics Deal," *Wall Street Journal*, August 5, 2008.

14. So-called "gay-index" research has discovered that high-tech talent is attracted to cities which, for similar reasons, are home to large gay populations. Richard Florida, formerly a regional economic development professor at Carnegie Mellon University in Pittsburgh, discovered that economic development was driven as much by where workers chose to live as it was by where companies decided to locate. He further discovered that indices of high-tech economic development generated a list of cities that looked very similar to the list of cities with large gay populations: San Francisco, Boston, Seattle, and Washington, DC. See Bill Catlin, "Gay Index Measures High-Tech Success," Minnesota Public Radio, June 5, 2001, archived at news.minnesota.publicradio.org. Subsequent to Florida's early work, he gained prominence as he published books such as *The Rise of the Creative Class* (Basic Books, 2002), his groundbreaking work highlighting the success of cities ranking high on measures of tolerance, arts and lifestyle, and technology; *The Flight of the Creative Class: The New Global Competition for Talent* (Collins, 2005), a thinly veiled indictment of Bush Administration labor market policies, immigration

policies, intolerance, and fiscal policies; and *Who's Your City?* (Basic Books, 2008), a reinforcement of the point that where you live matters enormously to your opportunities and personal development. Recently, Prof. Florida has moved to my hometown to take up a position as the head of a newly created research unit at the University of Toronto Joseph P. Rotman School of Management. He is a fan of our city's funky neighborhoods, such as Kensington Market, and its legendary Manhattan-like diversity. For an antidote to this viewpoint, see the counterintuitive, but no less empirical, perspective on technology entrepreneurs who have escaped the main hubs to work in far-flung, lower-cost, tech-friendly havens such as Bend, OR, Albuquerque, NM, Overland Park, KS, and Oklahoma City, OK, in Om Malik, "Escape from Silicon Valley," Business 2.0, November 10, 2004. The purported advantage these alternative business hubs have—such as cheap or free broadband access—will soon seem trite as this access spreads. Theories that speak to the clustering advantages of some locations seem to be triumphing over reclusive virtuality.

15. See "Does Values Research Explain Where Global Opportunity Lies?" Traffick.com, February 17, 2006. The underlying research on "post-materialism" has been led by Prof. Ronald Inglehart for many years.

16. The LAMP Stack is a web programming term that refers to the concomitant use of Linux, Apache, MySQL, and Perl/Python/PHP; respectively, all open-source or open-source-friendly server operating system, web hosting environment, web database programming, and custom programming languages. Beyond the LAMP stack lie similar programming languages such as Ruby on Rails that increasingly allow companies to hire programmers to customize applications, but without the licensing costs and restrictiveness associated with traditional proprietary languages and systems (such as Microsoft's .NET architecture).

17. Micromarkets based around a single fruit, vegetable, or legume seem to be one example of an "enthusiast area" that is currently underserved and perfectly tailored to online marketing. On the weekend of Saturday, August 27, 2005, 25,000 visitors once again descended on Zurich, Ontario, population 860, for the annual bean festival. It should be noted that Zurich is not The White Bean Capital of Canada. That distinction goes to Hensall, a few miles down the road. One of the experts cited in this book (who shall remain nameless) is a regular attendee of the Stockton Asparagus Festival in California. The festival's website estimates that the festival has a $19 million economic impact on Stockton.

18. Yahoo's Chief Scientist. Remember?

19. Nicholas Carr, "Is Google Making Us Stupid?," *The Atlantic*, July/August 2008, 56–63.

20. Myanmar's, to some.

Index

References to figures are in *italics*.

A

accounts
    campaigns and ad groups, 102–103
    historical performance, 141–142
    setup, 103–105
    sharing campaign access, 105–106
accuracy, 224
ad groups, 102–103, 116–120, 138
    granularity, 121–122
    limits on keywords per ad group,
        120–121
    multiple managers, 122
    naming, 125
    organization and bottom-line
        performance, 123
    overlapping keywords in different ad
        groups, 124–125
    post-click tracking, 123
    reevaluating structure, 125–126
ad networks, 14–15
ad placement, 215–216
ad position, 99, 203–205
ad rotation optimizer, 108–109
ad scheduling, 210
ad space, 216
ad tone, 216–221
Adapt, 205
AdGooroo, 188–189
Adhere, 12
AdRank, 133

ads, writing, 126–127
AdsBot, 148–149
AdSense, 21
    non-disclosure of details, 62
advertiser needs, vs. user needs, 52–53
advertising
    history of advertising on the
        Internet, 7–8
    limits, 6
    traditional vs. nontraditional
        media, 10–11
AdWords, 20–21
    Application Program Interface (API), 65
    early version challenges, 50–52
    ranking formulas in previous versions,
        138–139
    start of, 33–37
AdWords Editor, 208–209
AdWords Select, 52
affiliate marketing, 159–160
algorithmic changes, 22–25
Allen, Ray, 89
AltaVisa, 19, 40–41, 45, *82*
Amazon, 348–350
American Blind v. Google, 259
Analytics. *See* Google Analytics
Andreessen, Marc, 342
AOL, 350
AOL Search, 46
appropriateness, 229
aQuantive, 64
arbitrage, 144–145, 164

Ask.com, 15
Atlas Search, 205
auctions, on keywords and phrases in real
    time, 93–94
August National Golf Club, 354
authenticity, 8
average ad position, 94
awards, 13–14

B

B2B campaigns, 160
B2C campaigns, 161
Ballmer, Steve, 12
Balogh, Ari, 351
banned items, 57–58
        See also editorial policies
banner blindness, 80
banners, clickthrough rates (CTRs), 79
Beckwith, Harry, 328
bid discounters, 96
bid management tools, goal-based, 205–207
bidding at the keyword level, 207–208
bidding strategy, 205
bidding wars, 99–100
bid-for-placement advertising, 46
bids, upping, 253–254
The Big Red Fez (Godin), 90, 298
billing, 94
Blekko, 42
Blink (Gladwell), 144–145
The Boston Globe, 12
bounce rates, 273, 274
brand impact, testing, 238–239
brand lift, 13
Braverman, Jeff, 328–330
Brewer, Eric, 41
Brin, Sergey, 9, 24, 44
broad matching, 125, 183–184
        one-word broad matching and negative
            keywords, 249–250
        two-word, 248
        See also expanded broad matching;
            matching options

Buck, James Karl, 355
budget, daily budget setting, 106–108
Budget Optimizer, 157
business type, 286–287
business-to-business campaigns, 160
business-to-consumer campaigns, 161
buy-words, 96

C

Calacanis, Jason, 17
calls to action, 231–232
        testing, 235
Campaign Summary, 98
campaigns, 102–103
        Ad Scheduling and Serving, 108–109
        business-to-business (B2B), 160
        business-to-consumer (B2C), 161
        content targeting, 110–114
        country and language, 114
        daily budget setting, 106–108
        Edit Campaign Settings screen, 106, *107*
        information publishing, 163–165
        local, 162–163
        naming, 125
        professional services, 161–162
        search network partners, 109–110
        sharing access, 105–106
case studies, 143–145
        Brian's Buzz, 169–171
        FourOxen Corp., 172–173
        HomeStars, 147–150
        media company, 145–147
category pages, vs. single-product pages,
    321–324
Chrome, 340–341
Churchill, Christine, 189
clarity, 216
classified advertising, spending, 11–12
click auction, 47
click volume, 173–175
Clickable, 205, *206*
clicks, 95

clickthrough rates (CTRs), 56, 95, 140–141
    balancing with ROI, 221
    banners, 79
    for content targeting, 111
    forecasting, 175
Clif Bar, 8
cloud computing, 359
Comedy Central, 258–259
competition, 210–211
competitive intelligence, 188–189
comScore, 16, 84
Confessions of an Advertising Man (Ogilvy),
  217, 218
consumers, 4–5
content bidding, 113
content targeting, 110–114
    ads appearing near content, 254–258
    current affairs, 258–259
contextual advertising. *See* content targeting
ContextWeb, 261
conversion, barriers to, 299–300
conversion environment, 328
Conversion Optimizer, 208, 274–276
conversion rates, 100–101
    forecasting, 175
    launching a conversion improvement
      program, 253
    typical, 320–321
conversion scientists, 283
copywriting, 301–303
    See also writing ads
cost per acquisition. *See* CPA
cost per action. *See* CPA
cost per click (CPC), 95, 278–279
    on different matching options, 185
    forecasting, 173–175
cost per order, 270
country, 114
CPA, 88, 170, 270
CPC. *See* cost per click (CPC)
CPM, 87–88
crawlers, 39–41

credibility, 220
CTRs. *See* clickthrough rates (CTRs)
customer relationship strategies, 168–169

D

The Daily Show, 258–259
dayparting, 209–210
design cues, 303–304
differentiation, 237
direct mail, 90
direct marketing, spending, 11–12
disapproved keywords, 203
discussion groups, 359
dmoz.org, 41–42
double serving, 124–125, 130–131
DoubleClick, 14–15
Douglas, Diana, 163

E

eBay, 348–350
economists, 297
editorial policies, 34–35, 57–58
    See also privacy policies
editorial review, 127
    automated vs. human, 130
    delays and special rules, 129–131
    double serving, 130–131
    network partners, 130
    ramp-up timelines, 130
    responding to disapprovals, 127–128
    tips, 128–129
Eisenberg, Bryan, 286, 287, 297, 298, 299
emerging trends, 339–340
enhanced smart pricing, 112–113
exact matching, 183
    See also matching options
Excite, 40, *81*
expanded broad matching, 56–57,
  200, 248
    See also broad matching
eye-tracking studies, 79–80, 203

F

Fathom Online, 95
feed management, 19, 47
feedback, 35–37
    cycles, 86–87
filtering, 229–231
FindWhat, 49
first-page bids, 152
Fishkin, Rand, 18
fixed minimum bids, 150–151, 152
flair, 232
    vs. flat, 237–238
Fogg, B.J., 325–326
forecasting
    alternative to, 175–176
    clickthrough rates and conversion
        rates, 175
    cost per click and click volume, 173–175
FourOxen Corp., 252
Fox, Nick, 23–24, 60–61
Free Prize Inside! (Godin), 85, 156, 263
futurism, 335

G

Gauthier, Paul, 41
GEICO v. Google, 259
geotargeting, 77
Gladwell, Malcolm, 144–145
Gmail, 258
goals, 165–169
Godin, Seth, 7–8, 17, 84, 87, 90, 156, 238,
    263, 298
Goldman, Eric, 259
Golf Channel, 354
Google
    competitors, 345–347
    current competition, 50
    dominance in the marketplace, 81–83
    and DoubleClick, 14–15
    editorial policies, 34–35
    future of, 64–65

history of, 9–10
    mission statement, 56
    responsiveness of, 35–37
    service revolution, 62–64
    share of advertising online, 9
Google Ad Planner, 261–263
Google Advertising Professionals (GAP), 63
Google AdWords keyword tool, 185–187
Google Analytics, 61, 92
    core metrics, 273–274
    goals, 272–273
    testing sophisticated theories with,
        276–277
    vs. Urchin, 271
    See also web analytics
Google Base, 54–55
Google Book Search, 348–349
Google Checkout, 341
Google Chrome, 340–341
Google Conversion Tracker, 256, 274
Google Labs, 343–345
Google Maps, 343, *345*
Google Print, 348
Google Product Search, 341
Google Search, 43
Google Suggest, 344
Google Universal Search, 54
Google Website Optimizer, 61, 90, 311, 313
    planning and executing a multivarate
        test with, 313–319
    See also multivarate testing
Googlebot, 43
Googleplex, 24
GoTo.com, 46–47
Guerrilla Marketing (Levinson), 76
GWO. *See* Google Website Optimizer

H

high-class arbitrage, 144
Hilburger, Jimmy, 89
historical performance, 141–142
Hitwise, 17

Hitwise Search Intelligence, 189
HomeStars, case study, 147–150, 336
Hopkins, Claude, 227
hot sectors, 327–328
human enforcement, 137

I

IAB. *See* Interactive Advertising Bureau
Icahn, Carl, 352
idealogues, 297
imagining the perfect ad, 213–214
impressions, 94–95
inbound links, 26–27
index spammers, 22–23
information flow, control of, 60–62
information publishing, 163–165
information scent, 287–289
Infoseek, 40
Inktomi, 18–19, 41, 47
Interactive Advertising Bureau, 155
Internet advertising, history of, 7–8
Internet neutrality, 49
interruption marketing, 7
        See also surplus interruption
intrusive advertising, 91–92

J

Jaffe, Joseph, 3
Jaffray, Piper, 20
Jarboe, Greg, 18

K

Kaushik, Avinash, 270–271, 308
Keane, Patrick, 11
keyword arbitrage, 144–145, 164
keyword brainstorming, 195–196
        going narrow, 201–202
        solving your target market's problems,
          196–199
        variations, 199–201

keyword groups. *See* ad groups
keyword inventory, 55–56
        examples of unsold keyword inventory,
          191–193
keyword research, 189–191
        competitive intelligence, 188–189
        experimentation, 192
        generating a keyword list, 191
        Google AdWords keyword tool,
          185–187
        KeywordDiscovery, 188
        news, 189
        software, 93
        tools, 115–116
        TV, 189
        WordTracker, 188
Keyword Spy, 189
keyword stuffing, 23
keyword tracking, 209
keyword variations, 199–201
keyword-based advertising, 19–21
KeywordDiscovery, 188
keywords
        disapproved, 203
        inactive for search, 142, 151
        on landing pages, 324
        limits on per ad group, 120–121
        lowest-quality, 246–248
        negative, 249–250
        overlapping, 124–125, 130–131
        status, 142
        trademarks as, 259–260

L

Lamberti, James, 84
landing pages, 122, 142–143, 289–294
        design, 321–324
        keywords on, 324
        testing, 287
language, 114
LARABAR, 8
Levinson, Jay Conrad, 76

limits on advertising, 6
link farms, 23
linking campaigns, 18, 26–27
Live Search. *See* Microsoft Live Search
Livingston, Brian, 83
local campaigns, 162–163
Long and Winding Road Study, 155–156
Long Tail, 192–193
        See also tail
look and feel, 328–330
LookSmart, 48–49, 261

M

Marchex, 12, 261
Marckini, Frederick, 39
marketer mistakes, 279–281
MarketingSherpa, 17, 156, 163
matching options, 181–185
        CPCs, 185
maximum bids, 96–97
McDonald's, 223
media, traditional vs. nontraditional, 10–11
media buying, 353
media type, 215–216
Metacrawler, 45
Microsoft Live Search, 19, 38, 74
Miller, Scott, 307
Mills, Lee, 306
mindshare, 222
Miva, 15, 49, 261
multimedia ads, 13–14
multivarate testing, 226–227, 312–320

N

naming campaigns and ad groups, 125
natural search results. *See* web index results
negative keywords, 249–250
Net Words (Usborne), 227
network partners, 130
networks. *See* ad networks

Nielsen, Jakob, 53, 80, 85, 286, 287
Norvig, Peter, 23, 75
Notess, Greg, 39

O

Obama, Barack, 222
Obama Girl, 222
Occam's Razor, 270–271
ODP. *See* Open Directory Project
offers, testing, 235
offline marketing, 263–264
Ogilvy, David, 217, 218
online advertising
        size of the market, 12–13
        types of online ad formats, 13
online control panels, 12
online conversion science, 283–284, 285–286
        errors, 289–296
        principles, 296–304
ontology, 117
Open Directory Project, 41–42
Open Text, 45
optimizers, 22
organic index listings, 20
organic results. *See* web index results
organic searches, vs. paid searches, 27
Orkut, 341–342
overlapping keywords, 124–125, 130–131
Overstock.com, 297
Overture, 33–34, 38, 46–47, 56, 116
        ranking formula, 138

P

Page, Larry, 9, 44
PageRank, 23, 42–43, 73
pages viewed, 273
paid inclusion, 18–19, 47
        in directories, 48–49
        reasons for, 22–27
        See also Inktomi

paid search
    control over message, navigation, timing and exposure, 25–26
    predecessors in, 44–50
    ranking formulas, 137–139
paid searches, vs. organic searches, 27
Panama, 138–139, 260
pay as you go advertising, 89
PayPal, 348
pay-per-click model, 55
    pricing, 87–88
permission marketing, 7, 84–85
Permission Marketing (Godin), 7, 84
persuaders, 297–299
persuasion, 300–301
    copywriting, 301–303
    design cues, 303–304
    stereotypes, 303
Persuasion Architecture, 297, 298
phrase matching, 125, 184, 184–185
    See also matching options
Pickens, T. Boone, 352
placement targeting, 114
plumbers, 297–299
policies
    editorial, 34–35, 57–58
    enforcement, 59–60
    privacy, 58–59
    See also editorial review
pop-up ads, 58
portal suppliers, 41
portals, 15, 38, 81, 350–352
post-click tracking, 123
PowerBar, 8
powerposting, 118, 207–208
predecessors
    in paid search, 44–50
    in search, 37–44
preferred bids, 97
pricing model
    in early version of AdWords, 51–52
    pay-per-click model, 87–88

priorities, multiple, 221–224
privacy policies, 58–59
    See also editorial policies
professional services, 161–162
profit motive, 55
proxy metrics, 320
pure click arbitrage, 144
Purple Cow (Godin), 7, 27, 263

Q

Quality Score, 56, 59–60, 134, 135
    for ad ranking, 140–142
    avoiding low initial scores, 202
    details, 152
    historical data, 136
    and low CTRs on content placements, 258
    opinion and arbitrary determinations, 137
    predictive data, 136–137
    as a statistic, 277
Quality-Based Bidding formula, 57, 135, 138, 150–153, 202
    and instability, 276

R

Ramstad, Bob, 89
rank-checking tools, 39
ranking formulas, 137–139
    CTRs, 140–141
    goal of, 139–140
    historical performance, 141–142
    landing pages and website quality, 142–143
ranking methodology, 22–25
Rashtchy, Safa, 20
reach, 16, 49
Real Media, 15
real-time auctions on keywords and phrases, 93–94
relevance, 22
request marketing, 84–85
return on ad spend. *See* ROAS

return on investment. *See* ROI
revenue maximization, 56
revenue per click, 270
reverse bidding wars, 99
    See also bidding wars
ROAS, 269–270
ROI, 101, 269–270
    balancing with CTR, 221
ROI marketing, 85–86
Rubel, Steve, 169

S

sales-generation machine, 90–91
Sandberg, Sheryl, 53, 128
scheduling, 210
Schmidt, Eric, 44, 65, 351, 359
Scientific Advertising (Hopkins), 227
Scoble, Robert, 50, 169
screen real estate, 22
search, predecessors in, 37–44
search engine marketing
    affiliate marketing, 159–160
    strategies for small vs. large companies,
      157–159
    value of, 155–157
search engine optimization, 17–18
search engine results pages (SERPs), 55
Search Engine Visibility (Thurow), 18
search engines, user growth, 16–17
search marketing, 10
    ad networks, 14–15
    multimedia ads, 13–14
    search engine user growth, 16–17
    size of the advertising market, 10–12
    size of the online advertising market,
      12–13
    types of, 17–21
    types of online ad formats, 13
search penetration, 16
search quality, 23
search results, 72, 76
    separating from sponsored listings, 44
    See also web index results

SearchMonkey, 19
search-to-purchase scenarios, 72–78
seasonality, 327
segmentation, 277–278
Self-Counsel Press, 163
self-learning, 89
self-serve advertising, 89
Selling the Invisible (Beckwith), 328
SEM. *See* search engine marketing
SEMPO, 155
SEO. *See* search engine optimization
SES Awards, 14
share of searches, 16
Sherman, Chris, 39
Sherpa. *See* MarketingSherpa
single-product pages, vs. category pages,
    321–324
Site Match, 19
site search, 326–327
Skrenta, Rich, 42
Skype, 308–309, 348
Slegg, Jennifer, 21
social graph, 342
soft events, 312
sole advertiser, 193–195
spending
    classified advertising and direct
      marketing, 11–12
    large companies, 10–11
split-testing, 233
sponsored links, 75
sponsored listings, 19–21
    separating from search results from, 44
Spool, Jared, 287
Spyfu, 189
Stanford Persuasive Technology Lab, 325–326
statistical validity, 310–311
stereotypes, 303
Sterne, Jim, 270
Stevens, Mark, 85
Stockman, Marc, 284
story-telling, testing, 238–239
success, building on, 252–253

Sullivan, Danny, 17, 39
surplus interruption
    vs. user targeting, 4–6
    See also interruption marketing
Survival Is Not Enough (Godin), 87, 227

T

Taguchi testing, 226
tail, 250–252
    See also Long Tail
targeted advertising, vs. surplus
    interruption, 4–6
testing, 126, 214–215, 232, 233
    A/B or A/B/C, 306–312
    brand impact and story-telling,
        238–239
    on calls to action and offers, 235
    differentiation, 237
    differentiation of ad copy from other ads
        on the page, 236–237
    display URL, 239–240
    flair vs. flat, 237–238
    landing pages, 287
    multivarate, 226–227, 312–320
    protocols, 304–306
    selling solutions, 237
    split-testing, 233
    statistical significance in, 241–242
    syntax variations, 236
    Taguchi, 226
    tracking results, 240
    variables to test, 233–235
    word choice, 240
testing budget, 175–176
TheStreet.com, 284
thin-slicing, 145
third-party tools, assessing need for, 92–93
Thurow, Shari, 18
Tiger Direct, 156
time spent, 273
titles, matching to searched keywords, 228
Tolles, Chris, 42
Tomkins, Andrew, 337

tone, 216–221
Topiz.net, 42
total cost, 97
tracking, 240
    how it works, 268–269
    imperfections of, 269
    metrics to consider, 269–270
    post-click, 123
    See also web analytics
trademarks, as keywords, 259–260
Trader Corporation, 11
Traffic Estimator, 174
Tragedy of the Commons, 91
trends, 339–340
Twitter, 351
two-word broad matching, 248
Tyler, Nate, 23

U

Under Armour, 8–9
Universal Search, 133
upping your bids, 253–254
Urchin, 272
    Google Analytics vs., 271
Usborne, Nick, 227
user feedback, 35–37
    fast feedback cycles, 86–87
user intent, 83–84
user needs
    addressing, 54–55
    vs. advertiser needs, 52–53
user targeting, vs. surplus interruption, 4–6
user-generated content (UGC), 337
users, 4–5
    catering to, 214–215

V

ValueClick, 15
vanity searching, 100
Vertster Clickthrough Rate Validity
    Checker, 310–311
visibility, 203–205

W

Ward, Eric, 18
web analytics
    explosion of the industry, 270–271
    See also Google Analytics; tracking
Web Analytics (Kaushik), 271
web credibility, 325–327
web index results, 72–73
    See also search results
web properties, 16
website quality, 142–143
WordTracker, 188
writing ads, 126–127
    accuracy, 224
    ad space, 216
    ad tone, 216–221
    balancing clickthrough rates
      with ROI, 221
    clarity, 216
    credibility, 220

    imagining the perfect ad, 213–214
    media type and location, 215–216
    multiple priorities, 221–224
    multivarate testing, 226–227
    refining ads, 225–227
    resources on copywriting, 227
    six rules for better copy, 228–232
    Taguchi testing, 226
    testing, 214–215
    tone, 216–221
    See also copywriting

Y

Yahoo, 21, 48, 350
Yahoo Directory, 37–38
Yahoo Search Marketing, 38, 260–261
Yang, Jerry, 351
Your Marketing Sucks (Stevens), 85
YouTube, 342–343